The Best of

Vogue Knitting

Magazine

25 Years of Articles, Techniques and Expert Advice

Sixth&Spring Books
233 Spring Street
New York, New York 10013

Vice President, Publisher
Trisha Malcolm

Executive Editors
Rosemary Drysdale
Carla S. Scott

Editorial Director
Elaine Silverstein

Art Director
Chi Ling Moy

Book Editor
Erin Walsh

Graphic Designers
Marie Nguyen
Sheena T. Paul

Copy Editor
Kristina Sigler

Yarn Editor
Tanis Gray

Book Division Manager
Erica Smith

Production Manager
David Joinnides

President, Sixth&Spring Books
Art Joinnides

1 3 5 7 9 10 8 6 4 2
Manufactured in China

Library of Congress Control Number: 2006931206
ISBN: 1-933027-16-9
ISBN-13: 978-1-933027-16-6

Contents

CONTENTS

Foreword

I picked up my first pair of knitting needles at the age of 5, but I didn't get my hands on my first copy of *Vogue Knitting* until many years later, when I moved to New York and took a position with *McCall's Needlework & Crafts* magazine. (I grew up in Australia, and at that time the magazine didn't have quite the international reach it does today.) Once I did get hold of a copy, though, I was instantly hooked. And who wouldn't be? Here was page after page of incredible fashions that anyone with a little knitting knowledge could duplicate, along with all the advice needed to make things turn out as they should. When I was offered the opportunity to take over the helm of what truly is the "ultimate knitting magazine" in 1997, I didn't need to think it over. For me, working at *VK* is the ultimate definition of a dream job.

I'm continually amazed by (and very proud of) the talented teams, both past and present, that put each issue together—in particular, Carla Scott, whose technical expertise is unparalleled and who has worked on more *VK* issues than anyone; and Joe Vior, our longest-serving creative director, who takes our ideas and turns them into exquisite photographs and magazine layouts. From the editors, coordinators and assistants who help source all those great fibers, to our dedicated advertising sales staff and the print production and accounting people who take us to the printed page, I'm lucky to find myself with a hardworking crew who love the magazine as much as I do. Our fabulous book publishing group, a spinoff from the magazine, keeps building our brand and growing our influence, and they have done a stellar job on this book!

I owe a huge debt to all the *VK* editors who came before me: Polly Roberts, Marilyn F. Cooperman, Lola Ehrlich, Margaret C. Korn, Meredith Gray Harris, Sonja Bjorklund Dagress, Nancy J. Thomas, Margery Winter, Carla Scott and Gay Bryant. Each left an indelible mark on the magazine and helped shape it into what it is today.

The person who deserves the greatest accolades is our publisher and CEO, Art Joinnides. It was Art's brilliant idea to approach Condé Nast in the early 1980s and revive *Vogue Knitting* (which they had published from the early '30s through the late '60s), turning it into the modern version we are all so proud of. Without his vision, the legacy would not have lived on and evolved as it has over the past twenty-five years and as it will continue to do under his leadership in the future.

What's really kept *VK* growing and prospering are the thousands of knitters who've thumbed through our pages, re-created our designs and shared our passion for what can be accomplished with needles and yarn. We spent many hours scouring through back issues to find the articles we know you need at your fingertips to inspire and educate you. This book is our silver anniversary gift to you; we hope it compels you to keep knitting as we work toward our gold and diamond anniversaries.

Trisha Malcolm
Editor in Chief, *Vogue Knitting*

VOGUE KNITTING BOOK

FALL AND WINTER 1951

Directions for cover dress on page 76

50 CENTS

Knitting was hot when *Vogue Knitting* hit the newsstands in 1982, and in the 25 years since, we've seen lots of trends (and plenty of yarn) come and go. From Arans to amigurumi, big shoulders to big needles, sweater sets to scarves, *VK* has showcased it all, giving knitters of all ages and all skill levels something stylish to put on their needles and something beautiful to feed their souls. This book pulls together our favorite articles, ideas and advice from the past two-plus decades, all of it as relevant today as it was when first in print.

If there's one thing we've learned over the years, it's that the more things change, the more they stay the same. As our first issue went to press, knitwear was all over the runways, women were rethinking their roles at home and in the workplace, and making things yourself—whether it was a power suit or a mohair sweater—was something of a badge of honor. Twenty-five years later we find ourselves in a similar state, though this time, the need to knit seems more purposeful than practical. We're knitting to feed our souls and express our individuality, rather than to get the latest designer look at a discount. Still, there's a common thread that ties us to all the knitters who have come before and will come after—we want to challenge our skill, learn all we can and share our passion for yarn and needles with anyone who'll listen.

THE BACK STORY

VK first appeared on the magazine stands in the early 1930s (back then it was called the *Vogue Knitting Book*), a time when knitting was a practical as well as pleasurable pursuit. Condé Nast (the creators of *Vogue* magazine and bastion of all that's chic)

was the publisher, and the focus then (as now) was on fashion knitting. On the stands for a good 35 years, the magazine ceased publishing in the late 1960s, a casualty of a cultural revolution and the growing disdain for "women's work." A little over a decade later, fashion's focus on knitwear had rekindled an interest in knitting (sound familiar?), and Vogue Patterns, then a division of the Butterick Company, decided to test the crafting waters by including a few knitting patterns on the pages of its fashion sewing publication, *Vogue Patterns Magazine*. Readers began begging for more, and in 1982, Butterick's president and vice president, Bill Wilson and Art Joinnides (who later became publisher and now heads SoHo Publishing Company, the magazine's current publisher), decided that the time was ripe to relaunch *Vogue Knitting*.

The first issue of the new *Vogue Knitting* was put together by Polly Roberts, then editor-in-chief of *Vogue Patterns*. With the help of a talented art and editorial staff, she reached out to the top talents in the hand-knitting industry—designers, technical editors (Carla Scott, now *VK*'s executive editor, was among the first), yarn companies and some of the era's best-known knitwear designers: Adrienne Vittadini, Joan Vass and Carol Horn, to name a few. *Vogue Patterns'* connection with the top names on Seventh Avenue opened the door for designs from Perry Ellis, Calvin Klein and Donna Karan to appear on our pages. In the years that followed we've continued to add to the list, signing on Anna Sui, Michael Kors, James Coviello and rising stars Twinkle and Pierrot. The magazine also had plenty of substance to back up all that great style. Knitting legend Elizabeth Zimmermann began contributing technical

MASTER KNITTERS OF THE '90s

In the 1990s *VK* paid tribute to these talented women. From left to right: Mari Lynn Patrick designed six garments for the first issue and has been contributing designs (more than 300 at last count), articles and instructions ever since. Lily Chin submitted her first design to *VK* in 1987; today she's the face of the modern knitter, appearing on countless television shows, authoring books and designing her own line of yarns. Kristin Nicholas made her mark as design director at Classic Elite and later as an author and designer. Norah Gaughan, the queen of cables, is now the design director for Berroco, Inc., and the author of *Knitting Nature*. Nicky Epstein's artfully embellished designs are always reader favorites; her books *Knitting On the Edge, Knitting Over the Edge* and *Knitting Beyond the Edge* were instant bestsellers.

STAR QUALITY

More than one of our sweaters have hung from celebrity shoulders. From left, top row to bottom: Cindy Crawford, on the beach in the Spring/Summer 1986 issue, in a design by former editor Nancy Thomas. Jennifer Flavin on the cover of our 1994 crochet special. Carmen, modeling's grande dame, wearing a "Then & Now" design from the Winter 1996/97 issue. Stephanie Seymour in a Deborah Newton top from the Holiday 1986 issue. Supermodels Paulina Porizkova and Cindy Crawford in our Spring/Summer 1984 and Holiday 1986 issues, respectively. Actress Daryl Hannah was our Fall 2003 cover girl, Courtney Thorne-Smith promoted Knit for Her Cure in our Spring/Summer 2005 issue, and Karen Allen modeled her own designs in the Winter 2004/05 issue.

BEHIND THE SCENES

Big names have always worked behind our cameras: Patrick Demarchelier, Arthur Elgort, Richard Bailey and Dewey Nicks are just a few who come to mind. Paul Amato, who shot for our very first issue, is still with us today.

articles in 1985; later, her daughter Meg Swansen followed in her footsteps with a series of columns about knitting techniques. The magazine's list of contributors reads like a Who's Who of the knitting glitterati: Kaffe Fassett, Sasha Kagan, Debbie Bliss, Nicky Epstein, Kristin Nicholas, Brandon Mably, Norah Gaughan, Deborah Newton, Shirley Paden and Melanie Falick are just a few of the big-name knitters to contribute both designs and technical advice over the years.

Getting those first sweaters from swatch to printed page took a good deal of talent and a lot of hard work. In 1982 electronic publishing was as unimaginable as knitting blogs and LED needles, so nothing was done by computer. Charts and schematics were drawn by hand and every line of text had to be typeset in our EPS (Electronic Publishing Systems) department, then brought back down to the graphic designers who used X-Acto blades and tape to create "paste-ups" of each and every page. The advent of desktop publishing and digital photography has radically changed the way our pages go to press, but the attention to quality and detail fostered in those early years still remains.

Twenty-five years, ten editors-in-chief and hundreds of sweaters have come and gone since that 1982 issue. Through it all we've kept our commitment to quality and our excitement about taking on new challenges. Special issues focusing on such topics as knitting for kids and men were introduced in the 1990s; in 2000 we launched a Web site and began publishing four issues a year to help feed our readers' insatiable need to knit. Books have also become a big part of the *Vogue Knitting* experience. Our first foray into hardcover was *Vogue Knitting: The Ultimate Knitting Book*. Now fondly referred to as the "Vogue Knitting Book," or the knitting "Bible," it was first published in 1989 and has been reprinted many times. In 1998 we began publishing our own titles (under the Butterick Publishing Co. imprint), starting with the wildly popular *Knitting On the Go* series. These were followed up by gorgeous hardcover design compilations of some of our favorite sweaters from past issues (*Designer Knits* and *The American Collection* were among the first). In 2001 *VK* split amicably from the Butterick Company (now a division of the McCall Pattern Company) to start our own publishing house, SoHo Publishing Company, and our own imprint, Sixth&Spring Books (named for the cross streets where our New York office is located). From there we've launched two new knitting magazines, *knit.1* and *Knit Simple*. Our award-winning *Stitchionary* book series is fast becoming a must-have on every knitter's shelf, and we're continually looking for new ideas and new designers to keep the creative excitement of knitting alive.

In 2006 *VK* was named one of the *Chicago Tribune's* Top 50 Magazines, and, thanks to our stellar design team, won the American Graphic Design Award for Publication Design for our Spring/Summer 2006 issue. We're continually amazed by the people we meet, the things they teach us and the fabulous things our readers are making—all fueled by a passion for fiber and need to feel the click of needles beneath their fingers. As you read through the pages that follow, we hope you'll look back with fond memories, learn something new, be inspired to start yet another project and look forward with us to what the next 25 years have in store…. ⌒

COLLECTIBLE COVERS

You can't judge a magazine by its cover, but we sure get a kick out of designing one that's both attention-grabbing and appealing to knitters. Hang onto your old issues—many are completely sold out, and we've seen several fetching high prices on eBay. We continually run into readers who proudly inform us they have every issue since 1982—and sometimes earlier—in their personal collections.

THE DESIGNER DIFFERENCE

The relationships Vogue Patterns cultivated with the day's leading designers helped *VK* forge lasting relationships of our own. Back then Perry Ellis, Calvin Klein, Donna Karan and Joan Vass were the designers in demand; today it's Michael Kors, Anna Sui, Twinkle and James Coviello.

1. Perry Ellis, Winter 1990/91. 2. Calvin Klein, Holiday 1987. 3. DKNY, Spring/Summer 1991.

4. Joan Vass, Spring/Summer 1983. 5. Michael Kors, Holiday 2005. 6. Anna Sui, Winter 2005/06.

7. Twinkle, Fall 2006. 8. James Coviello, Holiday 2006.

A History of Knitting

by Sylvia Jorrin

Did you ever realize, when picking up your needles and yarn, that you were participating in history?

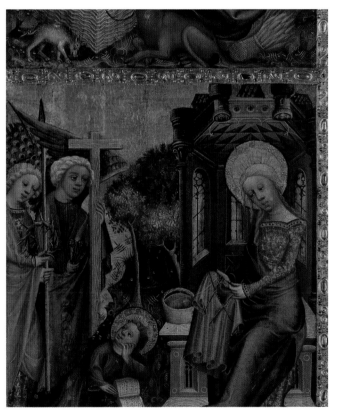

One of the earliest known depictions of knitting, this 14th-century painting by Master Bertram, "The Visit of the Angels," shows the Madonna knitting circularly.

Knitting originated about 3,000 years ago on the Arabian Peninsula. It was performed by the men of nomadic tribes using wool from the sheep and goats of their flocks. The wool was gathered and spun by the women, who did not knit. The men would knit as they tended the flocks, some as they stood on stilts so they could keep better watch over the animals.

The oldest surviving knitted samples that have been reserved from that time include a sock with the big toe knitted very much as our mittens are knitted today, to accommodate the fit of a thong sandal. The sock is knitted in stockinette stitch with no ribbing at the ankle. The heel is turned as we turn ours, but without any reinforcement. The slip-stitch "continental heel" appears to have been developed later. Excellent samples of these socks are in the Victoria and Albert Museum in London, England, and the Royal Ontario Museum in Toronto, Canada.

It is the legend that Christ's coat without seams, described in the New Testament, was knitted. This would explain why it could not be cut or divided and why lots had to be drawn for its possession. It possibly was made from the neck down, as we knit many of our "Norwegian" sweaters today.

KNITTING METHODS

Two methods of knitting originally were used. The first incorporated a knitting frame similar to the child's knitting spool with which we are familiar today. The frames were crafted in varying sizes, including some big enough that entire garments could be made on them. Circular frames produced tubular items, while straight frames produced flat fabrics.

The second method used two needles, each with one end quite smooth and rounded and the other hooked. The hook was used to draw the yarn through. These needles were used on through the 12th century, when the first pointed needles were devised.

By the 14th century, double-pointed needles were common. In fact, a 14th-century painting entitled "The Visit of the Angels" by the Master Bertram clearly depicts the Madonna knitting with double-pointed needles—and a set of five double-pointed needles at that. The painting, on exhibit at the Art Gallery in Hamburg, Germany, is of great interest to knitters since it shows that knitting in 1390 was much as it is today. In the painting, the Madonna keeps her yarn in a little basket by her side as she knits a short-sleeved tunic-like blouse. She appears to be picking up stitches around the neck as we often do when knitting the ribbing on a pullover.

KNITTING TRAVELS

Knitting gradually was introduced to other countries via Arabian traders and sailors. Knitters themselves, they took their craft with them on their travels and passed their techniques on to people they met in ports along the way.

Knitting spread east to Tibet in its early stages (never crossing the Himalayas into China until modern times), north to Spain and on throughout Europe. Although it originated on the Arabian Peninsula, it circled the Mediterranean but was not introduced in Africa until the influx of Europeans to that continent.

Egyptians also learned knitting from the Arabs, and knitting from 4th- and 5th-century Coptic Egypt has been found. There, the famous early Christian Coptic caps were first knitted. They were made in the round without seams and were worn by monks and missionaries.

KNITTING GUILDS

The Tudor and Elizabethan periods (1485–1603) marked the golden age of knitting. It was a time of great excellence in craftsmanship, when knitting guilds were formed in England, France, Germany and Italy to maintain high standards. Requirements were rigid. Boys were apprenticed to the knitting guilds and had to serve for six years, the first three spent studying under a master and the second three traveling to other countries to study new techniques. At the end of the six years, the apprentice was required to knit a rug four ells square (15 by 15 feet), which had to include in the pattern flowers, foliage, birds and animals; a beret; a woolen shirt; and a pair of clocked woolen socks. And he had to complete it all in thirteen weeks!

The apprentice first submitted his rug design in color graph form and swore it was his own original design. Since the gauge used for knitting the intricate rugs was only five to six stitches to the inch, the Tunisian stitch was sometimes used. It is a method of knitting into the back rather than the front of a knit stitch to give a tighter version of stockinette. It produces a light, hard edge, almost appearing as a woven stripe. This gave a firmer body to the rugs.

Master knitting was still a man's trade…the women, who did home-knitting, would spin and prepare the yarn for the men, just as the Arabian women did for the first knitters. They never were apprenticed to the guilds, but a widow of a master knitter could be admitted were her work thought to be proficient.

FAIR ISLE ORIGINS

We think of the popular Fair Isle sweater as having originated on Fair Isle itself, an island off the coast of England. But according to tradition, the people of the island learned color knitting from shipwrecked Spanish sailors during the time of the Armada. Look carefully at the pattern the next time you see a real Fair Isle sweater. In an authentic example you will be able to discern a motif representing a cross. The Spanish sailors knit their clothing in black and white, using the cross from the flag of their ships as a basic motif. It was referred to as the Cross of the Armada. The Islanders used their own heather yarns to knit the color patterns and always included the stylized Cross of the Armada.

Another sign of Fair Isle authenticity is that there should be only two colors on one line of knitting. The original Spanish patterns, which the people of Fair Isle adopted, were knitted only in white and black with occasional variations in red.

This is a fine example of the development of knitting. In the cross-cultural flow of commerce, trade and even war, techniques and patterns were exchanged knitter to knitter, as even now two knitters meeting will share methods, techniques and designs.

ARAN KNITTING

The Aran Isles, off the western coast of Ireland, and the ancient fishing villages of Cornwall and Devon are also important locations in the heritage of knitting. Each port had its own traditional fisherman's sweater, and one could tell where a fisherman was from by the sweater he wore. The sweater patterns have such names as "Rose of Sharon," "The Sacred Heart" and "Star of Bethlehem."

WOMEN KNITTERS

The first knitting machine was the stocking machine, invented in England in 1589 by William Lee. His wife hand-knit socks for sale, and so his invention helped lighten her work. The history of Mistress Lee's business is one of the earliest records of a woman earning money by knitting—previously a male domain. However, knitting was always regarded as a female accomplishment in the home. Some medieval documents even list a bride's ability to knit as part of her dowry.

SILK KNITTING

The introduction of silk changed the appearance of knitting in Europe. The increased availability of silk in the 16th century made possible expensive, luxurious stockings and garments that closely resembled brocaded and embossed woven fabrics. Often, gold and silver metal threads were used to outline patterns. In some instances of silk color knitting, the yarns were stranded, or left "floating," on the back of the fabric. Many historians think that the English and Continental knitting methods were both used so that the right and left hands could hold different colors at the same time to facilitate working elaborate patterns.

Silk stockings and clothing were prized by royalty and were responsible for the introduction of knitting to Denmark. In the 1500s the king of Denmark received a gift of a pair of embossed, knitted hose from Holland. He was delighted with his gift and wanted his own people to learn to knit. Therefore, he invited a group of Dutch knitters to colonize outside of Copenhagen. He gave them full rights as citizens and, in turn, they taught Danish women to knit.

In England, Queen Elizabeth was so pleased with silk knitting that, after wearing a pair of silk hose, she vowed she would never again wear woolen stockings. Some of her stockings are in the Victoria and Albert Museum. They seem to have been held up by garters, since the tops are knitted lace ruffles rather than any kind of rib. A version of this stocking is still worn in the British Isles—it is now ribbed for support, but the rib is hidden under a decorative cuff.

AMERICAN KNITTING

Knitting in the United States during the period of colonization was purely practical. Most knitting was done to make plain clothing—there was seldom time, and there were rarely materials, for the decorative. Women were the primary knitters, but children were expected to be proficient, too. Eventually, American knitters made bedspreads, lace and rugs that were sold to the Dutch settlers at the head of the Hudson River and to Canadians.

The Hopi Indians of the Southwest had been taught to knit by the Spanish explorers in the 16th century, and samples of their white cotton leggings, worn as part of their ceremonial costumes, have been preserved.

KNITTING MACHINES

The work of the knitting master was finished in Europe with the onset of the machine age in the early 19th century. In fact, the hand-knitting industry was one of the first to go, as more and more knitting machines were developed.

The decline of knitting was so widespread in England that in 1872, a law was passed making the teaching of knitting mandatory in schools to prevent the loss of the craft. Home knitting continued, and in many rural spots, hand knitting remained a cottage industry.

We have come full circle today. Millions of women are now knitting around the world, and it is again a serious craft passed on to future generations. For example, at the Waldorf Schools in Massachusetts, children make needles from dowels and then use them to knit their own socks and mittens.

We are enjoying a revival of the craft of hand knitting, regaining an appreciation of both the pleasure of making and wearing a hand-knitted garment. Cottage industries are evolving all around the country, creating a source of pride and honor in the craft and art of handwork. ⌒

So You Think You Know

by Lily M. Chin

One wonders what will happen when knitting is no longer the craft du jour. How can we ensure that those jumping on the bandwagon won't jump off? In the course of researching my book *The Urban Knitter*, I consulted a target group of twenty knitters in their twenties and thirties, the generation so very important to the continued good health of our craft. What are these knitters looking for? In what areas can we, as an industry, improve? I stipulated that we cover a range of skills, projects and materials. Here are the results. I think you will be surprised.

All of a sudden, knitting is the hot thing to do. Celebrities are showcasing their favorite hobby in public. Urban professionals are talking up its therapeutic appeal.

THE PARTICIPANTS:

Theresa Belville, 24, Morton, PA; stay-at-home mother

Jennifer Braico, 29, Madison, WI; copywriter

Anne Briggs, 26, Washington, D.C.; graduate student

Jamie Fife, 26, Colton, CA; employment services specialist

Emilyn Lee, 25, Singapore

Jessica Mikkelson, 24, St. Paul, MN; homemaker

Leslie T. O'Neill, 28, Oakland, CA; magazine editor

Erica Steedle, 24, Menlo Park, CA; classroom aide and former graphic designer

the Twentysomething Knitter

WHAT KINDS OF THINGS ARE YOU INTERESTED IN KNITTING?

Theresa: Garments and fun stuff for my kids [ages 8 months and 2 years], funky garments for myself, especially sweaters and shells. A diaper bag would be absolutely fabulous. A sweater vest for my husband that won't make him look like a middle-aged professor.

Jennifer: I started out making hats and bags. Also scarves—last Christmas I made four. I've moved on to sweaters, thankfully. I've also been knitting baby things—my sister-in-law is expecting her first child.

Anne: Mostly sweaters, but I'm trying socks, hats, mittens and even knit toys.

Jamie: Socks, hats, shawls, sweaters, especially Fair Isle and cable.

Emilyn: Sleeveless tops, sweaters, casual wear.

Jessica: Socks, sweaters, shawls, bags, cat toys, hats, mittens, scarves…

Leslie: I knit sweaters almost exclusively, but I also like the occasional pair of booties, as long as they have interesting construction and unusual stitch patterns.

Erica: Sweaters and other garments. I like classic styles—Arans, Fair Isles—and natural fibers.

WHAT KINDS OF PATTERNS WOULD YOU LIKE TO SEE MORE OF?

Theresa: Circular knitting. Why are almost all patterns in magazines for flat knitting?

Jennifer: I'd like to see more patterns for things knit in the round, especially for

children and babies. I can see myself altering patterns when I have more experience.

Anne: Modular patterns that include options for different neck shaping, sleeve length, etc., so that you can create a design that works for you with minimal hassle.

Jamie: I'm short-waisted, so I'd like to see more patterns for fitted or close-fitting sweaters—they're much more flattering on me. I also like cropped sweaters, but I have a hard time finding patterns; I always have to shorten the body myself.

Emilyn: Summer knits—tank tops, flared sleeves, bias shaping. Unusual designs that are hip and trendy.

Jessica: Plus-size patterns. The ones available are geared mostly toward older people. I have to come up with my own patterns, which takes too much time.

Leslie: It's difficult to find sweater patterns in any of the major magazines that appeal to someone my age. In three years, I've knit only one sweater from them, and that was for my mom. Too many of the sweaters look matronly, and the ones that target "young knitters" are boring and too simplistic or too self-consciously wacky or trendy. Sweater designers seem to think young knitters don't have advanced skills. I'd like to see more sweater patterns that are elegant but youthful; interesting but not trendy. I won't spend several months—and a lot of money on the finest yarns—knitting something that will look dated by the time I'm done.

I'd also like to see more truly masculine sweaters, appropriate for a guy in his early thirties. Most are for men my dad's age, or are just a woman's sweater in brown or gray. Why not more patterns? What happened to color?

Designers also don't seem to understand the way many women my age dress for work. I'd love to see more semi-tailored boxy cardigans that work with khakis, rather than the loose-fitting sweatshirt-type cardigans. I'd also like to see more sweaters designed at an Aran-weight mid gauge. I love using chunky yarn for the instant gratification, but you just can't wear those sweaters to work or to go out, at least not here in California.

The other end of the spectrum's just as bad. Finely knit sweaters require more time than most of us who work have. Even though I usually knit for a few hours each day, a pattern calling for anything smaller than twenty stitches to 4 inches demands more time than I want to give to a project. I'd like to be able to complete a few sweaters a year, so anything knit at about fifteen to eighteen stitches to 4 inches is doable in a reasonable amount of time and is wearable in a variety of normal situations.

Erica: I'd like to see more Alice Starmore-style colorwork—very challenging, very beautiful sweaters.

WHY DO YOU KNIT? HOW DID YOU GET STARTED?

Theresa: I got started as a freshman in college—it helped keep me focused. I knit now because it's portable, therapeutic, fun, therapeutic, satisfies my creative urges, therapeutic, keeps my hands busy at the playground, therapeutic, and brings me joy. Did I mention it's therapeutic?

Jennifer: I took a class a year ago at a local community college so I could be productive during the times my husband was in class. I had sewn as a kid and loved the idea of making useful things by hand. I was afraid at first that I'd get frustrated. But it's been just the opposite—I find knitting to be so calming.

Anne: My grandmother taught me to knit when I was 8 and I've been hooked ever since. It's my creative outlet, my chance to create something just because it looks good to me. I also knit when I can't find anything in the stores that appeals to my taste.

Jamie: I knit because I love it. It's an effective reliever of stress, which I have in abundant supply. My grandmother taught me to crochet, but I wanted to make wearable knit garments, so I bought a learn-to-knit leaflet and some knitting needles and taught myself how.

Emilyn: I knit because I can't cook! I knit because it's good therapy. I started knitting at 18 as a way to curb my temper, and my family sees a marked difference. I stopped knitting when I started working but picked it up again because I missed it too much.

Jessica: I knit because I enjoy the clicking of the needles, because it's relaxing and because I love to take a pile of yarn, or a smelly fleece, if I'm working with hand-spun yarn, and create something warm, soft and beautiful. I learned how to knit when I was little but it didn't hold my interest then. I picked it up again when I learned how to spin wool.

Leslie: I knit because it's relaxing and satisfying in a tactile, tangible way. I've always enjoyed expressing myself through clothing, and knitting reflects that sense of style. But when you get right down to it, knitting's just fun. I knit mostly after work, but sometimes, if my computer's slow and I'm working at home, I'll knit while waiting for the machine to catch up, or during conference calls. I knit in the car, while hanging out at my parents' or in-laws' house, or during any other spare moment that promises to be otherwise boring.

Erica: I knit because I love creating something from nothing. I've always been fascinated by colonial and pioneer life, the idea of living off the land and surviving by your wits. Knitting allows me to feel closer to that kind of life. I taught myself how to knit in college, after I broke up with my boyfriend. I was so busy concentrating on learning the techniques that I'd forgotten about my ex within two weeks.

KNITTING IS TRENDY AT THE MOMENT, ESPECIALLY WITH YOUR AGE GROUP. WHY?

Theresa: Our society is so fast-paced that we're yearning for a simpler, quieter life. Knitting is usually associated with "granny" types, but I think that's exactly what people my age are looking for—the quiet life we perceive our grannies had! In an age where you can buy a hand-knit sweater at Target for three times less than it'll cost you to make it yourself, it's obvious that knitting is serving some grander purpose. It soothes the soul. And it definitely keeps you sane when you have small children around.

Jennifer: People in their twenties have often been through a lot. Some have led unstable lives, with parents divorcing or moving around. Others have lived through the pressures of college, or are coping with first jobs. Things can seem out of control. But knitting has a beginning and an end, and you're totally in control. The end result is up to you, and that's very appealing. You learn a lot about yourself. That's important to me.

Anne: Part of the reason I knit might have something to do with the rise of Martha Stewart. She has raised the bar for what many women consider to be the ideal woman—business-savvy, smart and able to make ordinary life more beautiful, no matter the time or expense involved.

Jamie: Many people in my age group, much like myself, are going to school and working; some are even raising children. My generation is very health-conscious, and knitters my age find this hobby to be a better stress-reliever than overeating, smoking or drinking. Knitting is also a wonderful way to exercise creativity in a society that has a way of stifling self-expression and individuality.

Emilyn: I'm a bit of a pioneer, because knitting's not that common in Singapore. Labor costs are low here, and it's more convenient for people to buy ready-made knits. And our weather is warm year-round. You really have to be dedicated.

Jessica: We realize there's more to life than career and social life, and we really enjoy being able to make something. I love saying "I made this" and giving handmade items as gifts.

Leslie: For the same reasons people have always knit: to express yourself, to develop an individual sense of style, to show love for family and friends. Many writers have postulated it's a backlash against technology, but I disagree. I'm a technologist; I spend my days working in front of a computer, editing stories about computers, and I don't knit because of that. I knit because it gives me a creative outlet for color and warmth and softness.

Erica: It's part of a larger overall trend of getting back to the "authentic." People my age grew up in a plastic, electronic, TV-dinner world. Knitting puts you back in touch with things we hardly ever saw growing up. We probably romanticize it in our minds. When you spend the day surrounded by computers and cell phones and pagers, it's a relief to have something tangible in your hands and to watch it turn into something real right before your eyes. Knitting is humanizing in a dehumanizing world.

WHAT ELSE WOULD YOU LIKE TO TELL OUR READERS?

Jennifer: You can't lump people in their twenties together. That's true for anything, not just knitting. I think people this age are less homogenized than other generations. As a group, we don't have positive, defining, unifying hallmarks, the way others may have, such as witnessing people walk on the moon.

Jamie: I'd like to add that knitting has become quite an obsession. Since teaching myself to knit less than a year ago, I've amassed a sizable library, I have subscriptions to four knitting magazines, I've subscribed to Internet knitting lists, I have many knitting needles, and I have a huge mountain of yarn. I love the process, from picking the pattern, deciding on the materials and wearing the final product or giving it as a gift. Every spare moment I get, I knit or I read about knitting. I love that people are amazed that such a "young" person is practicing such an unusual craft. I only regret I didn't learn sooner.

Jessica: This surge of interest among twentysomethings doesn't just apply to knitting. Several people my age are involved with the local Weavers Guild—spinners, weavers, rug-hookers, dyers. I also know many people who sew and quilt. We've discovered what a great way this is to express our creativity, and we're working hard to help other people realize it as well.

Erica: I'm not sure I qualify as "hip." Most of the designs I see in magazines for people in my age group are a little too fashion-forward for me, and, as I said, I like classic styles. But that's mainly a matter of taste. I think the drive to knit is the same, whatever look you prefer.

These up-and-coming knitters inspire me. I can empathize with their frustrations, and I cheer them on when they succeed. But even though they have different reasons for knitting and may have different goals in mind, these new knitters, as a group, are the craft's lifeblood. We must do everything in our power to bring them, and others like them, into our ranks by talking up all that is great about our craft, whenever and wherever we can. Form guilds and other groups, then let others know about them. Post on the Internet. Casually mention to general user's groups and bulletin boards that knitting is your hobby and that it should be tried by one and all. Show off the fruits of your labor as an incentive, as if to say "You, too, can do this." The industry as a whole must offer patterns and yarns and accessories that interest these knitters, and all other potential knitters out there. Challenge them with just enough technique, yet don't intimidate. Offer simpler projects, but don't dumb them down. Make available sumptuous yarns to fit all budgets. Provide options for any mood and skill level. Educate and further hone skills. Continue to offer public events, like the Knit-Outs, to increase awareness and exposure. My greatest wish is to bring more young, new knitters into the fold. Once they've experienced the joys associated with our craft, they'll be ours forever. ⌒

The Knitting Revolution

by Meg Swansen

I pull out my well-organized folders of all the back issues of this magazine and am reminded of the various fashion trends: shoulder pads, fine yarn, bulky yarn, formfitting garments, balloon or oversized sweaters, hip length, mid-thigh length, textures, intarsia, etc. Various knitting traditions have also swept through the country, each in their turn: Arans, Guernseys, Fair Isle color patterns, lace knitting. With the exception of shoulder pads, all of the above remain fashionable to this day, which is one of the most pleasant aspects of this skill: knit whatever shape, color or texture appeals to you in whatever fiber you like.

As a lover of knitting techniques in specific, I am drawn to "innovations" in that field. I put that word in quotation marks because, as my mother wrote in her book *Knitter's Almanac:* "I very much doubt if anything is really new when one works in the prehistoric medium of wool and needles.... The earth is enriched with the dust of the millions of knitters who have held wool and needles since the beginning of sheep."

If you agree with Elizabeth Zimmermann, every exciting "new" technique is most likely a rediscovery of something achieved by one of our knitting predecessors. Case in

On a momentous anniversary such as this, my mind drifts back over the past twenty knitting years to see if there are summations to make, conclusions to draw or innovations to observe.

point: In her book *Traditional Knitting,* Sheila McGregor describes a pair of Turkish stockings dating back more than 1,000 years. They are knit from the toe up, with intricate color patterns, an afterthought heel and a lacing of twisted cord around the calf to hold the stocking in place. Ms. McGregor describes the cord as necessary, "in the absence of ribbing (a fairly recent development)...."—quite unimaginable if one adheres to EZ's theory. With all the knitting knowledge displayed in that pair of stockings, one can only assume that the knitter knew how to purl but chose not to put ribbing at the top. Or perhaps purl went missing for a while in certain parts of the world, until it was rediscovered and utilized in ribbings and textures.

When *Vogue Knitting* was restored to us in 1982, we had been using Steeks for only a few years but had never heard of the now popular Crocheted Steek.

The evolution of Tubular Cast On and Cast Off has been fascinating to observe, changing from a rather awkward multistep process to a streamlined one-step mode.

Knitting Back Backwards, One-Row Buttonholes, SSK, Short Rows and Wrapping, Invisible Casting On, dozens of variations of I-Cord: Most of these terms, which now roll so smoothly off our needles, were somewhat unfamiliar only a few decades ago. It is difficult to imagine that they have all recently been invented.

Perhaps the most significant change in knitting, obvious to those of us who have been obsessive about the subject for thirty or forty years, is the sudden, widespread popularity of hand knitting in this new century—particularly in the U.S. We knitters are now positively mainstream—most surprising to those of us who have determinedly knitted-on through decades when we were considered rather dowdy.

The current popularity is demonstrated most obviously by the long, year-round list of knitting retreats and conventions. When Elizabeth Zimmermann started the country's first Knitting Camp in 1974, who could have foretold the wave of similar gatherings that would sweep across America, not to mention the scores of Knitting Guilds scattered from coast to coast?

With the near-frenetic pace under which most of us operate today, small, portable knitting items, logically, have the greatest appeal to the busy professionals who have recently taken up the skill: socks, mittens, caps, scarves and baby items are a good way to experiment with patterns and textures, finish an item relatively quickly and enable you to keep your knitting at your elbow for a refreshing row or round in times of stress. The vast reservoir of untapped knitting knowledge will wait for you until you are ready to dive in—or perhaps inch in, one new technique at a time.

Dozens of articles have been written in a diverse array of newspapers and magazines, all attempting to explain this sudden "phenomenon" of intense interest in hand knitting. I'm perhaps too deeply involved in the subject to look at the trend objectively, but I like to think that scores of people have stumbled onto the happy realization that we all know so well: Knitting is soothing yet exciting, creative yet mindless, hypnotic yet energizing. This ancient and comforting craft also ties us to a simpler life and time, to something real and productive that makes use of our skill and imagination—a feature that has had great appeal, particularly in recent months.

Truly, this is an excellent time to be a knitter. So with our wool and needles at the ready, we brace ourselves to plunge boldly into the next twenty years.

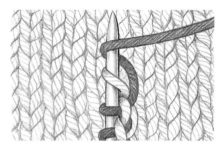

STEEK

Pick up stitches through the inside loop of the first stitch before the steek by inserting the needle into the stitch and wrapping the yarn around the needle.

KNITTING BACKWARDS: STEP 1

To practice KBB on stockinette, purl to the middle of the row. Turn the work around. The yarn will be coming from the left needle as shown. To continue the row, insert the tip of the left needle into the back of the stitch on the right needle.

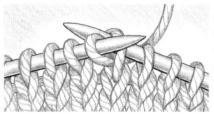

STEP 2

Wrap the yarn over the top of the left needle *counterclockwise* and draw through a loop as shown. If you wrap the yarn incorrectly, the result will be a twisted stitch.

I-CORD

The basic I-cord formula is: k3, do not turn, push the stitches to the end of the needle and continue to k3 as shown. Note: I-cord must be worked with double-pointed or circular needles.

GLOSSARY OF TERMS

STEEK extra stitches cast on at center front (for a cardigan) or at underarms (for a dropped shoulder) to permit circular knitting to continue all the way to the shoulders. The extra stitches are then secured by means of machine-stitching or crochet and cut open. A cardigan border is added and the sleeves are sewn or knitted into the cut armhole.

KNITTING BACK BACKWARDS (KBB) enables you to work back and forth without turning your knitting. This is especially useful for entrelac or for Aran bobbles. Plus, it's enormous fun.

I-CORD is the name Elizabeth Zimmermann gave to Idiot-Cord. She also came up with dozens of ingenious applications for this simple technique.

INVISIBLE or PROVISIONAL CASTING ON can be used as a temporary beginning. You may return to those stitches later and knit them in the other direction or weave them to the end stitches.

ONE-ROW BUTTONHOLES are just what they say.

SSK stands for Slip, Slip, Knit and is a left-leaning single decrease that mirrors the right-leaning Knit 2 Together.

SHORT ROWS AND WRAPPING is the technique that permits you to turn in the middle of a row or round and knit in the other direction—without leaving a trace.

TUBULAR CAST ON and OFF may be used for the most elastic ribbing imaginable—to the point where it is recommended you use a smaller-size needle for the Tubular part. It produces a mysterious rounded edging with no beginning or end. ⌒

INVISIBLE OR PROVISIONAL CAST-ON:
STEP 1

With two needles together, make a slip knot. Hold waste yarn beside the working yarn. Loop, working yarn under waste yarn, then over the needles as shown.

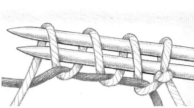

STEP 2

Continue looping under waste yarn until all stitches are cast on. Withdraw one needle; knit into the front loops on first row. Leave waste yarn in place until stitches are needed.

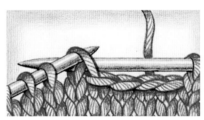

ONE-ROW BUTTONHOLE

Bring yarn to front and sl a st purlwise. Place yarn at back.

STEP 1 * Sl next st from LH needle. Pass 1st sl st over it; repeat from * 3 more times. Sl last bound-off st to LH needle. Turn. Using the cable cast-on wyib, cast on 5 sts: *Insert RH needle bet. 1st and 2nd sts on LH needle, draw up a loop, place loop on LH needle, rep from * 4 times more; turn.

STEP 2 Sl 1st st wyib from LH needle and pass the extra cast-on st over it to close the hole. Work to end of row.

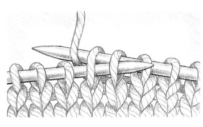

SSK

Insert the left needle into the fronts of the two slipped stitches as shown and knit them together.

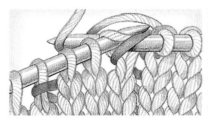

SHORT ROWS AND WRAPPING (KNIT SIDE)

When you have completed all the short rows, you must hide the wraps. Work to just before the wrapped stitch. Insert the right needle under the wrap and knitwise into the wrapped stitch. Knit them together.

Essay: Knitting for Victory

Chronicling a wartime tradition in America

by Anne Macdonald

Before American troops were called up in World War II, legions of knitters mirrored their foremothers' tradition and began knitting for their men. As the *New York Times* observed, "men have hardly time to grab their guns before their wives and sweethearts grab needles and yarn." That was back in 1940, but the observation needn't have been limited to World War II. Knitting during wartime is firmly rooted in American tradition.

Even in the decade before the American Revolution, as colonists increasingly defied the British, saucy Daughters of Liberty scoffed at imported textiles by sponsoring spinning and knitting bees on New England township commons or in parsons' manses. A Newport editor was impressed. Pointing to the "Knot of Misses busy at their Needles," he urged all the city's matrons: "Let the Knitting Needle be your Delight." As the rage for homespun yarns and handknits spread southward, a New Jersey colonist boasted to his local paper that within six months a "Lady of Distinction, tho' infirm, and of a very delicate constitution, has knit thirty-six Pairs of Stockings, besides having the care of a large Family."

Such zeal became commonplace during the ensuing Revolution, when colonial women, knitters since childhood, worked unstintingly to clothe their men. In some townships, the women donated knit stockings, gloves, or scarves in lieu of paying taxes levied for soldiers' clothing. Since wool was a precious commodity reserved for soldiers, women darned their own stockings

with ravelings from others, and flossed old silk gowns for thread to spin with cotton for knit gloves. Martha Washington's fervent knitting while visiting the General (whom she lovingly called "The Old Man") at camp inspired others to contribute thousands of new socks and to patch, darn or reknit discarded ones. When soldiers fought barefoot in the snow during the darkest days of Valley Forge, women drove their oxcarts loaded with knitting supplies along the blood-stained trail to the front.

Decades after the Revolution, a discovery at Bunker Hill recalled the selfless dedication of knitters throughout the colonies. While preparing a permanent monument to those buried as they fell, exhumers unearthed knit socks—precious relics of wartime devotion—mingled with the soldiers' dust.

Knitters also played an essential role during the Civil War. Following the South's secession in 1861, knitters on both sides packaged "delights of home" for their boys at the front—cushioning edible, potable (blackberry wine being a great favorite) and smokable goodies among mittens, socks, scarves and wristers. Eventually transportation bottlenecks made it impossible to direct parcels to particular boys. Compelled to act in concert, the women converted church or sewing circles into soldiers' aid societies, which collected and shipped provisions where needs were most acute.

Northern women established the United States

Sanitary Commission to coordinate efforts in behalf of soldiers. They met its expenses through vast metropolitan "Sanitary Fairs" and even had a song dedicated to their knitting efforts. "Knit! Knit! Knit!" urged their "fingers fleet" to fashion "nice warm socks for the weary feet." Southern women, with no such central organization, labored back-breaking hours to spare their soldiers nothing: "For four years we worked unceasingly, and even at evening parties the knitting needle was a regular attendant," one of them noted. "We were miniature knitting machines," boasted another. Still another recalled that "We spent all our spare time knitting socks…and we never went out to pay a visit without taking our knitting along."

Aid Society meetings became the focus of women's social life, and there were also groups for young girls, like Cleveland's "Busy Bees" and "Wide Awakes," Detroit's "Young Girls Stocking and Mitten Society" and Raleigh's "Young Ladies' Knitting Society." Although knitters had sacrificed individual packages for communal ones, they still craved personal links with donees ("How faithfully I tried to learn to knit and sew, ever cherishing the secret thought that, perhaps, in time I could send George a gift which would be the word of my own hands"). Many of them wadded notes into glove fingers and stocking toes. Before tossing her stockings into the society barrel, one proud knitter added: "The fortunate owner of these socks is secretly informed that they are the one hundred and ninety-first pair knit for

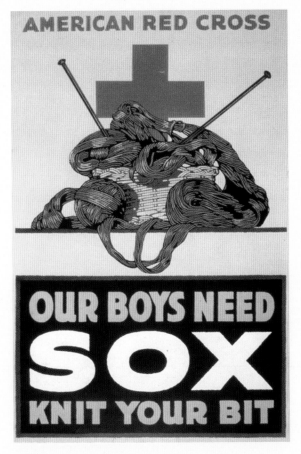

The Red Cross's "Our Boys Need Sox: Knit Your Bit" campaign, launched during World War I, became even more important during World War II, as knitters played a vital role in supplying soldiers with clothes.

our brave boys by Mrs. Abner Bartlett, of Medford, Massachusetts, now 85 years." Soldiers being soldiers, they probably fancied the notes that said, "And when from wars and camps you part—May some fair knitter warm your heart," and "Apples are good but peaches are better; If you love me, will you write me a letter?"

A lot of the soldiers responded. "I needed the stockings badly.… The maple sugar was a treat and

reminded me of the old times in the sugar camp at home," one wrote. "The mittens were just in time to do good service. The boys now gladly take the 'mitt' from the girls they left behind them," noted another. And there was this report: "We gave three rousing cheers to the ladies of the Hartford Soldiers' Aid Society. In this bleak December snowstorm, their hands and hearts are the warmer for what you sent." And this: "Your box recalled the pleasures of home (Grassy Pond, South Carolina) vividly to this war-torn soldier."

As in the Revolution, stockings were in critically short supply. One sister wrote, "If the stockings Uncle Sam provides are too thin, or too anything, let me know." Another sorrowfully returned to her Aid Society "Three pairs of socks, sent home in the knapsack of a dear brother who fell at Antietam." One leader even offered precious handknit socks to soldiers as a bribe to get them to wash their feet, and added a shirt and drawers in exchange for a "general ablution." Surveying their transformation, he whistled, "It looks as if Mother has been here!"

"Mother" was at it again half a century later in the "war to end all wars." Five widows of Civil War veterans at New York's Baptist Home for the Aged, now knitting for Sammy instead of Johnny Reb or Billy Yank, gamely challenged other knitters to beat their output, prompting newspapers to feature "knitters of the sixties." Everyone who could knit, did—from tiny 4-year-olds to Civil War veterans. They besieged Red Cross yarn depots. When the Navy League's Central Park Knitting Bee drew vast throngs of knitters, its chairwoman gloated that clicking needles echoed all the way to Berlin. One knitter acknowledged, "Knitting has

become your food and drink… Sundays, weekdays, midnight, crack of dawn, street car, parlor, kitchen, all times and places are one. They exist only for knitting."

This must have been true for Olivia Kindelberger, whose ten sweaters in less than seven days led to her coronation as "Champion Red Cross Knitter of New York." Leading town parades were platoons of knitters, their bosoms draped with bandoliers of khaki yarn, their needles tapping buckets to punctuate chanted mantras of "Knit Your Bit." Mormon women's strenuous knitting in church classes drew this rebuke from the General Board: "Our sisters will have plenty of time at home and in the work meetings to do all the knitting for which they can obtain yarn and thus assist the Red Cross cause." Knitting bags grew so emblematic of fidelity to war work that fashion magazines prescribed coordinating knitting bag with dress and hat. The ubiquitous bag even delineated characters in one-act plays presented to women's clubs or Red Cross gatherings: "dressed smartly but simply in tailored suit (and) carries cretonne knitting bag.… "A cheerful, motherly-looking person, well but comfortably dressed (and) carries a capacious, rather shabby knitting bag."

Knitting-infected vacationers at Atlantic City completed 10,000 sweaters in one season as novice stitchers sought instruction from the clusters of venerable pros hunched over workbaskets in hotel lobbies. Thus reinforced, the young drew knitting from rubber-lined knitting bags while ambling along the beach—and even, it was reported, floating precariously in inner tubes. It is no wonder that "Nettie's Knitting Nighties for the Navy" won hands-down as their favorite Boardwalk song. For non-knitters, after a futile attempt to organize a Nonknitters' Protective Association, it was farewell bridge and hello solitaire.

After the '20s, when war-spent knitters defected to other crafts, canny yarn companies launched such successful promotions to woo them back that the '30s produced a veritable knitting craze. Knitters were thus primed for wartime regeneration, when Bundles for Britain and war refugee organizations pleaded for warm clothes. After the American entrance into the war, the Army and Navy reported adequate supplies of "necessities," but knitters who felt compelled to knit anyhow created "comforts" for their men. Thousands, like the colonial "Knot of Misses," took up their needles, and in knitting helmets, gloves, sweaters and stretchy cotton bandages, they shared an experience not unlike that of their foremothers. One knitting veteran confessed to new recruits, "You see, I lost two sons in that other war, and somehow, doing this, I feel that I am helping to keep them warm."

Knitting clubs, like earlier Civil War Aid Societies, provided social outlets for women anxious about their men at the front. Even band leader Glenn Miller immortalized club meetings in his national hit "Knit One, Purl Two." *Popular Science* magazine, noting that knitting had become "an almost universal pastime among women," suggested lashing together cardboard tubes "such as the new linoleum is rolled up in" to form an umbrella-like stand that would allow each knitter to draw yarn from her own tube. When knitting-club wives of airmen training at Walla Walla, Washington, learned their husbands were headed for the South Pacific instead of Europe, they dispatched completed helmets and gloves to the Navy, grabbed their babies and headed home to mother. In 1945, Akron's Stitch and Bitch Club members dropped out one by one to greet their returning husbands, but thoughtfully rejoined when they realized one member's husband continued to be missing in action.

To World War II knitters, remembrances are still vivid. A knitter now in her seventies, who copied her infantryman brother's vest for two of his camp buddies, says proudly, "One went through the Battle of the Bulge, and the other went through the Italian campaign." A woman who knit bandages during her subway commute recalls: "I'd put fifteen to twenty stitches of Clark's Knit-Cro-Sheen cotton on a number four or five needle and just knit to the end of the ball." Another, confounded by an allegedly simple scarf, remembers, "I just knit those stitches until the end of the war!" One who in elementary school knit 6-inch "soldier squares" to be assembled into blankets, shudders, "I still avoid garter stitch like the plague!"

A wrenchingly familiar olive drab sweater is tacked to the wall of a case of Eleanor Roosevelt's needlework in the Hyde Park presidential library. A name tag (the kind used to mark clothes at camp) is the only indication that its young recipient was Joseph Lash, a soldier who survived to become the famous knitter's biographer many years later—a tender testament to America's wartime knitting tradition. ⌒

by Margaret Bruzelius

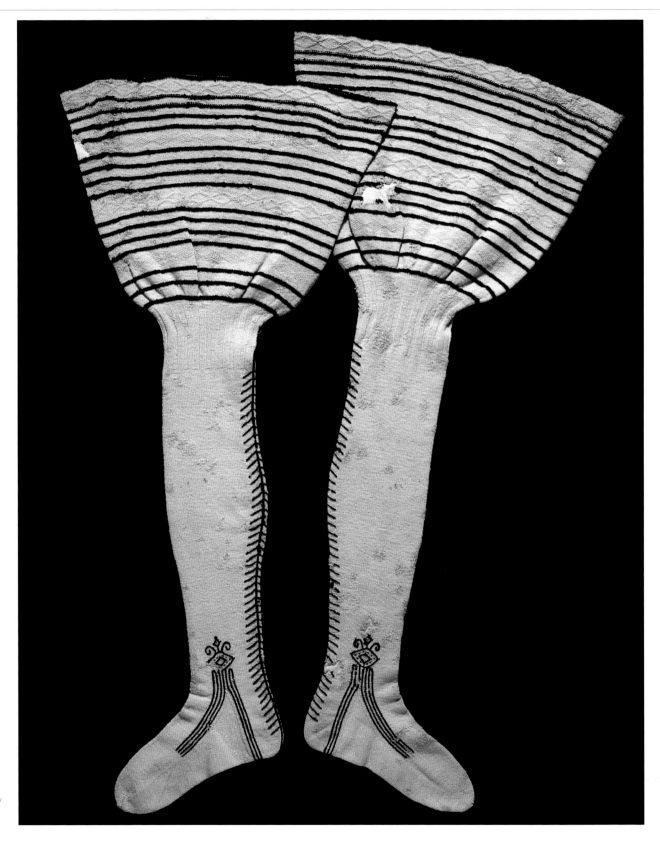

Pair of 17th-century Englishman's stockings, now sadly moth-eaten.

Where are the Knits of Yesteryear?

In the costume collection at the back of the Edinburgh Royal Museum of Antiquities stand three mannequins wearing the ordinary clothes of the 18th century—dull, shapeless garments made of rough cloth. Discovered accidentally hundreds of years later, these clothes belonged to men who were murdered and buried in an isolated spot. Because peat preserved their remains, we can see their loose and much-mended knit socks and a small knit purse decorated with a pattern of Greek keys and a picot edge. Coins found in the purse helped to determine its age.

The next case in the museum offers a dramatic contrast to the first. The figures in this case wear evening finery of the same period that's almost perfectly preserved. Compared to the longevity of these showy pieces, the existence of some patched and baggy socks and a single slender purse seems rare and indescribably touching. These remnants fortuitously preserved remind us how few knitted relics survive today. For though knitting is an ancient craft that may have been practiced by the Egyptians, only a few relatively recent and well-documented folk traditions—such as Fair Isle and Guernsey knitting—have come down to us over the years.

Why has so little lasted? One reason is that knitted garments have almost always been used for hard wear rather than show. The few articles that have survived have been distinguished by their rarity and fineness: beautiful knit ceremonial gloves of silk and metallic thread, silk shirts with astonishingly intricate patterns. Most other knitwear has been of the warm and flexible kind that bends and stretches with wearing, such as knit socks, gloves, caps and underwear. It seemed as ordinary to its owner as our cotton underwear does today. And it was just this type of clothing that was worn out and thrown away, even in thriftier times than our own.

Knitted garments have also traditionally been worked in wool, or, if they were very fine things, in silk, so that even someone's favorite clothes, meant to be saved, were vulnerable to moths. The Victoria and Albert Museum in London, for example, has a splendid pair of hose with a wide striped cuff that draped over a boot top. The socks are severely moth eaten, though they manage to maintain a jaunty air to this day.

Furthermore, unlike woven threads, which can hardly be taken apart, knitted yarn is easily unraveled. This meant that the yarn could then be used again to follow new fashions or to suit the tastes of a different member of the family.

But perhaps the most fundamental reason why knitted textiles have not survived is knitting's very simplicity. We naturally value what seems both mysterious and costly, and knitting is neither. Unlike weaving, which requires a loom and other equipment that must be mastered, knitting is easily taught with simple and inexpensive tools.

This view that knitting is familiar and ordinary diminishes our sense of knitwear's refinement and elegance, and also our desire to save it. As we learn about our knitting traditions, we should be wise enough to recognize the beauty of a process that simply by looping yarn through itself has kept us warm, comfortable and even stylish for so many centuries. After all, how often do we think, when we knit, that we are taking part in a tradition that goes back to the pharaohs? ⌒

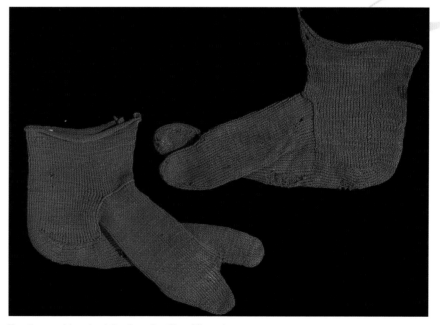

Egyptian sandal socks dating from the 4th or 5th century.

Essay: Nasty Knitters

A literary mix of knitting and mayhem

by Margaret Bruzelius

You may think of knitting as a peaceful activity for people of equable temperament who like to work with their hands—hardly the stuff of which murder and mayhem are made. But are you aware of another more sinister knitting tradition that lurks in literature? Here, leagues of ferocious women, knitting needles in hand, swoop down on their prey like Furies. For the creators of these characters, their knitting serves as a metaphor for their inexorable purpose.

The great-grandmother of these formidable women is certainly Mme. Defarge from Charles Dickens' *A Tale of Two Cities*. We first meet her in her husband's wine shop: "Madame Defarge was a stout woman…with a watchful eye that seldom seemed to look at anything, a large hand heavily ringed, a steady face, strong features, and great composure of manner…Madame…was wrapped in fur, and had a quantity of bright shawl twined about her head, though not to the concealment of her large earrings. Her knitting was before her, but she had laid it down to pick her teeth with a toothpick."

Like the inexorable Fates whose spinning determined the span of a man's life, Mme. Defarge's knitting carries the death sentence for the heartless aristocrats she despises. Indeed, on the reader's second encounter with her, Dickens makes the comparison himself: "…the woman who stood knitting looked up steadily, and looked the Marquis in the face…. He was driven on…the one woman who had stood conspicuous, knitting, still knitted on with the steadfastness of Fate."

Mme. Defarge's knitting, however, is not only a symbol of eventual retribution, but a record of the aristocrat's evil deeds. When a fellow revolutionary presumes to question her husband on her ability to maintain her list, he gets an unequivocal answer: "'Jacques,' returned Defarge, drawing himself up, 'if madame my wife undertook to keep the register in her memory alone, she would not lose a word of it—not a syllable of it. Knitted in her own stitches and her own symbols, it will always be as plain to her as the sun…. It would be easier for the weakest poltroon that lives, to erase himself from existence, than to erase one letter of his name or crimes from the knitted register of Madame Defarge.'"

Never in the novel does Madame Defarge appear without her knitting. When a government spy attempts to ingratiate himself with her, he compliments her on her knitting and asks what it is for. "'Pastime.' Said Madame, still looking at him with a smile. 'Not for use?' 'That depends. I may find a use for it one day. If I do—well…I'll use it!'" The spy retires, discomfited, but not before Madame has included his name on her fatal list. Indeed, even innocent strangers are subjected to her ferocity. When one presses her to reveal what she is knitting, "'Many things,'" she replies," 'For instance …shrouds.'"

Dickens' chapter titles—"Knitting," "Still Knitting," "The Knitting Done"—attest to the symbolic significance of his character's busy fingers. After her death, her friend, The Vengeance, missing her at the guillotine, laments, "'Bad Fortune!...and here are the tumbrels! And Evrémonde will be dispatched in a wink, and she not here! See her knitting in my hand, and her empty chair ready for her….'" The other knitters continue in their places: "Crash!—a head is held up, and the knitting-women, who scarcely lifted their eyes to look at it a moment ago when it could think and speak, count One."

Although Dickens' vengeful Mme. Defarge has no equal among literary knitters, many mystery writers have combined knitting and mayhem. Agatha Christie also used the motif of a knitted secret in one of her early yarns of Middle East derring-do, *They Came to Baghdad*. Victoria, the heroine, considering whether a knitted message could be managed, says, "'Oh, I think you could…. Plain and purl—and fancy stitches—and the wrong stitch at intervals and dropped stitches. Yes—it could be done…. Camouflaged, of course, so that it just looked like someone who was rather bad at knitting and made mistakes…' Suddenly, with a vividness like a flash of lightening, two things came together in her mind …the man with the ragged hand-knitted red scarf clasped in his hands…and together with that a name. *Defarge*."

This insight turns out to be the vital link needed to unmask a dastardly plot for world domination. In the final unraveling, Victoria asks the kindly British agent (this is before the days of George Smiley) if there was really a message in the scarf. "There was a name," he replies, "the scarf and the 'chit' were the two halves of the clue…."

Of course, Christie's most famous detective, M. Hercule Poirot, does not number knitting among his eccentricities. However, Miss Jane Marple, an equally illustrious Christie creation, is not only a formidable sleuth but also an indefatigable knitter. Here is one typical description from *A Murder Is Announced*: "She had snow white hair and a pink, crinkled face and very soft, innocent blue eyes and she was heavily enmeshed in fleecy wool. Wool round her shoulders in the form of a lacy cape and wool that she was knitting and which turned out to be a baby's shawl."

Miss Marple, selfless creature that she is, never seems to knit anything for herself, but instead turns out endless items for babies. Time after time she draws out information by placidly sitting and knitting. As one of her interlocutors says in *A Pocket Full of Rye*, "It's nice in here today…with the fire and the lamps and you knitting things for babies. It all seems cozy and homely and as England ought to be." Indeed, knitting is so much a part of Miss Marple's persona that we often hear of it only when she puts it down or loses her ball of wool. But while she may seem completely unlike the proletarian Mme. Defarge, she is just as tireless in her pursuit of justice. One of Christie's detectives even compares her to Nemesis as well: "Miss Marple was very unlike the popular idea of an avenging fury. And yet…that was perhaps exactly what she was."

A literary contemporary of Miss Marple's, Miss Maud Silver is another invaluable aid to Scotland Yard and a tireless knitter. She is the creation of Patricia Wentworth, whose introduction to any tale is a set piece whose focal point is Miss Silver and her gently clicking knitting needles. Unlike Miss Marple's rather vague projects, Miss Silver's are detailed, as in *The Case of William Smith*: "three pairs of stockings each for Johnny, Derek and Roger," or "she had finished the pair of leggings for little Josephine and had begun a coatee to match them." She is described as knitting so quickly that socks seem to revolve as she works them. Needless to say, she, too, always gets her man.

But knitters are not always on the side of justice. In Ruth Rendell's story "A Needle for the Devil," Alice Gibson discovers in knitting a method for controlling her violent temper: "Alice had never thought of knitting. Knitting was something one's grandmother did…. But if Pamela could make the coat…she was very sure she could. And it might solve that problem of hers which had lately become so pressing…." Alice becomes an expert knitter.

Late in life she unfortunately decides to marry, and her husband cannot bear to watch her knitting. Deprived of her therapy, Alice lies awake at night, dreaming of projects she may not start. Her temper rises and rises until she finally finds a new use for a knitting needle—with consequences fatal to her husband.

Another mystery writer, Harry Kemelman, shares Miss Rendell's view about knitting needles' possibilities, and in *Tuesday the Rabbi Saw Red* he supplies an ingenious new use for one. Once again we are presented with an industrious, selfless knitter at work on "Christmas presents for nephews and nieces. I start early enough, but I always seem to be rushed toward the end. I keep three or four projects going all the time…." This murder is not the result of knitting deprivation, but involves the craft as an essential part of *modus operandi*.

But the final word on the fatal aura of the knitter must be left to Ogden Nash in his poem "Machinery Doesn't Answer Either, But You Aren't Married to It."* For those of us who are at a loss to understand the thread of menace that these authors see in our quiet occupation, he articulates the rage of the non-knitter—and takes his quiet revenge:

Sometimes she knits and sits,
Sometimes she sits and knits,
And you tell her what you have been doing all day and you ask what she has been doing all day…and you speak tenderly of your courtship and your bridal,
And you might as well try to get a response out of an Oriental idol,
And you notice a spasmodic movement of her lips,
And you think she is going to say something but she is only counting the number of stitches it takes to surround the hips;
And she furrows her beautiful brow, which is a sign that something is wrong somewhere and you keep on talking and disregard the sign,
And she casts a lethal glance, as one who purls before swine,
And this goes on for weeks
At the end of which she lays her work down and speaks,
And you think now maybe you can have some home life but she speaks in a tone as far off as Mercury or Saturn,
And she says thank goodness that is finished, it is a sight and she will never be able to wear it, but it doesn't matter because she can hardly wait to start on an adorable new pattern,
And when this has been going on for a long time, why that's the time that strong men break down and go around talking to themselves in public, finally,
And it doesn't mean, that they are weak mentally or spinally,
It doesn't mean, my boy, that they ought to be in an asylum like Nijinsky the dancer,
It only means that they got into the habit of talking to themselves at home because they themselves were the only people they could talk to and get an answer. ⌒

*From the collection "Verses From 1929 On," by Ogden Nash, from the book *Many Long Years Ago…* (Little, Brown).

Patterns of History

by Kelly Hargrave Tweeddale

Although historians know little about the origins of knitting, many believe it was practiced as early as the 4th century by nomads roaming North Africa.* Later, Arab traders adopted the craft, which helped them wile away the hours as they traveled across deserts in camel caravans. This spread knitting to Tibet, to Egypt, and eventually to sailors of the Mediterranean, who exported it to ports of call along their trade routes.

Early evidence of multicolored knitting—now unfortunately lost—is said to date back to the Egyptian Copts of 600–800 A.D. During that period, the Egyptians were already known as master textile artists; they used knitting primarily for socks. Even the earliest relics reflect an extensive knowledge of color and design. The Copts produced intricate patterns through a stranding technique, combining such colors as red, dark and light blue, ocher, white, pink, green and brown.

These highly sophisticated patterns were apparently designed as defenses against the "evil eye." Some of them even took the shape of an eye, which was supposed to stare back at the evil one and counteract its harmful gaze. According to another common belief, a complex motif would trap that gaze and prevent it from doing damage. Many knitted symbols were used to ward off the evil eye, including crosses, the letter S, and the phoenix, representing eternal life. But the strongest protection was a pattern that included the threatening gesture of an upraised hand.

In 1272, Marco Polo recorded that the monks of St. Barsauma in Persia had knitted woolen girdles reputed to have great healing powers. By then, the Church had probably fostered the highest standards of medieval knitting, Pope Innocent IV was said to have been buried in 1254 wearing a pair of knitted altar gloves, as was the bishop interred at the cathedral church of Rome in the 14th century.

Monks weren't the only knitters of that period. Thirteenth-century nuns are credited with knitting the cushion covers found at the monastery of St. Mary of Huelgas in Spain. Founded near Burgos in 1187 by King Alfonso VI of Leon and Castile and his

What do the Copts of Egypt, Queen Victoria and Coco Chanel have in common? They all were knitters. Indeed, since the craft first arose, knitting has been associated with countless cultural groups and historical figures, from Pope Innocent IV to Mary Queen of Scots.

This portrait of the Prince of Wales made Fair Isle pullovers and vests immensely popular.

* Other articles in this book state that knitting originated earlier and in a different region. Current experts acknowledge that the true date and time of origin is unknown.

wife Eleanor of Aragon, the monastery was a royal abbey for nuns of high birth. Designed for the royal family, the cushions served as sacred pillows at burial. The cushion of Mafalda, made for the illegitimate son of Alfonso VIII, is a prime example of the period's most intricate color and pattern work.

It wasn't long before knitting appeared in paintings as a sacred craft, practiced by what art historians call the "knitting Madonnas." In 1345, Ambrogio Lorenzetti painted the Holy Family, with Jesus as a child resting one hand on his mother's arm. In this enchanting scene, Mary knits in the round, using a purple yarn and four needles. At her side are about a dozen spools of yarn.

The most famous of the knitting Madonnas is part of an altarpiece entitled *Der Besuch der Engel bei Maria* ("The Visitation of the Angels to Mary") [see page 11]. Painted around 1400 by Master Bertram of Minden, it depicts Mary in a room knitting a small crimson shirt on four needles. She has almost finished the garment and is ready to bind off. The child Jesus lies on the grass in the garden, completing a picture of domestic tranquility.

Later, knitting achieved a kind of nobility. Even before the craft became fashionable, Mary Queen of Scots, age 9, wrote notes in her Latin reader on how to make decreases in the leg of a stocking. By February 8, 1586—the day of her execution—many aristocratic ladies favored knitted clothing. According to one account of that event, Mary herself wore "her nether stocks of worsted, coloured watchett, clocked with silver, and edged at the tops with silver, and next her legs a pair of Jersey hose white." (In other words, white stockings under sea-blue socks with a silver decorative edge.)

Probably the most notorious knitter of all time was actually a fictional character—Madame Defarge, the leader of the female rabble in Charles Dickens's *A Tale of Two Cities*. In that classic, Dickens describes the women knitting as they watched the guillotine: "All the women knitted. They knitted worthless things; but the mechanical work was a mechanical substitute for eating and drinking: the hands moved for the jaws and digestive apparatus: if the busy fingers had been still, the stomachs would have been more famine-pinched…on the women sat, knitting, knitting. Darkness encompassed them…where they were to sit, knitting, knitting, counting dropping heads."

Madame Defarge and the bloodthirsty *tricoteuses* of the French Revolution showed that the lofty art of the aristocracy had become a craft for the masses.

And the masses produced their own folklore, such as the story surrounding the origin of Fair Isle knitting. The story goes that the Shetland tradition was suddenly enriched in 1588 when *El Gran Griffon*, a ship from the defeated Spanish Armada was wrecked on one of the Fair Isles. The Spanish sailors who abandoned ship wore brightly patterned knitted garments, each decorated with what came to be known as the Armada Cross. Since then, that cross has distinguished authentic Fair Isle knitting.

But most of that is legend. In fact, there was no cozy exchange of knitting techniques. After the wreck of *El Gran Griffon*, the Fair Islanders, afraid that the influx of unwelcome visitors would cause famine, hid their food and animals. Many of the Spaniards died of starvation. Others, weak from hunger, were set upon by the islanders and hurled from the high cliffs into the sea. Eventually, the Spaniards sent a small boat to mainland Shetland for help, and the surviving men were returned home.

Shetland Islanders were famous during the Victorian era for the quality of their lace knitting. They made shawls from the finest Shetland wool, plucked from the necks of their sheep and spun into yarn as delicate as cobwebs. A thousand yards of yarn could be spun from a single ounce of that wool. And the work was so fine that a shawl measuring 6 square feet could easily slip through a wedding ring—indeed, it became known as the "wedding-ring shawl." To promote their business, the Shetland Islanders presented Queen Victoria, herself an avid knitter, with a pair of lace stockings and gloves. With her royal blessing, Shetland lace achieved world renown.

By the 1920s, knitwear was burgeoning. Coco Chanel and Elsa Schiaparelli brought sweaters and cardigans into fashion, leading to a popular song entitled "All the Girls Are Busy Knitting Jumpers." In 1924, Chanel designed the costumes for Diaghilev's ballet *Le Train Bleu*, in which dancers portraying flappers and their boyfriends wore hand-knit bathing suits and golfing jerseys. The latter was patterned after the Prince of Wales's eye-catching Fair Isle pullover. In *A Family Album*, published in 1960, the prince wrote:

"I suppose the most showy of all my garments was the multicolored Fair Isle sweater, with its jigsaw patterns, which I wore for the first time while playing myself as Captain of the Royal & Ancient Gold Club at St. Andrews in 1922."

Today, however, designers find inspiration all over the world, and in many historical periods. As a knitter, you can still create an air of royalty with a Fair Isle pullover. Or you can fend off the evil eye with an Egyptian border, or put romance in your wardrobe with a touch of Shetland lace. The possibilities are endless. So why not work the patterns of history into your next knitting project? ⌐

Yarn Behavior and

by Mari Lynn Patrick

When knitting is a passion, our desire for new yarns to pass through our fingers cannot be contained. As today's knitting market is inundated with a wide array of fiber choices, we want you to be informed of new developments, not just what is available, but how each of these yarns behaves when put to the ultimate test. We hope to leave you with a fresh understanding of the world of yarns perfect for spring and transseasonal knitting.

COTTON YARNS

Cotton is an all-American wardrobe staple, worthy of praise for its wash-and-wearability and soft touch next to the skin. Medium to heavyweight cottons work best when made into easy-fit garments. Very fine cotton works beautifully into a dense elastic fabric when knit along with a strand of matching elastic thread. All cotton fabrics can suffer some drag or droopiness when knit up, so very shaped garments should probably be avoided. The overall finished weight of a garment knit in 100 percent cotton may affect your design choice.

When it comes to choosing a yarn for your spring project, you will find the varieties of fibers are indeed vast, the weights fall across the scale and the color range is simply delectable. Luxury blends in cashmere, silk and wool are balanced against sporty contenders in cotton, linen, rayon, Lycra blends and acrylic tapes.

COTTON/ACRYLIC BLENDS

Blending cotton with synthetic fibers is often the solution to some of the weight and elasticity problems of 100 percent cotton. Blending with polyester, acrylic, microfiber and/or nylon helps create a lighter fabric. Acrylic also adds elasticity and, because it is so receptive to dye, expands the color possibilities.

COTTON/WOOL BLENDS

This is one of the best marriages in yarns today. Wool provides memory elasticity, while cotton's dry hand helps to firm up wool's fuzzy density, providing a cooler fabric perfect for transseasonal wear. The two fibers absorb dye differently, creating creamy color with a lot of depth. Doubling the yarn creates chunky texture, the elasticity of the wool allows the design to keep its shape, and cotton keeps the finished fabric cool enough for warm weather.

LIGHTWEIGHT WOOLS

Most knitters are familiar with the properties of wool—it's strong, flexible, forgiving, and wonderfully warm. Summer-weight, or tropical, wools are often sportweight, babyweight or fingeringweight yarns. They have all of the benefits of their heavier cousins, but create a lighter, cooler fabric. When knit with a fine needle, they provide a deeply elastic fabric. Use a larger needle, say 5 or 6 sizes bigger than the size suggested, and they work into a light, airy fabric that will still hold its beautiful shape.

100 PERCENT SILK

The sheen and drape of silk is unparalleled in lightweight luxury and refinement. It

Misbehavior

works up into sensuous garments that are best worn close to the skin. Silk offers wonderful definition for stitch patterns—fine details will show up beautifully—so think lingerie-influenced camisoles. Silk's only drawback is its tendency for surface pilling.

COTTON/SILK BLENDS

Cotton and silk blends are another perfect coupling. Silk adds sheen to cotton's simple side, and cotton cuts back on silk's tendency to fray.

100 PERCENT CASHMERE

This scarce commodity, forever the aristocrat of fibers, is the hand-knitter's ultimate dream. Soft, lightweight and gorgeous to the touch, cashmere takes every range of subtle color dye to perfection. It is perfect for wearing year 'round and close to the skin. The yarn is time-consuming to produce, making it the most expensive yarn available to the hand-knitter.

CASHMERE BLENDS

The next best thing to cashmere, and certainly no slouch, is a cashmere blend. Since twinsets are designed to be bodywear, the best twinset will always be a cashmere or cashmere blend—the ultimate fiber experience for the body.

100 PERCENT LINEN

Pure linen is an extremely dry-handed, hard-structured yarn that stands up very well on its own. It works very well on a large needle—too small a needle can make a fabric that is very coarse. Linen's drawback is that it can be scratchy, so you may need to wear something between your skin and the sweater.

LINEN BLENDS

Linen blended with cotton or viscose gives a more drapey, less harsh fabric than 100 percent linen alone. The different ways the fibers take dye can give a subtle two-tone or heathered color effect.

RAYON TAPES

Rayon, or viscose, is a less expensive alternative to shiny, slinky silk. The yarn has beautiful elasticity, and its flat-tape construction cuts down on the fraying and pilling problems associated with silk. Rayon tape comes in various styles—sometimes shiny, sometimes stiffer and more substantial, but whatever type, be careful not to steam press, or your work will collapse and flatten. Expect some s-t-r-e-t-c-h with wear.

ACRYLIC TAPES

These are very versatile yarns that are often blended with viscose or rayon. As with any textured novelty yarn, seaming is best accomplished by crocheting together from the wrong side using a slip stitch.

CHENILLE

Chenille is fast becoming a new basic summer yarn, in either 100 percent cotton, cotton/acrylic, or viscose blends. Its velvety surface can be dressed up or down, making it a versatile fiber for any wardrobe. On the down side, the yarn has a tendency to "worm," and it has almost zero elasticity. As a result, ribs will not pull in and turtlenecks can look limp and lifeless. Finish chenille designs with flat simple crochet edges; for turtlenecks, avoid ribs completely and work decreases all around, in a similar way to shaping a hat crown.

LYCRA BLENDS

These very modern yarns are made with maximum stretch and shape memory—perfect for an active lifestyle. They can be slightly harsh when knitted up, so choose a Lycra yarn blended with a soft fiber for close-fitting garments.

METALLIC BLENDS

Metallic fibers blended with rayon, cotton or other basic fibers are returning to hand knitting in a big way. Metallics have a reputation for being stiff and scratchy, but breakthroughs in the manufacturing process are changing the character of this fun fiber mix. ⌒

Woolgathering

A joy to wear, wool can be easy-care, too.

by Donna Bulseco

Remember the day you decided that "just this once" it wouldn't hurt to throw your favorite wool sweater in the washing machine? Or when your spouse put your cherished cardigan in with the other washables and what emerged from the dryer was a doll-size replica of the sweater you could never live without?

Wool, like many other precious commodities, has to be treated with care in order to avoid the *I Love Lucy* episodes in all of our lives. And because of wool's beauty and durability, the lessons are worth learning. History shows us that wool can last for centuries: woolen cloth was found when the tombs of Egyptian pharoahs were unearthed. The early Romans took scrupulous care of wool—on their sheep—protecting the unshorn fleece with cloth or skins and washing, combing and oiling their flocks three or four times a year in order to produce a lustrous, wavy wool.

Nature and technology have produced an endless variety of types of wool. Lambswool, for example, is a fine, very soft yarn shorn from sheep up to 7 months old; it is identified by the round end or tip of the fiber, which shows it never has been cut. And then there's merino wool, which comes from merino sheep, one of the breeds most highly prized throughout history. (At one time, Spanish law prohibited the export of the Spanish merino flock with laws punishable by death.)

The Romans took scrupulous care of wool, washing, combing and oiling their flocks a few times a year.

More recently, science has come up with a machine-washable wool to prevent the "incredible shrinking sweater" scenario. In the last twenty years, scientists have wrestled with the unique properties of wool. Their aim has been to arrest or transform what causes damage to the fiber when washed, while maintaining the favorable qualities of wool—its resilience, luster and absorbency.

But the very properties that make wool so desirable also create the problems in the laundry room. Wool is a living fiber, its basic structure made up of cells growing from the inner follicles in the skin of sheep. Each wool fiber has a layer of microscopic scale-like structures which overlap like fish scales, allowing the fibers to move only in one direction. When wool is subjected to the heat, moisture and friction in a washing machine, the fibers become entangled with one another, causing felting or matting. Wool is unique in that it is the only fiber that has the ability to felt. Once the scales of the wool fiber interlock, however, the wool fiber cannot return to its original position. Consequently, when subjected to heat, moisture and agitation, the wool becomes bulkier and smaller; it shrinks and felts.

The importance of proper care is to maintain all of the special qualities of wool. (Those properties were so highly treasured in England during the Crusades that wool was used as a king's ransom to free Richard I, who was captured by John, Duke of Austria.) What are some of those precious characteristics? Wool is extremely durable. Under a microscope, a single wool fiber looks like a tiny coiled spring. This single fiber can be twisted and turned 20,000 times without breaking. What gives wool its resiliency is its natural crimp—it can be stretched 30 to 50 percent beyond its original length and rebound without damage. Even when twisted out of shape or subjected to strain, wool cells continue to resist damage and return to their original alignment.

Wool is also absorbent. While its outer scaly covering resists moisture, it has an inner protein cortex that absorbs water. In fact, wool can absorb up to 30 percent of its weight in water without feeling damp. Therefore, wool has the ability to absorb natural perspiration and release it gradually, preventing chills under a variety of weather conditions and making it comfortable to wear year-round.

In addition, wool gives more warmth than any other fiber—with the least weight—and shields the body from either colder or hotter air, regulating the body's natural temperature.

While there are many practical reasons why we choose wool, we also favor its beautiful hand and its vibrancy of color. Wool absorbs dye completely, and resists fading from outside forces like the sun, perspiration or pollution.

MACHINE-WASHABLE WOOL

For those who have resisted starting a knitting project in wool because of the time and effort involved in caring for wool sweaters, the machine-washable yarns are a beautiful alternative to acrylics. All of the properties that wool lovers embrace can be found in Superwash wool.

The idea behind Superwash wool is to arrest the felting process in order to avoid any further shrinkage. In simple terms, the Superwash process involves a mild chemical treatment that is applied to the fiber, forming a microscopic film of resin that evenly coats the fiber's surface. By covering the fiber, the film reduces friction, and consequently eliminates entanglement. The resin, which weighs no more than 2 percent of the total weight of the wool, is not diminished by washing and wearing because it is held permanently in place by chemical adhesive bonds. The treatment allows the wool fibers to move in either direction, and it is this freedom of movement that prevents felting.

SELECTING A SUPERWASH

By knitting with machine-washable wool, you eliminate many of the care problems you may encounter once the sweater is completed—from shrinkage to staining to felting. Many yarn companies offer yarns that have been treated with the Superwash process, which means the yarn has met the specifications set by the International Wool Secretariat that qualify it to be machine washed and dried.

Check your local yarn store to see what machine-washable wools are available to you. Then ask for appropriate patterns for that yarn, or look through knitting magazines and books for those styles applicable to the weight of wool you'd like to use.

CARE TIPS

Although Superwash yarns can be machine washed and dried without shrinking or fading under normal laundry conditions, it is wise to follow a few simple care instructions to achieve the best results.

- Turn the garment inside out.
- Machine wash at the gentlest cycle, usually mild detergent at 100°F (37.7°C), or at the warm setting. Because wool readily releases soil with mild washing, it is unnecessary to use hot water.
- A normal rinse and spin cycle is all that's necessary to finish the process. The regular spin cycle that extracts water and speeds the drying process does not damage Superwash wools.

- Tumble dry at a normal setting for about 15 to 20 minutes. Check periodically so that you do not overdry. You may also dry your sweaters in the open air on a towel placed on a flat surface or on a mesh sweater dryer.

- To reblock your sweater, draw an outline of it on brown paper or take measurements of the body length and width, and sleeve length and width, before you wash. Remove the sweater from the dryer while still slightly wet and block to desired dimensions.

- Use a light touch when pressing with steam, and never press completely dry. Do not iron the sweater as you would a shirt. Using a damp press cloth, lower and lift the iron instead of sliding it across the garment. Never press the ribbing. Press at right angles to the ribbing edge to avoid stretching.

Machine-washable wools are precious. Be sure to store your sweaters in a cool, dry area. After washing, fold sweaters and place in a well-sealed garment bag, cedar chest or acid-free tissue paper, taking care not to pack sweaters too closely. Use cedar chips or mothballs as extra protection.

Finally, make special-care labels for all of your sweaters. List fiber content, whether or not they are machine washable, and date made, on labeling tape marked with indelible ink. Once you get used to washing Superwash wool sweaters, you may forget what happens when you wash regular wool!

WOOL'S BEAUTY AND PRACTICALITY ARE DUE TO ITS COMPLEX INNER STRUCTURE. HERE, THREE MICROSCOPIC VIEWS OF AN INDIVIDUAL FIBER.

Each wool fiber has a built-in three-dimensional crimp—a combination of a sideward bend and an up-and-down twist, as illustrated on the right. Up to thirty crimps per inch can coexist on a wool fiber. Scientists believe they result from the uneven development of the fiber's interior cortex cells. These crimps decrease when the fiber is wet but promptly reassert themselves on drying. They are thus the basis of wool's elasticity. They also give wool its superb tactile

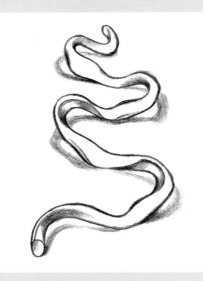

hand, its loft and its good cohesion. What's more, because crimps are constantly trying to maintain their natural convolutions, the individual wool fibers tend to keep repelling one another. This results in a retention of air within the yarns—or the knitted surface, or weave, of a woolen fabric. What it means is year-round insulation and comfort.

Under an electron microscope, the surface of a wool fiber is shown to have a covering of thin, scaly cells that overlap like the shingles on a roof. [See the illustration at right].

As a result of heat, moisture, or friction—the conditions in a washing machine and dryer—these scales tend to interlock and fuse, causing felting and—ultimately—shrinkage. The remedy is the Superwash process: the application of a mild chemical that evenly coats the surface of the fiber with a microscopic resin. The film—no more than 2 percent of the wool's weight—reduces friction and eliminates entanglement. Chemical bonds hold it in place—it can't wash out, so Superwash wool can safely be machine washed and dried.

The cross-section of a wool fiber, shown at right, reveals a dense mass of interior spindles, or cortical cells. Each cell is made of amino acids—the building blocks of life. These

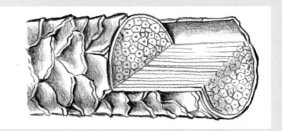

acids—up to nineteen of them have been counted—join together to form long cross-linked (or chemically bonded) chains. Such cross-linkage allows for wool's amazing resiliency. And because its chemical bonding is so active, wool accepts both acid and alkali dyes. It lastingly, brilliantly absorbs a wide range of colors. ⌒

The Cashmere Craze

by Melanie Falick

Ask Edith Eig, owner of La Knitterie Parisienne in Studio City, California, what's driving her yarn business these days and the answer you're likely to receive is "cashmere, cashmere, cashmere!" It's not only Eig's Hollywood clientele who are clamoring for the luscious yarn. Shop owners all over the country are noticing an increase in sales and interest in luxury fibers. "Cashmere is selling for us like wool was in the past," says Lindy Phelps, co-owner with Beryl Hiatt of Tricoter in Seattle. At stores as geographically diverse as Angel Hair Yarn Company in Nashville, Tennessee, and Three Kittens Yarn Shoppe in St. Paul, Minnesota, customers are stitching up everything from lace to baby gifts in this luxurious fiber.

Knitters across the country are taking their needles for a luxurious spin.

LOOKING FOR LUXURY

Mary McGurn, owner of colorful Stitches in Lenox, Massachusetts, reports that it is the large number of new, young knitters at her store who are fully embracing the cashmere craze. She is somewhat awed by the adventurous yarn choices of her novice knitters. "They're fearless," she says, "they'll knit a cashmere scarf as a first project." Edith Eig has noticed a similar trend with her young clientele. "They're knitting cashmere on small needles—size 4s," she says. "They don't care how long the project will take. They just love the feel of the yarn."

What's the driving force behind the demand for cashmere and other luxury yarns? Linda Skolnik, owner of Patternworks in Poughkeepsie, New York, takes a philosophical view. "We're knitting for self-fulfillment, for the same reason that we go to art museums," she points out. "We are no longer picking up our needles to save money; it's hardly possible. We knit during our very limited—and precious—free time and want to work with the best and most interesting materials we can afford."

McGurn points to the ready-to-wear market, which is pushing the "good life" in a big way. "Cashmere is everywhere, from the Lands' End catalog to every department store." Fashion aficionados view the growing interest in cashmere as part of a millennial trend toward understated self-indulgence and a growing demand for comfortable garments that are both warm and lightweight. No longer afraid to splurge for quality, today's consumers

Baby cashmere goats from Mongolia.

crave beautiful things. Call it the "cashmere mystique." "Wearing cashmere is like a green light to a world of sophistication, wealth, gentility and art," says Lisa Parks, a knitwear designer in Pontiac, Michigan. "My knitters want to make heirloom pieces," explains Three Kittens owner Karen Weiberg, "and cashmere endures."

But don't overlook the purely economic component—in recent months cashmere has become more affordable. Thanks to the loosening of communist restraints on Chinese and Mongolian herders and a drastic cut in demand from Japan (traditionally a huge importer of cashmere products) as a result of that country's faltering economy, raw cashmere prices are down. A glut of cashmere on the world market is another reason cashmere sweater sets are popping up in every price range.

QUALITY COUNTS

Even with market prices falling, cashmere handknitting yarn is still one of the most expensive fibers out there, and quality varies. Marilyn Ackley of Cashmere America, a cooperative of about 125 American cashmere growers, suggests letting touch be your guide when choosing a cashmere yarn. "If a yarn feels good between your fingers it will feel good when it is knit up," she explains. Ackley suggests consumers avoid cashmere yarns in which coarse, straight, stiff "guard" hairs are visible (an indication that the fiber may not have been processed carefully) and yarn that shows small white specs of dander (more prevalent with hand-spun than machine-spun cashmere). Spinning expert and Cashmere America consultant Marilyn Merbach suggests you test cashmere quality by holding a piece of yarn between your hands and rubbing up and down on it firmly. Cashmere that frays, fuzzes or breaks may not be a good investment; if the yarn holds together, it's probably good quality. For added insurance, Ackley suggests purchasing a single skein, then knitting a swatch and washing it to see how the yarn behaves. Good quality cashmere lofts, or "blooms," after washing. The fiber releases a

very subtle, soft fuzz that sits atop the fabric like a cloud or halo. However, "if that halo gets too long or looks excessive, the yarn wasn't spun tightly enough," adds Merbach. Because cashmere fibers are relatively short (about 1½ to 3 inches) and fine, they require several twists (about five to twelve per inch) to hold together. Yarn that doesn't have enough twist is likely to pill excessively; yarn with too much twist will feel harsh.

KNIT KNACK

Lovely as it may be, cashmere is not suited to every knitting project. Ackley advises taking advantage of the fiber's natural assets—smoothness, softness, drape and warmth—by using it to make simple, lightweight garments such as scarves or sweaters with uncomplicated silhouettes. "Cashmere has less elasticity than wool," she explains, "it drapes rather than bounces back." Ackley also points out that cashmere ribbing will not pull in as much as wool ribbing; you'll need to use smaller needles and/or fewer stitches to get similar results. Another good choice for cashmere is lace—Ackley advises using a pattern that incorporates sections of plain knitting, since smooth areas (such as those worked in stockinette stitch) will feel better against the skin than large areas of texture. Baby garments are another wonderful outlet for cashmere. Decadent and somewhat impractical, perhaps, but Ackley points out that the small size of these pieces makes them relatively inexpensive to knit, and parents (who always think their babies deserve the best) adore these heirlooms.

When exploring the world of luxury fibers, don't overlook cashmere blends. Not only are these yarns usually less costly than pure cashmere, they are also more versatile. Blends of cashmere and merino are more elastic than pure cashmere and luxuriously soft. The addition of wool can also "bulk up" cashmere, creating a chunky yarn that isn't overly warm. Cashmere blended with silk has an attractive opalescent luster (an attribute completely lacking in pure cashmere), beautiful drape and improved stitch definition. Cashmere-silk blends have less loft than pure cashmere and cashmere-merino blends. Blends made with less than 30 percent cashmere should be evaluated carefully—they may not be worth the price. Cashmere (and the allure attached to it) may be used to catch the knitter's attention, but the properties that make it so special may be obliterated by the fibers that make up the majority of the yarn's content.

TAKE CARE

When it comes time to launder a cashmere hand knit, Merbach suggests hand-washing in hot water with a gentle washing medium (such as Ivory Liquid or Dawn). Keep the water temperature the same for both washing and rinsing (you don't want to "shock" the fibers) and remove water from the garment gently, without twisting or pulling. To dry, lay the garment flat in an area away from direct sunlight and gently reshape.

A small amount of pilling is inevitable with cashmere garments (the same is true of other soft fibers, such as angora, qiviut and merino), especially if the yarn was spun loosely. Merbach advises gently pulling on pills to remove them.

"Pilling doesn't indicate poor quality," points out Beryl Hiatt of Tricoter, "it's just part of the experience of hand-knitting with fabulous soft fibers."

While the extra cost and care that come with knitting cashmere can be daunting, once knitters feel the fiber running through their fingers, there's no turning back. "I have customers who won't knit with anything else," says Hiatt. McGurn agrees, "Once you've tried cashmere it's hard to give up!" Some knitters who suffer from carpal tunnel syndrome and other joint problems report that it is less taxing on their wrists than many other fibers. So even if cashmere proves to be a passing trend among the fashion conscious, it's likely to become a mainstay for knitters. Cashmere, like all the little luxe "extras" in our lives, enriches what is already a supremely gratifying experience. ⌐

WHAT IS CASHMERE?

The name cashmere is the result of confusion that arose when the fiber first appeared in Europe. Luxury textiles of the day were often imported from the Kashmir region of India, so merchants mistakenly assumed that Kashmir (cashmere) was the source for this sumptuous fiber. Cashmere is derived from a breed of goats (Capra hircus) indigenous to Asia that are genetically capable of producing a fiber that meets specific standards for length, fineness and performance. Pashmina, the finest, lightest, softest cashmere available (and currently the rage among fashion cognoscenti), comes from a goat that lives in the Himalayas.

Fiber from cashmere-producing goats has two main components: the outer "guard" hairs, which are coarse and typically straight, and the fine undercoat (known as down). While all the goats of the Capra hircus strain are genetically capable of producing these components, whether or not a particular goat produces cashmere from year to year depends on several environmental factors, including weather, terrain and diet. To determine whether or not a goat has produced a fiber that qualifies as cashmere, the goat is combed or shorn and the down is evaluated by a "classer" (a professional trained to judge cashmere) for diameter, length and crimp (waviness). True cashmere fiber does not exceed 18.5 microns (about a third of the diameter of a human hair—top-quality cashmere is even finer), is usually at least 1¼ inches (3.25cm) long, and is extremely wavy. Fiber that meets these standards can be labeled pure cashmere, though quality varies depending on how well these standards are met and how the fiber is prepared for spinning, spun, and dyed.

Exploring Yarn Substitution

by Mari Lynn Patrick

Choosing the right substitute yarn is most important. For the first time, we're identifying yarns by a new code. Here, we explain what the symbols in the code mean and how they can help you make yarn substitutions with confidence.

Today most yarn labels carry gauge symbols that conform to the Craft Yarn Council's Standard Yarn Weight System. This article anticipates the current system by several decades! We have included here the standard weight chart (which also appears in every issue of *Vogue Knitting*).

Standard Yarn Weight System

Categories of yarn, gauge ranges, and recommended needle and hook sizes

Yarn Weight Symbol & Category Names	1 Super Fine	2 Fine	3 Light	4 Medium	5 Bulky	6 Super Bulky
Type of Yarns in Category	Sock, Fingering, Baby	Sport, Baby	DK, Light Worsted	Worsted, Afghan, Aran	Chunky, Craft, Rug	Bulky, Roving
Knit Gauge Range* in Stockinette Stitch to 4 Inches	27–32 sts	23–26 sts	21–24 sts	16–20 sts	12–15 sts	6–11 sts
Recommended Needle in Metric Size Range	2.25–3.25 mm	3.25–3.75 mm	3.75–4.5 mm	4.5–5.5 mm	5.5–8 mm	8 mm and larger
Recommended Needle U.S. Size Range	1 to 3	3 to 5	5 to 7	7 to 9	9 to 11	11 and larger
Crochet Gauge* Ranges in Single Crochet To 4 Inch	21–32 sts	16–20 sts	12–17 sts	11–14 sts	8–11 sts	5–9 sts
Recommended Hook in Metric Size Range	2.25–3.5 mm	3.5–4.5 mm	4.5–5.5 mm	5.5–6.5 mm	6.5–9 mm	9 mm and larger
Recommended Hook U.S. Size Range	B–1 to E–4	E–4 to 7	7 to I–9	I–9 to K–10½	K–10½ to M–13	M–13 and larger

*** GUIDELINES ONLY: The above reflect the most commonly used gauges and needle or hook sizes for specific yarn categories.**

Certainly, substituting one yarn for another was easier when most yarns fell into four main categories—baby/fingering, sport, worsted/4-ply, and bulky. Now there are so many different kinds of yarns that many fall in between these four categories. In addition to yarns, there's a vast range of novel materials. With this array of choices, the problem of interchanging yarns seems greater than ever before.

Of course, the only yarn which will duplicate the look of the yarn shown in our photographs is the original yarn. Even if you get the exact gauge with another yarn, this different yarn will give your garment a different hand, weight and sheen. To select a yarn other than the original, first match up yarn type, using the yarn type symbols if they are given. Then compare the new yarn carefully to the sample on the photo page. Use the gauge symbol to select the yarn weight. Experiment to find the correct needle size to get the gauge, determine the total amount of yarn needed, and you are ready to knit.

GETTING THE GAUGE

Needle size isn't important. When you work in stockinette stitch, there's a range of needle sizes for each weight of yarn that will give a rounded-off number of stitches when making a 4"/10cm–square swatch. Depending on the tension (how tightly or loosely you knit), you can find a perfect needle size to achieve the gauge you want. You may have to try one or two sizes above or below the stated needle size before you get the exact gauge.

HOW MUCH YARN?

To decide exactly how much of a substitute yarn to buy, use the *yardage* as a guide, not the weight in ounces or grams. Yardage (and meter length) is always stated under "Materials" in *Vogue Knitting* instructions. Multiply the total number of balls you need by the number of yards/meters in each ball to determine how much yarn to purchase. Since yardages per ball vary greatly, check carefully when exchanging one yarn for another.

YARN SYMBOLS

If a knitting project uses a special type of yarn, the appropriate symbol is given. If a knitting project uses plain yarn, no symbol is provided.

When making substitutions, it is important to remember the character of the yarn. Cotton, rayon and silk yarns stretch and change shape when worn, while wools or synthetic blends retain their original shape. Tapes and ribbons give a unique dimension to the knitted texture, while mohairs and angoras impart a special lighter-than-air appeal. Tweeds and variegated yarns perform an allover, subtle color dance, so a sweater may look ordinary if the replacement is a plain, flat yarn. On the other hand, if a sweater has a complex patterning, all knitting efforts may be buried if you substitute a highly textured yarn.

"Pay attention to gauge" is the primary rule for all knitters and the most important thing to remember when interchanging yarns. The yarn categories have been restructured to group yarns by their gauges, not by the old standards of fingering, sport, worsted and bulky. There are six gauge symbols now:

1. Fine Weight (29–32 stitches per 4"/10cm).

    This category includes lightweight dress yarns, baby and fingering yarns, and some of the heavier crochet cottons. The average range of needle sizes is U.S. 0–4/metric 2–3½mm).
2. Lightweight (25–28 stitches per 4"/10cm).

    Sport yarn, sock and sweater yarn, and U.K. 4-ply fall into this group. Lightweight sweaters, socks, gloves, dresses and children's wear are often made from this weight. Needle size range is U.S. 3–6/metric 3¼–4mm.
3. Medium Weight (21–24 stitches per 4"/10cm).

    The majority of yarns available are included in this group. This is the weight most often preferred for garments, afghans and accessories. This includes the knitting worsted and U.K. double knitting group. Needle size range is U.S. 6–9/metric 4–5½mm.
4. Medium-Heavy Weight (17–20 stitches per 4"/10cm).

    The yarns in this group could be called heavy worsted. They are used almost as frequently as medium-weight yarns. Needle size range is U.S. 8–10/metric 5–6mm.
5. Bulky Weight (13–16 stitches per 4"/10cm).

    These yarns could be called bulky or chunky, and are often used for outerwear. A double strand of a medium (knitting worsted) weight yarn usually gets the same gauge. Needle size range is U.S. 10–11/metric 6–8mm.
6. Extra-Bulky Weight (9–12 stitches per 4"/10cm).

    Most of the heaviest yarns available are included in this group. They're used for the same items as bulky-weight yarns, above. Needle size range is U.S. 11–15/metric 8–10mm.

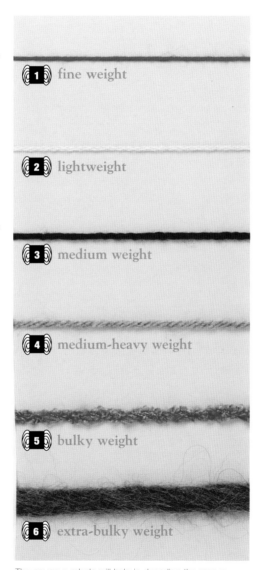

The gauge symbols will help in decoding the proper weight for your substitute yarn.

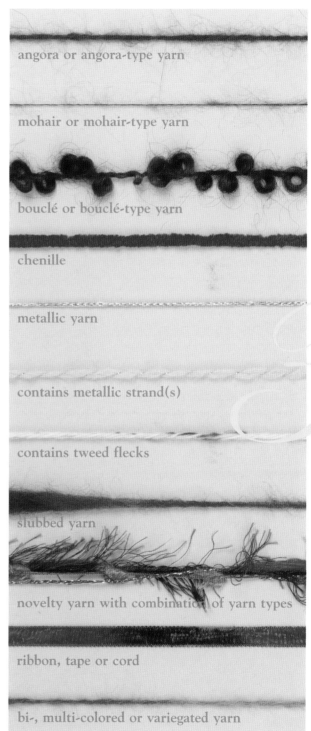

When choosing alternative yarns, read yarn symbols to determine fiber content; texture plays an important part in substituting yarns.

Organic Yarn: Nurturing

by Barbara Albright

Nature With Knitting

What makes yarn organic? Unlike the more nebulous term "natural," "organic" has long had a good working definition, thanks to farmers and other producers who established voluntary certification programs. And now a version of that definition is a matter of law: In 2002, the United States Department of Agriculture put in place a set of strict national standards. While the focus is setting guidelines for organic foods, the standards apply as well to the production of animals and plants used as sources of fiber. Those who violate the rules will be fined up to $10,000 for each infraction.

The key is how the animal or plant is raised, but the standards also dictate how the fiber itself is processed. To qualify as organic, a fiber must meet the following criteria:

• Wool-producing animals must graze only in organic pastures and be given non-genetically modified feeds.

• The animals must not receive routine antibiotics, wormers or other medications.

• No chemicals should be applied topically to control parasites.

• Fiber-producing plants such as cotton must be grown without the use of synthetic pesticides and fertilizers.

When we put on a sweater, most of us don't give a thought to its animal or plant origins. Though we have long been careful about what we put *in* our bodies, we are only now becoming concerned about what we put *on* them. Increasingly, fiber producers are seeking to do the right thing for Mother Earth, and consumers are looking for organic products that support an eco-friendly, sustainable way of life.

• No bleach or other chemicals may be used to wash or scour the fibers, and they may not be treated with mothproofing or flame-retardant finishes.

• The yarn must be spun using organic spinning oils, not petroleum-based oils.

• Organic fibers must be handled separately to avoid contamination.

However stringent these requirements, claims on labels of yarn that meets them will be limited to "made with," as in "made with organic cotton," according to Sandra Marquardt, coordinator of the Fiber Council of the Organic Trade Association, which protects the integrity of organic standards and promotes organic products in the marketplace.

There are several reasons to choose yarn with the organic label. One is that by doing so, knitters are supporting a system of agriculture that works to build healthy soil and a clean environment. Another plus is that organic fibers are a great choice for people with multiple chemical sensitivities or for those who think they may be allergic to wool. (In fact, they may be reacting adversely to the chemicals in the soaps or oils with which the wool was processed and finished, not the wool itself. Wool fiber is very

Pakucho organic cotton, made by cooperatives in Peru.

porous, and toxic products can never be eliminated completely.) If organic fibers sound right for you, keep your eyes and ears open for people farming in a sustainable manner in your area. Getting to know the producers of your fiber helps you get back in touch with the earth. Thinking local also cuts down on the amount of fuel needed to transport the fiber.

COTTON

Cotton crops around the world are routinely treated with fertilizers, pesticides, growth regulators and defoliants, putting both workers and consumers at risk. In fact, Lynda Brown in *Organic Living* estimates that cotton production accounts for nearly 25 percent of the total global insecticide market. When cotton is farmed organically, however, farm workers are not exposed to toxic chemicals that can harm them and pollute the ground water or soil. After cotton is grown and picked, the fiber is separated from the seeds, carded and then brushed. Then, to be considered organic, the cotton must be spun with beeswax. (In contrast, the ring-spinning process does not use wax or additives of any kind. Open-end spun yarn is less expensive but uses paraffin wax.)

SILK

Silk is made from the fine, long fiber produced by the silkworm for its cocoon. It can be grown commercially or cultivated in the wild. Conventional silk is made by boiling intact cocoons and unwinding the single silk strand onto reels; only a few moths are allowed to emerge to populate the species. Silk is produced in this manner so the fibers won't be broken and can be reeled off in a continuous strand.

Worms that live naturally in tropical or semitropical forests produce tussah, or wild silk, which is gathered after the moth emerges from its cocoon. The fiber, generally stronger and more resilient than cultivated silk, is hand spun by softening the cocoon with soap and then pulling the fiber from it into a yarn. Because silkworms eat all types of trees, the silk varies from beige to brownish in tone. It dyes beautifully, with the colors softly muted by the beige undertones. Because tussah silks are wild-crafted, they can be considered organically raised.

WOOL

The use of pesticides in wool production is widespread. Noxious chemicals are employed in sheep-dipping, a common way to control parasites. The process can harm not only the farmer and the animal but also the environment, since a pollutant

residue is often dumped into waterways.

To ensure the animals' safety and natural productivity, organic-livestock producers commit to breeding sheep in a chemical-free environment. In fact, "organic wool" is defined by the way the livestock is raised:

- Animals must be fed 100 percent organically grown feed (grains) and forage (pastures).
- Use of synthetic hormones, vaccinations and genetic engineering is prohibited.
- Producers must encourage livestock health through good cultural and management practices.

The term does not yet apply to what happens to the wool once it is processed. Those standards, however, are being developed by the Organic Trade Association and will be passed on to the USDA for consideration in its development of federal standards for organic-fiber processing.

For sources of organic wool, visit the Organic Pages Online at www.theorganicpages.com. Search for Fiber and Textiles, then Wool Fiber.

WASHING ORGANIC FIBERS

Right now there are no regulations in place for certified organic washing of organic textiles, so we went to hands-on experts in the field. David Ritchie of Green Mountain Spinnery recommends Eucalan, saying, "We've been assured it is not petroleum-based." Robin Collier of Tierra Wools says, "We hand-wash raw wool with a plant-based detergent such as orange oil or soy soap. I'd like to experiment with yucca root, a traditional Navajo soap. And we're looking at earthworm enzyme detergents, which seem promising."

MOTH PREVENTION

Says David Ritchie: "The Textile Museum in Washington, D.C., says that freezing wool for a sustained period will kill moths." Adds Robin Collier, "We suggest storing wool in cedar chests or with a sachet of cedar shavings, juniper and sage. Some of the natural dyes we use, such as indigo and sage, act as natural moth repellents." ⌒

ABOUT ORGANIC YARNS

The Organic Trade Association, P.O. Box 547, Greenfield, MA 01302; (413) 774-7511; fax: (413) 774-6432; info@ota.com; www.ota.com.

United States Department of Agriculture, www.ams.usda.gov/nop.

The Business of Bliss

by Daryl Brower

Have you ever daydreamed about working with wool spun from your own private flock or knitting on your front porch as the spring lambs frolic at your feet? Judy McDowell, Kat Smith and Winnie Johnson have made that dream a reality. Shepherding their budding flocks hasn't allowed them to give up their day jobs, but all three are spinning themselves a nice little sideline (and a whole lot of serenity) in wool and needles.

HIGH FIBER

Misty Meadow Icelandics
Minnetrista, MN

Judy McDowell swears she fell in love with knitting from the first stitch. She may not have picked up her first pair of needles until she was 25, but she's had a lifelong passion for fiber, one that led her to dive into life on a sheep farm.

In 1989, while house hunting, Judy and her husband Tom came across a 10-acre farm that was perfect for raising an Icelandic breed of sheep being introduced to the U.S. at the time. "They're just incredible animals, descendants of the flocks brought to Iceland by the Vikings in 1000 A.D.," says Judy. Because they had led such an isolated existence, the sheep had never been crossbred, meaning that they were genetically identical to their ancient ancestors. The result is a fleece known for its wonderful array of natural black, brown, white and gray spotted colors.

In 1994, Tom and Judy purchased two lambs (a ram and a ewe), making their flock of Icelandics one of the first in the U.S. Today they care for twenty-five registered purebreds, though the number can swell to as many as forty during lambing season. The couple still work full-time for the Three Rivers Park District (Tom as director, Judy as a special services manager), but the farm remains a family affair, with kids Emily, 11, and Zack, 8, helping

Judy McDowell examines her "harvest."

out with the chores. Tom handles the breeding, selling and day-to-day management of the larger flock; Judy focuses on developing yarns and marketing them to the public.

"Tom loves caring for the sheep and is very aware of how each one is doing," Judy explains. "I'm excited by the fiber end of it."

When shearing time rolls around, the farm becomes party central. Tom hires someone to help with the shearing, and family and friends head over to pitch in. Those friends often include parents and students from the Waldorf School that Zack attends. "Knitting and fiber arts are a big part of the curriculum there," says Judy, who just completed training to become a Waldorf instructor. "So coming out here to see how wool goes from sheep to sweater is really a great thing for the kids."

"We make hand spinners happy" is the motto by which the McDowell family lives. "We have customers who reserve fleece from a particular ewe months before shearing," says Tom, who is happy to fill such requests. The rest of the yield is sold as clouds or roving on the Misty Meadow Icelandics Web site, reserved for Judy's own hand-spinning and -dyeing experiments, or sent to a mill in Taos, New Mexico, that spins it into yarn to Judy's specifications.

Judy is also branching out into design and ready-to-wear. With the help of her sister-in-law, who lives in Manhattan, she's working on a line of mittens and other accessories to sell in boutiques in New York and other metropolitan areas. "I've always wanted to try it," she says. "So I am."

For Judy, country life was a big change. But for someone who lives and breathes fiber, life on a sheep farm is a perfect fit. "You develop this incredible connection to the seasons," she explains. "I connect in ways I never could have as a suburbanite.

"I spin out on the front porch in the summer—it's wonderful to sit there and listen to the lambs or watch the sheep out in the field. In the fall we're busy with shearing, and in the winter I do most of my knitting—it just feels right to have something warm evolving in my hands."

A DREAM JOB

A DREAM JOB

Stonesthrow Farm
Wallingford, VT

Growing up in suburban Ohio, Kat Smith fantasized about owning a farm where she could keep horses. The purchase of a house in Vermont helped her finally realize that dream, though not exactly as she had imagined it. She cleared some land on the 6-acre property for a pasture and purchased two sheep, which she intended to use as "living lawn mowers." That all changed when she took a spinning lesson.

"I learned to spin, fell in love with the sheep and never got the horses," she says, laughing. Nine years later the flock of two has grown to twenty-five (four different breeds in all) and has been joined by ten Angora goats that provide a constant source of entertainment. The goats also provide the gorgeous mohair fleece that Kat has introduced to her hand-spinning business. As for the sheep, she keeps their fleece covered throughout the year to keep dirt, hay and other vegetation out, which allows her to spin their wool without processing it after shearing. The result is a strong and lustrous fleece that she sells at sheep and wool festivals in New York, Vermont and New Hampshire.

"My fleece comes from Cormo, Shetland, Blue Face Leicester and Romney breeds, so I have a broad spectrum of fine to strong in browns, black, grays of all kinds and white." A professional comes in twice a year to do the shearing, an event that Kat says is her favorite time of the year. "It's fantastic. I get to see the 'crop' I've been watching and waiting a year to harvest," she explains. The day also turns into a pseudo block party, with friends and neighbors coming over to help.

Except for the shearing, Kat—who works full-time as a nurse at the local hospital—runs the farm and does the spinning single-handedly. Not that she's complaining. "I love this life," she says. "I love the rhythms of the year, watching the lambs leap and play. What could be better?"

WOOL AND A WARM WELCOME

The Woodland Cottage
Elk River, MN

Winnie Johnson turned to knitting at an early age. "I grew up in a family of quilters, but I wanted to try something a little different," she says. Over the years her enthusiasm for knitting and weaving grew, and she decided it would be fun to raise her own sheep and spin her own yarn. That decision came as a revelation. "One day," she says, "I realized I lived in the perfect spot," a 45-acre hobby farm in Elk River, Minnesota, that she and her husband Russ have occupied for the past twenty years. "I had a friend who was also interested, so we bought a few sheep and a spinning wheel that we traded back and forth and taught ourselves to spin."

Winnie Johnson greets a friend.

The size of the flock has fluctuated over the years, from two to as many as twenty-five. Six sheep are currently in residence, along with the bees Russ keeps for honey. Winnie—who also substitute teaches—hires a pro to handle the shearing. She then custom-spins and hand-dyes the fleece into wool sock and mitten yarn.

Two years ago, Winnie and Russ decided to expand into the bed-and-breakfast market. "My mother lived in a three-bedroom house on a lovely wooded lot across the road," explains Winnie. "When she passed away, we had to decide what to do with the property." Selling it was one option, but Russ had a better idea. Aware of how much Winnie loved teaching—she has been dispensing knitting, quilting and weaving advice for as long as she can remember—he suggested opening a B&B catering to fiber lovers that would offer workshops and classes in knitting, spinning, dyeing and weaving as well as the usual home-cooked breakfast and countryside peace and quiet.

Today the house across the lane includes a spacious workshop filled with roomy tables, cutting mats, sewing machines, looms, spinning wheels and quilting frames. Candlemaking, spinning, quilting and felting classes are offered, though guests can also bring along an instructor or ask Winnie to custom-design a program for their stay. Some visitors arrive with no itinerary in mind, working at their own pace on a project of their choosing or just sitting in the yard watching the sheep and lambs frolic in the fields. "The idea is to relax and enjoy a craft you love," says Winnie. "I'm just here to help."

OUT OF SITE

Looking for more information about raising a flock of your own? Check out these Web sites:

- www.woolandfeathers.com provides support and direction for hobby farmers.
- www.farminfo.org includes advice and articles for raising all sorts of livestock (sheep included).
- www.frelsifarm.com/farm_resources.htm offers informative articles on small farming, including one on starting a flock on a shoestring budget.

EXPERT ADVICE

Tamara Burke raises Icelandic sheep on the Farm at Morrison Corner in Mansfield, Vermont, and provides advice and support for small farmers through her award-winning Web site, www.woolandfeathers.com. She advises would-be shepherds to consider the following before starting a flock of their own.

WHERE SHOULD YOU PURCHASE YOUR SHEEP?

Research the different breeds and ask others in the business for names of reputable breeders. Resist the temptation to bring a cheap "starter flock" onto your property, says Burke. "Cheap sheep can bring with them perfectly loathsome diseases and problems that are there to stay once they're on your farm. Inferior genetics will yield inferior fleece, and you'll have higher vet and feed bills to contend with."

Registered sheep can cost from $400–$2,000 apiece, but you can find quality sheep at a more budget-conscious price. "Many farms will sell you unregistered sheep on the cheap," says Burke. "If you decide to register them later, you can sell the lambs at a premium; the farm will charge you the difference and send you the papers." If breeding and lambing aren't in your plans, there's an even less expensive alternative. "Buy wethers [neutered males]," says Burke. "You'll get a perfectly adequate, and quite friendly, little flock."

HOW MANY SHEEP DO YOU NEED?

Between six and twelve animals—a ram, a wether and four breeding ewes—is enough to keep a good spinner knee-deep in fleece. "Your ewes will throw their own replacements, you'll 'roll' your wether every few years, and your ram will need to be replaced every three years or so," Burke explains. Keep in mind that the bigger the flock, the bigger the investment in space, feed, fencing and shelter.

If you plan to spin only for yourself, a smaller flock will do, but make sure to have at least two in every pen. "Sheep are flocking animals," says Burke. "Leave one alone and it will get weird." If your flock will include a ram, make sure you have a wether to keep him company during the times he'll be penned separately from the ewes. A wether is also an ideal companion for new animals that must be quarantined before being introduced to your existing flock.

IS IT LEGAL?

Is the area in which you live zoned for sheep? Is there a limit to the size and number of buildings you can put on your property? Does your community have fencing requirements? Burke knows of a local lodge that purchased several llamas for pets and fiber and to draw in business. "When they went to the town to get their barn-building permit, they were turned down cold. The town board decided the lodge was not a farm, and that the animals were there to be mobile billboards. The barn permit was denied, and they were forced to sell the animals at a catastrophic loss." Knowing what type of shelters you are allowed to build will save a lot of aggravation down the road.

WHERE WILL YOU HOUSE THE SHEEP?

A securely fenced pen or pasture is essential for keeping the sheep in and neighborhood dogs and other predators out. If you plan to raise both a ram and ewes, you must provide separate accommodations. Burke cautions against relying on regular fencing to do the trick: "A motivated ram can bash his way through a solid fence," she explains. "Plan on either welded steel livestock panels, or fence your rams and ewes on opposite sides of your house so they can't see each other. You must also provide shelter from the elements and a dry area on which to stand and lamb."

WILL YOU BE ABLE TO FEED THEM?

"An appalling number of new shepherds get a sturdy breed like Icelandics or Shetlands and think all they have to do is put them out on scrub pasture," says Burke. Not so. Sheep need fresh water, shade, a salt/mineral supplement and a good supply of hay for the winter months and times when grass is in short supply. If you're planning on becoming a "backyard" shepherd, Burke advises purchasing feed in small quantities and making certain it is stored securely.

HOW WILL YOU MAINTAIN THE HEALTH OF YOUR FLOCK?

You'll need a qualified veterinarian with livestock experience to provide both well and sick care for your animals. But perhaps more important than a vet is another supportive farmer. "Buy your sheep from someone who is willing to be there for you," Burke advises. "Paying a little extra per sheep from someone who is willing to help you get started is well worth it when you're lambing for the first time and have a question at 4 o'clock in the morning. Your vet is going to charge you to answer a simple question. Another shepherd is going to laugh about it with you." ⌣

Essay: Starting Early

A class of young children, even the early grades, can learn to knit. The trick is choosing easy projects and suitable material and translating the process into a story.

by Margaret Bruzelius

How did you learn to knit? At your mother's knee? Or your grandmother's? If you were born in the United States, you undoubtedly picked it up from a friend or family member, because knitting has never been part of American school curriculum.

Recently, however, there has been a surge of interest in teaching children to knit, as teachers have discovered that it helps their students master penmanship. Through knitting, children develop fine motor skills, not to mention a pride in accomplishment that prepares them for more difficult academic tasks.

Still, the only schools I've found that teach knitting to all pupils (not only the girls) are the Waldorf schools, which follow the philosophy of turn-of-the-century Austrian educator Rudolf Steiner. These private schools encourage the natural creativity of children by instructing them in drawing, needlework and dancing as well as reading, writing and arithmetic. Needlework training begins in the first grade with knitting, and continues in succeeding grades with embroidery and crochet. Children resume knitting in the fifth grade, when they learn to make socks or mittens. At some Waldorf schools, the students even make their own knitting needles by sanding down one end of a wooden dowel and fastening a knob to the other.

Elisabeth Radysh teaches needlework at the Waldorf school in New York, where I sat in on first- and fifth-grade classes. The Swiss-born instructor, who learned to knit from her mother, works with all grades in twice-weekly, 40-minute sessions. She introduces her first-graders to knitting by showing them how to make simple finger loops—first a slip knot, then a finger chain—using a cord approximately twenty-four inches long.

In the Steiner method, teachers often relate abstract concepts to the natural and cultural phenomena that surround a child (numbers, for example, are associated with units found in nature or in familiar stories—one sun, two eyes, three kings, four seasons and so on). With that in mind, Elisabeth has developed stories that help children to visualize each step of the process she is teaching. The first slip-knot loop is a little bird that sits on a branch (the stretched-out cord). When the children form new loops by drawing the cord through loops they have already made, new birds have come to sit on the branch. Once the cord is full of loops, the child pulls the ends and makes all of the birds fly away, so that only the branch remains.

After perfecting the finger loops, the children learn to fasten off the end of the chain, join the ends together, and make a crown. Each child is then crowned in front of the whole class. Fifth-graders I spoke with could still remember how proud they felt when they had mastered the loops and were crowned.

Next, the first-grade class moves on to knitting. Each child has a pair of 10"/25cm, size 10 (6mm) wooden needles and a small ball of yarn, which is wound around a message, a folded drawing by a classmate. Elisabeth casts on for the first project (she finds casting on much easier to teach once the children understand basic knitting moves).

Between needlework classes, all of the students' knitting is kept in a big basket. At the beginning of each session, the children rearrange their chairs in a circle, then Elisabeth selects two children, one to read out the name on the large tag attached to each child's work, the other to hand out the work.

All the children take on the same project, a scarf made up of garter-stitch squares, 18 stitches by 24 rows, in various colors. Elisabeth teaches the Continental method of knitting, in which the yarn comes from the left hand. Again she presents the process as a story: the mother bird (the right needle) swoops down to the branch (the left needle), picks up the baby bird (the stitch), gives it a worm (the new loop formed by the yarn) and then hops off the needle. Children trying to remember all the steps can be heard around the circle murmuring to themselves, "Here comes the Mama bird; then she gets the worm…no, she picks up the baby bird first…."

By translating the movements of knitting into a story, Elisabeth avoids dry explanations that 6-year-olds would have difficulty remembering. She never needs to mention either needle, only the mother bird and the branch holding all her babies. Stitches picked up inadvertently are adopted babies. (One boy, asking Elisabeth for help, said, "My mother bird seems to have adopted a *lot* of babies.") Dropped stitches are babies that have fallen from their nest; Elisabeth helps the mother bird place them securely back on the branch.

In the first-grade class I observed eighteen boys and girls sitting in a circle knitting. Naturally some were better than others, but all had completed at least one color square, and many were working on a third or fourth. There was great excitement when a student, reaching the end of his ball, was able to unfold the message inside. Each message was shown around the circle.

Not everything was so easy. The children had trouble remembering how to turn the needle after reaching the end of the row—Elisabeth was constantly pointing out that the baby bird could not hop off the end of the needle that had the knob on it. And students relied on Elisabeth to attach a new color. Yet all of the children clearly enjoyed the work (although the presence of a visitor was inevitably distracting), and Elisabeth's announcement that the session was almost over was met with cries of "Aaaaw!" and "Just a few more minutes, Mrs. Radysh!"

Eventually, after putting the fringe on the scarf, the students move on to a garter–stitch cat and projects requiring varying degrees of skill. By fifth grade they have acquired enough skill in handwork to make

knitting bags embroidered with their names. Most of the fifth-graders I saw were knitting socks, although a few were tackling mittens or caps. All were able to work on double-pointed needles and to achieve shaping that goes into a sock. And like the first graders, they really seemed to enjoy the work.

Outside of the Waldorf Schools, where needlework is part of an educational philosophy, knitting classes tend to reflect the individual efforts of a single teacher. Sister John Margaret, who teaches first grade at St. Dominic's School in Springfield, Kentucky, added knitting to the curriculum simply because she thought her students might enjoy it. Born in Ireland, she herself had learned to knit as a little girl. But only as her teaching progressed did she realize that the knitting helped her students learn handwriting. Sister John Margaret teaches knitting to both boys and girls, showing them how to make purses, slippers and pot holders.

Since many schools remain reluctant to support knitting classes, the classes often depend on the enthusiasm of one teacher, rather than on the system as a whole. Some schools, meanwhile, are expanding crafts activities as they receive pressure to provide extended afternoon programs. But all of the teachers I spoke with agreed on one thing: that children are enthusiastic about learning to knit.

If you are interested in teaching children to knit, here are some tips I gathered from the experts:

Begin by selecting the right materials. Worsted-weight yarn and size 10 (6mm) needles are best for most beginners. And the needles should be 10"/25cm or shorter, in either plastic or wood (aluminum needles tend to be too slippery for the novice). Some teachers also recommend circular needles.

After that, find an easy project, such as a scarf, or slippers formed out of a folding rectangle. Teach the basic knit stitch first, and casting on later.

And do think in terms of a story. In researching this article I heard several knitting mnemonics: Elisabeth's birds; a story about a little man who goes in the door, gets his hat, and hops off the needle; and one about a horse going into a corral, being roped, and then let out to ride. ⌒

How to Gauge It Properly

However tempting it may be to begin knitting a new project right away without first testing your gauge for an exact match to that given in the instructions, all your hours of knitting may just end up in ripping out a partially completed sweater. Now is the time to take the time to test your gauge.

Gauge defines the number of stitches needed to make a garment as shown in a photograph. It is the measurement of the number of stitches for each inch/cm of width, and the number of rows for each vertical inch/cm. For example, 4 sts = 1"/2.5cm or 9 sts = 2"/5cm. Gauge is rarely measured in half inches or half stitches.

If you're following a pattern, you'll undoubtedly want to duplicate a sweater just as it's shown. First you must select the size you'll want to knit, according to your bust measurement. Then check the final knitted measurements. There will very likely be a difference. This is the allowance for ease and design. You don't have to account for it; it's been "programmed" into the instructions.

Stitch size is readily influenced by needle size. Under Materials or Gauge, you'll be advised which size needles are likely to produce the required gauge. The size of the

In any *Vogue Knitting* instruction, near the top, directly under the description of required materials, you'll find a brief (and very bold) description of the GAUGE. Although often considered tedious and time-consuming, knitting a gauge swatch is the single most important key to a successfully completed garment. By selecting the right size of needles, the correct weight of yarn, and "getting your gauge," you ensure the proper fit, one that accurately duplicates the designer's style and intent.

needle is selected by the designer or instruction writer, according to the "size" (thickness or thinness) of the yarn.

There's also an "unknown" factor involved in gauge that only you can decipher, and that's your tension: the amount of stress you exert on the yarn as you knit. Like fingerprints, tension is a unique, personal factor, and as experienced knitters know, it varies with moods, seasons, maybe even with yarn color. If, on occasion, you're unusually tense, you may not be able to achieve the consistently required gauge. So put that project away for a while. (But…since knitting is just the thing to soothe frazzled nerves, try practicing a new pattern stitch instead. Or knit pot holders…they can use the tight gauge.)

Choose your needles. The size given in the instructions is only a suggestion. If you know you knit tightly, try a size larger needles; if you know you knit loosely, try a size smaller needles. By all means, always test your gauge with the suggested size needles first. Be sure you're using the size recommended for the body of the garment…ribbing is often done with smaller needles.

Knit a sample swatch with the exact yarn you plan to use. Cast on enough stitches so that your swatch will measure approximately 4"/10cm wide. If, for example, the required gauge is 6 sts = 1"/2.5cm, cast on 24 sts. Work in stockinette stitch (St st), unless the gauge is specifically given in a pattern stitch. A gauge given in a pattern stitch, particularly if it's a stitch you've not tried before, may be the perfect opportunity to try out the pattern before you begin the sweater.

Knit up your 4"/10cm swatch with enough rows to make it 4"/10cm long. Then carefully remove the swatch from the needles and pin corners to a flat surface. Do not stretch or pull your swatch when pinning—just let it lie flat and pin the corners. Using a tape measure or stitch gauge, count the number of stitches in 4 inches. Be sure to count only the stitches in the center of the swatch, omitting the selvage stitches. (Hint: To stop yourself from cheating at this point, try to "forget" the gauge you're aiming for.) Then measure the same way vertically. If your stitches tally with the given gauge, you're all set to start.

If you wound up with too many stitches, your tension is too tight, or you will need larger needles. If you wound up with too few stitches, your tension is too loose, or you will need smaller needles. Remember, even half or a quarter of a stitch is out of gauge, and will only be compounded over the full width and length of a garment. If you have either of these problems, try again with needles two sizes larger or smaller. This way, if you still don't get the gauge, you'll know you need the needle size in between.

If your swatch contains the right number of rows (vertical measurement) but is slightly too wide, the yarn is probably too slack between stitches. To correct, gently tighten your tension or hold on the yarn after inserting the needle into a loop, but be sure to release your tightened hold on the yarn as you throw it to form the next stitch.

Once you know you've reached the correct gauge, you're ready to begin knitting a wonderful new garment with all you've learned about your tension and the gauge in mind. Remember that although gauge should remain a constant in any garment, your tension in hand knitting constantly changes with every stitch or change of pattern. The slight variations subtly produced with each stitch are, in fact, what make hand knitting such a beautiful craft! ⌒

Measuring stitch gauge with a tape measure.

Measuring row gauge with a tape measure.

Using a stitch gauge.

On Gauge

by Meg Swansen

THE RIGHT TOOLS

You may discover a marked fluctuation in your gauge when working on needles made of different materials. Nickel-plated, enamel-covered, wood, bamboo, aluminum or plastic needles can produce varying results. Wood and bamboo have greater surface friction and the wool slides along more reluctantly—making them excellent for beginning a circle in the middle, when you have nearly as many needles as you have stitches. The new nickel-plated "Express" or "Turbo" needles are the opposite: the stitches slither along this material quickly, as if under their own steam. The nickel coating is particularly useful if you tend to knit tightly.

You may knit differently on the same diameter needle in a 16"/40cm versus a 24"/60cm circular, as the business-end of each needle is a different length. Circular needles 24"/60cm and up have a longer end than 16"/40cm or shorter needles, making them more comfortable to grasp. Unless you like the security of tucking the end of a long single-pointed needle under your arm, I recommend that you knit large flat pieces

GAUGE (yawn)...yes, it can be tiresome, but we all know that it remains a critically important key to achieving successfully fitted garments. There are many variables out there that can sabotage an accurate gauge reading, and they can be different for each knitter.

back and forth on a circular needle. The bulk of the work will be in your lap instead of weighing down the ends of the needles, tiring your hands and wrists and possibly affecting your gauge.

Be aware that the diameter of the same size needle may differ slightly from brand to brand—as will different needle gauges of different brands. The implement you use for measuring the finished fabric may also trick you. Cloth or plastic tape measures can stretch, shrink or bend, distorting your readout. For greater accuracy use a metal ruler, a carpenter's measure or one of those cute spring-return nylon-coated fabric tape measures.

Uff...all these warnings. It's a jungle out there, and the best advice is Keep On Knitting to familiarize yourself with your tools and to discover your own idiosyncrasies.

SWATCH TOPPER

Making a gauge swatch needn't be unpleasant if you adjust your attitude a bit. Instead of knitting a relatively useless oblong, turn your swatch into a swatch cap and appreciate the opportunity to familiarize yourself with the wool, needles and pattern before you launch into the main project. A cap will also provide a large surface on which to measure. The more inches/centimeters you measure, the more accurate your gauge of stitches per inch/centimeter. As an added bonus you'll end up with a matching hat.

Naturally, the style of garment and the chosen material need to be considered—an authentic fisherman's Guernsey worked in traditional 5-ply wool is so firmly knitted that it practically stands by itself, while gauge for a mohair garment is generally quite loose and relaxed. Unless you are following directions stitch-for-stitch and must match the given gauge, I think it is more important to be pleased with your swatch first and not even worry about what the gauge might be. Hand-spinners know that their wool usually dictates the gauge to them, regardless of their attempts to sway it.

Change needle sizes until you like the look and feel of your swatch in relation to the project you have in mind, then measure the gauge you are getting and calculate accordingly. "What size needle do I need?" is a question that only you can answer. Just last week I was told about a knitter who was in despair over her finished, ill-fitting sweater. When asked if she had double-checked her gauge for accuracy, she said that she had been much too busy to knit the gauge swatch herself; her neighbor had knitted it for her!

If the garment is to be knitted in the round, the swatch should also be circular. If the garment has color or texture patterns, so should the swatch. Knitting versus knitting and purling, color pattern, and texture pattern all have an affect on final gauge. For a swatch cap, make an educated guess at the needle size and the number of stitches you will need for a 20–21"/50–53cm circumference hat and cast on. If you are in a hurry, cast on invisibly so you needn't plow through the lower ribbing. Knit 5–6"/12.5–15cm vertically, steam-block (by puffing at the swatch with your steam iron; do not press the fabric) and check your gauge. Prevent the lower edge from curling by running a needle in and out across it. Now you can launch into the garment itself and finish up the hat later.

If you don't want to take time to knit a swatch cap, consider beginning on a sleeve and using it to measure your gauge.

CIRCULAR KNITS

You can make a flat "speed swatch" for a circular garment as follows: cast on about 6–8"/15–20cm of stitches onto a circular needle (incorporating any color or texture design) and *knit across. Now, don't turn, but slide the stitches back to the left-hand end of the needle and pull out a long length of wool(s) to span the width of the swatch. Knit across again with the lengths of wool hanging loosely across the back. Repeat from *. See? You are knitting only from the "right" side and not purling back. Work 5–6"/12.5–15cm, steam-block the swatch and take a measurement. Keep the ruler well away from the selvages, as they will most likely be distorted. I prefer the pull-out-loops method as opposed to break-the-wool(s)-at-the-end-of-each-row, because I may run out of wool with just a few rounds left to knit...I can then triumphantly rip out my swatch to finish the project.

With all this fuss about accurate gauge, keep in mind that you are dealing with a malleable fabric, and blocking (if working with wool) can work wonders to lengthen, shorten, widen or narrow a too-short, too-long, too-wide or too-skimpy body or sleeves. Remember, however, that when you stretch the wet fabric width-wise, you are taking up some of its length. By the same token, yanking it longer will make it narrower. Those of us who knit with wool depend upon its forgiving and obliging nature. If we happen to be a fraction of a stitch off from our calculated gauge, proper blocking will not only smooth out all the uneven stitches, but can also overcome minor miscalculations.

It is my intention only to alert you to potential pitfalls, not to frighten you. If you are nervous or worried as you knit you are probably defeating one of the main reasons you decided to knit in the first place, and your gauge is liable to tighten. There once was a perspicacious knitter who always kept a special "slipper-in-progress" in her basket. It had to be knitted quite firmly, and she reached for it whenever she had had a fight with her husband. After she calmed down again, she pulled out her "regular" knitting and carried on. ⌒

Purl When You Can

by Meg Swansen

We know that a slab of stocking stitch, when left to its own devices, will roll at all four of its selvages and, unless we want a signature J. Crew sweater, we must install something at the lower borders of body and sleeves to prevent the edges from curling. There are plenty of well-known non-curling treatments:

- Garter stitch
- Seed or moss stitch
- K1, P1 rib
- K2, P2 rib
- Checkerboard rib
- Diagonal rib
- Corrugated rib
- Hems
- Sideways (perpendicular) border
- Cabled or Aran border
- Twisted garter stitch
- Doubled or tripled I-cord

I'm sure there are plenty more, as well as a number of additional variations. However, several years ago, none of the options I've listed here suited the plan I had for a new design: an allover patterned cardigan with wide vertical underarm panels of a different pattern motif running up either side of the body and the underarm of the sleeves. I had planned corrugated rib for the lower edge, but wanted to begin the side panel chart immediately after casting on. The panels were wide enough that I was certain they would roll at the lower edge.

What if I were to stick purl stitches into the panel sections to prevent curling? But when you purl a stitch of one color into another color, you form a purl-blip (which certainly can be a design feature—as in Bohus knitting), which I did not want for this rather traditional Norwegian-style sweater. OK, I decided, I'll only Purl When I Can, which in this instance meant whenever I had a white stitch above a white or a black stitch above a black.

I did just that, purling into both the pattern and the background at every possible opportunity, and it lay beautifully flat at the cast-on edge. That success emboldened me to try the same technique around the entire circumference of a color-patterned sweater. I was excited at the possibility of beginning the pattern straightaway—no ribbing, no border, no waiting and no curling. However....

You know that garter stitch is perfectly square as opposed to the slightly oblong nature of stocking stitch. When I introduced so many purl stitches into a color motif, it became square—which meant that the design around the lower edge looked flattened compared to the unpurled motifs in the rest of the body. So I ripped back to the beginning, (cast on 10 percent fewer stitches than originally called for), reversed the colorwork and worked the first vertical repeat of the pattern. Once the Purl When You Can part was done, I switched the colors back and increased 10 percent (to the full wanted body circumference). I rationalized that I would have had to do something like that even if the purl stitches hadn't flattened the pattern, because once I increased, the motifs no longer lined up with each other vertically. The result was quite nice.

On my next sweater, I experimented by Purling When I Could into the background color only, while keeping the entire pattern in stocking stitch. It worked. I reversed it on a subsequent garment by working the motif in purl and keeping the background in plain knit. Aha, success again.

I continue to push the possibilities by purling fewer and fewer stitches, and am rather startled to find how relatively few purl stitches are necessary to keep a flat lower edge. The charts below demonstrate what I'm talking about:

A: Here is a chart with all the "possible" purl stitches marked with a horizontal line through them.

B: Here is the chart again with only the background purled.

C: The same chart with only the motif purled. Doesn't look as if it has enough purl stitches to work, does it? I would be tempted (superstitiously) to purl those initial background color stitches on the first pattern round [as shown in chart C]. Since I always knit in the round, I needn't worry about the "wrong side," but have added instructions in parentheses.

Why not experiment with a few allover patterned hats? I know there is a finite number of "required" purl stitches lurking out there—below which I will defeat my purpose, but I haven't reached it yet.

Knitting Onward…Meg

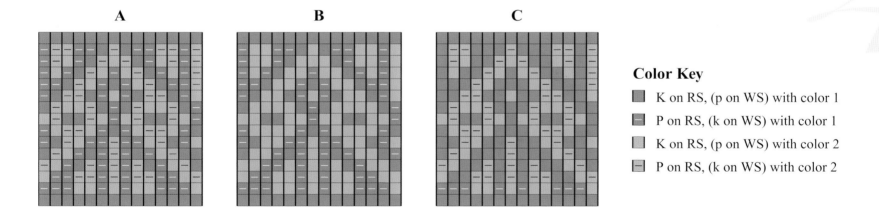

A **B** **C**

Color Key

■ K on RS, (p on WS) with color 1

▬ P on RS, (k on WS) with color 1

□ K on RS, (p on WS) with color 2

⊟ P on RS, (k on WS) with color 2

Essay: How I Discovered

by Barbara G. Walker

Back in the Old Stone Age when I was in college, the in thing for girls to do was knit argyle socks for their steady boyfriends. I didn't have one of those useful male attachments, a steady boyfriend. But I thought it might improve my image if I sat in class knitting socks like everyone else. I asked an expert argyle-knitter to teach me. She tried. Unfortunately, I was an abysmally slow learner and an uncoordinated klutz.

My first project was a small shapeless swatch demonstrating holes, knots, split yarn and dropped stitches. It was good for nothing except maybe to wash a car, but it was thrown away before the car got dirty enough. With no regrets whatever, I said goodbye to knitting. I figured if I wanted to do something with my hands I could always doodle, play solitaire, hook a rug or paint my room. Who needed knitting? My real interest at the time was riding horses. I hoped somehow to earn enough money to buy a ranch in Wyoming and breed mustangs.

Years later, as a wife and mother with no ranch, no mustangs and only moderate funds, I got the urge to try knitting again. I loved sweaters with the handmade look—so expensive to buy. Even if the price should be right, a store-bought sweater might be an acceptable size and shape but a wrong color. Or it might be a pullover when I wanted a cardigan. I yearned to create my own exactly-right sweaters with the aristocratic aura of the handmade. Next winter, I told myself, I will master knitting.

Since I had married I had made it a habit to set a course of study for myself each fall, to fill in spare time during the cold months. I would collect all the books in the library on my chosen subject, read them and take notes. In this way I studied architecture, astronomy, geology, ancient history, psychology, painting, sewing, folklore, anthropology and much else year by year. This year I began by buying some yarn and needles and a paperback learn-to-knit booklet published by a yarn company.

My knitting was as clumsy as I remembered, but this time I persevered. In due course the learning passed from my head into my fingers. I got the rhythm. But halfway through my first plain stockinette sweater, I struck another snag—boredom. I thought: Knitting is dull, dull, dull. How can a person make the same motions over and over? Knit another row, purl another row. Is that all there is to it?

Knitting...and Why

Of course, like any beginner, I was naïve. When I studied the pictures in knitting magazines, it began to dawn on me that this was not all there was to it. There were different-looking textures, fancy lacy patterns, embossed patterns, twists, cables. I wanted to know how all these were made. I read and practiced. I looked for a nice big book that would give directions for many patterns. There was no such book published in the U.S. at the time, so I began my own collection. I copied patterns from magazines, foreign books, old pamphlets, yarn-company publications. I began to invent my own patterns by trying out variations.

This initial collection formed the basis of my first published book, *A Treasury of Knitting Patterns*, which I thought must be quite complete, with its directions for about 550 patterns. Wrong again. Two years later I had over 700 additional patterns gathered from back issues of knitting magazines, from correspondents' contributions, from a private library of old pamphlets, from the Library of Congress collection, even from an archeological text that yielded a pattern more than 2,000 years old, taken from a dig in Mesopotamia. These went into *A Second Treasury of Knitting Patterns*.

Then I stopped collecting and concentrated on inventing. From my own designs evolved the subsequent ten years' production of the following: swatches and knitted projects for photographs in my next five published books; 79 blouses and pullover sweaters; 33 suits and two-piece dresses; 28 knitted handbags; 27 cardigan sweaters, 25 table mats and doilies; 18 skirts; 17 bed-size afghans; 16 hats; 15 scarves or shawls; 12 pillows; 12 capes or ponchos; 11 one-piece dresses; 7 coats; 6 pants; 6 wall hangings; 5 knitted lampshades; 4 lace tablecloths; 3 neckties; 2 swimsuits; and one—no, not a partridge in a pear tree—bedspread. Plus commercial designs. On seeing my album of photographs, visitors often ask, "Who could find time to do all this?" I have a standard answer: I didn't watch television. Not at all. It's astonishing how much time one has for creative activities when the idiot box is eliminated from one's life.

Naturally, that's not the whole story. I was altogether addicted to working out the puzzles of patterning and garment shaping that I set for myself. I knitted day and night. I never wasted a minute in life's miscellaneous waiting spaces: offices of dentists, doctors, pediatricians, veterinarians; train stations, bus terminals, airports; as a passenger in any form of transportation; waiting for coffee to perk, for hair to dry, for guests to arrive, for a concert to begin, whatever. I knitted. I knitted so many acres of yarn that a friend said I should create a house-cozy to keep our house warm in winter.

In my own way I even solved the problem so many dedicated knitters complain of: idea explosion. This is what happens while you are working on one project and suddenly think of six more ideas you want to try right away. It's always an effort of will to hang in there and finish the job in hand before rushing on to the next. My solution was to stop creating full-size garments and start creating miniature garments for dolls, which can be finished sooner, so many more ideas can find expression in any given time period. This is still my hobby.

Doubtless I'll keep on inventing puzzles for myself to solve until I am hauled away to the great yarn shop in the sky. Others who have become hooked on this endlessly fascinating craft will know exactly what I mean. There will never be Knitters Anonymous, because we addicts don't want to be cured. ⌒

Knitting the Best Way

Continental vs. American

by Elizabeth Zimmermann

There are two distinct ways to handknit: the continental, or German, method and the American, or English, way. The results, when performed correctly, are identical. However, both ways have drawbacks and these will be tackled anon.

In continental knitting, the yarn is held over the left forefinger and regulated by the other fingers. The right-hand needle digs into the stitch on the left-hand needle and hooks the yarn through it to make a new stitch. The stitch through which it has been hooked has now attained its mission in life and become part of the fabric.

In the American method, the yarn is held in the right hand, over the forefinger and under the others which regulate the tension. Some knitters wind the yarn around various fingers, starting by one or more winds around the little finger (I always imagine this can result in more tightness than is necessary). The knitter then digs the right-hand needle point into the first stitch on the left-hand needle, wraps the yarn around the right-hand needle, and hoicks the new stitch through. To each his or her own.

The American method, when reduced to its essentials, can be by far the fastest in the annals of handknitting. However, one must be armed with two of those 14"/35cm double-pointed needles and a knitting pouch which is strapped to the right hip. The right-hand needle then has its right end firmly secured in the pouch. Its left end is held by thumb and forefinger of the left hand. The free right hand can feed the yarn and hook through the stitches at surprising speed—Mary Thomas (a truthful knitter) says 200 stitches a minute! I've been privileged to watch Freda Veitsch of Burlington, Ontario, perform this feat. I assure you that I couldn't count the stitches; her fingers were a blur.

The American method suffers under a slight disadvantage: When one works a pattern stitch involving knit and purl stitches, the right forefinger must guide the yarn behind the needle for a knit stitch, and in front of the needle for a purled one. This slows matters down a bit.

Handknitting is an ancient and beguiling skill—no loom, no machine, no need even to look. Except, that is, when your right-hand needle sends you a message that it can't find its way into the next stitch. Perhaps the stitch is twisted, split, or has been inadvertently dropped. For a few seconds, pay attention to this mishap, fix it, and then let your eyes return to what they were doing before.

The continental method also has a disadvantage, which must be tackled before it becomes too firmly entrenched: When purling, it is simpler to put the right-hand needle down *over* the yarn before hooking the purled stitch through. This causes the stitch to lie *backwards* on the right-hand needle after it has been worked. When one comes upon it in the next row, it must be dug into from the *back* to save it from becoming twisted.

I tell you, it's a hard life!

However, I've saved marvelous news for the end and will start with a sound piece of advice. Familiarize yourself with both methods. Work 5 stitches the unfamiliar way today, tomorrow work 10, then 15, and so on. It may never be as fast as your original way, but it will have a surprising and rewarding usefulness.

Knit a Fair Isle or Scandinavian sweater involving color patterns, *employing both methods alternately*—the color of which there are the most stitches by your original method, the other by the other method! Keep the carried yarn loose across the back by pulling the work to the right at each color change. You will soon acquire the skill of keeping the "carries" at the proper tension. If they are too loose, they can always be pulled up later. If too tight you are sunk and will have to rip, unless you want a tight, unyielding, puckered sweater. ⌒

Splicing Yarn

A smooth transition

by Meg Swansen

Once you have become a True Knitter (whom I define as one who must knit every day), finishing details often are no longer a chore, but a pleasure. I can vividly remember my early knitting days when I felt that I could not be bothered to darn in the loose ends (who was going to look at the inside of my sweater?). I now find great gratification in finishing a garment properly and thoroughly, though it has nevertheless become a game of mine to avoid finishing details whenever possible.

Part of the game involves splicing in each new same-color skein. I did not set out to learn this subtle and seemingly insignificant detail, but was backed into it by unsuccessful attempts to invisibly deal with wool ends on reversible items such as afghans and lace shawls—where there is nowhere to hide. Indeed, if you are knitting an afghan back and forth, you may leave ends at the selvage only and cleverly hide them there. However, this is not always an option. Consider a circular lace shawl: While not always reversible, it is generally transparent enough to cause the usual finishing choices to be quite visible, and there are no selvages to duck into. If you work duplicate stitch or weave in the ends, it will double the thickness of the fabric and be obvious, as will a diagonal skimming of wool across the back.

Splicing is the answer. I now splice in new matching skeins on all my knitting, reversible or not. Whether you are working in the round or back and forth, you may splice at any point of the row or round. Naturally, if you are introducing a new color there must be an end, but this tail will allow you to disguise the "jog" in circular knitting. The direction in which you darn the end can align the first stitch of the round to the last and eliminate the mismatch.

Two-ply wool is the easiest to splice (I refer to it as "wool" and not "yarn," for splicing success is guaranteed in wool; with synthetics you're on your own). Leave a 5- to 6-inch tail of the old wool and pull out a 5- to 6-inch tail from the new skein. Untwist each strand, separate it into its component parts and break off (do not cut) 3 to 4 inches of one of the plies from each piece. Now overlap the two ends on your palm—so that the long end of one strand meets the broken end of the other strand—

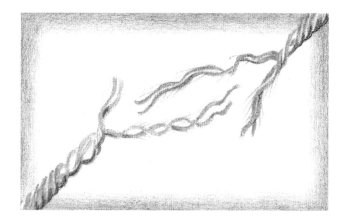

and do a "spit-splice," i.e., dampen the other palm and briskly rub the ends of the wool together for about five seconds. The combination of moisture and friction will heat and fuse the wool fibers to each other. Some types of wool blend together more readily than others so I sometimes add some twist to the spliced section until I have knitted 3–4 stitches across it, and then I release the additional twist. The result is an invisible join of ends with no discernible anomalies. If you find the concept of a "spit-splice" unappealing, you may keep a moistened sponge by your knitting chair.

For a 3 (or more)-ply wool, break off each separate ply at a different length so you have a staggered array of ends, which, when laid over each other and spit-spliced, will result in a solid stand of 3 (or more)-ply. If you are using a single-ply (or roving) wool, un-spin a 3- or 4-inch length on each of the two ends and draw them out to reduce the thickness before splicing. The objective here is to achieve the original diameter after the two ends are overlapped and fused.

Now then, not only will you have more beautifully finished afghans and lace projects, but on your next single-color sweater you will have only the cast-on and cast-off tails to deal with. ⌐

Essay: Fussy Knitting

by Meg Swansen

Dear Knitter,

Technical knitting questions are a frequent occurrence in my life, and I often get article ideas from the queries that come through. Fairly oft heard is: "When I work ribbing or cables, the left side of the last knit stitch (that is followed by a purl stitch) is sloppy. How can I fix it?" An important thing to establish is, How much do you care? One of my slogans has always been "A repeated mistake is a new design"; because that sloppy half-stitch is consistently made, it actually produces a uniform design of its own. Are you philosophical about mistakes, accepting them as part of the way you knit? Or are you bothered by them? If the latter best describes you, you may be a fussy knitter. Here are some other "fussy" examples:

• You fastidiously mirror-image any paired increases or decreases. That is a personal and secret pleasure, for most likely you will not be praised or rewarded for paying attention to such subtle details. Mirror-imaged cables and color-pattern motifs are much more noticeable; others may be pleased by the symmetry, even if they acknowledge it only subconsciously.

• You may cast on only one way, regardless of the circumstances. Or, you may use a different cast-on method for every situation.

• On a plain stockinette-stitch sweater, you add Phoney Seams to the sides of the body and underarms of the sleeves to give a snappy appearance (when was the last time you heard that adjective?). It's most helpful when blocking the garment, to ensure that the body is not torquing.

• You insist on tracking down the exact yarn used by the designer.

• When the instructions blithely say, "Increase 27 stitches, evenly spaced around," you most likely turn to *Sweater 101* or *Sweaters From Camp* and apply the simple formula to find how many stitches are between the increases. If, for instance, the answer is "Inc every 7th stitch 6 times, then every 8th stitch 21 times," do you spread out the sevens among the eights so they are properly dispersed? If so, you definitely qualify as a Fussy Knitter.

• I-cord solutions are ready-made for you: You can eliminate the frontal droop of a finished cardigan or tighten up sagging shoulders with an I-cord shoulder holder. You can neaten the selvages of a knitted-in saddle shoulder by means of Built-in I-cord. The fussy embellishment possibilities of I-cord are endless.

It has been pointed out to me that a growing segment of the knitting community is becoming so meticulous and fussy about their work that their attitude teeters on the edge of neurosis. If the goal is perfection, some say, why not buy a commercially made garment, or switch from hand to machine knitting? Those are the knitters who cherish and appreciate the slight imperfections in their work and consider them to be the little idiosyncrasies that hallmark a hand-knitted garment.

Actually, I subscribe to both ways of thinking. Though I am quite fussy about my knitting, my lumpy hand-spinning efforts don't seem to improve with practice. Thus, I've decided that I like my hand-spun

wool to look hand spun. If I wanted a perfectly uniform yarn, I would use commercially spun wool. So, though I understand the drive for perfection (if a job is worth doing, etc.), I have also finely honed the art of rationalization when perfection cannot be achieved.

Anyway, back to the sloppy half-stitch. Here are some possible solutions I have gathered over the years:

• Work the last K and the first P very tightly.

• Wrap the wool the "wrong" way (clockwise) around the needle on the last K stitch, as it uses less length and will be snugger. Then knit into the back of the resulting twisted stitch the next time you meet it.

• P into the back of the first P stitch, which will tighten the K stitch to its right.

• Or, try this new idea from Amy Detjen:

On 2/2 ribbing, or on any cable that has two knit stitches preceding a purl stitch, knit into the first of the two knit stitches but do not remove it from the left needle. Now knit into the second stitch and slide both stitches off the left needle at the same time. Amy discovered that, for her, the distortion was coming from the stretched first stitch and was being transferred to the left side of the second stitch.

Any of the above may (or may not) work for your style of knitting, so give them a try...or ignore them altogether. After all, this is your knitting, and you may be as fussy or as cavalier about the results as you choose.

Knit on, Meg ⁓

Decoding the Cables

Symbols replace written instructions

by Carla S. Patrick

Any knitter who's created a gift for a loved one knows that knitting has a language of its own. Now, knitting instructions are becoming a means of universal communication. "Symbolcraft," which uses international symbols instead of words, is the wave of the future in knitting instructions. An easy alternative to the tedious reading of a pattern's many rows, it can also expand your knowledge of knitting's structure.*

Reading Symbolcraft is no different than interpreting other charts used in knitting. Each square represents one stitch and one row. The odd-numbered rows (1, 3, 5, etc.) are listed on the right-hand side of the chart. Unless otherwise stated, these are always right-side rows and are read horizontally from right to left. The numbers on the left-hand side of the chart are the wrong-side rows, and are read from left to right.

Let's look at the symbols themselves. You will notice that the chart resembles the pattern on the right side of the work. When seen from the right side, knit stitches look vertical. Therefore, the symbol ⊡ represents a knit stitch (in stockinette stitch), which is knit on the right side and purled on the wrong side. Purl stitches, which have a horizontal shape when viewed from the right side, are represented by the symbol: ⊟

Note that when reading the right-side rows, you work the stitches as they appear on the chart. When reading the wrong-side rows, you work the opposite of what is shown. This may seem difficult at first, but you'll find that practice makes these charts easier to follow than written instructions.

Although there are many possible symbols to show a particular stitch, we have chosen the most universal ones, which appear in Japanese instructions and most closely resemble the finished product. Here is a listing of some common stitches along with a detailed description of how to work them. ~

*The chart below shows one way of representing cables. There are many others. Be sure to read the key to the specific pattern you are using.

⊡ **Stockinette Stitch** Knit on the right-side rows, and purl on the wrong-side rows.

⊟ **Reverse Stockinette Stitch** Purl on the right-side rows, and knit on the wrong-side rows.

Six-stitch Cable Crossed to the Right Slip next 3 sts to cable needle (cn), and hold to *back* of work, k3, k3 from cn.

Notice how the 3 long diagonal lines are slanted to the right. In order to slant these sts in this direction, you must always place the slipped sts to the back of the work. Work the sts slanting to the right, and then work the sts that were held in back.

Six-stitch Cable Crossed to the Left Slip next 3 sts to cn and hold to *front* of work, k3, k3 from cn. These 3 long diagonal lines are now slanting left. Therefore, the operation is just the opposite of the right slant.

Eight-stitch Cable Crossed to the Right Slip next 4 sts to cn and hold to *back* of work, k4, k4 from cn. The principle here is the same as that used for the six-stitch cable, except that you use 8 sts.

Eight-stitch Cable Crossed to the Left Slip next 4 sts to cn and hold to *front* of work, k4, k4 from cn.

Three Stitches Crossed Right (Over 4 sts) On right-side rows: Slip next st to cn and hold to *back* of work, k3; p st from cn. On wrong side rows: Slip next 3 sts to cn and hold to back of work, k next st; p3 from cn.

Notice the symbol to the left of the 3 slanted lines. This represents the p st on the right-side rows and the k st on the wrong-side rows, which are both held to the back of the work. In this case, the stitches are shifted *every* row.

Three Stitches Crossed Left (Over 4 sts) On right-side rows: Slip 3 sts to cn and hold to *front* of work, p next st; k3 from cn. On wrong-side rows: Slip next st to cn and hold to *front* of work, p3, k st from cn.

In this instance, the small symbol is at the right of the slanted lines. It also represents the p stitch on the right-side rows and the k st on the wrong-side rows.

Three Stitches Crossed Right (Over 5 sts) Slip next 2 sts to cn and hold to *back* of work, k3, p2 from cn.

Three Stitches Crossed Left (Over 5 sts) Slip 3 sts to cn and hold to *front* of work, p2, k3 from cn.

Four Stitches Crossed Right (Over 6 sts) Slip next 2 sts to cn and hold to *back* of work, k4, p2 from cn.

Four Stitches Crossed Left (Over 6 sts) Slip 4 sts to cn and hold to *front* of work, p2, k4 from cn.

Four-Stitch Right Cable Sl 2 sts to cn and hold to *back* of work, k2, k2 from cn.

Four-Stitch Left Cable Sl 2 sts to cn and hold to *front* of work, k2, k2 from cn.

Right Cross (over 5 sts) Sl 1 to cn and hold to *back* of work, k4, p1 from cn.

Left Cross (over 5 sts) Sl 4 sts to cn and hold to *front* of work, p1, k4 from cn.

by Mari Lynn Patrick

When your knitting magazine arrives and you start thinking about the designs you're going to make, look through the instructions for the corresponding schematics. Schematics are small-scale drawings of the sweater pieces, and they can help you make sound final choices. Schematics show precisely how a sweater is shaped and include details which might not show in the fashion photograph. Also, a close look at the schematic may reveal that the pattern uses a sleeve style which you find unflattering, helping you to avoid this style.

If you're a skilled machine knitter, you can rely solely on the schematics to execute an exact and speedy replica of the hand-knit version. And whether you knit by hand or machine, if you like to innovate, schematics can provide the shape for original designs. Simply "plug in" your own stitch pattern, change the yarn or change the gauge.

Aside from all these reasons for reading schematic diagrams, each time you familiarize yourself with a new pattern, it expands your knowledge of knitted fit. It helps you to understand how an 11"/28cm armhole actually fits against your arm, and where a 30"/76cm-long sweater hits your hips. As you build your personal sweater repertoire, you learn what styles are most suitable for you and can steer away from fit disappointments. You can knit it, wear it and love it, and that's what it's all about!

Schematics prove the axiom that good things come in small packages! These mini-drawings offer valuable help before you begin, while you're knitting, and when it's time for blocking. They're educational, too, even if you're just browsing.

So you can use schematics to the greatest advantage, let's look at a typical front/back [Diagram 1] and sleeve [Diagram 2]. This explanation applies specifically to *Vogue*'s schematics, but the basic principles apply to the schematics in other knitting instructions, too, even if the schematics are set up a little differently.

The first thing to notice is that the drawings are positioned in the way the sections are to be knitted—in this case, beginning at the lower edge and knitting up to the top. When sections are knitted from seam to seam, the schematic is printed sideways. When a dolman sleeve sweater is knitted in one piece from sleeve cuff to sleeve cuff, this schematic, too, would be shown on its side.

Now let's find out what the numbers and lines on the front/back schematic [1] mean:

A – the width across the back, or the width across the front at the bust. This

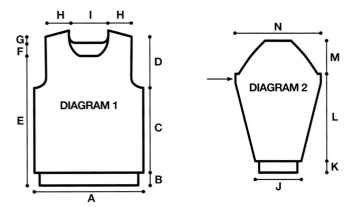

measurement is usually the same for back and front in a pullover. When doubled, it gives you the finished bust measurement. You'll notice that the line extends past the ribbing at the lower edge as the ribbing usually pulls in and doesn't match this width measurement.

B – the depth of the ribbing. The depth of the ribbing or other lower edge detail corresponds to the instructions. It's the first vertical measurement given on the right side of the schematic. It will also tell you the depth of a hem that is later turned up to the inside. The turning line will be indicated by a horizontal broken line.

C – the length to the underarm. This is measured above the lower edge ribbing and up to the underarm. Notice that each of the measurements on the schematic's right side is an increment and is marked between two dots. These marked increments are particularly helpful if you are planning to shorten or lengthen your sweater.

D – the depth of the armhole to the shoulder. This measurement is given in the instructions for the back under "armhole shaping" to "shoulder shaping." Whether the armhole is straight or curved, take this measurement flat, and vertically from the first armhole bind-off. Do not curve your tape measure along the shaped armhole edge.

E – the length from lower edge to first neck shaping.

F – the depth from front neck to back neck. This increment, when added to "G," gives you the number of inches/cm that the front neck is dropped from shoulder edge.

G – the depth from back neck to shoulder. This shows how much the back neck is dropped compared to the shoulder at the armhole edge. This doesn't reflect the slope of the shoulder, which is a slant of about ½–1"/1.5–2.5cm—shoulder slope is determined by stepped bind-offs, not this depth measurement.

H – shoulder width. This is determined by the number of stitches bound off for each shoulder divided by the stitch gauge.

I – width of the neck. Neck width is measured straight across, not along the depth or curve of the neck, front or back. It is determined by the total number of stitches bound off for the neck divided by the stitch gauge. Add "I" and both "H's" together and you'll get the cross back measurement (the width across the back between the shoulders).

The lines and numbers on the sleeve schematic [2] mark off increments in a similar way:

J – width of the sleeve. This measurement is taken above the cuff ribbing, and includes any increased stitches on the first row above the ribbing.

K – depth of the cuff ribbing. This measures the ribbing before the stitch pattern begins.

L – sleeve length to underarm. This is the length that is knit, in pattern, above the cuff and up to the underarm. If you plan to change the sleeve length, the schematic shows you where to add or subtract at the top of the sleeve—this is done in the straight portion just beneath the shaping at the underarm (indicated by our arrow).

M – sleeve cap depth. This length measurement is determined by the number of rows needed to arrive at the top of the sleeve cap shaping, and is proportionate to the depth of the armhole.

N – sleeve width at upper arm. This measures the sleeve at the upper arm, and is figured according to the final number of stitches in the sleeve after all increases are made. You'll also see this measurement given under "Knitted Measurements" in the instructions. If you have fitting problems at the upper arm, compare this measurement to your figure as a check before you knit.

After you've completed your sweater pieces, there's one more useful role for the schematic drawings. When blocking, have a tape measure and your schematics handy. Pin down all your pieces, using the schematic measurement—front on top of back, and sleeve on top of sleeve (or pin each piece separately). Pat or slightly stretch the pieces to shape them correctly. When dry, the pieces will "remember" what you've learned from the schematics. ⌣

by Carla S. Patrick

1. WHAT DO THE SQUARES MEAN?

Each square represents one stitch when you read the chart horizontally. Each square represents one row when you read the chart vertically.

2. WHAT DO THE SYMBOLS MEAN?

In color charts, as shown in samples 1 and 2, the symbols stand for colors; this type of chart is used for Fair Isles and scenics. In stitch charts, such as sample 3, the symbols stand for types of stitches; this kind of chart is used for Arans and lace patterns, among others. Stitch charts use universal symbols to indicate stitches.

Refer to the key to determine what the symbols represent. As you can see from the key for chart 1, a square with an "X" equals color A, and a blank square equals color B. Similarly, in chart 3 a square marked ⊞ equals a knit stitch (k on right side, p on wrong side) and a square marked ⊟ equals a purl stitch (p on right side, k on wrong side).

Now that rich colorwork and stitch patterns are in fashion, knitters who know how to read charts are a giant step ahead. If you long to make a beautiful Fair Isle or scenic-design sweater but need help understanding what charts are all about, here's where your questions are answered.

3. WHAT DOES "REP" MEAN?

Many charts say "rep"—which means repeat—both for stitches and for rows. It means you must repeat the symbols within the lines over and over until you get to the end of the row; for example, in chart 1, the repeat is 8 stitches. In the same way, repeat the rows as many times as the instructions state; for example, in chart 1, repeat rows 1–8.

Let's say you are working with 96 stitches and following chart 1. Reading from right to left, work the first row from the chart as follows: Work 2 stitches with color B, 2 with color A, repeat [6 stitches with color B, 2 stitches with color A] 11 times, then work the last 4 stitches with color B.

After working rows 2–8 from the chart, begin with row 1 again. Repeat this sequence of rows as many times as stated in the instructions.

4. WHAT IS THE PURPOSE OF "BEG" AND "END"?

If working with a chart which shows a large repeat, you won't always be able to use complete multiples of the repeat for the sweater size you are making. Therefore, you

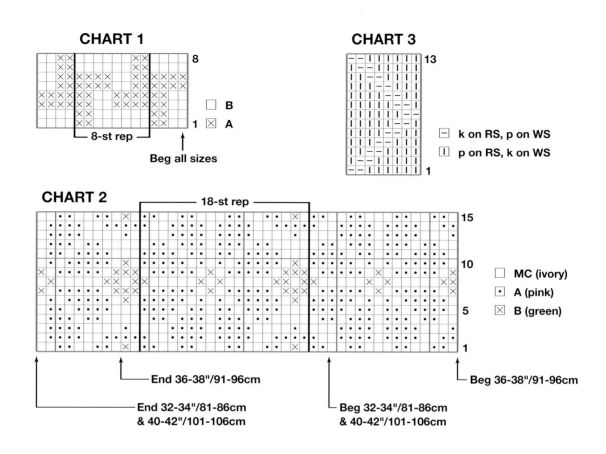

CHART 1

8

☐ B

⊠ A

8-st rep

Beg all sizes

CHART 3

13

1

⊟ k on RS, p on WS

Ⅰ p on RS, k on WS

CHART 2

18-st rep

15

10

5

1

☐ MC (ivory)

▪ A (pink)

⊠ B (green)

End 36-38"/91-96cm

End 32-34"/81-86cm
& 40-42"/101-106cm

Beg 32-34"/81-86cm
& 40-42"/101-106cm

Beg 36-38"/91-96cm

can't simply repeat as described above. You must begin (beg) and end working at a certain point.

For example, let's say you are working with 54 stitches following chart 2, making size 36–38"/91–96cm. Reading from right to left, to work row 1, begin at the first square, work to the repeat line, repeat the 18 stitches within the lines twice, then work the last 2 stitches beyond the repeat line.

On some smaller charts, the beginning and ending points are unimportant. On these charts, the repeat may have a few stitches of the pattern on each side.

5. IN WHICH DIRECTION SHOULD CHARTS BE READ?

The most common way to read a chart is to read the **right-side rows from right to left,** and the **wrong-side rows from left to right.** Always read a chart this way unless the instructions tell you to read the chart differently.

For example, here is how the first two rows of chart 3 would look written out:

Row 1 (RS) *K6, p2; rep from * to end.
Row 2 (WS) *P1, k2, p5; rep from * to end.

6. HOW DO YOU FOLLOW FULL-SIZE CHARTS THAT SHOW SHAPING?

Let's say you are following a full-size sleeve chart which shows the increase stitches on each side. The written instructions may also explain how to do the increases on the sleeve; these instructions will correspond to the chart.

The increases are shown on the chart so you can see how to work the pattern into the increases. You only need to make the increases once, working either from the written instructions or the chart.

As you can see, reading a chart is not difficult at all. However, before starting to knit, study the chart and the instructions so you understand how to handle the color or stitch pattern. For an easy-to-follow guide, graph out the entire chart for the size you are making. ⌒

Charting a Steady Course

by Sally Harding

CHARTED DIRECTIONS

Knitting patterns of all types can be written in chart form—from simple knit and purl combinations to intricate cables and lace. Charts for colorwork stitches, however, are the most commonly used because they eliminate the need for rows and rows of complicated written instructions.

Those familiar with cross-stitch embroidery or needlepoint will understand colorwork knitting charts quite easily. Each square on the chart represents a stitch, and each line of squares, a row. The individual squares are either colored in or contain a symbol to indicate the color to be used. One of the advantages of these charted patterns is that they transcend the language barrier. A chart knitter can work from international charts without a translation.

Whether knitting a colorwork pattern from purchased instructions or creating your own colorwork designs, you will find that a basic understanding of charts makes the going easier.

READING COLORWORK CHARTS

Although colorwork charts are easily understandable, they do require intense visual concentration and can frustrate even the most patient knitter. This may be due to a knitter's eyesight, the chart's size, the complexity of a pattern containing a great number of colors, or a combination of all three. Before beginning a knitting pattern which requires working from a chart, make sure that you can distinguish the chart's symbols without straining your eyes. Examine the chart carefully: Place a ruler under one of the more complicated rows and see if you can read the pattern with ease. If not, there are a couple of tips that may help.

One way to make a chart more readable is to have it enlarged by a photocopying service. No matter how much sympathy knitting-pattern publishers have for their readers, they usually can't print charts as large as they would like to because of space limitations. But a larger chart is not always the answer to easier reading. It may be that the color symbols are not easily distinguishable from one another. If this is so, try using colored pencils to copy one repeat of the chart onto large-squared graph paper. Colored squares which match your yarn colors can make chart reading a breeze.

WORKING CHARTED PATTERNS

Always make a sample swatch of your colorwork pattern before you start a sweater. This will allow you to check the stitch gauge *and* become familiar with the chart. A newcomer to charts might like to try following the simple chart opposite. (If you haven't mastered colorwork knitting yet, however, you should practice it without a chart before attempting chart reading.)

Your chart will usually indicate how many stitches make up a single repeat. In this case, it is 8 stitches. Begin by casting on a multiple of 8 stitches using color A. Knit one row and purl one row, then begin the first chart row. Just as you knit from the bottom upwards, so do you read a chart. The first chart row is the first row at the bottom of the chart. Knit across the row, changing color as indicated on the chart and reading the chart from right to left. Carry the color not in use loosely across the back of the work. The pattern repeats every 8 stitches, so keep repeating this same 8-stitch repeat until your row is complete. On the next row, read the chart *from left to right* while purling across the row, changing colors as indicated. Continue in this way, reading the chart from right to left on right-side rows (knit rows) and from left to right on wrong-side rows (purl rows). You might like to place a ruler under the row you are working on and move it up as you progress. Keep careful track of which row you are working on. After row 21, the entire pattern repeats again.

The shapes on your knitting will not look exactly like the chart. The tree shapes will appear slightly less elongated. This is because a stitch is not an exact square, but is more rectangular in shape. You should always keep this in mind when designing your own patterns.

Working colorwork patterns from charts is probably a slower process than other types of knitting, but many experienced knitters prefer the challenge of colorwork knitting. And, the results of your patient work will give you a great deal of satisfaction and years of pleasure! ⌒

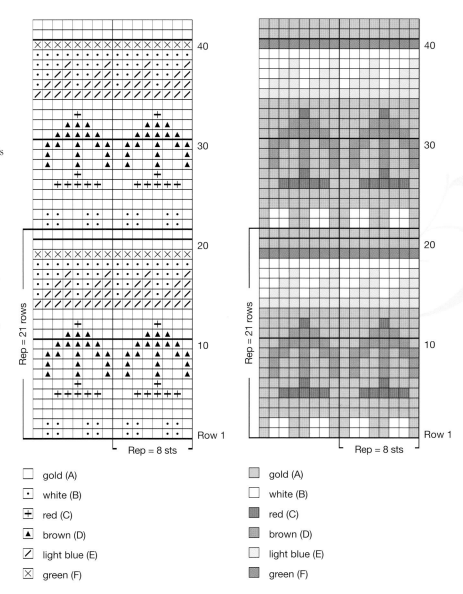

	gold (A)
·	white (B)
+	red (C)
▲	brown (D)
╱	light blue (E)
✕	green (F)

	gold (A)
	white (B)
	red (C)
	brown (D)
	light blue (E)
	green (F)

When this article was originally published, color printing was not as common as it is today, so the article explains how to read a chart that uses black-and-white symbols to represent different colors. Because most charts today are presented in color, we have added a new, full-color version of the original chart.

Working Mosaic Patterns

by Barbara G. Walker

Mosaic patterns have been special pets of mine since I first coined the term in my *Second Treasury of Knitting Patterns* and invented many new mosaics for subsequent books. The mosaic technique is fun and easier for inexperienced knitters than other kinds of color knitting.

The only stitches needed are plain knit stitches, slip stitches, and sometimes purl stitches (if stockinette-type fabric is wanted). There are no bobbins, no stranding and no changing colors in the middle of a row. Each color is used alone for two whole rows: one right-side row, and the following wrong-side row, which work and slip exactly the same stitches. Colors are changed only at the right-hand edge, every other row. All slip stitches are slipped as if to purl. When stitches are slipped, the yarn is always held to the wrong side of the work (that is, with yarn in back (wyib) on right-side rows, with yarn in front (wyif) on wrong-side rows). These are the basic rules for mosaic knitting.

Sound simple so far?

Now let's consider the new graphic way of giving mosaic directions on charts. An easy basketweave mosaic on our example chart shows a pattern with 8 stitches and 16 rows to each repeat. Exact multiples aren't necessary in mosaic knitting, so you can cast on any number of stitches to try out this pattern. Start with at least 2 or 3 repeats' worth of stitches. Cast on with a light color, A. Knit one (wrong-side) row. Join a dark color, B. Prepare to work the bottom row on the chart.

Row 1 begins with a black square at the right-hand edge, denoting color B. This is the first right-hand edge stitch of the first right-side row, which is NOT part of the pattern. Each right-side row begins with this extra edge stitch, to tell you which color to use for that row.

NOTE: If the right-hand edge stitch is black, as on Rows 1, 5, 9 and 13, all BLACK stitches on that row are knitted, and all WHITE stitches on that row are slipped wyib. If the right-hand edge stitch is white, as on Rows 3, 7, 11 and 15, all WHITE stitches on that row are knitted, and all BLACK stitches on that row are slipped wyib. This is the

From Charts

whole secret of reading the "pictures" on mosaic charts. Read each row from right to left, the same way the knitting goes.

Thus, the example chart tells you: **Row 1** (right side): With B, k1, *sl 1, k7; rep from *. Knit the last stitch on your needle.

The chart's equivalent of the asterisk is the vertical REPEAT LINE just after the right-hand edge stitch. When you reach the left-hand edge of the chart, return only as far as this repeat line for the next pattern repeat. Do not include the right-hand edge stitch in the pattern.

You can end your row anywhere on the chart, but always knit the last stitch on your needle, whether the chart calls for a slip stitch there or not.

Wrong-side rows (2, 4, 6, etc.) are all worked as follows: With the same yarn as the preceding row, knit (or purl) the same stitches of that color that are now on the needle. Slip the same stitches of the other color that are not on the needle, wyif, which, of course, is to the wrong side of the work. In circular knitting, all the stitches are slipped wyib.

Don't look at the chart to work wrong-side rows. Look as your needle. The colors of the stitches tell you what to do. Every wrong-side row copies the preceding right-side row, so the two are combined in one horizontal line of squares on the chart.

Row 3: With A, k1, *k1, sl 1; rep from *.

Row 5: With B, k1, *k4, sl 1, k3; rep from *.

Row 7: With A, k1, *k3, sl 1, k1, sl 1, k2; rep from *.

Row 9: With B, repeat row 5.

Row 11: With A, repeat row 3.

Row 13: With B, repeat row 1.

Row 15: With A, k1, *k1, sl 1, k5, sl 1; rep from *.

With the final wrong-side row, there are 16 pattern rows.

HINTS: To keep your place on the chart, lay the edge of a card or ruler along the top of the row you're using. This will show you a picture of your work as it proceeds. You can check the actual knitting against the pattern that appears on the chart.

When changing colors at the right-hand edge, drop the yarn you have just used to the front of the work, and pick up the other yarn behind it. This makes a series of neat, easily counted stripes up the side edge.

For a stockinette-type fabric, purl all stitches that are worked on wrong-side rows. For a garter-stitch fabric, knit all stitches that are worked on wrong-side rows. For a combination, knit wrong-side rows of one color, purl wrong-side rows of the other color.

Charts help you keep mosaic patterns correct while increasing or decreasing. You can draw your own shaping pictures by adding or subtracting squares at the edges. Just remember to knit the first and last stitches of every row. ⁓

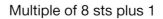

Multiple of 8 sts plus 1

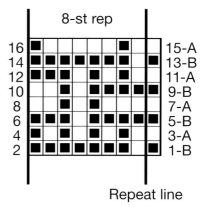

Repeat line

Essay: Copyright and Knitting:

"Copyright" is a legal right that is given to the creators of original works, including literary,

by Lance D. Reich

My wife, an avid knitter and blogger, often chats online with fellow stitchers. Because I am an intellectual-property attorney, my wife constantly fields questions from her knitting friends about copyright issues—for instance, Is it legal to make a photocopy of a purchased pattern? Unfortunately, American copyright law is not black and white, so many times I can quote only the guiding legal principles, which of course never makes anyone happy.

Below are some questions I am asked repeatedly by knitters who are confused about what they can and can't do when it comes to sharing patterns and information. I have tried to provide general guidelines, not from a point of view of skirting the law but for the honest knitter simply trying to make sure that his or her conduct does not constitute copyright infringement. Though I have shared with you matters of law, this is not a legal article in the sense that I will immediately cite the legal authority for my statement. References are listed at the end for those who wish to study these issues in more detail.

WHAT IS A COPYRIGHT?

"Copyright" is a legal right given to the authors or creators of original works of authorship, including literary, dramatic, musical, artistic and certain other intellectual works in many types of media. In the U.S.,

the Copyright Office is housed at the Library of Congress, which allows the copyright holder to register the copyrighted material. It is important to note that copyright *automatically* attaches to an original work regardless if it is published or unpublished, or whether the copyright is registered. The owner of the copyright has the exclusive right to reproduce the work in copies, to prepare derivative works based on the original, to distribute copies of the work to the public by sale or other transfer of ownership (such as licensing), and to display the copyrighted work to the public.

It is also important to know what copyright *cannot* protect, such as works that lack originality, are pure logical and comprehensive compilations (phone book listings, for instance), works solely in the public domain, and facts, ideas, processes, methods and systems described in the work. To qualify for copyright protection, a work must be original to the author; "original" means only that the work was independently created (as opposed to being purely copied from other works) and that it possesses at least some minimal degree of creativity. Further, originality does not signify novelty; a work may be original even though it closely resembles other works, so long as the similarity is fortuitous and not the result of copying. For example, assume that two knitters, each ignorant of the other, create identical patterns. Neither work is novel, yet

both are original and, consequently, copyrightable.

WHAT IS "FAIR USE"?

One other common principle in copyright law is the "fair use" doctrine. It is this fairness rule that allows a person to reproduce copyrighted material for purposes such as criticism, comment, news reporting, teaching, scholarship or research. In determining whether the use made of a copyrighted work in any particular case is a fair use, several factors are considered: the purpose and character of the use, including whether such use is of a commercial nature or is for nonprofit educational purposes; the nature of the copyrighted work; the amount and substantiality of the portion used in relation to the copyrighted work as a whole; and the effect of the use on the potential market for or value of the copyrighted work. In many of the frequently asked questions, the concept of fair use is central to determining if the copying is potentially infringing.

DO COPYRIGHTS EXPIRE?

Yes, they most certainly do. Once the copyright expires, the work is in the "public domain," and anyone can freely copy and disseminate that work. The rules for determining when a copyright expires are complicated and depend on when the work was created. The modern law for works created on or after January 1, 1978, is that

A Matter of Principle

dramatic, musical, artistic and other works in many types of media.

they are automatically protected from the moment of creation, with an ordinary term lasting for the author's life plus an additional seventy years after the author's death. In the case of a joint work prepared by two or more authors who did not make a "work for hire" for another, the term lasts for seventy years after the last surviving author's death. For works made for hire, and for anonymous and pseudonymous works (unless the author's identity is revealed in Copyright Office records), the duration of copyright will be ninety-five years from publication or 120 years from creation, whichever is shorter. For works created before January 1, 1978, the term of copyright is very complicated, so I will not go into it except to say that copyrights can last a very long time—well over 100 years in some instances—so do not assume the copyright has expired just because something is quite old.

WHERE DO COPYRIGHTS COMMONLY APPEAR IN KNITTING, AND WHAT IS PROTECTED IN A COPYRIGHTED KNITTING PATTERN?

In knitting, copyrights are most commonly encountered in printed knitting patterns and separately in finished garments. A copyright typically exists only for unique elements in the exact media in which the work is expressed. If the copyright is for a knitting pattern, then protection extends only to copying of the physical pattern or derivative portions of the pattern. To the extent that the pattern contains very well-known instructions that cannot really be called original to the creator of the pattern—such as very old patterns on which the copyright has expired—a copyright would cover only the exact pattern with all of the elements; only the original (not well known) aspects of the pattern are protectable by copyright. Consequently, only substantially identical copying of such a pattern could potentially infringe such a narrow copyright.

DOES A COPYRIGHT OF THE PATTERN EXTEND TO GARMENTS MADE FROM A COPYRIGHTED PATTERN?

No. A copyright for the pattern covers only copying and derivative works from the physical pattern itself, such as a photocopy; a copyright does not extend from the knitting pattern to a clothing item made from the pattern, although a person or entity can register copyrights for both. There could be other issues here too, such as purchasing the copyrighted pattern under a license that restricts your use, or other intellectual-property violations from making the garment, but the copyright of the pattern protects only against copying the pattern. For example, if you purchase a pattern with no restrictions, you could sit with a friend and both knit separate garments from the same pattern. (This also assumes that the garment made from the pattern does not have its own separate copyright.) You should note that many pattern-publishing Web sites list explicit terms under which you can copy and use patterns from their site, such as specifically limiting production of garments from the patterns, and you should abide by these terms.

CAN I SELL OR DONATE ITEMS I MAKE FROM A COPYRIGHTED PATTERN?

It depends on how you purchased the copyrighted knitting pattern—either outright or subject to a license. If you bought a copy of the pattern with no written restrictions on use, then you should be able to sell or donate whatever you like from the pattern because the copyright for the pattern does not otherwise extend to items made from the pattern; if the ultimate garment itself is copyrighted, however, you could infringe on that copyright. (Most designers include such restrictions next to the copyright symbol on their printed patterns.) If you purchased the pattern pursuant to a written license that limits your activities, you may be restricted in what you make from the pattern. For example, if the knitting pattern has a written license enclosed with it, or has a disclaimer at the bottom of the pattern that says in purchasing the pattern you are getting only a license to make items from the pattern for your personal use and are not allowed to resell the items, this could constitute a limitation on your actions. (This magazine, for instance, prohibits the sale of garments made from its patterns.) A good rule of thumb is that if you are unsure if the garment produced from the pattern is separately copyrighted, it is better not to sell or donate a garment made from the pattern.

HOW MUCH NEEDS TO BE CHANGED FROM THE ORIGINAL COPYRIGHTED WORK FOR IT TO FALL OUTSIDE THE COPYRIGHT?

People often tell me that they heard that if you change 10 percent of the copyrighted material, you no longer infringe. I call this the "10 Percent Myth." There simply is no set "amount" of deviation from a work that will fall outside the scope of the original copyright. To specifically answer the question, the best I can do is quote a court that said: "There are no absolute rules as to how much of a copyrighted work may be copied and still be considered a fair use." The real question about avoiding infringement is qualitative and not quantitative, e.g., what is copied and what is changed, and will vary case to case.

WHAT CAN I DO WITH AN OUT-OF-PRINT PATTERN BOOK?

The short answer is that even if the book is out of print, you still have to respect the copyright if there is an enforceable copyright claim that clearly marks the book. There are some reasonable steps you can take, though, to mitigate any potential fallout should you exceed fair use of the out-of-print book. One court commented that longer portions copied from an out-of-print book may be fair use because the book is no longer available and,

presumably, there is little market effect produced by the copying. However, the same court found the argument convincing that damage to out-of-print works may in fact be greater since permissions fees may be the only income for authors and copyright owners. If you want to make copies from an out-of-print book, you can contact the publisher or author to seek written permission. Search the Library of Congress for this information; or, contact the Copyright Clearance Center (www.copyright.com) to find out whether it represents the owner of the copyright. If you have made a documented and legitimate attempt to seek permission to make copies and your actions prove fruitless, it is hard to see how the dormant copyright holder could come after you for anything other than making you stop, but it is always possible. Given that there are statutory damages for copyright infringement—$750 to $30,000 per infringement, and up to $150,000 per infringement if determined to be willful—any potential infringement always needs to be taken seriously.

CAN I MAKE A COPY OF A PATTERN FOR A FRIEND?

No. This would specifically be infringement because you are copying the work to deprive the author of a sale. You should have your friend buy a copy of the pattern for him/herself.

CAN MY LYS MAKE COPIES OF PATTERNS FROM MAGAZINES OR THE INTERNET FOR CUSTOMERS, EVEN IF THE PATTERNS ARE NOT TO BE SOLD?

No. This conduct is infringement as it would deprive the author of a sale; i.e., the customer would otherwise purchase a copy of the pattern if you did not give it to them.

CAN I COPY KNITTING PATTERNS FROM A LIBRARY BOOK?

Libraries and archives are authorized under the copyright law to furnish a photocopy or other reproduction of a copyrighted work, but one of the specified conditions is that the photocopy or reproduction is not to be "used for any purpose other than private study, scholarship or research." If a library user makes a request for, or later uses, a photocopy or reproduction of library materials for purposes in excess of "fair use," he or she may be liable for copyright infringement. Therefore, you should treat the library book under loan as a book you own and not copy the book to the extent that would exceed fair use. Remember that one argument for your having exceeded fair use is that you deprive the author/creator of a sale by making a copy. So when you copy one or more patterns from a book, you need to reasonably say that you would not have otherwise purchased the book to get the copies.

CAN I MAKE PHOTOCOPIES OF A COPYRIGHTED PATTERN TO TEACH CLASS?

The issue about teaching and fair use was extensively addressed in the case of Basic Books, Inc. v. Kinko's. In that case, publishing houses in New York brought suit against Kinko's, alleging copyright infringement. Kinko's basically copied excerpts from textbooks and other materials without permission, compiled them into course "packets," and sold them to college students. The court ultimately found that Kinko's was liable, as its copying was of the important portions of the works and unfavorably impacted on the publishers' sales of their books and collections of permissions fees. The same principles would apply to copying and supplying a knitting pattern to teach a class; i.e., is the class for profit, are you using the complete copyrighted pattern, are you depriving the pattern's creator of sales, etc. My advice to those teaching for-profit knitting classes would be to use a pattern that is original to you, is not copyrighted, or that you have express written permission to copy and use.

IF I OWN A COPY OF A PATTERN (SUCH AS FROM A MAGAZINE), CAN I POST THE PATTERN ON MY BLOG?

No. The ownership of the magazine or other print is really just ownership of a physical copy, as opposed to ownership of the actual copyright. The owner of the copyright is the only person or entity that can rightfully make a copy of the copyrighted work. Entities that purchase the copyright for a work from others own the copyright just as if they were the original owners.

CAN I POST A COPY OF A PATTERN ON MY BLOG OR ON THE INTERNET EVEN IF I DO NOT INTEND TO SELL IT?

No, you can't post the pattern or the magazine photograph of the completed garment. The right of "display" is an express right reserved to the copyright holder. Furthermore, you could be facilitating infringement by others as any screen can be captured on the Internet.

CAN I PHOTOCOPY MY PURCHASED PATTERN?

Yes, you can photocopy it for your own use, but no, you cannot copy it for others or to sell it. The line here is pretty clear: You can make copies of your purchase — that is, the physical item—for yourself because you purchased a "copy"; but you cannot make another copy for use by others or sell another copy. You can sell your purchased copy or give it to another as long as you then destroy your own copy. Hopefully, these answers to the common questions I field can at least give an overview of where copyright issues are involved in your knitting. Let me conclude by saying that your gut reaction is probably an excellent guide when deciding whether or not to make a copy of a copyrighted item. ⌒

RELEVANT WEB SITES:
U.S. Copyright Office: www.copyright.gov
Fair use guides: fairuse.stanford.edu;
"Crash Course in Copyright"
(www.utsystem.edu/OGC/IntellectualProperty/cprtindx.htm)
Specific issues for libraries:
www.librarylaw.com

How to Cast On: Seven

Selecting a cast-on method is the first decision made when knitting. To help you make that

by Mari Lynn Patrick

Arrival at the perfect ending depends on getting off to a great start. In knitting, the starting point is the cast-on edge, for which there are a variety of methods. There is a perfectly simple cast-on for beginners, a somewhat to very elastic cast-on for ribbed edges and a more stable cast-on for lie-flat edges. There are also two versions of a tubular cast-on edge, both of which imitate the machine-knit, cast-on edge.

Although you may prefer to stay with the one technique that you feel best suits all your knitting styles, why not experiment with one of the methods outlined here?

MAKING THE FIRST STITCH

The first stitch of every cast-on method is actually a slipknot, made as follows:

Wrap yarn around index and middle fingers to form a loop. Pull up the loop through wrapped yarn, forming a new loop.

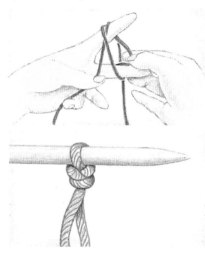

Place the new loop on the needle and tighten it by pulling on both ends of yarn. After the first loop is complete, you are ready to continue with any one of the cast-on methods given.

SIMPLE METHOD

An easy-to-learn, rather loose edge that's great for beginners.

Place a slipknot on needle, leaving a short tail. Hold needle in right hand. Wrap yarn from ball around left thumb and hold with other fingers in left palm.

Insert needle through strand at front of thumb.

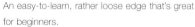

Slip this loop onto needle, pulling yarn from ball to tighten. Continue in this way until all stitches are cast on.

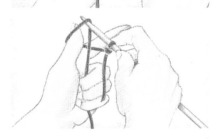
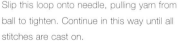

THUMB METHOD

Make a slipknot on needle. With needle in right hand, wind yarn around left thumb from front to back.

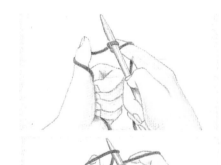

Insert needle into loop on thumb.

With right index finger, wrap yarn from ball over the needle as if knitting. Then, with the needle, draw the yarn through the loop to make the stitch. Take thumb out of the loop and pull left-hand yarn to secure the stitch.

If cast-on edge is too tight, try using two needles held together, then simply pull out one needle when all stitches are cast on.

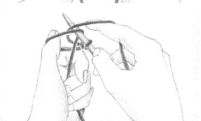

Ways to a Perfect Start

choice, here are techniques for a variety of cast-on edges.

TWO-NEEDLE CAST-ON

Casting on using this method is in effect knitting the stitches on. It's best used when a loose edge is required.

Place slipknot on left needle. Insert right-hand needle from front to back into this stitch and pass the working yarn around the needle as if knitting.

Draw right-hand needle through the first stitch as if knitting, but do not slip the first stitch off needle.

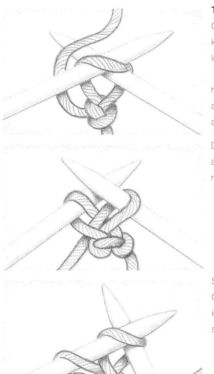

Slip this new stitch onto left-hand needle. Continue to add stitches in this way, working into each subsequent stitch instead of the slipknot.

CABLE CAST-ON

The cable cast-on is a sturdy yet elastic edge and is my own personal favorite. It has a slightly decorative rope appearance that always looks even and neat.

Repeat steps 1, 2 and 3 of the two-needle cast-on. Once the first new stitch is slipped to needle, instead of knitting *into* the loop on the needle, work in this way.

Insert right-hand needle *between* the slipknot and the next stitch on needle.

Pass yarn around needle as if knitting; pull loop through.

Place the new stitch on the left needle. Repeat these steps, working between first and second stitches on left-hand needle.

TUBULAR CAST-ON

This duplicates a machine-knit edge.

Using a long strand of contrasting waste yarn and needles to be used for ribbing, cast on half the number of required stitches for the ribbing. Drop waste yarn. With working yarn (MC) [purl 1 row, knit 1 row] twice.

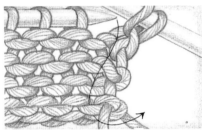

*Purl the first stitch on needle, then insert tip of left-hand needle downward into the first MC loop, connecting 2 waste yarn loops from the cast-on row below. Slip this loop onto left-hand needle and knit this stitch through back loop. Repeat from *, ending with the last full MC loop being picked up and knit after the next-to-last stitch on needle has been purled, purling the last stitch on needle, then picking up and knitting the half-loop of MC at the very edge.

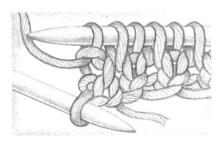

All stitches for ribbing are now on needle and waste yarn may be removed. The first row of ribbing will be worked over an even number of stitches and will begin with purl 1.

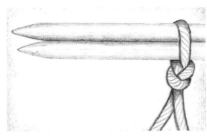

OPEN CAST-ON

This is a cast-on method used when stitches are to be picked up and worked later, such as for hems or special edges.

Using two needles held together, begin with a slipknot.

Hold a long strand of waste yarn beside the slipknot and take the working yarn under the waste yarn and then behind it again until all stitches are cast on.

Before knitting, withdraw one needle, then knit into the front of the loops on the first row. Leave waste yarn in until you are ready to pick up stitches and add your edge later.

Turkish Cast On

by Meg Swansen

Turkish may not be the proper name for this method, but I learned it while embarking on a Turkish stocking from the toe up. I now use Joyce William's adaptation (from her book *Latvian Dreams*), and she refers to it as Eastern European Cast On.

Whatever its name, it is an intriguing, invisible way to cast on when a closed end is your goal (sock toes, glove-finger tips, round shawl beginnings, purse bottoms, etc.). Once you grasp the concept, you'll find that it's not difficult.

Since you need two same-size 24"/60cm circular needles, it may help a great deal, as you learn this method, to use two different-colored needles; I use one bamboo and one silver-plated. As previously stated in this series, I have eliminated slipknots from my knitting, but in this instance one is required for about two minutes.

On the bamboo 24"/60cm needle, make a (temporary) slipknot. Hold both needles in your left hand, pointing to the right, with the silver needle parallel to, and above, the bamboo one [Figure 1].

Bring the working wool behind the silver needle and wrap it fairly loosely around both needles—from left to right [Figure 2]. Wrap a number of times equal to half the total desired number of stitches.

Pull the bamboo (bottom) needle to the right, so its loops are on the cable section, and let it dangle there [Figure 3]. *Grab the other end of the silver (top) needle and knit all its loops, then pull the silver needle through so the new stitches are on the cable section.

Turn the work.

Slide stitches to the tip of the bamboo needle. Remove and undo the temporary slipknot and let it hang. With the working wool coming from the last stitch on the silver needle, knit the stitches on the bamboo needle [Figure 4]. Pull the bamboo needle through so the new stitches are on the cable section. Turn. Slide stitches to the tip of the silver needle. Repeat from * [Figure 5].

As I read over what I had just written, it sounded garbled and slightly nuts, but as you have most likely discovered with other knitting instructions, when you actually have the work in your hands, and carefully follow the instructions, the directions become more intelligible.

Think of a favorite technique that you can now do in your sleep. Can you remember how awkward and plodding you felt when you first learned it?

Onward, Meg ⁓

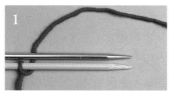

Hold 2 circular needles parallel to one another, having a temporary slipknot on the bamboo one.

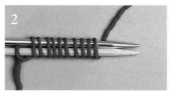

Wrap yarn around both needles a number of times equal to half the desired number of stitches.

Pull the bamboo needle to the right so its loops are on the cable section and let it dangle.

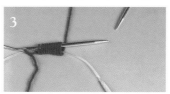

After knitting all loops on the silver needle, pull it through, turn and knit the loops on the bamboo needle.

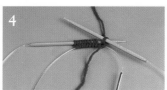

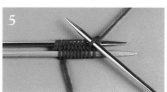

As you alternate between the two needles, a sided, seamless piece of knitting will form.

by Meg Swansen

According to Montse Stanley's wonderful knitting compendium *The Knitter's Handbook*, there are more than forty different ways to cast on. That information rather takes a knitter's breath away; it is both comforting and daunting at the same time. I began as most of you did: I picked a favorite all-purpose way to cast on and added variations as specific needs arose. At present I have a small but useful collection of eight or nine methods that I use most frequently and that have (so far) covered all of my requirements. I would like to describe each of them to you in this ongoing series.

I'll begin with my fave, which is usually referred to as Long Tail Cast On but is also known as Single Needle, or Two Strand, Cast On. Many knitters refer to it simply as Regular Old Cast On (terminology is one of the few bugbears in this beloved discipline of ours). Long Tail is my favorite because it can be performed at great speed—when faced with the task of casting on 412 stitches, speed can be a consideration—and it is beautiful to behold.

This method is known as Long Tail because you must begin by pulling out a long tail of wool. How long, you may ask? Ah, good question. There was extensive discussion of this topic recently at Knitting Camp, with all kinds of solutions being offered. For instance: Wrap the wool around the needle 10 times. Unwrap it. Measure it. Divide the number of stitches you plan to cast on by 10. Multiply the result by the length of the 10-wrap strand and pull out that amount of wool, plus a little more. There were other quite scientific strategies described; they were impressive and yielded an accurate result. To my mind, however, they eliminated all the fun.

I prefer my mother's method: Grab the end of the ball of wool, roll your eyes to the heavens and go into a trance. Begin pulling out lengths of wool until...*there*. Stop. This is the place. Start casting on and the game is under way. Will you make it? The suspense will sustain you, and the satisfaction of achieving your wanted number of stitches with a few inches of wool left over is enormous. But what if you don't make it?

Trick #1: You are 40 stitches away from the number you need and the tail is becoming alarmingly short. Are you holding the tail wool over your forefinger? Unless you are using a very fine needle, the thumb wool uses much less length per stitch than the forefinger wool. Switch places—put the tail wool over your thumb and the ball wool over your forefinger. There will be a tiny twist in the selvage, but I defy anyone to spot it.

Trick #2: You are 40 stitches away from your wanted number of stitches and you have totally run out of tail wool. If you cleverly wound a center-pull ball, take the outside strand, leave two longish ends and keep going. Yes, you will have to darn them in later, but it's better than having to rip back 372 cast-on stitches. (Speaking of ends, you may choose to use two separate balls of wool at the outset and never have to worry about the length of the tail, but you will then have an extra end to darn in and will deprive yourself of the game to boot.)

Wait a minute: I almost forgot! Please do not make a slip knot at the outset (I have eliminated all knots from my knitting); instead, drape the wool over the thumb and forefinger of your left hand and grab the two tails with your remaining fingers. With the needle in your right hand, dive down into the space between the traversing strand and your palm. Point the needle toward you and up to the ceiling. There. That twisted loop is stitch number one and you have eliminated the bulky knot. [Figures 1 and 2.]

You may know the Backward Loop Cast On [Figure 3] as the simplest method for beginners. Although I use it for buttonholes and plain-color steeks, I do not recommend it for starting a sweater because, when knitting the first round/row, you will find the bit of wool between the loops growing longer and longer; it is a relatively unstable cast on. As you work the Long Tail method, study your hands: That loop over your thumb forms the simple Backward Loop Cast On we just talked about, but, before you release it, knit into it by hooking the forefinger wool through the loop. What a good deal—casting on and knitting the first round/row at the same time.

You can achieve an identical result in a slightly different manner [Figure 4]: Hold the needle and strand #1 in your right hand, loop strand #2 around your left index finger as shown, insert the needle into the left-hand loop, throw strand #1 around the needle and hook it through. This is a more graphic representation of knitting into the backward loop.

Once you've cast on, study the result. Which side is the "right" side? Let us get queries like this out of the way at the beginning: Both "wrong" or "right" in knitting are largely subjective. Since you are in charge of your own knitting, you are the one to decide such questions.

One side of Long Tail Cast On resembles outline stitch in embroidery; the other side has little purl bumps. Pick the side that pleases you most to be on the outside, unless you plan to add a hem to the finished garment later on. In that case, arrange to have the outline stitch on the "public" selvage of the garment. When the sweater is finished, you can come back to the cast-on edge and knit up stitches into the purl bumps (behind the outline stitch) for the hem. The outline will serve as a nice sharp hem turn, and by now you may have decided what message you want to knit into the hem. As you can imagine, there are many reasons to wait until the last minute before committing this sweater to a specific recipient.

Onward, Meg ~

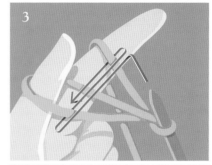
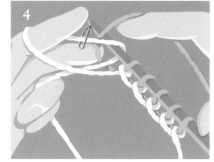

Knitted-On Cast On

by Meg Swansen

KNITTED-ON CAST ON IS A GOOD, stable way to begin a piece of knitting and is also useful when you have to add on stitches in the middle of a project. It seems to have slightly more elasticity than the Long Tail method [page 76], and it also may help to prevent corrugated ribbing from curling.

If you already know this cast on, you most likely get started with a slipknot. I have a thing about knots in my knitting; I do not want any and would grit my teeth every time I had to make one for this technique. Now, thanks to Nancy Robinson's clever solution, I have finally eliminated the last "necessary" knot. Here's how: With a short tail and your hands set for Long Tail Cast On, work the twisted loop and cast on one stitch in the manner described in the previous issue and shown in the first two steps at right. Transfer the needle to your left hand and proceed to knit on the number of additional stitches you want in one of these two ways.

METHOD #1 is my fave: Begin with Nancy Robinson's No Knot method, then *put the tip of the right needle between the two stitches on the left needle and hook the working wool through. Put that loop on the left needle. Repeat from * to achieve your wanted number of stitches.

QUERY: Should you put the loop on the left needle frontward or backward? Test both choices by knitting on a dozen stitches with one method, followed by a dozen with the other; choose the one you like best. The superiority of one method over the other is purely subjective; just be consistent throughout.

METHOD #2: Begin with Nancy Robinson's No Knot method, but this time *put the tip of the right needle into the stitch on the left needle (as opposed to between the stitches); hook the working wool through and place the resulting loop onto the left needle. Repeat from *. Take a look at each method and choose your favorite.

A TRICK FOR EITHER METHOD (this idea is from Mary Hall): When you have achieved the wanted number of stitches, you may be displeased with the way the final cast-on stitch slants to the right on the needle and how the bottom of it merges with the penultimate stitch. The remedy, to be used on the last stitch only: Before you place the final loop onto the left needle [Figure 3], bring the working wool to the front, between the final loop and the left needle. Now place the last stitch on the needle and take the working wool to the back (under the needle), ready to begin knitting. See? That final stitch now lines up perfectly with its sisters.

Knit on, Meg ⁓

To begin the No Knot method, wrap the yarn around your hand and place needle under strand as shown.

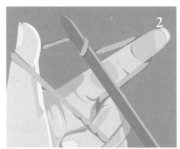

Twist the needle around the yarn to make the first loop. This eliminates the usual knot.

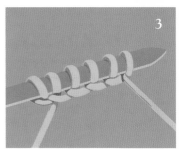

When using the Knitted-On method, before placing the final loop onto the needle, bring the yarn to the front, then slip on the stitch.

Austrian Variation
Plus K & P Cast on

by Meg Swansen

The Austrian method is a cast on that Yvonne Cutright learned during a research trip to Austria to study Bavarian Twisted Stitch. This variation is standard among knitters in that area and is used to prevent a lower edge from curling. Also, it is relatively elastic and quite simple to learn.

Set up your hands as for Long Tail Cast On and make the twisted-loop first stitch [page 76]. Go up into the thumb loop and, instead of grabbing the near forefinger strand, take the far finger strand and hook it through the thumb loop. Reset both thumb and finger and repeat this action. Yes, it takes a bit longer to have to reset both digits, but you will soon fall into a pleasant rhythm.

I usually use regular ole' Long Tail when I am casting on for a ribbed border. However, if I am feeling particularly fastidious, I have several options open to me to cast on in Knit and Purl.

Example #1: Work two stitches in regular Long Tail method (for K2), then, for P2, think of Long Tail Cast On in mirror-image. Pretend your forefinger is your thumb and *bring the needle up under the far finger strand, over the near finger strand, hook the far thumb strand (from underneath) and pull it through the finger loop [Figure 1]. Reset your left hand and repeat from asterisk. See the purl bump on the front of the needle?

You can achieve a very slightly different appearance from the following Purl Cast On variation—and you can decide which pleases you most. As above, work the regular Long Tail method for the knit stitches. For the Purl: Take the needle behind the near finger strand, down into the thumb loop and up under the near thumb strand. Now back over the near finger strand, under the near thumb strand and through the finger loop [Figure 2]. Whew! As complex as that sounds on first reading (and trying), you may well surprise yourself with how easily it flows after about forty or fifty repetitions. The hand-brain connection is a wondrous thing.

Knit on, Meg ⌢

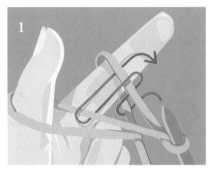

To work the purl version, grab the underneath strand from around the forefinger and pull it through the thumb loop as shown.

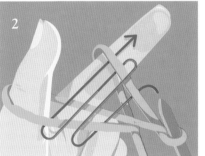

An alternative purl version can be tricky to master, but is worth trying.

by Meg Swansen

As with the Turkish Cast On installment, I cannot vouch for "Latvian" being the proper title for this technique, but here is how I learned it: Joyce Williams was at work on her book *Latvian Dreams* and was shown a pair of beautiful hand-knitted Latvian mittens with a mysterious lower edge. She was told that the technique was unfamiliar even to the Latvian knitting community in Minneapolis. Rising to the challenge, Joyce, from memory alone, figured it out herself. Not one to stop in the middle of a project, Joyce also discovered a method for a matching cast off—so both of these techniques are presented here with her kind permission.

Set up your hands as for Long Tail Cast On [page 76] and make a twisted loop for stitch #1.

A) Reset your left hand and put your thumb into the strand the "wrong" way—i.e., lower wool coming from needle goes around your thumb clockwise [Figure 1]—and knit into the BACK of that strand.

B) Work a regular Long Tail Cast On [Figure 2].

Alternate A and B; end with A.

Flipping the thumb-wrap back and forth is an excellent mental exercise as, initially, your thumb balks at the unfamiliar direction. Persevere, however, and you will eventually be able to retrain your thumb for every other stitch. (Truthfully, I still have to concentrate on each stitch, but, I rationalize, it keeps my knitting brain on its toes.)

As in most of knitting, you also have another choice, and Amy Detjen has come up with this alternative:

Alternative A) Let your thumb go into the strand the way it wants to (with the wool going around it counterclockwise); send the needle straight down between the two wools and hook the far thumb strand onto the back of the needle [Figure 3], then knit the finger wool through.

Alternative B) As above. Alternate A and B.

Isn't this a beautiful cast on? Little couplets of stitches have been wrapped snugly around their base. Actually, the mittens Joyce studied used a double strand of wool over the thumb and a single strand over the forefinger (as shown here); then the handsome horizontal wrap is more pronounced and stronger.

Joyce's matching Latvian Cast Off is a very elastic sewn technique and is worked while the stitches are still on the needle. If you used a double thumb wool to cast on, then use a double thread to cast off: With a blunt sewing-up needle, bring the wool through the first stitch from back to front.

A) Two stitches to the left (the third stitch in line): Go through the stitch (under the needle) from front to back and pull the wool through [Figure 4].

B) One stitch to the right, come through the stitch (under the needle) and UNDER the previous wool loop [Figure 5].

C) Two stitches to the left, repeat A.

D) One stitch to the right, come through the stitch and OVER the previous wool loop [Figure 6].

Repeat from A through D.

During this series I have had several calls from knitters wanting to know if there is a matching cast off for some of the cast ons I have described. Use Joyce as an example, and study the cast-on stitch movement closely, then experiment to see if you can determine how to reproduce it at the other end. Elizabeth Zimmermann duplicated Long Tail Cast On with her casting on and off. Tubular Cast Off matches Tubular Cast On perfectly. There is a Picot Cast Off to match Channel Island Cast On, and now Joyce has nailed Latvian Cast On and Off. See what you yourself can come up with.

Knit on, Meg ~

Cast on

1 Set up thumb into loop opposite to the one used for the regular long-tail cast on (yarn wraps round the thumb counterclockwise), and hook finger-wool through far strand.

2 This is a regular long-tail cast on with the yarn doubled over the thumb.

3 Shown here is the alternative method for working step A.

Cast off

4 To work the cast off, insert the sewing needle through the stitch that is two stitches to the left.

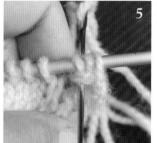

5 Come back through the stitch, one stitch to the right and UNDER the previous loop.

6 Or, come back through the stitch, one stitch to the right and OVER the previous loop.

German Twisted Cast On

by Meg Swansen

This wonderful method was first taught to me by the talented designer Betts Lampers, who referred to it as Elastic Long Tail Cast On. Several years later I found it in Montse Stanley's *Knitter's Handbook*, where it is called Twisted German Cast On. For the sake of political correctness, I have renamed it German Twisted Cast On.

It is, indeed, a more elastic version of Long Tail Cast On [pages 76–77], which makes it a good candidate for the beginning of a wide rib or even a lace project. Equally important, with a purl bump both fore and aft, it is ideal for corrugated ribbing because it helps prevent the little curl many knitters get along the lower edge when they use regular Long Tail Cast On.

This variation has a few extra twists and turns: Set up your hands as for Long Tail: the wool is draped over the thumb and forefinger of your left hand, and the two tails are held by the other three fingers. With the needle in your right hand, dive down between the strand and your palm, turn the needle toward you and up to the ceiling. That twisted loop is stitch #1, and a knot has been eliminated [Figure 1].

As you pull the needle down, a loop will form, emanating from your thumb [Figure 2]. Move the needle under both of those thumb strands, come over the top of the far strand and down into the loop. Come out of the loop in front of the near strand and reach over to grab the near forefinger wool. Now comes the only tricky part: In order to take the forefinger wool down into the thumb loop, you have to open it up by bending your thumb away from you. See the loop appear? Now you can draw the finger wool down through the loop, release both thumb and forefinger and reset your hand for the next stitch.

Cast on 20 stitches, then study what you have made. See the purls on either side? Now cast on 20 Long Tail stitches and compare the differences in appearance and stretch. The few extra moves in the German variation slow the process down a bit, but with practice, a nice, steady rhythm will develop.

Knit on, Meg ⌒

For the No-Knot method, wrap the yarn around your hand; place needle under strand and twist it around as shown.

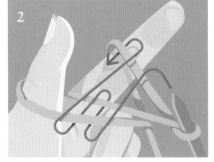

Maneuver the needle over and under the strands as shown to create the cast-on stitch.

How to Bind Off

Tips and specifics on how best
to work the last row

by Mari Lynn Patrick

As much as we all do love to knit, binding off may well be the most satisfying of all knitting procedures. It signals that we are near the finish of a piece and locks in the many hours of loving work. Binding off can also give shape to a piece, such as in the curve of an armhole or the roundness of a sleeve cap. It also serves as the first step in the two-step horizontal buttonhole, and it is even used throughout some three-dimensional stitch patterns.

There is a large array of bind-off methods, from the basic one, with which most of us are familiar, to more specific techniques, such as suspended and invisible bind-offs for ribbing edges. There is also a decrease bind-off for holding together stitches in patterns that spread out too readily. There are many decorative bind-offs to suit perfectly an edge that will later stand on its own, such as the outer edge of an afghan, a baby's jacket or a fine pointelle knit in cotton.

There are more ways than one to fasten off your knitting.
Here's a primer on six of them, from plain to decorative,
firm to elastic.

THE BASIC METHOD

Always suitable, the basic method is one of the beginner's first-learned techniques. Sometimes this method will leave an edge that is tight, in which case you can bind off firmly with a needle two sizes larger than that used for your work. To keep the continuity of the patterns in your piece, always bind off stitches as they present themselves: that is, knit the knit stitches and purl the purl stitches, unless otherwise stated in the instructions.

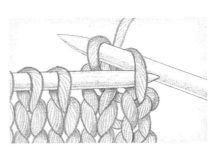

Working on the right side of the work, knit the first two stitches in the normal way. Insert the left-hand needle through the first stitch.

Take the first stitch over the second stitch and off the needle. Continue working in this way: knit each subsequent stitch and always work with two stitches on the right-hand needle.

To fasten off the last stitch, for each method of binding off, cut the yarn, leaving a desired length and pull the end through the remaining loop and tighten.

SUSPENDED BIND-OFF

Although this is a similar method to the basic bind-off, it has the advantage of producing a more flexible edge and is thus particularly suitable for ribbed edges.

As in the basic method, work the first two stitches and pull the first stitch over the second, but this time leave the pulled stitch on the left needle.

Then work the next stitch.

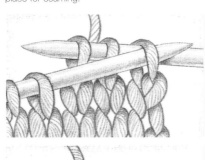

Drop both stitches from the left needle at the same time. There will always be two stitches on the right needle.

Continue to work across in this way until only two stitches remain. Knit these two stitches together and fasten off.

DECREASE BIND-OFF

Here is a solution for pattern stitches with a great deal of lateral spread, such as allover traveling cables or double knitting. The decrease bind-off method pulls the stitches together to hold them in place for seaming.

Work as for the basic method, but first work three stitches onto the right needle. Then pull the first stitch over the next two stitches. To keep the edge elastic, use a needle three times larger than that used for the work and always knit the stitches to be bound off, except in double knitting, where the stitches should be worked as knit and purl.

Two stitches remain on the right needle.

CROCHETED BIND-OFF

When fairly inelastic yarns, such as cottons and silks, are used, a crocheted bind-off is useful for a firm but elastic finish. Somewhat decorative, it also works to edge accessories and baby clothing, and it serves as a good base for crochet edges to be added later. You should use a crochet hook of a comparable size to your knitting needles.

Using the crochet hook instead of a knitting needle, insert the hook knitwise into the first stitch. Pass the yarn around the hook.

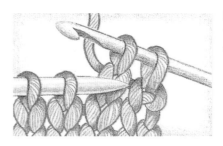

Pull up a loop and let the first stitch fall from the needle. Pull up a loop through the next stitch in the same way.

Then pass yarn around the hook and pull a loop through both of the stitches on the hook. Continue across the row in this way.

SEAM BIND-OFF (THREE-NEEDLE BIND-OFF)

An ideal method for joining shoulders or any two pieces with an equal number of stitches, this bind-off method accomplishes binding off and sewing together all in one step. When each piece is completed, simply place the stitches to be joined later on holders or draw the yarn through the stitches on the needle with a sewing needle.

Hold the right sides of the pieces together and work from the wrong side, with each piece on a separate needle. Using a third needle of the same size, knit together one stitch from the front and one stitch from the back needle.

Work the next two stitches together in the same way. Then pass the first stitch over the second one. Continue to work across the row in this way.

To achieve a raised effect that is the same on both sides, bind off in single rib: that is, knit together the first two stitches and purl together the next two stitches.

PICOT EDGE BIND-OFF

Of the many decorative bind-offs, the picot edge bind-off is one of the prettiest and simplest. Decorative bind-offs of this nature are used widely in traditional fine-lace knitting—such as tablecloths and other articles knit with tiny needles using gossamer-weight cottons and threads. This decorative edge is ideal for the subtle trim of a pointelle sweater or for baby clothes and blankets.

Using the basic method, bind off the first one or two stitches of the row. Then, *cast on two stitches along with the single stitch which remains on the right-hand needle; bind off all the stitches on the right-hand needle to form the picot (including the stitches just cast on); then bind off an additional two stitches form the left-hand needle*. Repeat the steps between asterisks to the end of the row. You can, of course, vary the number of stitches between each picot as well as the number of stitches used in each picot, as desired.

BIND-OFF TIPS

- Use a needle two sizes larger than the one you were working with to loosen up a tight edge.
- After binding off along edges to be seamed later, such as those of a shoulder, leave a yarn end long enough for sewing the pieces together.
- When worked from both edges of the work (such as those of a shoulder or armhole), binding off is usually done at the beginning of a row to avoid cutting and reattaching the yarn. For this reason, there will be one more row on one side than on the other. This will have a minimal effect on the finished result and should be of concern only when a very bulky yarn or a pattern stitch with very few rows per inch is used.
- When binding off vertical cables that are interspersed among other more stable patterns, working two stitches together across the cable will make them lie flat like the rest of the piece. Be sure that you bind off on the correct row of the cable pattern. Ideally, you should bind off on a row that is halfway between the cable twists. If you bind off immediately after a cable twist row, the fabric will pull in very tightly. If you bind off immediately before the next cable twist (that is, you have worked a number of rows without twisting), the piece will stretch out and may be wider than your desired finished measurement.
- When binding off across the top of a sleeve cap that will later be a puffed sleeve, you can pre-gather the stitches by working two or three stitches together across the last few rows while binding off.
- Whenever possible, to aid in seaming, bind off from the right side of the work. This will create an even ridge, making it easier to sew the seams. ⌒

Correcting Mistakes
Solutions to Most Knitting Blunders

by Corinne Shields

All of us make mistakes or change our minds, so it's good to know how to fix things. Three problems—a stitch backwards on the needle, unwanted increases and incomplete stitches—often puzzle beginners. Even experienced knitters find it valuable to know how to deal with dropped stitches and how to unravel back to correct a problem. In the methods described here, the words "strand" and "loop" are often used. "Strand" refers to the working yarn before it becomes a stitch, and "loop" is the completed stitch.

Dropped, twisted and unwanted extra stitches have a mischievous way of cropping up in everyone's work. These nuisances are easy to repair. Here's how.

TWISTED STITCH

If a stitch on the needle looks wrong, it may be on backwards. If you work it as it lies, by inserting your right needle knitwise under the part that is in front of the left needle, you will produce a twisted stitch.

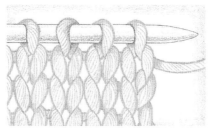

The front of the loop is behind the needle, the back of the loop in front. Whether the stitch is to be knitted or purled, you can leave it in place and cope with it very easily.

To knit the stitch, insert right needle (behind left needle) through it from front to back and knit (that is, knit through the back loop).

To purl the stitch, insert right needle in the back loop from back to front and purl.

UNPLANNED EDGE INCREASES

Should you find extra stitches at the edge of your work, look for situations like these:

(last row purled) The yarn has gone over the needle to the back.

(last row knitted) An extra stitch made same as above.

In both cases, two strands appear in front of the needle. If you work both, you will have an extra stitch.

To avoid this problem, at the end of knit rows, drop the yarn and leave it at the back of the work, then turn the work.

At the end of the purl rows, drop the yarn and leave it at the front of the work, then turn the work.

EXTRA STRAND OVER NEEDLE

If you work the extra strand, you will have an additional stitch and a hole, often mistaken for a dropped stitch. There are two possible causes, both occurring on the previous row.

A strand between two loops usually happens between a knit and a purl stitch when the yarn was taken to the correct side over instead of under the needle. Drop the strand off the needle and later adjust stitches on both sides to even it out.

A strand passing either in front of or behind a loop results when the strand was not pulled through the loop to complete the stitch and both loop and strand were transferred to the right needle.

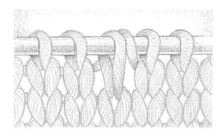

An incomplete purl stitch on the previous row appears with a strand crossed behind the loop.

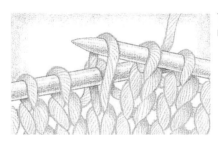

To correct, insert the right needle through the loop purlwise, lift it over the strand and off.

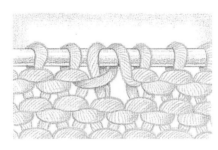

An incomplete knit stitch on the previous row has a strand crossed in front of the loop and on the needle incorrectly.

To correct this stitch, insert the right needle through the loop knitwise, lift over the strand and off the needle.

In both cases, the now completed stitch is ready to work.

THE UNPLANNED DROPPED STITCH

If you should happen to lose a stitch by dropping it, remember that it won't drop far and it won't leave a big hole. It can be easily fixed in one of the following two ways:

If you drop a stitch and have gone only a row or two beyond it, a crochet hook (size B/2.00mm is suitable for most yarns) will fix it. It is easier to pick up a stitch on the knit side of the work. If the purl side is facing you, turn the work around.

Work to where the stitch should be. Gain length on the strands above it by borrowing from the stitches on each side.

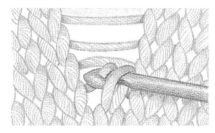

To knit the dropped stitch: With right side facing, insert the hook through the loop and under the first horizontal bar above.

Pull the strand through to form a new stitch. Continue up the ladder in the same way. Be very careful to use the first strand above the loop each time. If you need to purl as well as knit up the ladder, in a moss stitch for example, you can do that quite easily by alternating knit and purl stitches.

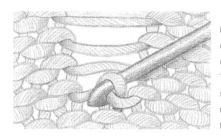

To purl the dropped stitch: With the loop behind the first strand, insert the hook upside down through the loop from back to front on top of the strand. Pull the strand through the hook. The hook will be in position to knit the next strand, so if you want to purl it, you must remove the hook and reinsert it from back to front.

After all strands are picked up, ease the yarn from several stitches on each side over the entire area.

If the dropped stitch is down several rows, this method is impractical because it produces a tighter section. You can either catch the dropped stitch with a sewing thread the same color and fasten it on the back, or you can unravel back and rework correctly.

THE INTENTIONAL DROPPED STITCH

If you discover a small mistake several rows down, you don't have to rip out all of your work. Work until you are above the faulty stitch.

Drop the necessary number of stitches down to the row of the error, fix it and work the stitches back up. The procedure is the same as for the unplanned dropped stitch except that you need not borrow yarn from the side stitches to make new stitches.

UNRAVELING

Sometimes taking out stitches or rows is the only answer. If the mistake is on the working row, you can easily unravel stitches to the error. If the bad stitch is only two or three stitches back, you may prefer to transfer them rather than take out and redo them. In transferring a stitch, the needle is inserted the same way whether it is a knit or purl stitch. To move the stitch from the left to right needle, the right needle is inserted purlwise. To transfer a stitch from the right to left needle, insert the left needle from front to back behind the right needle. The transferred stitch will then be on the needle in proper position for working.

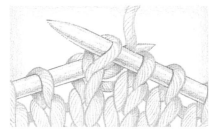

UNRAVELING A FEW STITCHES BACK ON SAME ROW

To rip back on the working row, hold the work in the direction you are knitting and maintain tension on the yarn.

Insert the left needle under the front of the stitch below the first loop on the right needle and move it to the left needle. Pull the right needle out of the loop and tighten the yarn to undo it. Continue in the same way to the faulty stitch, fix it and continue knitting.

UNRAVELING SEVERAL STITCHES BACK ON PREVIOUS ROW

Reverse your work so that what was the right needle is in your left hand; in other words, the opposite direction from which you were working. Hold the yarn as usual and maintain tension as you go. Insert the right needle purlwise through the stitch below the loop on the left needle. Pull the left needle out of the loop and tighten the yarn to undo it.

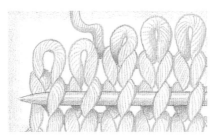

A quick way to unravel many stitches: Weave the right needle under the front and over the back of several stitches below the loops before dropping the loops. Continue across until you reach the mistake, fix it, reverse your work to normal position and proceed.

UNRAVELING ON THE PREVIOUS ROW

Simple errors, such as having knitted a stitch that should have been purled, can be corrected quite easily. Work to the place you want to correct. Place the faulty stitch on the right needle without working it. Insert the left needle under the front of the stitch below and slip the right needle out. With the right needle, pull the loop free. The loop has become a strand, and whether you want to knit or purl the stitch determines what you do.

To knit the stitch, put the strand on the left needle to the right of the loop. Lift the loop over the strand and off, with the strand, now a loop, remaining on the left needle.

To purl the stitch, put the strand on the left needle to the left of the loop. Insert the right needle purlwise through the loop and over the strand. Pull the strand through, dropping off the loop.

The new loop will be on the needle backwards, so when you transfer it to the left needle to be worked, put the left needle in from front to back.

UNRAVELING DOWN SEVERAL ROWS

Sometimes, all you can do is unravel back to the mistake. Unravel your knitting back to the row you wish to fix. It is a bit tricky to return stitches to the needle in the correct position. Check our diagrams for twisted stitches as you reknit this row. A second method is to unravel to one row before the mistake row, finally unraveling the stitches back onto the needle stitch by stitch.

Try these techniques. Mastering them is not difficult, and when you do, you'll find correcting mistakes less frightening. ⌢

Undoing Disasters

by Elizabeth Zimmermann

In couture knitting, techniques are translated from dressmaking. The result: more professionally finished handknitted garments. Why do so many knitting disasters seem to occur in the most visible section of a lovingly handknitted sweater, namely the upper center front—the point where eyes are focused as their gaze roams about during many conversations? Let us try to cope with simple technical errors before they become too deeply entrenched. Even several rounds (or rows) later, these blips can be eliminated easily. Review your masterpiece every few rounds (or rows) and cope while the coping is good.

Few mistakes are fatal. Even a split stitch (the only genuine "mistake" of which I am aware, for all others have their place in various patterns) can be rectified. When you spot a split stitch, trace it up to the needle, and drop the stitch down as far as the split. Then, with a medium-sized crochet hook, hook it up again to its place on the needle, "knitting" it from the front or "purling" it from the back as the fabric demands [see the illustration at left].

If the split stitch has given birth to two stitches instead of one, it will, in its corrected form, be too loose. This looseness must then be eased into the stitches on each side alternately. The result at first may not be absolutely perfect, but by grabbing the fabric and giving it a good yank in all directions, one can cause their unevenness almost to disappear. After the first washing it will be gone completely.

Twisted stitches and stitches worked incorrectly are cured by the same method. However, if a *dropped* stitch manifests itself a couple of inches/cm down, there is no wool available for hooking up its descendants (or shall we say those stitches which should have arisen from it?). In this case, the wool must be borrowed from the right and left of every alternate row—a tight business, but possible, and even tolerable after the first few washings.

If you discover a cable that has been worked in reverse, drop down *all* its stitches to this point. Pick them up on a double pointed needle, and work the tiny rows up again, cabling correctly.

May I add that it is *most* advisable to inspect your knitting every few rows, to ease correction of the above slip-ups while they qualify as minor, but not irrevocable, mistakes?

Some larger emergencies come to mind. **Ribbing too loose around the lower edge of the sweater**—take 6 lengths of elastic thread and skim them through the back of the first 2–3"/5–7.5cm (or depth of the ribbing). Grab all the threads and pull them up to the wanted fit. Knot the beginnings to the ends; snip off the surplus thread (rather a waste of elastic, but better than a never-worn sweater). To pull in a neckline, one or two lengths of elastic will suffice.

Sweaters that ride up at the back and droop down in the front—slightly more work but worth it. Insert one or more sets of 2-row, "short-row-like" additions fairly evenly spaced up the back. This is achieved by snipping one stitch (don't faint) at the middle of the back, and unraveling the stitches in that row almost to the side seams in either direction (leaving about 3 stitches on each side). Place the lower stitches on the needle, work 2 rows on these stitches, and laboriously weave the stitches together again (see my article, "Weaving? Grafting? Kitchener Stitch?") [p. 104]. Each time you do this, you are adding to the back length almost ½"/1.5cm if your gauge is 5 rows to 1"/2.5cm. If it is necessary to add 1 or 2"/2.5–5cm, you will have to repeat this process 4 or 5 times at evenly spaced intervals.

Sleeves too short—if worked downwards, no problem: Lengthen the ribbing. If worked upwards, you cannot unravel. BUT, snip a stitch just above the ribbing (about 2 rows above) in the same manner as described above for lengthening and back. Take out one round (or row) and set aside your ribbing. Pick up stitches on your sleeve, knit down to wanted length, and weave the sleeve and ribbing together again. This is most practical in stocking stitch (stockinette stitch) or garter stitch. In color or texture patterns, the weaving can be tricky.

This covers the most usual trouble spots. Let me know if you have any other knitting bugbears. ⌒

Easy Sleeve Pick-ups

by Mari Lynn Patrick

This bias-knit diagonal cable pullover, with a set number of cables along the shaped armhole edge, can be easily picked up in the 9-stitch multiple of the pattern. This design first appeared in the Fall 1998 issue.

A clever alternative to traditional sleeve construction—knitting from the armhole down to the wrist.

Classic sleeve styling has usually focused on knitting sleeves from a cast-on cuff up to the top, with increases to fit the upper arm, and sometimes a sleeve cap to fit the armhole. With the recent fashion trend toward innovative clothing construction, hand-knitwear designers have been inspired to try new methods of construction.

An easy alternative to the classic sleeve is to pick up stitches around the armhole, then to knit with decreases down to the cuff. With 25 years' experience in this industry, my own involvement with hand-knitwear has always been twofold: creative and technical. Creative in that I try to work each idea just once, so that I am continuously stimulated to formulate something new. Technically, I think and plan within the bounds of a design that can be successfully duplicated by the knitter at home. As an avid home knitter myself, I am always looking for the perfect marriage of these two basic elements.

The innovative method of the knit-from-the-armhole sleeve construction is a signature of the successful ready-to-wear designer Joan Vass, whose many exquisite designs have been featured in VK. The technique is especially effective when working with tape yarns, where seaming is more visible. The armhole seaming strand is eliminated, making the joining flawless. If you have knit from a Joan Vass pattern, you will know that the elimination of seams by picking up stitches along the edges of a garment is a special construction element she has perfected.

STRAIGHT ARMHOLE PICK-UPS

The silhouette that has dominated knitwear design for the past ten years, for women, children and men, has been the T-square-style with a straight armhole. It couples ease of knitting with ease of wearing, and has universal appeal. For the novice knitter, there are countless patterns from which to choose, but a trained eye can point out some of the subtle pitfalls of this design style. First, sweater pieces are blocked, then shoulder seams are joined. Markers are placed along the armholes to accommodate the sleeve upper-arm width, then the sleeves are sewn in between the markers. This seaming stage often highlights any mistake, be it inaccurate stitch gauge or visible, uneven seaming.

After blocking and sewing shoulder seams, picking up stitches along the armhole edge from the right side of the garment can eliminate these problems and result in even spacing of stitches and virtually invisible seaming. A knit 1 (garter stitch) selvage stitch (or selvage stitch of your choice) is especially recommended along all garment edges for accurate pinpoint pick-up. You can actually count each garter ridge along the selvage edge, 1 ridge representing 2 rows. Based on the stitch-to-row ratio, you may not actually pick up 1 stitch in every 2 rows along the edge, but counting the number of ridges will help determine how many stitches to pick up for each ridge. You may want to pick up 1 stitch in every 2 rows (or ridge) along the pick-up line, then increase evenly along the first row to achieve the correct stitch count.

SHAPED ARMHOLE PICK-UPS

The shaped armhole has definitely returned, be it square, angled or curved, and the result is a more tailored fit along the shoulders and less sleeve "drag" at the cuffs.

The technique for picking up stitches along a shaped armhole is in essence the same as for the straight armhole, but really works best on sleeves that are designed to fit close to the body, upper-arm and wrist measurements. Also, the amount of fabric cut out at the armhole, that is, the number of stitches decreased, should not exceed 2–2½"/5–6.5cm for the best hang of the sleeve [see diagram, A-B, opposite]. This 2–2½"/5–6.5cm difference in length will be taken up around the armhole when worn and will fit comfortably.

When picking up, begin at the edge of the armhole and pick up stitches right around the angle or curve as you would on any other shaped seam edge. I find this shaped pick-up works best with stitches that have lateral stretch, such as ribs or cables that result in a close-to-body, tubular fit.

RECONSTRUCTING AN EXISTING PATTERN

The technique can easily be applied to existing patterns. As well as providing ease and visual neatness, it is a method that allows for length adjustability, a great asset for children's designs or "custom" knitting. After basting or seaming, you may actually have a fitting before binding off to be sure the sleeve length is perfect for the wearer.

Be sure to choose a style with sleeves that fit into one of the categories described. Sleeve caps with a height of more than 2"/5cm and armholes that are cut in at more than 2½"/6.5cm are styles that will not work.

To figure the stitches and rows needed, read the sleeve pattern backwards. You will need a calculator and paper to make notes before actually rewriting the sleeve construction.

From the sleeve pattern, determine the number of stitches at the upper arm (the stitch count after all increases are made). Also determine the sleeve cuff stitch count (number of stitches cast on). If your gauge is 22 sts x 28 rows = 4", then the 1" gauge is 5.5 sts x 7 rows = 1" (for practical purposes, only inch calculations are used). If the first increase above the cuff is on the 8th row and each subsequent increase is every 8th row 12 times more, then increases will take place over a span of 15" (13 x 8-104 ÷ 7 rows = 14.8" or 15"). If the total length of the sleeve is 20", of which 2" is the cuff and the first increase occurs 1" (8th row) after the cuff, work 2" even at the top of the sleeve, then decrease 1 stitch on next row and every 8th row 12 times more (2" + 15" + 1" + 2" = 20"). After the last decrease, work 1" even, then work the cuff in reverse and bind off.

This example is simplified to give a basic understanding of the process; remember that the calculator does the hard work when tricky 1" gauges (such as 3.75 stitches = 1") are involved.

CIRCULAR SLEEVE KNITTING

You may go a step further and eliminate the underarm sleeve seam by knitting a sleeve in the round. This can be done by working with double pointed needles or by first picking up with a 16"/40cm circular needle, then changing to double pointed needles as the sleeve narrows.

Decreases may also be worked in innovative ways, either evenly spaced around for pattern continuity or along the center of the sleeve (not the underarm side) if your goal is to highlight the decorative decreases or a pleated or welt detail.

One of the critical elements in knitting is getting a perfect fit. The standard measurements [see charts] for the standard sizes in clothing are used routinely for the sizing of all garments.

Because the top-of-sleeve-to-cuff length measurement in this type of pattern is going to be based on the varying body width of the style, the actual measurement needed is the center-back-neck-to-cuff measurement (D-E). To determine sleeve length from this measurement, measure the knitted piece (or schematic) from center back to neck shoulder edge or half the cross back measurement. (Cross back is the measurement taken across the back above the armhole shaping, A-C). Subtract this width from the total length on the chart for your size, and you are left with the total sleeve length.

Whether you choose to adapt one of the many patterns suitable for this construction element, to better understand an existing pattern, or to design your own style, you can apply this time-saving technique with ease.

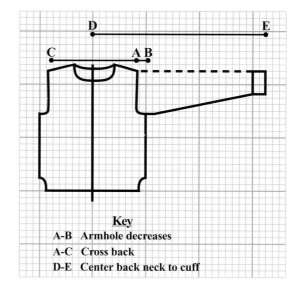

Key

A-B	Armhole decreases
A-C	Cross back
D-E	Center back neck to cuff

CENTER BACK NECK TO CUFF MEASUREMENTS

BABIES				
Size	0-3 mos.	6 mos.	12 mos.	18 mos.
Inches	10½"	11½"	12½"	14½"
CM	26.5	29	32	35.5

CHILDREN							
Size	2	4	6	8	10	12	14
Inches	18"	19½"	20½"	22"	24"	26"	28"
CM	45.5	49.5	52	56	61	66	71

WOMEN					
Size	XS	S	M	L	XL
Inches	27"	28"	29"	30"	31"
CM	68.5	71	73.5	76	78.5

MEN					
Size	S	M	L	XL	XXL
Inches	32"	33"	34"	35"	36"
CM	81	84	86	89	91.5

Cabling Without

by Meg Swansen

I often make a game of my knitting by peppering it with assorted little made-up challenges. I believe that Right and Wrong are subjective in hand knitting, and I have accumulated my own personal set of "rules" to see if I can avoid my less-than-favorite knitting activities. For instance, I will go to great lengths to avoid having to break the working wool. I eliminate seams whenever possible, I try to substitute knitting for sewing (such as knitting a sleeve into an armhole rather than sewing it in), and I like to see how wide a cable I can execute without having to scrounge about for a cable needle.

The smallest possible cable you can make, which is also called a Traveling Stitch, is relatively easy and a good place to begin, as it utilizes only two stitches. Call the first stitch A and the second stitch B. Those two stitches may travel to the left or to the right.

Working a Left Twist requires the first stitch to travel over the second stitch and lean left; there are several means to achieve this:

You may work the two stitches out of order by knitting into the back of B, then into the front of A and sliding them both off the L needle together. (Yes, this twists B—but it will not show as it is tucked behind A.)

You can knit into the front of B from behind, but it is quite a contorted move and may stretch and distort the stitch.

You may reverse the order of the stitches before you knit them by dropping A from the needle and then, from behind A, slipping B to the right needle, picking up A on the left needle, and replacing B. Now knit them sequentially. If you practice this method, you may surprise yourself at how quickly you can fall into the rhythm of the technique…and your possible squeamishness at dropping a live stitch off the needle will eventually be dispelled!

Working a Right Twist needs the second stitch (B) to travel over the first stitch

When you drop the cable needle, you pick up speed and fluidity.

(A) and lean right. Again, choices abound:

You may leave both stitches on the L needle and knit B and A together, then knit A again and slide them both off the needle.

You may pass over A and knit B first, then knit A and slide them off together.

You may reverse their positions by slipping them both off the L needle. With the R needle, grab B from in front of A and snag A with the L needle. Put B back on the needle and work them sequentially. Be careful to put stitches back on the needle facing the same way they were before you slid them off; in other words: do not twist the stitch unless you are knitting Bavarian Twisted Stitch patterns.

Please be assured that you can probably execute the moves described about five or six times in the time it takes to read and understand the verbal description.

Can you tell that I favor reversing the position of the stitches before working them? With practice it becomes rhythmical and fast with a minimum of distortion.

Now what about a wider cable of 2 over 2, or 3 over 3? It is easier to "lose" a stitch in those situations, so, for greater security, there is an easy-to-work (though verbose-to-describe!) method: Let's say you're going to twist 2 over 2 to the left; the first pair we'll call A and the second pair B. Slide all 4 stitches to the R needle (photo 1).

a Cable Needle

With the L needle, grab the A pair from in front (photo 2).

Slip the 4 stitches off the R needle—letting the B pair fall free for just a moment (photo 3).

With R needle, from behind, pick up the B pair and put it back on the L needle (photo 4) and knit all four stitches sequentially (photo 5).

Whew! Trust me, with repetition it really does become a swift and fluid move.

To cable to the R, proceed as above, but grab the A pair from behind, slide the 4 off the needle, letting B fall free for a moment, then pick up B from in front with R needle. Put the B pair on L needle and knit the 4 stitches sequentially.

I can usually manage 3 over 3, but when it gets to 4 stitches over 4, I scrounge around for a dp needle (or a bobby pin or sewing-up needle or even a smooth stick) and am grateful for the assist.

For a cable where one stitch is pulled over 3 or 4 stitches, you can still manage on your own. Let's say it is a 9-stitch Fishbone. The 4th stitch will be pulled over the front of the first 3; the middle (neutral) stitch remains a plain knit; and the 6th stitch will pass over the front of stitches 7, 8 and 9.

OK—the 9 stitches are on the L needle, skip over stitches 1, 2 and 3, and knit stitch 4. Now knit 1, 2 and 3, and slide all four of them off the left needle. Knit the 5th (center) stitch.

Slide the 6th stitch off the needle and nail it down with your left thumb as you knit 7, 8, and 9. Now grab stitch 6 and knit it.

If you feel daunted by the above, remember that the concentrated activity of cabling takes place only every few vertical inches…you'll have smooth sailing of plain knit and purl in between the exciting cable-round.

Onward, Meg ⌒

Four-Stitch Left Cable: Insert the right-hand needle through next 4 stitches on left-hand needle as shown, and slide them to the right-hand needle.

With the left-hand needle in front, grab the first "A" pair of stitches on the right-hand needle.

Slip the 4 sts off the right-hand needle, letting the second "B" pair of stitches fall from the needle and stay at the back of the work for just a moment.

Place the 2 free stitches at the back onto the right-hand needle, as shown.

Then slip the stitches from the right-hand needle to the left-hand needle, as shown, and knit all 4 stitches sequentially.

The Wayward Cable

by Meg Swansen

Before I describe how relatively easy it is to repair the mistake, first let us define "mistake." Some are obvious and irrefutable, but others are subjective. For instance, if you are knitting a specific color pattern from a book or magazine, you have an anticipated and fixed image of the outcome. If you veer off the chart by a stitch or two when you begin a new round or row, the color pattern will be altered. Is it "wrong" or is it just different? If you are able to look at it objectively, it may very well be superior to the chart you were originally following and you have a lovely and unique new pattern.

Designer Joyce Williams created a magnificent Bavarian Twisted Stitch vest, encrusted with scores of different cables and traveling-stitch designs and worked at an incredibly tiny gauge. At about underarm height, Joyce began—inadvertently—to work a double cable from the inside out instead of from the outside in. She didn't notice it until she was nearly finished with the garment and decided to leave it in, as she actually preferred the "mistaken" cable to the "real" one. And, when studying the vest, one is so taken by the overall beauty of the design and the skillful knitting that so far no one has yet noticed the discrepancy unless Joyce points it out.

You're in your favorite chair, knitting along happily on an Aran or cabled sweater. You pause briefly and spread your work out on your lap to admire the progress you've made and to encourage yourself onward. Uh-oh. A large and glaring error reveals itself in the form of a cable crossing the wrong way (or crossing in the wrong place), and it happened 14 rows ago. Your heart sinks. This intricately cabled project is very slow-growing and you are loath to rip out all those hours of work. Well, you needn't rip the entire thing.

I continue to make real mistakes on a regular basis. One of the most blatant was on a 27-stitch wide cable from Barbara Walker's *Charted Knitting Designs*. It was the focal point down the center back of a cardigan, and the error was dozens of rounds back when I finally spotted it.

OK: Slide the stitches involved off the needle (in my case, 27 of them). Pull out each row until you have a frightening series of gigantic ladders in a tangle down the back of your work. When you reach the offending row, rip it out and stop. The 27 stitches of the row before the error will be patiently waiting to be picked up onto a dpn. Have a second dpn at the ready.

You will now knit up the vertical cable stitches again, using the ladders in proper order (see illustrations). To determine the correct order, pull gently on the strand you think is next in line. Note where it joins the knitted fabric on the sides and look for a tightening of that first stitch. Make sure it is the next sequential row before you start the repair.

The first row will most likely be the mistaken-cable row where you initially went the

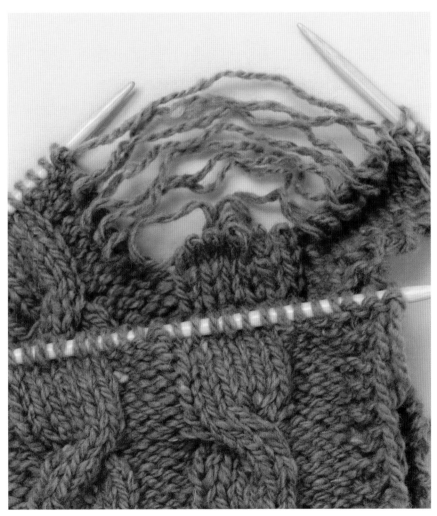

Front needle: The right-hand cable is crossed the wrong way.
Back needles: The wayward cable has been ripped down to the row where the error occurred.

wrong way. Re-knit the cable(s) in the proper direction across all stitches. *Return to the right end of the needle; find the next row's ladder and knit it across. Repeat from * (maintaining continuity of the pattern) until you are back at the top.

Now, that sounds very simple—and it is—but there is a potential pitfall (PP): It is a rare occurrence when the amount of wool in the ladders is equal to the amount of wool needed to knit the row. Invariably you will have a tiny bit too much or too little wool. Fudge. If you end up with a big, sloppy stitch at the left side, feed the excess wool back through the stitches to the right and even it out as best you can. And, vice versa, if you run out of wool at the left-hand end, go back over the stitches just knitted and sneak a bit of wool away from each of them to feed the final stitch(es). Perhaps I should not even tell you about this PP—maybe it's just me. (It always reminds me of packing a suitcase to return home and not having room for the identical articles you originally brought.) May all YOUR ladders be just the right length!

One more thought about cables. For years I struggled to count the rounds between cables to be sure they were of equal height. Then knitting instructor Charlie Hada showed me a very cool trick: With a dpn, dig down into the inevitable hole that forms wherever cable stitches have been crossed. Poke the dpn back to the front just below the working needle. Stretch the fabric over the dpn and count the horizontal bars across it; one bar for every round/row knitted. Isn't that neat?

When dealing with color-pattern errors, you have to be the judge. If the mistake is more than just one or two rows away, it may be easier in the long run to rip the whole thing back and re-knit. I usually give the quick-fix a try first—then determine whether it is a correction I can live with, or if it looks too messy and must be ripped out. Working with wool raises the odds considerably—even my lumpy-looking knitting smoothes out when properly blocked. The deciding factor is whether YOU and you alone will ultimately be pleased with the repair. And—as you are cogitating that point—remember that Attitude is Everything: If you will forever be pointing out the mistake to every passing knitter, then rip it back. If you can keep your mouth shut, not one in a hundred observers may ever notice. Onward. ⌐

Essay: Knitting Mysteries

by Meg Swansen

How can a three-stitch I-cord produce a perfect four-sided square? I don't know either, but try this: with a pair of dpns, cast on 3 stitches, do not turn, but *slide the 3 stitches to the other end of the needle and knit them. Repeat from * ad infinitum and, after a few inches, a tiny circular cord will emerge from your needles. That is basic Free Standing I-cord (one of dozens of applications of this simple technique).

Now then, if instead of working all knit, try K1, **P1**, K1 for a few inches (see illustration). See? A four-sided square cord, knitted on 3 stitches? Wait. Before you all come running in with perfectly logical and easily understandable explanations, I request that you do not tell me, please. The above is just one of several knitting mysteries I have come across over the years, and I cherish being mystified. If I studied this conundrum at length and in solitude I could probably figure it out, but I much prefer to be baffled and in awe of the beauty and enigma of the outcome. Sometimes analysis is destructive of things magical.

What else? The relationship of stitches to rows is fraught with mystery. New knitters are usually told that, in plain stockinette stitch, the basic ratio of stitches to rows is 5 to 7 to equal 1 square inch/2.5cm. That is often the case. However, shift from plain stockinette to color-pattern knitting and you may notice the numbers move closer to each other; your stitches are squarer (is there such a word? Well, you know what I mean). Now, move from horizontal or vertical color patterns to diagonal designs and things change again: you may end up with a perfectly square stitch-to-row ratio! Is that not a wonderment? And the beauty of it is that you may design specifically for this mysterious happening. For instance, if you work a diagonal color-pattern across the upper reaches of a drop- or modified drop-shoulder garment, you may then knit up stitches around the armhole in sequential color-pattern—continuing the design unbroken all the way to the cuff. As you look at the finished sweater, you are sure the yoke was worked from cuff to cuff in a smooth flow of pattern—even though you know the sleeves were knitted separately and perpendicularly to the body. I've done a number of designs utilizing this beautiful bit of knitting sorcery.

Further to the stitches/rows ratio variations: I know knitting buddies who have made identical garments (same instructions, same wool, same needles), achieved identical stitch gauges, but their row gauges were not even close to matching each other!

The Jogless Jog [page 134] is something I came up with in cold blood as I was working out a design for a Swedish dubbelmössa (a traditional long, color-patterned hat knitted in a tube and tapered at each end). When finished, one end is punched into the other, then a deep cuff is turned up, making four thicknesses over your ears and forehead). When I envisioned the item being photographed for a magazine, I was seriously offended by the horrible jog that occurs when a circular pattern meets itself again at the beginning of the round. Ordinarily, that jog is placed at an unobtrusive spot, like a side seam; but on a hat there is nowhere to hide, AND, it is amazing how frequently the non-knitting wearer dons the hat with the offending jog smack dab in the center-front.

The solid stripes of 2 or 3 rounds that separate the pattern motifs are the most offending jogs. I tried everything and anything I could think of before stumbling across the following: At the end of the first round of a new color, pick up the right side of the stitch in the row below (it will be the "old" color), put it on the L needle and k2tog! The first stitch of the round now becomes the last stitch of the previous round as it changes color like a chameleon. The move is so simple, yet at the same time so mysterious. I didn't ask any questions; I was just grateful to have found this solution and I use it in awed humility. And it works.

There are other jogless techniques that, alone in a quiet room for half an hour, I can understand. But as they flick past during the actual knitting, I categorize them as Knitting Mysteries. For instance, to cause an alternate-color speckle pattern to come out evenly, be sure you are working on a multiple of two MINUS one (or two PLUS one) and there will be no discernable beginning/ending.

Over the years I have learned that one is not supposed to use exclamation points during "serious" writing, but this article would be sprinkled with them if you were to hear me read this text aloud.

My mysteries may not be your mysteries. The techniques I have listed here may be perfectly comprehensible to you—yet you may be stymied by items I find crystal-clear. Hang onto your own personal enigmas and be careful about revealing them lest some kind knitter explain them to you and the mystery melt away. To me they are part of what keeps knitting so continuously intriguing. ⌒

Easy Shaped Pick-ups

by Mari Lynn Patrick

With some advance planning, picking up stitches is a simple operation. Begin planning early, as you shape the edges from which you'll pick up stitches. As an example, we've chosen to show a round neckline, but the same principles apply to other neckline styles and shaped edges such as shoulders and armholes, too.

To shape most round necks, begin by binding off a given number of stitches at the center of the piece. Then, working each side with separate balls of yarn, continue to bind off given numbers of stitches in decreasing quantities.

If you bind off stitches only at the beginning of each row, you'll have a jagged edge with stepped bind-offs. When it's time to pick and knit stitches around the neck edge, it's often difficult to pinpoint where the needle should be inserted. Or, you may find there are holes forming along the pick-up line.

To avoid these drawbacks, use the sloped bind-off method on each side of the center bound-off neck stitches.

SHAPING WITH SLOPED BIND-OFFS

Step 1 Work to the last stitch of the row previous to the bind-off row. Do not work this stitch. Turn the work.

Step 2 Slip the first stitch from the left-hand needle to the right-hand needle, and pass the slipped stitch of the previous row over this stitch—the first stitch is bound off.

Step 3 Then work the next stitch on the left-hand needle and continue to bind off as you normally would.

You can use this method for necks, armholes, shoulders or any other place where you have repeated bind-offs. Also, you can use steps 1 and 2 when you are decreasing one stitch at each end of every other row.

SELVAGE STITCHES

After completing the sloped bind-offs, work selvage stitches along the straight edge. Selvage stitches can be used at any or all edges of a sweater to make a neat and even line for seaming as well as for picking up stitches. These stitches are worked in the

You've just finished knitting all the pieces for your sweater. After blocking, everything looks great. You've mastered the art of sewing it all together, but now it's time for picking up stitches around the neck, and you're stumped. If you've ever wished for an easy way to handle pick-ups, here's the answer!

first and last stitches of a row, and using them on the pick-up edges of your sweater gives you a double advantage. First, it gives you a longer loop to pick up easily, and second, this long loop actually represents two rows of knitting, making it easier to count the rows.

If you work selvage stitches by this method, you'll create an even, looped edge:

On the right side of the work: Work all stitches as you normally would to the last stitch. Slip this last stitch knitwise (as to knit) to the right-hand needle.

On the wrong side of the work: Purl the first stitch, then work all stitches in pattern as you normally would to the last stitch. Slip this last stitch purlwise (as to purl) to the right-hand needle.

PLANNING FOR PICK-UP STITCHES

When picking up stitches, plan ahead so you can distribute them evenly around the curved and straight edges. Without a plan, you might find you're three-quarters of the way around the edge but only halfway through the stitch count needed. If you try to squeeze the pick-ups into the last little quarter segment, you'll end up with a lopsided edge.

To plan in advance for pick-ups, mark off the edge with pins or yarn markers at even intervals—about every 2"/5cm (Figure 1). Divide your stitch count evenly to figure how many stitches you need to pick up at each interval. Be sure to pick up the correct number of stitches so you can work a full repeat of the pattern. For example, for a k1, p1 ribbing, you'll need to work with a number of stitches evenly divisible by 2, and for a k3, p2 ribbing, you'll need a number which is evenly divisible by 5.

What if there is no given stitch count? As a rule of thumb, pick up 1 stitch for every bound-off stitch on straight edges; pick up 2 stitches for every 3 rows along sides of rows. Since this is only a guide, experiment picking up the number of stitches that looks neat in the first two intervals only on your marked edge. Or, use your gauge swatch for a trial run. Work the desired depth of your band, and bind off. If this small segment has an elasticity that seems neither too loose nor too stretched, then you're ready to proceed with the edging.

GETTING READY FOR PICK-UPS

Here are some tips to help you prepare for picking up stitches:

- If using straight needles, sew the left shoulder seam only. Make sure the markers are placed evenly around the neck edge.

- Plan to use knitting needles at least two sizes smaller than those used to knit the sweater, whether your edge is in ribbing, garter stitch or rolled stockinette stitch. This ensures a flat, firm, yet elastic edge.

- If making a stockinette-stitch neckband in a contrasting color, make the pick-ups in the same color as the sweater body. Switch to the contrasting color on the first knit row of the neckband.

- If, despite your efforts, the edge seems too uneven for smooth pick-ups, try working a row of single crochet to even if off. Then, pick up one stitch in every single crochet stitch.

PICKING UP STITCHES

With the shaped edge fully prepared, you can use any of the following three methods to pick up stitches.

With one needle: With the right side of the work facing you, and working around neck edge, begin at the right back shoulder (the open, unsewn seam). Insert the right-hand needle from front to back in the first bound-off stitch, and wind the yarn around the needle as if knitting; bring this loop through to the right side—1 stitch picked up and knitted. Continue in this way, working from right to left around the entire neck edge (Figure 2). Work the next row from the wrong side.

With two needles: With the right side of the work facing you, begin at the right

back shoulder (the open, unsewn seam). Insert the left-hand needle from front to back in the first bound-off stitch. Leaving a 4"/10cm end, hold the yarn ready for knitting and insert the right-hand needle into the loop on the left-hand needle as if knitting. Wind the yarn around the needle and pull the loop through to the right side—1 stitch picked up and knitted. Continue in this way, working from right to left around the entire neck edge (Figure 3). Work the next row from the wrong side.

With a crochet hook: With the right side of the work facing you, begin at the right front shoulder (the open, unsewn seam). Hold the working yarn, the knitting needle and your sweater in your left hand. Then, insert the crochet hook from front to back in the first bound-off stitch, draw up a loop and place it on the needle; pull the loop snugly—1 stitch picked up and knitted. Continue in this way working from left to right around the entire neck edge. Work the next row from the right side.

Whichever method of picking up stitches you adopt as your favorite, be sure none of the stitches are twisted when you work the next row. If you need to untwist a stitch, knit or purl into the back loop of each twisted stitch on your next row. Keep your pick-ups neat and even, and your hand-knit sweater will look beautifully finished. ⌒

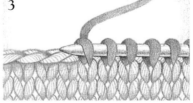

Vogue's Finishing School

A cram course in putting your knits together

by Nancy J. Thomas

If you were to ask knitters or crocheters how they felt about finishing and sewing sweaters, most would probably give you the same answer. They may love to knit and crochet, but they don't care for finishing and sewing. They may even go to great lengths to make garments with as few seams as possible—to avoid sewing. All needleworkers do understand the value of good finishing techniques, but often the process remains an elusive skill that few have properly learned. The primary emphasis of knitting and crochet classes is stitches and garment making; finishing is quickly becoming a lost art. A good professional finisher is worth her weight in gold and may charge almost that much for her services and expertise!

Finishing isn't a difficult skill to master. With a bit of practice and our *Vogue* professional tips, even a novice can sew and finish a sweater with ease.

TIPS FROM THE PROS

- Before you begin, carefully read the pattern's finishing instructions. The designer has painstakingly worked out the specifications of your pattern. Assemble your sweater in the order suggested in the pattern for best results.

- To make the process of stitching together a sweater much easier, first block or press all the pieces. Check both your pattern and yarn care label for the blocking or pressing instructions for your sweater.

- Avoid using highly textured or very heavy yarn to assemble your sweater. Untwisted yarn called "roving" yarn, which pulls apart easily, is also not a good choice for stitching. The best choice for sewing is a flat, firm yarn that approximates the color of your sweater. Remember to use a stitching yarn with the same properties as the yarn of your sweater. A washable sweater teamed with dry-cleanable stitching yarn would be a definite "mismatched" combination.

- Although basting is time-consuming, it can be very helpful. Basting allows you to have an excellent "preview fitting" and make minor adjustments before sewing. Basting also keeps your seams neatly in place, thus making your sewing job much easier. If you can't be persuaded to baste, careful pinning is the next best choice.

- Use needles especially designed for yarn to aid in professional finishing. These needles have large eyes that the yarn easily passes through. Yarn needles are either plastic or metal and have blunt-ended points. Experiment with different types and use the type of needle with which you feel most comfortable.

- To professionally set-in your sweater sleeves, mark the center point of the top of the sleeve and pin or baste in place at the shoulder seam. Ease in the sleeve on either side of the shoulder seam. Baste or pin carefully and try it on before you sew the sleeve in place.

- For sweaters or other garments with stripes or bands of colorwork, take care to match at the seams before stitching.

- To pull in droopy shoulders or reinforce shoulders (especially important for heavy sweaters and coats), stitch a piece of seam tape to the shoulder seam, easing in fullness.

SEAMS

There are three basic seam finishes which are most commonly used. Each one has advantages and disadvantages.

THE INVISIBLE SEAM – This seam is preferred by many experienced finishers. It will not, however, work on every garment or seam. Work these seams from the right side of your garment. This method produces a neat, flat seam that is practically "invisible" and is best for side seams or shoulder seams that have the same number of rows or stitches and that match up evenly.

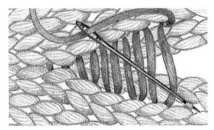

INVISIBLE SIDE SEAMS ON STOCKINETTE STITCH

To work the invisible seam on stockinettte stitch, line up the rows, edge to edge, with the right sides facing you. Attach the yarn at the lower edge of the seam. Working alternately on each side, insert the needle under the horizontal bar (ladder) of each stitch taking in a half or whole stitch on both sides. The seam will fall to the wrong side of the garment.

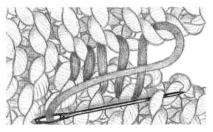

INVISIBLE SEAMS ON GARTER STITCH

The garter-stitch seam is worked very much like the stockinette-stitch seam. Working from the right side, place the two edges together, matching the rows. Attach yarn and insert needle through lower edge of stitch on one side and then insert needle into upper edge of stitch on opposite side. Repeat along seam edge.

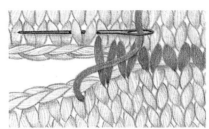

INVISIBLE SHOULDER SEAM

With right sides facing you, align seams. Work back and forth into the row next to the bound-off edge, inserting the needle under one stitch and pulling it through alternately on each side. Insert needle under stitch, pull needle through and then through stitch on the opposite side.

THE BACKSTITCH SEAM – This seam gives a firm finish, which makes it an excellent choice for heavier sweaters and coats. The backstitch seam can also be used on crocheted garments. It is the best method to use on areas that don't match up row to row or stitch to stitch, and can be used to take in fullness or make a deeper seam. Backstitching is also the best finish to use on curved seams.

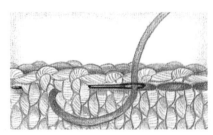

BACKSTITCH SEAM

With the right sides of the knitted pieces together, baste or pin the pieces, taking care to match patterns and stripes. To begin the seam, insert the needle from front to back through both thicknesses and make a stitch approximately ⅜"/1cm long. Continue making stitches of the same length, inserting the needle back into the middle of the space between where the needle was inserted and where it emerged.

THE CROCHETED SLIPSTITCH SEAM – This seam can be used in the same ways that you would use a backstitch seam.

Pin the right sides of the pieces together. Using a crochet hook of a compatible size, insert the hook through both thicknesses, wrap the yarn around the hook and draw a loop through. Insert hook through the next stitch, wrap the yarn around the hook and draw a loop through the work and through the loop on the hook. Continue in this manner along the seam.

Once you master the techniques, you will be well on the way to giving your sweaters a real "vogue" finish! ⌐

Weaving? Grafting?

by Elizabeth Zimmermann

Today I did a super-foolish thing: left home without a blunt wool-needle. Since I was at the weaving point of my current knitting-project, I was completely hamstrung until I arrived home again. Being an ambitious creature, I *did* try to weave by the classic method of "place-stitches-on-two-needles-wrong-sides-together-knit-first-stitch-on-front-needle-pull-wool-through-slip-stitch-off-needle" routine, becoming in the process totally ham-handed and frustrated, and suddenly conscious of the fact that this is how most knitters weave. Or graft. Or perform Kitchener-stitch.

Having now woven my shoulders according to logic and convenience, I'm feeling better, and realize that no time must be lost in letting other knitters in on the act. As follows: Start off by acquiring a suitable blunt wool-needle (hereinafter WN). I do *not* mean a tapestry-needle. A blunt wool-needle can be found in any drygoods store usually attached to a card which also harbors a leather-needle (you'd be surprised how helpful it is on occasion), a strange, semicircular upholstery-needle, and several other exotic breeds of needle, which you never know when you may need—the whole card-of-tricks sells for under a buck. If you can find a wool shop with WN by the dozen, they are a marvelous investment, and can be placed in useful spots: in your money-purse, in the car, in odd coat-pockets (being blunt, they won't prick you) or tossed loose in your knitting-bag.

The WN weighs about ½ of an ounce (2½g) and is 2½"/6.5cm long, including a ⅝"/1.5cm eye—super-easy to thread—and provided with a convenient groove above it so that it does not have to be tugged at. It is so easy to thread that I've just threaded one with my eyes shut. (Something I've never attempted in my life!) Double the fluffy end of a piece of wool, pinch this end together with thumb and forefinger and just push it through the wool-needle eye. Lo! threaded.

Kitchener Stitch?

Now to weave with this marvelous tool: For stockinette-stitch weaving, place the two pieces to be woven on two needles right sides up, facing each other with a good end of wool coming from the right-hand end. Thread it through WN. Now put WN through first stitch on front needle from below, leave stitch on needle, and pull wool through. * Now, on back-needle, put WN down through first stitch, slip stitch off needle, put WN up through 2nd stitch, leave this stitch on, and pull wool through. Now, on front-needle, put WN down through first stitch, slip this stitch off, put WN up through 2nd stitch, leave this stitch on, and pull wool through. That's it! Simply repeat from *. You are weaving, you are grafting; you are Kitchenering [see illustrations].

To weave reverse stockinette stitch, work as above as on the smooth side. Ribbing and pattern stitches can be woven only when the knitted grain runs in the same direction, i.e., top to bottom. If woven head-on to each other they will be half-a-stitch off, and not worth weaving. Cast off and sew together.

And, by the way, the term "Kitchener stitch" was contributed to the American language through Alfred, Lord Kitchener, during World War I, when, hearing that U.S. women were "knitting comforts for the boys in the trenches," he contributed his very own sock directions, which included a grafted toe. ⌐

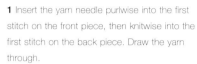

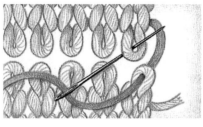

1 Insert the yarn needle purlwise into the first stitch on the front piece, then knitwise into the first stitch on the back piece. Draw the yarn through.

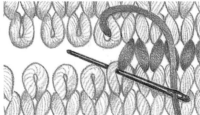

2 Insert the yarn needle knitwise into the first stitch on the front piece again. Draw the yarn through.

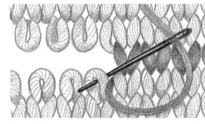

3 Insert the yarn needle purlwise into the next stitch on the front piece. Draw the yarn through.

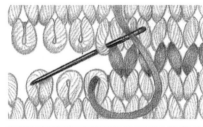

4 Insert the yarn needle purlwise into the first stitch on the back piece again. Draw the yarn through.

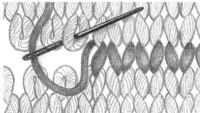

5 Insert the yarn needle knitwise into the next stitch on the back piece. Draw the yarn through. Repeat steps 2 through 5.

by Mari Lynn Patrick

PLAN AHEAD

When designing a garment, buy the zipper along with the yarn so you can match colors and plan length. If you're new to zipper installation, be sure to choose a yarn with minimal surface texture. Mohair and bouclé can get caught in the zipper teeth, and you'll want to avoid costly accidents.

The style of garment will determine your choice of zipper. Separating zippers are used for cardigan or jacket fronts that open fully. Separating zippers are available in a wide variety of colors and three standard types. Coil and molded plastic zippers are the least bulky of the three, and are a good choice for lighter-weight hand knits. Use a zipper with metal teeth for heavier-weight jackets. A regular dressmaking zipper, one that's held together at the base, is meant to be set into necklines or skirt seams.

While it is best to choose a zipper that matches the length of your garment's opening, both separating and regular zippers can be shortened to achieve a perfect match. A separating zipper is shortened at the top. To shorten, close the zipper and mark each side of the tape at the point where you want the pull tab to stop. Open the zipper and cut the tape ½"/1.25cm above the markings. Using a double strand of thread, whipstitch tightly around each side of the coil. Trim away the coils above the whipstitches with small, sharp scissors. A regular zipper is shortened at the bottom. To shorten, close the zipper and mark the point where you want the opening to stop. With the zipper closed, whipstitch tightly across the zipper teeth, forming a new stop. Cut away the excess zipper below the new stop.

EDGE DETAILS

Inspect the zipper on a ready-made garment and you will see it is usually hidden under some sort of flap. Sometimes very fine zippers are hidden between two layers of fabric, but this detail is usually too cumbersome for the working of hand knits.

Often the selvage stitches of a knitted piece are too uneven to serve as a neat flap. In most cases, you'll want to work a stabilizing edge after your pieces are knit.

Adding a zipper to hand knits has always been a sticking point among the circles of hand-knitters that I know. It must be the idea of a hard finish to the warm and cozy knitting experience that doesn't seem to fit. But with the beautiful selection of zippered jackets currently in style, the thought of installing a zipper is becoming hard to resist.

A simple edge of single crochet, evenly spaced, is one of the easiest edge stitches. Or, if you prefer to knit, simply pick up stitches evenly along the front edge, then bind off (on a wrong-side row) knitwise. For lighter-weight yarns, two rows of garter stitch also work nicely.

Each stitch forms a base for the zipper to be sewn in. Sewing along the pick-up line will turn the edge into a small flap. A wider stockinette-stitch band, doubled with a turning ridge, may be worked to accommodate a heavier zipper, though this is only recommended for very fine yarns that are tightly knit, to avoid additional bulk.

After the pieces are blocked and the stabilizing edge has been worked, the zipper can be inserted. You will need a fine, sharp needle and matching thread for hand sewing. Machine stitching is not recommended for hand knits, as it can cause the fabric to stretch, resulting in a puckered edge. ⌒

STEP 1 Decide at this point whether the zipper will show or be hidden by the flap. If you have a heavy zipper with a decorative pull, you may want to sew just the edge, leaving the zipper's teeth completely free. If you prefer your zipper to be hidden by the flap, pin the fabric so it meets at the center of the zipper teeth.

Work from the right side of the piece with the zipper closed. Pin one half of the zipper to one center front at even intervals. If the flap will hide the zipper, be sure it fully covers the zipper stop at the lower edge. Baste very loosely with contrast thread approximately ½"/1.25cm from the center of the teeth through the zipper tape and knitted fabric.

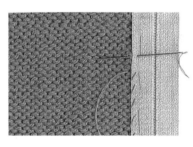

STEP 2 Turn to the wrong side and whip-stitch the edge of the tape in place. Check that the zipper zips and unzips freely, then reinforce the zipper base by turning under the tapes at both ends. At this point, unzip the zipper completely to free the other half of the zipper tape. Pin, baste and sew the other half of the zipper.

Joining Shoulders

by Meg Swansen

So varied are the methods of constructing a hand-knit sweater that you can produce scores of differently shaped garments without ever even encountering a specific shoulder seam. However, when confronted by having to join the front to the back of a sweater at the shoulders, decisions must be made.

Sometimes, the style of the garment will make the decision for you. If you are knitting a dropped-shoulder or Norwegian-style sweater, the top of the sleeve will not sit on the actual shoulder point, but will be about one-third of the way down the upper arm. Because of this, the weight of the sleeve will drag on the shoulder line, and if you have an infirm seam it will stretch and result in "gorilla sleeves." (Perhaps this sparked the idea to put a buttonhole in the ribbed cuff for the wearer's thumb to poke through—as seen in Vibeka Lind's *Knitting in the Nordic Tradition*—thus combining sweater and half-mittens?)

The need for a firm shoulder seam will lead you either to cast off the body stitches and sew the seam together, or to use some form of the 3-Needle Cast Off to unite the raw stitches. In my early knitting days, I would cast off the stitches and sew up the

Having trouble getting it together? Tips, tricks and techniques for a flawless finish.

seam. Now, one of my games is to knit the entire garment and avoid sewing whenever possible, so I choose other means. I use the 3-Needle Cast Off to knit the shoulders together [see page 85]. This is the most basic method of several variations. If you wish to pursue this technique further, look up Priscilla Gibson-Roberts's *Salish Indian Sweaters*.

If you choose the aforementioned basic 3-Needle Cast Off method, you are now faced with the question of whether to work the technique from the outside or the inside of the garment. I have a very decided opinion about this—purely personal and based on appearance. When worked from the inside, the visual result is that of a not-too-successful attempt at grafting, as the seam line usually dimples in. I have known meticulous knitters who require the rigidity of this type of seam to work the cast off from the inside and then weave together the rows on either side of the dimple over the top of the knitted seam for a smooth and invisible join.

I much prefer to work the 3-Needle Cast Off from the outside, as I admire the look of the handsome ridge it produces. Be aware that the front and back views of this ridge are different from each other. For visual consistency, knit both seams in the same direction: from armhole to neck edge on one shoulder, then from neck edge to armhole on the other.

Another variation, which will result in a more pronounced seam line, is to incorporate I-cord into the mix with a 3-Needle I-Cord Cast Off. Set up the stitches in the same manner as described above and cast 2 (or 3) stitches onto the third needle. Slip them to the front or back needle and *K1 (or 2) I-cord stitches, slip last I-cord stitch, k2tog (one each from front and back needles), pass the slip stitch over the k2tog (psso), and replace all I-cord stitches to one of the left needles. Repeat from * across raw stitches. If you are using a strongly contrasting color for the I-cord, employ Joyce Williams's method of adding a yarn over after slipping the last I-cord stitch as described in her book, *Latvian Dreams*). Then pass both the yarn-over and the slipped stitch over. This will serve as a built-in outline stitch to cover the inevitable blip of body color that will poke through the base of the I-cord.

If you are knitting a vest or a Shetland wool sweater with set-in sleeves, you may opt to use the beautiful and magical technique of weaving the shoulders together (also called grafting or Kitchener stitch) [see page 104]. There will be no weight on a vest shoulder and minimal draft on a lightweight wool sweater when the armhole sits squarely on the shoulder top.

On a Fair Isle vest I designed recently, I wanted the final OXO pattern to look like a saddle across the top of the shoulders. Rather than struggle to weave two halves of a color pattern together, I worked as follows: Start by imagining a typical Fair Isle design with wide bands of OXO motifs alternating with narrow, patterned bands or "peeries" [see page 128]. Each band is separated by one round of plain background color. You have steeked and shaped the armholes and neck and are nearing the final desired length. Knit the last peerie pattern around the top of the body. Now put the back stitches on a piece of wool and working back and forth across the front only, knit the final OXO. Fold the OXO over the top of the shoulder and weave the raw stitches to those waiting across the back, leaving the center-back stitches on the thread for the final neck border. The row of weaving will form the plain, unpatterned round between peerie and OXO. This method is both lovely and a bit mysterious; the fold-over method will also serve to slightly lower the back of the neck.

As usual, the choices described here are just a smattering of those that exist. Try some of the above and keep your eyes peeled for additional options.

Onward, Meg ⌒

3-NEEDLE I-CORD CAST-OFF

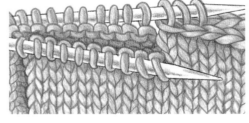

Knitted Hems

Easy ways to avoid the familiar pitfalls

by Elizabeth Zimmermann and Meg Swansen

A HEM! We haven't noticed these on knitted garments of late, and suspect they are out of favor for several reasons:

- flaring around the lower edge
- a noticeable dimpling where they are sewn to the inside of the garment
- a tightness around neck and cuff hems
- an obvious purl round for the "turn" in an otherwise purl-free garment.

You can correct all the above, and have some fun as well.

To begin with, always work the hems—whether cuffs, neck or lower edge—last. A hem should have neither a cast-on nor a bind-off selvage. The dimpling mentioned above is not caused by poor sewing so much as by sewing down an inelastic selvage to the back of a totally elastic fabric. Casting on and binding off simply cannot "breathe" with the garment. SO, in order to avoid the problem, we simply will eliminate them both. How?

Suppose you are beginning your sweater at the lower edge. Cast on, using the long-tail method. This produces a pretty border on one side that resembles outline stitch in

By applying these techniques, you can make a smooth, attractive hem—without such worries as unwanted flaring and dreaded dimpling.

embroidery; the other side has little purl bumps. Consider the outline-stitch side to be the "right" side, and knit on up the sweater. When the body is finished, return to the lower edge to knit the hem. With the "right" side facing you, knit up into the little purl bumps behind the outline stitch, one stitch for each cast-on stitch. You will note that the outline stitch makes a nice sharp fold for the hem [Figure 1].

To prevent the flaring problem, you have several choices. You can use a lighter-weight wool for the hem itself. Or, if this is not feasible, decrease 10 percent of the stitches by working k8, k2tog around *after the first round* of the hem. You may want to use a needle one size smaller as well to help the hem hold in.

Now, if you've been thinking ahead, you will see how we are about to solve the dreaded dimpling pitfall. We will not bind off, but will sew the stitches down right off the needle, one at a time, with a sharp metal sewing needle. Sliding off 10 to 15 stitches or working directly from the needle, skim lightly through the back of the fabric (making sure to stay on one horizontal row of the sweater) and then sew through the raw stitch. This will permit the hem to be as elastic as the garment [Figure 2].

With all the above in mind, we will now let you in on what we consider to be the reward of the whole procedure: the message that is incorporated into the hem. What shall it be? The name of the recipient? Perhaps with the date and the name of the sweater? (Do you always name your sweaters, too?) Maybe a private joke or (if the circumference permits) a limerick? And which way up should we knit the message? So that, when the hem is folded back, the words will be easily legible to (A) the wearer or (B) the observer?

Get yourself some knitter's graph paper and chart out the words. We usually make our letters 5 rows high. But, you may want a speechless hem with a pretty color pattern instead…which reminds us…for a super-neat job: When knitting the hem in a contrasting color, work the last 2 hem rounds in the predominant color of that to which it will be sewn. Since the hems are worked last, you can be thinking about all these things as you knit the body and sleeves.

The foregoing applies to cuff hems, as well as round necks.

Boatneck hems are another matter. A boatneck is really only a horizontal slit across the top of the body. A hem will have to lie flat as it travels around the 180-degree corners…seemingly a tricky bit of business.

After you have knitted up all neck stitches for the hem, mark the three corner stitches at each side with a safety pin. Work around, and increase 1 stitch each side of the 3 marked stitches every round for the entire depth of the hem. This is a fierce increase, but necessary in order to provide sufficient fabric to make the turns [Figure 3]. Sew the raw stitches down right off the needle—particularly important for any kind of neck hem, as a bind-off edge may well prevent the sweater from going over your head!

But enough hemming and hawing. Go knit yourself ahem! ⌐

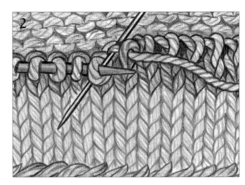

PICKING UP FOR THE HEM

With the outline stitch (right side) facing, insert the needle into the purl bump behind the outline stitch. Wrap the yarn around the needle and pull up a loop. Work one stitch in each bump.

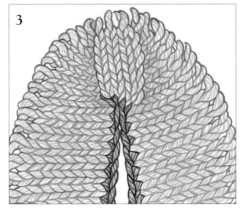

SEWING DOWN THE HEM

Sew the open stitches of the hem to the body by inserting a sewing needle into part of one body stitch (to prevent the stitching from showing on the right side) and through one stitch on the hem as shown. Keep the hem even by sewing through stitches along the same horizontal row of the sweater.

BOATNECK HEMS

You must work rapid increases on either side of the neck opening. Mark the three corner stitches. Work a "make one" increase on either side of these stitches on every round. This will allow the hem to lie flat when sewn down.

Delving Into Pockets

by Mari Lynn Patrick

POCKET LININGS

• You can make a separate pocket lining or knit the lining while making your front(s). Separate linings should be made before other pieces of your sweater. To make a lining, cast on 2 stitches more than the number of stitches to be bound off for your pocket opening. When desired pocket depth is achieved, slip stitches to a holder so that your next row will be worked from wrong side. BE SURE TO MAKE LININGS IN THE SAME COLOR AND PATTERN AS YOUR SWEATER.

• If your yarn is very bulky, knit the top 1½–2"/4–5cm of your pocket lining in the same yarn as used for the sweater front and the remainder in a lighter-weight yarn.

• Fabric pockets, which are folded in half and hem-stitched, can be used in place of knitted pocket linings to reduce bulk. Just remember to knit a 1½–2"/4–5cm pocket lining to prevent the fabric from showing on your finished sweater.

• When your sweater is knit in a double strand of yarn, hidden pocket linings should be done in a single strand. Check the gauge on your single strand.

• A pocket lining can be knit as a double length with a separate needle and then folded in half on wrong side and worked back in place with the remaining stitches [Figure 1]. Sides of the lining are stitched closed, and pocket lining stays free. This type of lining should only be made for a lightweight garment.

POCKET SIZE AND PLACEMENT

If you have never made pockets, or wish to add pockets when the pattern doesn't call for any, begin by deciding on the pocket size and where you wish to place the pocket(s). The average size for a woman's pocket is 5–6½"/12.5–16.5cm wide by 5–7"/14–17.5cm deep. You can add 1"/2.5cm to that in each direction for men and subtract 1"/2.5cm or more for small children.

The lower edge of a horizontal or patch pocket should end no further than 21 or 22"/53 or 56cm down from the shoulder on a woman's sweater. If your sweater is short, 22"/56cm or shorter in length, you should plan a vertical or side seam pocket for easier wear. Horizontal or patch pockets should be placed from 2½–4"/6.5–10cm from each side of center front edge and can end at the top of the ribbing or higher if

There are few among us whose hands don't reach for pockets at our sides as soon as we've put on a new garment. It must be the easy relaxed feeling we get that urges us to do so. What garment to feel more relaxed in than a hand-knit sweater? There is no reason to feel intimidated about adding your own pockets—just follow along with us and use these guidelines. You'll soon be a pocket professional, too!

sweater is extra-long.

A scaled-to-size sketch of your front pieces will best illustrate your pocket placement BEFORE you start knitting.

PATCH POCKETS

Patch pockets may be the easiest to knit, but neatly sewing them to your fronts can be tricky! Hems of ½"/1.25cm can be added on 3 sides to give a sharp turning edge to your pocket. For example, work ½"/1.25cm tightly in stockinette stitch, then purl the next row on right side for turning ridge and work even for ½"/1.25cm more and cast on 2 to 4 stitches at the beginning of the next 2 rows for side hems. Work inside stitch of each side hem in a slip stitch for turning ridge to the end of your pocket. The last ½–¾"/1.25–2cm can be worked in ribbing or your chosen edge stitch before binding off.

POCKET OPENINGS

Horizontal

Work with your stitch gauge to determine the pocket opening's size, placement and number of stitches to bind off. Bind off on the right side of work the desired number of stitches (or slip stitches to a holder). If your gauge is 6 stitches = 1"/2.5cm and you want a 5½"/14cm-wide pocket, you would multiply 5½ by 6 = 33 stitches to be bound off. On the next (wrong side) row, join your separate pocket lining to your pocket opening as follows: Work across stitches of front to last stitch before opening and with wrong side of pocket lining facing, work last stitch of front together with first stitch of lining—then work across lining stitches (from holder), working last stitch of pocket lining together with first stitch of front—work to end—pocket lining joined.

Vertical

If you want a pocket opening on the front, work in pattern to the placement of the pocket opening, attach a separate ball of yarn and bind off 1 or 2 stitches, then continue along the pattern to the end of the row. Work in pattern on each side of the pocket opening with separate balls of yarn to the planned pocket depth. To rejoin the pocket opening, beginning on right side of front, work in pattern to the pocket opening, cast on 1 or 2 sts, drop second ball of yarn and continue to the end of the row.

To make a pocket lining in the side seam on the back section of your sweater, cast on stitches for desired lining width to each side seam and work to planned pocket depth. Bind off these stitches and continue on back as before [Figure 2].

You can also pick up stitches later along the outside pocket opening (nearest seam edge) and knit these stitches for pocket lining [Figure 3]. Or simply make a separate lining and sew in.

Slanted or Curved

SLANTED openings are worked in the same way as vertical openings with decreasing at inside edge of opening (side nearest center front) worked to desired slant. The outer side of the pocket opening is worked straight with a separate ball of yarn, as for a vertical pocket opening. BE SURE that your number of stitches cast on for the lining is at least 3–4 stitches WIDER than the total number of stitches decreased for slant.

CURVED openings are worked in a similar wary to the slant pocket opening—take inspiration for your shape from an armhole curve with its bind-offs and decreases. Both slant and curved pockets are definitely for more experienced knitters.

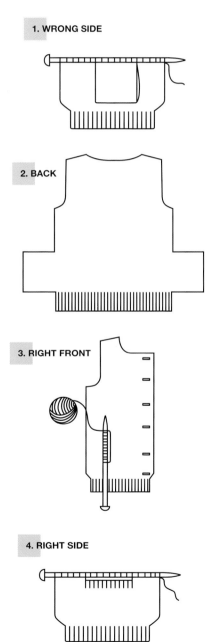

1. WRONG SIDE

2. BACK

3. RIGHT FRONT

4. RIGHT SIDE

POCKET EDGES

Ribbing to match that of a sweater's edges is frequently used as a pocket edging. Pick up the stitches along the bound-off edge with the same size needle used for edge ribbing, adding 2 or 3 stitches. Work edge for ½–¾"/1.25–2cm, then bind off loosely enough so that edge is elastic. Garter stitch also makes a neat edge and should be worked tightly without increases. You can also experiment with seed stitch, rolled reverse stockinette stitch, or crocheted edges.

If you want to avoid picking up and sewing down pocket edges, there is an ingenious way to knit edges into fronts BEFORE binding off. First, plan your edge to begin at ½–¾"/1.25–2cm down from top of pocket opening. On the next right-side row, centering pocket where desired, work pattern to designated stitches for pocket opening, place a marker, then if you are working ribbing, increase 2 to 3 stitches across pocket area (BEING SURE to begin and end with the same stitch), place a second marker, and complete your row. Continue in pattern on stitches at each side of markers and work pocket edge in ribbing as established, slipping markers on every row, for ½–¾"/1.25–2cm. On the next right-side row, bind off stitches between markers in rib, and pocket edging is complete [Figure 4]. Then follow steps for inserting pocket lining on next row.

SEWING POCKET LININGS

Before sewing, pocket linings should be blocked to size along with the other pieces of your garment, then sewn to the wrong side of fronts using an overcast stitch. First baste or pin linings in place so that stitches and rows match exactly—straight seaming is important! Next, carefully take single stitches so that seaming is invisible on the right side. ⌒

by Mari Lynn Patrick

Sewing techniques can correct less-than-perfect buttonholes at the finishing stage—the buttonhole band can be backed with ribbon or tape, or the buttonholes can be reinforced with sewing thread by hand or machine. But, as the handknitting purist knows, the ideal way to finish a sweater is with yarn only and working totally by hand. Some knitters even split the yarn to sew on their buttons.

Here are some helpful tips to improve your hand-knit buttonholes:

• Pre-plan buttonhole placement by making the left (button) band first; on men's sweaters, make the right band. Then place markers along the band for easy counting when working the buttonhole band.

• When spacing buttonholes along a band, be sure that the first and last buttonholes are not more than ½"/1.5cm from the upper and lower edges. Then space the other buttonholes so there are the same number of stitches or rows in between each buttonhole.

• When working buttonholes in a front ribbed band, center buttonholes in the ribbing. For example, if you have a vertical band 7 stitches wide, center a 3-stitch

Flat, even, hideaway buttonholes certainly identify the best of the very best knitters. If you're an otherwise excellent knitter who's bothered by buttonholes that gape and gap, here's how to refine your technique and join the elite.

buttonhole. This leaves 2 stitches on each side to frame the buttonhole. Always try to have at least 2 stitches on each side of the buttonhole so the garment buttons neatly.

• For horizontal bands, when stitches are picked up along the front borders, work buttonholes in the center row. For example, a 7-row band should have buttonholes formed on the 4th row.

• If you are working with a slippery yarn and anticipate sloppy buttonholes, add one strand of the same-color sewing thread when working the buttonholes. This stabilizes the buttonhole.

• If you are working an edge in single crochet, you can work a simple buttonhole with a method similar to a knitted buttonhole. Skip the desired number of stitches for the buttonhole, then work the same number of chains over the buttonhole opening. On the second row, work a single crochet into each chain, not over the chain, to keep the buttonhole from stretching.

• A crochet chain loop at the very edge of a band or border makes a quick and easy buttonhole.

- There is no rule for determining button size in relation to buttonhole size. As a guide, you can measure the buttonhole width flat, and add ¼–½"/5–13mm. This gives you a button size that fits snugly.

There's more than one way to make a buttonhole, and we offer three methods which follow. The simplest method is the eyelet buttonhole, the most frequently used the 2-row buttonhole, and for an extremely neat-looking buttonhole, try the 1-row buttonhole.

EYELET BUTTONHOLE

This buttonhole [Figure 1] is made in the same way as a knitted eyelet—with a knit 2 stitches together and a yarn over (k2tog and yo). This method is limited to lightweight yarns and tiny baby buttons, or to very bulky yarns with small buttons.

TWO-ROW BUTTONHOLE

This method forms horizontal buttonholes [Figure 2], which are quite satisfying in most cases. A given number of stitches is bound off at evenly designated intervals on the first buttonhole row. Then the same number of stitches is cast on over each set of bound-off stitches in the second buttonhole row.

With this type of buttonhole, you may want to go one step further at the finishing stage of your garment. Split the yarn, stitch all around the buttonhole; use a buttonhole stitch to keep all the stitches flat [Figure 3]. Unless you're working with a very fine strand of yarn, try not to place too many stitches around. This will stretch the buttonhole out of shape—something to avoid when you want buttonholes at their very best.

ONE-ROW BUTTONHOLE

These directions for a one-row buttonhole [Figure 4] are adapted from *A Second Treasury of Knitting Patterns* by Barbara Walker. The photo shows buttonholes worked from the wrong side (top) and right side (bottom).
- Knit to the first buttonhole. With yarn in *front* of work, slip first stitch from left-hand to right-hand needle, then place yarn in back of work and leave it there.
- Slip next stitch from left-hand to right-hand needle and pass the first stitch over it; one stitch bound off. Continue to bind off stitches in this way until the stated number of stitches are bound off.
- Slip the last bound-off stitch back to the left-hand needle and turn work.
- Place yarn to *back* of work (behind needles). Then cast on the same number of

stitches bound off for buttonhole, plus *one extra stitch*. Use the cable cast on as follows: *Insert right-hand needle between the first and second stitches on left-hand needle, draw through a loop, and place loop onto left-hand needle for first cast-on stitch; repeat from * until all stitches are cast on. Before slipping the last loop on the left-hand needle, bring yarn to front to form a dividing strand; turn work.
- Slip the first stitch from left-hand to right-hand needle, then pass the extra cast-on stitch over it to close buttonhole. Then continue to work across row, working each buttonhole in this way. ⌒

Block That Knit!

Blocking takes quite some time, but it ensures a superb-looking, well-fitting garment. When done properly, blocking is even more rewarding, in that the finished product reflects all of your care, patience and expertise. In addition to giving desired final shape and dimension to each sweater piece, blocking will ease stitch irregularities, smooth small bulges caused by increases and decreases, and smooth and straighten curled edges. Above all, it insures intermeshing size and shape so that sewing your sweater together is a breeze.

Blocking is necessary for most garments made of natural fibers. It is not effective for garments made of synthetics. For synthetics, follow the directions on the yarn label whenever they are given. The process of blocking, quite simply, involves stretching or molding the pieces of a garment to their finished measurements; pinning them into position, dampening them and letting them dry naturally so that they "remember" their final shape.

If your knitting instructions don't give finished measurements, you can calculate them. *Simply divide the number of stitches in a row by the gauge.* For example: To find the

Knitting is tremendously rewarding—not only in terms of relaxation, but also in the satisfaction you get from creating a beautiful custom-made garment. It requires lots of time and dedication. Think of those times when you're binding off the last piece of a sweater…you can hardly wait to put it all together. But one task remains that makes all your hours of work even more worthwhile: BLOCKING.

back width measurement from side seam to side seam, count the number of stitches in a row, then divide by the number of stitches in an inch/2.5cm, according to your gauge. So if you have 60 stitches across, and your gauge indicates 4 stitches in an inch/2.5cm, you'll know that your piece should measure 15"/38cm across. To determine the proper length, follow the same procedure, counting the rows.

To block, you will need a flat padded surface into which pins can be pushed. This surface can be made to any size, but must be larger than the largest piece you intend to block. You may also use a dressmaker's cutting board or a purchased blocking board. Or, you can always use a folded blanket, covered with a sheet. You will also need a ruler, tape measure, *rustproof* pins, two terry-cloth towels and a plastic sheet to cover your board.

Find a convenient spot (away from major household traffic) for the board. Keep pets off limits and instruct the curious that this is a no-touch project.

The back of a sweater gets first priority, followed by the front, sleeves and pockets. Mount the plastic sheet securely and smoothly over the board. Wet a bath towel, wring out excess moisture and place over the sheet. (If you are blocking a particularly large piece, you may need to lay down two damp towels first.)

With the right side down, begin carefully pinning your back piece. Pin carefully, stretching or molding and shrinking your piece to the finished measurements. First pin across the bust/chest measurement, from one armhole across to the other. If you find any sizing discrepancies, gently and firmly smooth and pat the piece until it takes on the desired dimensions. Then pin from the center back to the bottom. *Do not pin the ribbing.* Work around the piece in this manner, according to the diagram, until your piece is secure. Be sure your pins are close enough together (½"/13mm) so that sides and other straight edges are smooth and do not curl between pins. Wet and wring out an additional towel or towels and completely cover the piece. Leave undisturbed until everything is dry. Then, and only then, should you remove the pins.

Repeat this process for all pieces, being sure that all side seams, sleeves and shoulders are equal to their corresponding areas of the back.

If desired, after your garment is sewn together, the seams *only* may be pressed to flatten them. It is a good idea to test your iron's temperature on your gauge swatch. From the wrong side, using a press cloth, gently guide the tip of your iron along seams to open and flatten them. Be sure to let the garment completely cool from the heat of the iron before finally wearing your sweater with all the pride you deserve!

SOME FINAL TIPS:

- With some very lightweight wools, cottons, linens or silks, or with a natural-and-synthetic-blend yarn, it may be necessary to use only one damp towel, just to cover your piece.
- You can pin lacy and very lightweight knits on a dry board and cover with a damp cloth or sheet that is not as heavy as a towel.
- If you have worked with a 100 percent synthetic, your pieces should match the finished dimensions quite accurately. In this case, you may simply press your pieces with a warm iron and a damp pressing cloth. Be certain to test your yarn's reaction to heat first by trying this on your gauge swatch.

Fine Finishing: Selvages

by Catherine Lowe

WHAT IS A SELVAGE?

Contemporary knitting manuals use the term selvage to refer to decorative border stitches worked along the sides of a piece of flat knitting, or the stitches along the vertical edges of a garment piece that either become part of a seam or are used for finishing. Couture knitting uses selvage stitches along the non-horizontal edges of a garment piece to create a seam allowance: one or more stitches are added to the edges and worked in a pattern that is clearly distinguished from the main stitch pattern.

CHOOSING AND USING SELVAGES

While many knitters are familiar with a single-stitch selvage, in couture knitting a more substantial selvage is preferred. Usually worked over 2 stitches, a selvage may be worked over 3 or more stitches and may vary along a single edge of one garment piece in both number of stitches and pattern. Selvages may be interrupted, added after a portion of the piece has been worked, or worked differently along each edge of a single piece. Because the number of selvage stitches, their pattern and necessary characteristics are determined by the construction or finishing technique to be used on the edge in question, it is essential to think through all aspects of the garment before beginning and plan the edges accordingly. Various selvages should be swatched with the main stitch pattern and their behavior analyzed. Above all, the selvage must not interfere with the main stitch pattern.

In couture knitting, techniques are translated from dressmaking. The result: more professionally finished hand-knitted garments.

CONSIDER THE FOLLOWING WHEN CHOOSING SELVAGE STITCHES

- A selvage must clearly distinguish itself from the main stitch pattern.
- Gauge is as crucial to the choice of selvage as the main stitch pattern. The selvage must match the main stitch pattern in row gauge, otherwise it will distort the edge.
- Selvages should measure ⅜–½"/1–1.25cm when used for seaming and may be lightly steamed open on the inside.
- To reinforce points of stress, use at least a ½"/1.25cm selvage and tack down inside.
- Selvage stitches must be added to pattern stitches, and stitch counts for cast-on and bind-off rows need to be adjusted.
- All shaping should be executed within the main stitch pattern, not the selvage.

- Selvages are not included in schematics or garment measurements.
- Additional selvage stitches need not be added to stitch patterns that already incorporate an edge stitch. Here, the edge stitch itself may be treated as a selvage and additional pattern stitches added to compensate for lost width. If the edge stitch creates too much bulk when turned to the inside for seaming or stitch pick-up, a multiple-stitch selvage that lies flat may be preferred.

WHY USE SELVAGES?

- To produce a firm edge that can be used to stabilize stitch patterns and set gauge.
- To provide a clear line for seaming and stitch pick-up.
- Rows are readily identifiable and countable, and an accurate rows-to-stitches-picked-up ratio is easily achieved.
- Yarn and color changes can be worked at the outer edge of the selvage rather than at the edge of the garment piece.
- Selvages clearly delineate the garment piece, making precise measurements possible.
- Garment pieces may be blocked using wires or pins in the selvages without distorting the edges of the main stitch pattern.
- To reinforce points of stress.
- For knitters whose gauge tends to vary at the edges of their knitting, selvages provide the stitches needed to maintain gauge across the pattern stitch.

BASIC SELVAGES

Understanding the structure and inherent characteristics of a selvage is essential to its successful use. When swatching, look at how different selvage stitches behave with respect to the main stitch pattern and choose the one that exhibits the characteristics needed for its particular role.

One-stitch selvages:

Even if a garment is to be worked without full selvages, it is advisable to add a single stitch along the non-horizontal edges of garment pieces—not only to facilitate construction, but to ensure no actual width is lost when seaming. When working garter, seed or moss stitch, a single-stitch selvage is often sufficient. A version of a slip-stitch selvage works especially well with these stitches. If a single-stitch selvage is to be used with a complex stitch pattern, a simple stockinette selvage is a good match, while a seed-stitch selvage pairs well with slip-stitch, mosaic, and knit-in-the-row-below patterns.

Two-stitch selvages:

These are well suited to vertical seaming in mattress stitch and using the running threads between the first or last pattern stitch and the selvage stitch next to it. This selvage is usually achieved by working the selvage stitches next to the main pattern as knit stitches, creating a column of seed stitch, while the outer stitches are worked in one of several ways, depending upon how flat the selvage needs to be.

Three-stitch selvages:

When the selvage must lie flat under the adjacent garment piece, adding a column of purl stitches between the main stitch pattern and a flat 2-stitch selvage will force the selvage to turn out along the edge of the garment piece rather than fold back under it. This is crucial when the selvage is to be used for stitch pick-up rather than seaming.

A FEW FAVORITE SELVAGES

The stitches below are excellent starting points, but do not hesitate to experiment beyond these suggestions.

ONE-STITCH SELVAGES:

Twisted Slip Stitch (good for stockinette):
(RS): wyif, sl selvage st at beg of row as if to p tbl; *work across main st pat*; k selvage st at end of row
(WS): wyib, sl selvage st at beg of row as if to k, **; p selvage st at end of row

Slip Seed Stitch:
(RS): wyib, sl st as if to k tbl;**; k1 tbl
(WS): same as RS

TWO-STITCH SELVAGES:

Penultimate Chain Selvage
(excellent for vertical seaming at a fine gauge or when bulk is not consequential):
(RS): wyib, sl st as if to k, p1; **; p1, k1

(WS): wyib, sl st as if to k tbl, k2; **; k3

Slipped Double Garter

(excellent for vertical seaming).

(RS): with yib, sl st as if to k tbl, k1; **; k2

(WS): same as RS

THREE-STITCH SELVAGES:

Purl Double Garter

(excellent for stitch pick-up to work adjacent garment piece)

(RS): wyib, sl st as if the ktbl, k1, p1;**; p1, k2

(WS): wyib, sl st as if the ktbl, k2;**; k3

A note about selvages and ribs

Ribs, when used as borders and cuffs, do not do well with selvages. If a rib border is to be seamed, work on a number of stitches that is one more than the required count, making sure that the two end stitches match (both knits or both purls). Use mattress stitch to seam and work in the loops (rather than the running threads) of the two end stitches. The result is an invisible seam with no break in the continuity of the ribbing. ⌒

Slipped Double Garter

Purl Double Garter

Essay: Knitting Back Backwards

An easy way to purl back—from the right side

by Elizabeth Zimmermann and Meg Swansen

Planning to knit popcorns? Or a saddle shoulder? Or short rows to raise the back of the neck? This technique will save you time and trouble.

Let us begin by defining our terms. Knitting is traditionally worked from the left needle onto the right needle. Stockinette is achieved by knitting on the right side and purling back on the wrong side. And knitting back backwards? That is the process of knitting stitches from the right needle onto the left needle.

You may know a left-handed knitter who works in this fashion and calls it left-handed knitting. We find this confusing, as both left and right hands are involved with knitting in either direction. When working back and forth to produce stockinette and using the knitting back backward (KBB) method, you will actually be purling back from the right side. If the concept is new to you, thinking about it may produce that through-the-looking-glass feeling, and you may ask, why bother?

Our chief pleasure is simply in learning a new knitting technique, but there are plenty of practical advantages as well. How about putting in short rows to raise the back of the neck? Or a saddle shoulder uniting two halves of the body? And when was the last time you knitted a bobble or popcorn in Aran knitting? Remember the slight feeling of frustration—especially when knitting a large body-section—as you had to turn the whole piece around merely to purl 4 or 5 stitches, then again to purl? We calculated that the flipping took more real time than the actual knitting and purling. Ah, well, to achieve your objectives in knitting, no amount of time and trouble is too great. However….

There is a knitter and lace designer named Lois Young. She is a left-handed person, and does all of her knitting in the KBB manner. She is a charter member of our summer Knitting Camps, and, over the years, nothing we could do or say would tempt her to try knitting in the other direction. We believe that some left-handed people think they cannot knit the way right-handers do, because they confuse the natural awkwardness we all feel when first learning to knit with the fact that they are left-handed. Wouldn't Continental-style knitting be ideal for left-handers? The wool is held over the left index finger, and the left hand does most of the work.

Be all that as it may, about seven years ago we began knitting entrelacs, the stitch pattern that resembles a wide basketweave. It is initiated by knitting a series of small triangles: k2, turn, p2, turn, k3, turn, p3, turn, k4, etc. Well! It didn't take long to start mentally rummaging around, looking for a more expedient method. Lois Young! We'd been observing her peculiar manner of knitting for years, and, sure enough, adapting her method on every second row enabled us to knit smoothly back and forth without turning the work.

To teach ourselves this "new" technique, we began by purling back, and as we were doing so, we peered over the top of the needles to see just what was happening on the right side of the work. Ahhh—the needle goes into the stitch *that* way; the wool wraps around the needle in *this* direction.

To practice KBB on stockinette, purl to the middle of the row. Turn the work around. The yarn will be coming from the left needle as shown. To continue the row, insert the tip of the left needle into the back of the stitch on the right needle.

Wrap the yarn over the top of the left needle *counterclockwise* and draw through a loop as shown. If you wrap the yarn incorrectly, the result will be a twisted stitch.

NOW: In the middle of this purl row, we turned the work around and duplicated all the moves we had observed from the other side. The wool is coming from the left needle. The tip of the left needle goes into the back of the stitch on the right needle. The wool wraps over the top of the left needle counterclockwise (this is critical: if you wrap the wool clockwise, the result will be a twisted stitch). It is then hooked through the stitch and pulled off the right needle. Doesn't that feel strange? And you needn't switch the wool from hand to hand. So when you change direction, Continental knitters become "throwers," and vice versa.

Another lovely advantage is that, for some knitters, their KBB gauge matches their forward gauge, whereas their purling-back does not. If you find this to be the case, think of it: you may achieve a circular gauge swatch by sneakily working back and forth on just 25 to 35 stitches. And the front of the work is always under your eye.

Once you feel comfortable with KBB, you may wish to experiment with other stitches. All in all, we find knitting back backwards to be a lovely, satisfying and useful skill. ⌒

Centering a Color Pattern

by Meg Swansen

With more and more knitters designing their own garments, the question of how to center a color pattern is being asked with increasing frequency. As usual, there are so many variables that a quick, pat answer is not an option. At the outset, let me establish that I knit all my color-patterned sweaters in the round and that my side "seams" are simply two diametrically opposed stitches within the tube.

For visual symmetry, it is critical that the motif be perfectly centered on the front and back of the body of a pullover. This is less vital with small-repeat patterns, but it is still important.

The example shown on these charts is a 28-stitch Norwegian Rose motif, and you must first decide which stitch you consider to be the midpoint—the center of the rose, or the stitch between two roses [see page 124]. Note that the final stitch at the left end of the chart on page 124 is the same as the first stitch of the motif, so stitch number 29 is the first stitch of the next repeat.

A PULLOVER

You have worked a swatch, established your gauge and multiplied it by the wanted body circumference. But what if that number is not divisible by twenty-eight? If you need only a few stitches (more or less) to come out evenly, here are three possible ways to fudge:

• Alter your stitch count up or down (the actual number of stitched affected will be small, so it won't make much difference).

• Redesign the motif slightly, adding or subtracting a stitch or two.

• Alter your stitch gauge up or down a fraction by changing your needle size, which will alter the total number of stitches you need.

Once you have worked that out, you can proceed happily to the underarms (or to the lower neck edge if you are knitting a straight dropped-shoulder shape).

However, when working with large stitch repeat motifs, it is likely that the number of body stitches you require will not be tamed into fitting your stitch count merely by fudging. But don't despair; you are far from being defeated. Three *more* choices are available to you:

- Mark the side "seam" stitches. Now, with the motif centered on the exact middle stitch of the back, count forward in increments of the pattern repeat to the marked side stitch. You will be somewhere within the motif repeat when you hit the "seam" stitch. Mark that point on your chart; pivot and read the same chart line in the other direction. Follow around the seam stitch on the other side, making sure the motif is perfectly centered in the middle of the front as you go by. You should be at the same (starting) point in the chart as the other underarm line.

- Proceed as above, but turn the pivot stitch into a seam stitch by keeping it in the background color throughout.

- If you don't like the Rorschach design at the sides, establish a vertical side panel

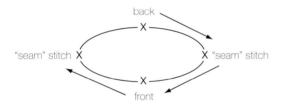

to use up the extra stitches. This panel can be as small and simple as 3 vertical stripes of K1 dark, K1 light, K1 dark, or it can be 5, 7, 9 or 11 stitches wide with a pretty little motif of its own.

As the "seams" become pivot stitches, vertical stripes or panels, the partial motif will make a mirror image as it bounces off itself (or off each of the side stripes or panels) and form a new and intriguing motif of its own. A side-panel pattern may begin at the lower edge of the body and continue, unbroken, down the underside of the sleeve to the cuff.

A CARDIGAN

This can be as simple as centering the motif in the middle of the back and counting forward to the cardigan steek. Remember to add another stitch to the total to provide a matching "balance stitch" on the other side of the center steek. But look out: If the pattern is not mirrored at the underarm, the motifs will not align at the shoulders. If

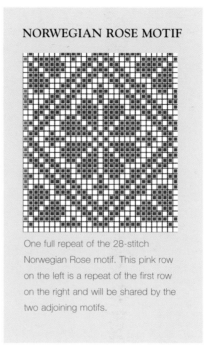

NORWEGIAN ROSE MOTIF

One full repeat of the 28-stitch Norwegian Rose motif. This pink row on the left is a repeat of the first row on the right and will be shared by the two adjoining motifs.

that idea bothers you, mirror the motif at the underarms using one of the methods described for a pullover.

When using horizontal bands from several different charts with no unifying or aligning pattern repeat between them, you may do as you wish for the lower patterns—but when you begin to knit from the chart that will end up at the shoulders, the design must be mirror-imaged at the underarms or it will be annoyingly misaligned at the shoulder tops.

All of the above is applicable to texture motifs as well.

Using these tricks, you can adjust a given color pattern to fit any stitch count for any size, at any gauge.

Onward, Meg ⌒

OPTIONS FOR CENTERING A COLOR PATTERN

1

Here are two examples of how to bridge a 9-stitch side-seam-panel:

Left: Make the panel something completely different, or

Right: Meld the 2 partial repeats into a new design shown here between two arrows.

3

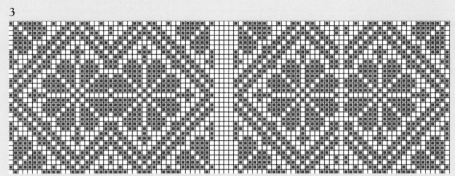

The pair of patterns on the left share a pivot stitch at the underarm. The pair on the right are separated by a "seam" stitch.

2

Here are two more triple sets of a partial motif meeting at the underarm. The upper row and the lower row have been interrupted at different points within the Norwegian Rose. In both rows:

Left: A "seam" stitch

Middle: 3-stitch vertical stripe

Right: A pivot stitch

It does not matter where you are within the pattern; some new Rorschach design will emerge.

4

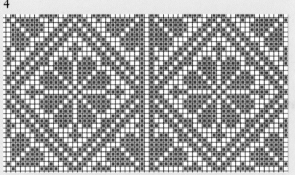

If you require only an additional 6 sts for the circumference, this shows 3 sts separating the two motifs at the side "seam" (kept in dark, light, dark).

by Meg Swansen

EPS stands for Elizabeth's Percentage System, the "E" being my mother, Elizabeth Zimmermann. Her Percentage System is a simple method for calculating the proportions of a sweater and how they relate to each other. Besides being a knitter, Elizabeth was also a painter, trained at the Akadamie in München, Germany, and I have always believed that EPS hatched in her brain as a result of the anatomy classes she took there.

EPS will enable you to design your own custom-fitted garment, with the two essential requirements being an accurate gauge readout and the circumference of the sweater body at the widest part (usually around the chest). If you multiply one by the other, you will have 100 percent, or [K], your Key Number. Other sweater measurements will be a percentage of [K].

Let us use the example of an average-to-large-size seamless pullover—about 45"/114cm around—knitted in a medium-weight wool that yields a gauge of 4 sts to 1"/2.5cm. Four sts x 45"/114cm = 180 sts = 100 percent, or [K].

For this size, you will need seven 4-ounce skeins of wool, a 24"/60cm circular needle for the body and yoke, and a pair of 16"/40cm circular needles and a set of dp needles for the sleeves; the size of the needle is up to you. I knit fairly loosely and used a #7/4.5mm needle to obtain this gauge.

The body is knitted from the lower edge to the underarms; then knit the sleeves from the cuffs to underarms and unite the three parts. At that point, you may knit any of twelve different yoke shapes, from a raglan to a saddle shoulder to a set-in sleeve; they all begin in the same manner.

STARTING AT THE LOWER EDGE: If you want a ribbed border to fit the hips snugly, cast on 90 percent of [K] (180 x .90 = 162 sts) and perhaps use a smaller-size needle. For K2, P2 ribbing, change the number to 160 or 164 for an even multiple of four. (K1, P1 ribbing needs only to be divisible by two.) When you have ribbed to wanted depth, increase up to [K] in the first stocking-stitch round.

If you choose a hem as shown on the Lake Blue version here, it will be knitted last, but please use Long-Tail casting on to facilitate that. Arrange matters so that the outline-stitch side becomes the "right" side; it will replace the purled row usually

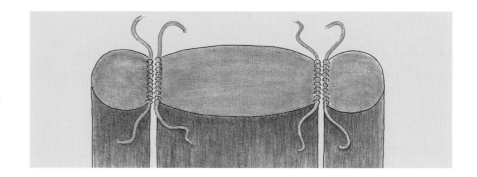

needed to turn the hem. You want a hem to fall relatively straight, but to prevent it from flaring, cast on 95 percent of [K]: 180 x .95 = 171. Think ahead: you will be increasing twice at the side "seams" in increments of 4 sts at a time (about 4"/10cm–5"/12.5cm apart vertically) as you head for [K] (180 sts), so make it 172 cast-on stitches. Once all that is decided, off you sail, working the plain old soothing, hypnotic stockinette stitch round and round until you reach that famous distance: wanted length to underarms. (Phoney Seams and Short Rows on the body are optional. See any of EZ's books for them.) Put the body aside.

SLEEVES: The cuffs will be about 20 to 25 percent of [K], depending on the style. A good way to double-check is to wrap the ribbing (or the yet-to-be-hemmed lower edge) loosely around your wrist. Keep it pinched closed as you slip your hand out, then count the stitches.

RIBBED CUFF, BLOUSED SLEEVE: Work the ribbing to wanted depth. Now you can make a bloused sleeve by increasing severely in the first stockinette-stitch round. Then work straight to about elbow length, where you will increase at the underarm to approximately 34 to 37 percent of [K]. Knit straight to wanted length. You may choose to taper the sleeve above the ribbing instead of blousing it.

HEMMED CUFF, TAPERED SLEEVE: After about an inch or so of plain knitting, taper the sleeve gradually: mark the center three underarm stitches and work a M(ake) 1 on either side of the marked stitches every fifth or sixth round until you have approximately 34 to 37 percent of [K] stitches for the upper arm. Work straight to wanted length. I like to knit both sleeves more or less together—a few inches on one, then catch up with the other. That way I do not have to remember my increase sequence.

Before you unite the sleeves and body, put the underarm stitches on pieces of wool (as shown above). How many, you may ask? EPS tells us 8 percent of [K]: 180 x .08 = 14.4. I will change that to 15 stitches to provide a center stitch for the Phoney Seam. Be sure to carefully center the underarm sts directly above the shaping on the sleeve and directly above the side "seam" stitch on the body.

UNITE SLEEVES AND BODY: Matching underarms, knit across the front (or back) of the body, continue around one sleeve, across the other side of the body, and around the second sleeve. There. All sleeve and body sts—minus 4 x 8 percent—are now on one needle. As you head for the 40 percent of [K] neck opening (180 x .40 = 72 sts), you must decide which style of sweater you want to knit. I will choose the simplest: a pair of yokes with the shaping worked in three concentric rings; I have amended Elizabeth's original formula to allow for a larger upper arm.

The yoke depth—in inches—turns out to be equal to about half the body width, but is rarely greater than 10"/ 25.5cm, regardless of girth. I always measure the yoke diagonally from the underarm; others measure it straight up and down. Stay alert!

Knit one or two rounds plain on all stitches, paying no attention to those messy sections of sts-on-a-thread at the underarms. To assure a proper fit, the back must be raised (which lowers the neck front). I like to insert a pair of short rows at the bottom of the yoke, then another pair at the top. If you are knitting a color or texture pattern into your yoke, it may dictate the location of the short rows.

SHORT ROWS AND WRAPPING: Knit to 15 sts past the front sleeve/body join. Wrap (that is, slip next st to R needle, bring wool to front, replace slipped st. Wool is now wrapped around the slipped stitch—keep it quite loose). Turn and purl (or do not turn and knit back backwards) to the same point on the other side of the front. Wrap (loosely). Turn. Knit to within 5 sts shy of the first wrap. Wrap. Turn. Work to 5 sts shy of the second wrap. Wrap. Turn. Knit a complete round on all sts, knitting the slipped stitches together with their wraps. Done. Four extra rows introduced. Knit until half the yoke has been worked. With my 10"/25.5cm-deep yoke, that is 5"/12.5cm.

FIRST DECREASE RING: Beginning somewhere behind the left shoulder, *K2, K2tog. Repeat from * around. You have decreased one quarter of the stitches. In a plain sweater such as this, I like to disguise the decreases by working this round and the next in purl. It looks like strings of necklaces—or pearls/ purls. Knit another one quarter of the yoke depth (2.5"/6.5cm for me).

SECOND DECREASE RING: K1, K2tog around; a one-third decrease. Knit the final quarter.

THIRD DECREASE RING: K2, K2tog, K2tog around; two-fifths decrease. You should now have about 40 percent [K] sts. Work another two sets of Short Rows and Wrapping as before.

NECK BORDER: If your sweater has a very large circumference, your 40 percent [K] neck opening may be too wide. If you choose a ribbed crew-neck border, you may now decrease as many stitches as necessary, hidden in the first round of ribbing. Bind off loosely. If the contrary is true and 40 percent looks too skimpy, reduce the severity of the final decrease round to end up with more stitches. You are in charge.

For a hemmed neck, purl one round, switch to a lighter-weight wool and knit about an inch. Increase so the hem will lie flat on the widening yoke. Knit another ½"/1.5cm–1"/2.5cm. Sew down the raw stitches as described below.

WEAVE: The final trick that will make this garment totally seamless is to weave (or Kitchener stitch) the raw stitches at the underarms. Put the 15 upper sts-on-a-thread onto one dp needle and the lower sts on another. Now, at each end of each needle, find a sloppy thread, twist it, call it a stitch and put it on the needle and weave 17 to 17. Be sure to use a blunt sewing-up needle to prevent splitting stitches. This little maneuver should take care of any holes at the corners; if it does not, work a kind of duplicate stitch around the hole to snug it up.

FINAL HEMS: Using a lighter-weight wool to prevent bulk, knit up one stitch for each cast-on stitch into the purl bumps behind the outline stitch. If you must use the same sweater wool for the hem, knit one complete round, then decrease 10 percent (K8, K2tog). Work the hem to wanted depth—knitting in a two-color secret message to the wearer, if you wish. Knit the last two rounds in the color to which the hem will be sewn. Slide about 10 to 15 sts off the needle at a time and, with a sharp sewing-up needle, tack each raw stitch down by skimming through the inside of the body fabric, then through the raw stitch. Keep it loose. During the final blocking, you can make up for slight miscalculations in length or circumference).

There. Isn't that lovely? What color will you make the next one? ⌒

Fair Isle Knitting

by Elizabeth Zimmermann

I remember the splendid Fair Isle jumpers (or jerseys) from my early youth when great boxes of them would come from Shetland "on appro" (on approval). What a sight! The most beautiful hand-knit sweaters and lace shawls. My sisters and I selected those we couldn't resist, put the resistible ones back in the box along with a check, and shipped them back to Scotland. The fact that I can't remember any squabbling about who got to keep which artifact I will attribute to the most ladylike behavior of all present.

Find Fair Isle on the map. It lies alone between the Orkneys and the Shetlands off the northeast coast of Scotland. It is sparsely inhabited by people, but richly in habited by sheep, which produce the truly exclusive wool (wonderfully soft and springy, with an important felting property) that is so necessary to the unique quality of the finished garment.

There is a tendency these days to call any color-pattern knitting "Fair Isle," but actually Fair Isle is a specific and succinct type of color-pattern knitting. The style was made famous by the Prince of Wales, who went golfing in his Fair Isle vest and wore it while sitting for his portrait [see page 28]. If you look at this painting, you will note that the V part of the V-neck rides up terribly. We know how to avoid that now: One stitch

What, exactly, are peerie patterns? And steeks? How many stitches in a float? Colors in a round? The opinionated knitter explains.

for each row is picked up along the diagonal of the V-neck; if a portion of the V-neck is worked straight, pick up two stitches for every three rows along this section. I always think of the honesty of the painter, painting just what he saw...obviously not a knitter! The prince established the popularity of the most common type of Fair Isle, which has OXO as the main motif. (To the British OXO also means a beloved species of bouillon, made with a beef flavor.) The OXOs are usually 13 to 15 rounds high, knitted in bands around the sweater, and separated by smaller bands, three to five rounds high, referred to as "peerie" patterns. Sometimes the OXOs will be an allover interlocking pattern, and sometimes you will see them knitted in vertical columns. Even more important than the motif is the use of color. The original sweaters were knitted in the natural colors of the sheep, sometimes blended, sometimes dyed reddish purple, yellow and orange with lichen. I prefer the muted colors: beige, cream, silver, moorit, lovat, natural black and so on. The actual use of these colors is more like painting than any other knitting I've done. Hold one color in each hand, and it feels rather like painting with two brushes and never having to rinse off either! In a single 15-round motif, the colors will shade from dark to light and back again, and, typical of Fair Isle, the background may shade itself in the opposite direction. Real Fair Isle designs never carry more than two colors in a round, and never cause you to have a carry (float) greater than five stitches.

Once embarked upon, Fair Isle knitting seems to instruct the fingers, and through them it gives you the faculty of invention and a feeling of historical continuity. The traditional sweaters are always worked in the round, using four double-pointed needles and a knitting pouch, or a circular needle. You will be hard pressed to find a Fair Islander purling back in color pattern. I've heard that some island knitters, having knitted the circular body and reached the underarms, will knit across the front, break the two wools, rejoin them at the right-hand side of the piece, and knit across again. They would rather darn in those hundreds of ends than purl back in two colors...and who can blame them? Usually the sweaters and cardigans are knitted entirely in the round, and the armhole openings and cardigan front are cut into the fabric. This is where the unique felting property of the wool comes into play: you need not machine-stitch each side of the cut as the Norwegians do, but employ a "steek"—a method of cutting into some extra stitches that have been cast on (or wrapped around the needle) specifically for this purpose. Since machine-knitting is rather inorganic to knitting (nailing into place an otherwise elastic fabric), the "steek" is a pleasing option.

So, if you've never knitted a two-color pattern before, why not start right off with some real Shetland wool, a 16"/40cm circular needle and about 100 stitches. Choose one of the 900(!) Fair Isle patterns in Sheila McGregor's splendid book *The Complete Book of Traditional Fair Isle Knitting*. Now try knitting the way "other people" knit (with the wool in your other hand). It will feel awkward at first, and five minutes of practice will do nicely for the first day. Next day: six minutes. Make a game out of it.

Naturally you'll have a favorite hand; use it for the color of which there are the most stitches. Be sure to carry the unused color loosely across the back of the work (no need to pick up the new color from under the old!), and see what emerges. ⌐

This felted Fair Isle bag, designed by Nicky Epstein, appeared in the Holiday 2006 issue.

Knitting in the Round

by Nancy J. Thomas

I must admit that I am strictly from the "straight knitting needle school." We are the most difficult to convert to circular knitting needles. As a knitting editor, I felt I must be "well-rounded," so to speak, and with some reservation, plunged ahead. Above all, I was leery of giving up my neat, compact needles that slipped conveniently into a case for a bunch of messy plastic wires. I also happen to be lazy enough to want the needle numbers printed clearly on the needle head. Most importantly, I had been knitting with straight needles for years—why change? Putting my doubts behind me, as I hope you will too, I began to find out why converted circular knitters are so unwavering in their devotion to circular needles.

The first reward you'll find in circular knitting is that you won't have to stitch together side seams. What a blessing! You can do rows and rows of stripes and colorwork patterns that will match perfectly—no seams! Also, when working in stockinette stitch, you'll never have to turn your work around and purl. You just merrily knit every row—round after round. One of my favorite reasons for using circular needles is that it is impossible to lose the second needle that always manages to disappear in even the most

The use of circular needles versus straight needles is a controversial subject in the knitting world. Elizabeth Zimmermann, the "guru" of circular knitting, will tell you adamantly that her straight knitting needles "gather dust in a jar." If you aren't familiar with the joys of circular knitting, read one of Elizabeth Zimmermann's books, and you'll gain insight into the vast world of circular knitting.

organized tote bag. Your stitches are also far less likely to drop or slip off the needle. Watch a seasoned circular needle user—she will probably lift the needle ends and slide all the stitches onto the center wire before she packs away her knitting.

If you fumble to find a good way to balance the second needle while knitting, you probably knit in what is called the English method. You may tuck the needle under your arm or figure out some unusual ways to balance the free needle. You'll be pleasantly surprised to learn that with circular knitting needles there is no need for such a balancing act because your second needle has no end. This will probably increase your knitting speed. To any addicted knitter, it's like opening the "gates to heaven" to find that she can knit even faster.

Although you can always use circular needles in place of straight needles for any type of knitting, circular needles are essential for both knitting in the round (tubular) and for large flat pieces. Circular needles are available in various sizes. The most common are 16"/40cm, 24"/60cm, 29"/80cm and 36"/90cm. The smaller circular needles are good for items such as hats or neckband and armband edges. The two medium sizes are the most common for tubular sweater making. The largest is best for knitting large shawls, afghans, skirts or dresses—garments that require numerous stitches to be worked at one time. As a general rule, don't use a circular needle that is longer than the width of the stitches you are working on. You'll have to pull your stitches around too tightly to attach the ends, stretching your work.

Circular needles are all made of plastic wires, most with either plastic or metal ends. You can buy sets of circular needles with interchangeable wires. Just make sure that the needle you select is smooth where the wire and needle point meet, to keep from snagging your knitting.

Use a needle gauge to determine the size of your circular needles. Pass the needle through a hole in the gauge. If it passes easily through the hole, try the next hole size. Does it stop at the point and not pass through at all? The correct needle size is the first hole, not the second. You may need to try several holes before you find your correct needle size. This may sound complicated, but it will get easier as you become more familiar with your circular needles and the needle gauge. If you are creative, you can devise a system to arrange your needles by size, or mark them so that you won't need to use the needle gauge.

HOW TO WORK IN ROUNDS

Cast on as you normally would for 2-needle knitting. The first few rounds are usually the most difficult. Slip a marker onto the needle at the beginning of the first round, before your first cast-on stitch. Marking the beginning and end of your round is essential, especially when working complicated patterns of colorwork. When joining, take care not to twist your stitches. Begin with the first cast-on stitch and work your stitches around to the marker, slip the marker and continue with your next round. Some knitters prefer to knit one row before joining their work. This may help you avoid twisting the stitches, especially if you are a novice circular knitter. Work your first and last stitches tightly on the first few rounds to avoid holes.

A sweater pattern that calls for straight needles can be done on circular needles by adding your front and back stitches together and casting on the total number at one time. If you have never attempted this process, carefully choose a simple pattern for your first project. You may become frustrated if you have to work out complex stitch patterns in the round from a sweater designed to be done in rows. If you are working on a sweater which requires increases at the side seams, you may wish to place a second (different colored) marker between the point where your second side seam falls. When you reach the armhole shaping, you can place either front or back section on a holder, and continue working with your circular needle back and forth in rows. When one side is completed, go back and work the stitches from the holder. Sleeves are not generally done in the round on circular needles, but they can be worked back and forth in rows with the circular needle.

WORKING IN ROWS ON CIRCULAR NEEDLES

Cast on as you would for knitting in the round. Begin your knitting or purling in the last cast-on stitch. Work to the end of the row but do not join work. Turn your work around and work on the reverse side just as you would for straight needle knitting. For instance, when knitting a cardigan, work back and forth in the rows working the back and fronts on circular needles all at once. You may find it a help to mark crucial points, such as side seams, with markers. If the pattern is a complicated cardigan pattern with many stitches, it's wise to use some form of row counter because if one row of the back is off, you'll be ripping out not only the back, but the two fronts as well.

These are the basics of circular needle knitting. I must admit that I am nearly converted. Now tell me how to organize these untidy "wires," and I'll be all set!

Two-Color Knitting

by Meg Swansen

Are you beguiled by the array of magnificent color-pattern designs spread before you—
yet feel intimidated by the thought of working with two colors at once? If the answer is
"yes," this article is directed at you, for there really are no knitting skills beyond your
grasp...you have only to want to learn them. Each new technique you acquire reinforces
the knowledge that all types of knitting are basically simple, merely requiring—as does
any skill—inclination and practice.

Once you decide you are going to learn color-pattern knitting, the next decision will
be how to hold the two colors—and in this you have a number of choices with which to
experiment. I am not didactic about knitting and do not believe there is a Right or a
Best or an Only Way to knit. Beware of the Knitting Bullies lurking out there who leap
at the chance to tell you that you're not holding your needles "properly"—or executing
a technique the "right way." Foosh! If you are getting the results you seek, then you are
doing it right. However, it doesn't hurt to be on the lookout for a smoother or quicker
method, or a new variation to an old technique. Over the years you will find your
knitting style evolving to suit your comfort and proclivity...that is what happened to my
two-color knitting technique.

TWO HANDS ARE BETTER THAN ONE

Originally, my mother taught me to hold one color in each hand. As a Continental
knitter with the working wool over my left index finger, this meant that I had to learn
to throw the second color with my right hand. The initial awkwardness was comparable
to the first time I strapped skis to my feet...how could knitting feel so klutzy? My
mother's method of instruction was to ease me into the technique slowly by practicing
on a plain bit of knitting: the first day I knitted 5 stitches the "new way," then went
back to my familiar left hand. The second day I knitted 10 stitches with my right hand,
the third day 15, etc., etc. At first the little multiples of 5 stitches stood out like a sore
thumb, but with perseverance they gradually began to disappear into the rest of the
fabric. You may never feel as facile with your new hand as you do with your original
hand, but you will gain enough competence to produce beautiful color pattern knitting.

There are advantages to the two-handed method—you never have to put down one
color and pick up the other; both colors are always poised and ready to be worked. And
if you keep one skein on either side of you the two colors will never become entangled.

EASING THE TENSION

A critical factor is the tension at which you work the two colors. New color knitters often give themselves away by producing a puckered fabric; they carry the second color too neatly across the back of the work. You need to loop the second strand almost sloppily to assure that the finished knitting will lie flat. A too-loose carry may be tightened after the fact; but there is no remedy for a too-tight carry except ripping—unless you alter your attitude and decide that you intended to make a smocked-looking fabric in the first place...for a much skinnier person.

There are a number of techniques you can employ to keep the carried loop loose enough. One rather unique method for use with a circular needle was promulgated by Gertrude Taylor in the now out-of-print *America's Knitting Book* and has been adopted by designer Joyce Williams: Keep your tube of knitting inside out and hold the circular needle so that the nylon cable is nearest you and the needle ends are away from you. Even though the work is inside out, you are knitting (and looking at) the "right" side on the inside. This forces the carried color to travel across the outer circumference of the fabric. This seemingly insignificant added distance will help to keep the pattern stitches relaxed. Continue to experiment and practice and you will no doubt invent your own techniques.

I confess to being a time-and-motion-freak in regards to my knitting, and back in the early '60s I felt hampered by the slowness of throwing the second color with my right hand. At the time, we were importing *Binge*, a beautiful book from Sweden. The cover photograph featured a closeup of a pair of old knitting hands with two wools being carried over the left index finger. The knitter simply snagged the color she/he wanted. My initial attempts to copy this method were thwarted, as I was unable to control the tension of the unused color in a multi-stitch carry. As practiced, my hands took over from my brain and independently switched the second color to the middle finger of my left hand. I have been color-knitting like this ever since and have yet to find another knitter who works in a similar fashion. To assure looseness across the back, I cause the wool to travel over the fingers of my stationary right hand where it grips the needle. As you practice whichever method you decide upon, observe your hands as they evolve their own idiosyncrasies to provide the speed, comfort and results you want.

Once your color-knitting technique is secure, you may step into designs of extreme complexity, but keep in mind that many exceedingly striking color patterns utilize only two colors at a time. Of course, this is Your Knitting and all decisions about style and design are entirely up to you. Onward. ⌒

FACTORS TO CONSIDER

• Be aware that your stockinette gauge will most likely be different from your two-color gauge. Be sure to work a color-pattern swatch for a color-pattern garment.

• You cannot see the design as you purl back in color-pattern—consider knitting in the round on a circular needle with the front of the work always toward you (and no seams), OR practice knitting back backwards. The latter will keep the front of the work facing you. As you knit the stitches from the R needle onto the L, you will actually be purling back, but from the front side.

• Hold the same color in the same hand throughout the project: many knitters insist fanatically upon this or, they say, the design will be distorted. I agree with this tenet, but only when working alternate stitches (speckles) of two colors. When working a large color pattern, I often switch fingers so that the color with the most stitches will be over my more comfortable index finger. You will have to discover if your style permits switching fingers or hands in mid-design. The same holds true for carrying one strand over or under the other consistently throughout the project.

• Weaving or twisting the two colors around each other between each stitch. Aargh! Certainly do that if it pleases you, but you need not trouble with it except in certain circumstances. When working isolated motifs (intarsia) or long carries of more than an inch/2.5cm, twist the two wools around each other. But for regular small-repeat color-patterns like Fair Isle knitting, simply strand the carried color loosely across the back. Also, there is nothing to stop you from altering a given chart: If you find an 11-stitch carry, try adding a contrasting color on stitch number 6 and break the 11 solid stitches into two 5-stitch carries. When you must twist, there are lovely techniques for "trapping" the carried strand without having to put down either color. Knit half the distance to be carried with color A. Put your right-hand needle into the middle stitch as if to knit, and wrap color B around the needle but do not complete the stitch. Now wrap color A around the needle, then unwrap color B and complete stitch with color A. See how cleverly it catches up color B? This method is relatively simple and in time you will turn it into a smooth series of moves which will hardly slow you down at all.

Smooth Transition

Aunt Jean's invisible jog—a new and simple technique for circular knitting row by row

by Cindy Sauerwald

"Aunt Jean's Invisible Jog" is a new technique that makes knitting color, texture and pattern in the round look exactly like the pattern chart, stitch for stitch and row for row. With this new technique, the "jog" created by knitting in the round (in "spirals") no longer exists and, therefore, the arduous chore of floating the beginning of the round to the right and left for circular color patterning is eliminated.

This all started in December of 1995 when I opened Aunt Jean's Handiworks, a shop in Clinton, New Jersey. One of my knitting instructors, Nancy Oakes, and I decided to put a pattern book together (one of many soon to come). Nancy has been knitting and designing for years and has tons of gorgeous sweaters she wants to share with the world. She doesn't like patterning—I do. So we thought we'd team up.

One sweater of Nancy's, a pullover with a large gauge of 4 stitches to the inch, contrasting-color garter-stitch wrapping around the sweater in several places, and a color pattern with a large repeat, created quite a dilemma for me. I decided the route would be to go circular so sizes could be done in 3-inch increments. I would, however, get that awful jog in the garter stitch and pattern at the side "seam," and with a large gauge and contrasting colors, it would be very noticeable.

So, the research started to see if anyone had found a way to totally eliminate the jog. I floated the beginning of the row to the right and left between XOX patterns, but the number of stitches between the pattern repeat changes and it was difficult to do. I don't like to think too hard when I knit—it's supposed to be fun! Meg Swansen showed us how rounds of solid color can be knitted without the dreaded jog, but I couldn't find anything that totally eliminated it in a colorwork pattern. I "knitted in circles" for days trying all kinds of things: adding stitches, floating stitches, dropping stitches, even trying to simulate what is done in circular crocheting to eliminate the jog—adding a stitch at the beginning of a round. Nothing seemed to work.

I was just at the point where I was going to learn to live with the jog when magic happened! "Aunt Jean's Invisible Jog" came into my head: instead of trying to add the stitch at the beginning of the round, as is done when crocheting, the last stitch of the round needed to be dropped one stitch. So, I slipped the first stitch to make this happen! I knitted frantically to see if it really worked—it did!

TIPS AND TRICKS

- Because the first stitch of the row is slipped, it tends to elongate a little. Be gentle and try not to yank and pull on the stitch when you slip and knit it. If you have trouble with your stranding tension, slip 2 stitches purlwise at the beginning of the round and move your marker over 2 stitches each row, marking the chart accordingly. This makes the transition a little smoother.

- Try not to stop at Marker A. This will prevent the slipped stitch from being elongated and keep you from losing Marker A in the carpet. If you do stop at Marker A, slip a few stitches from the left to the right needle before setting it down.

- If you lose your marker and don't know where you are, look to see where the row is incomplete. Finish the row if you need to, and look at the back of the work to see where you knitted your last stitch. Slip the first stitch, place Marker A, and off you go!

THE TECHNIQUE

Step 1–Mark the Pattern: To follow the pattern while making "Aunt Jean's Invisible Jog," mark the pattern chart as shown in Figure 1. With a pencil, place an "I" on the chart between the first stitch cast on the needle and the second stitch. Continue marking spaces between stitches up one row and to the left one stitch. (Marker A will be placed here during knitting.)

Step 2–Knitting Directions: To try this out, get some leftover contrasting yarn and cast on 40 stitches on four or five double pointed needles. I suggest using 100 percent wool to experiment with initially. Superwash wool is slippery and cotton is a little more difficult to strand. Refer to Figure 1 as you knit, and in the last rows of garter stitch, try using needles two sizes smaller, because the garter stitch has a wider lateral spread. Remember, you are knitting in the round, so check to see that the cast-on stitches are not twisted when joining.

Row 1: Join by slipping the first stitch purlwise. Place Marker A on the right needle. Knit to end of row—to Marker A—following the chart for this row. You now have one jogless row completed.

Next Rows: Remove Marker A. Slip the next stitch purlwise. Place Marker A on the right needle. Knit to end of row—to Marker A—following chart for this row.

Last Row: Bind off. When stranding, follow all of the same principles as you have done in the past. That's it in a nutshell!

CIRCULAR KNITTING ROW BY ROW

The reason "Aunt Jean's Invisible Jog" always looks and knits exactly like a pattern chart, stitch for stitch and row for row, is this: when the last stitch of the row is knitted, the stitch one row below this stitch is a slipped stitch and drops this last stitch to the right location for the row to be continuous and unbroken. The beginning and end of the row meet on the same level—we are knitting row for row on circular needles—the jog [shown in Figure 2] disappears! Since we no longer end the round one row higher than the beginning stitch of the round, the "spiral" that forms during regular circular knitting no longer exists and floating the beginning and end of the round to the right and left is eliminated. Keep in mind that "Aunt Jean's Invisible Jog" doesn't necessarily start and end where the knitting pattern instructions do. It just floats along doing its own thing. ⁓

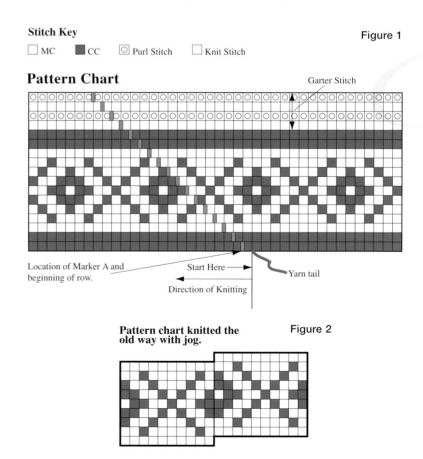

Stitch Key   **Figure 1**

☐ MC   ■ CC   ⊙ Purl Stitch   ☐ Knit Stitch

Pattern Chart   Garter Stitch

Location of Marker A and beginning of row.   Start Here →   Yarn tail

Direction of Knitting

Pattern chart knitted the old way with jog.   **Figure 2**

A Norwegian Classic

by Elizabeth Zimmermann

When you hear the words "Norwegian sweater," you, like me, probably think of those splendid Luskofte ski sweaters—the ones with bold two-color patterns across the chest and upper arms and speckles knitted into the lower body and sleeves. When I first came across that name, I romantically assumed that "lus" meant little "lights." Nothing of the kind. "Luskofte" translates as a much more down-to-earth "lice jacket"!

The original garments, produced in Setesdal in the mid-1800s, were knitted very firmly in natural cream and dyed black wool. I've heard that the large, fairly solid patterns across the chest were designed to provide extra warmth and protection for the wearer. There are several books available containing photographs of early Luskofte sweaters (now museum pieces): *Knitting in the Nordic Tradition*, by Vibeke Lind; *The Complete Book of Traditional Knitting*, by Rae Compton; and *The Complete Book of Traditional Scandinavian Knitting*, by Sheila McGregor. In them, you will note a large slug of plain white at the lower edge of the sweater, where colors are not carried, thus eliminating bulk. This was not seen, being tucked into the high-waisted, bibbed trousers. (It was considered extravagant to use the more expensive dyed wool in an area

As simple as it is splendid, the traditional Luskofte sweater requires no armhole shaping, no purling—just lovely circular knitting.

that would never be revealed publicly!) The black and white wool was highlighted by the most elaborate and colorful embroidery on felt cloth, sewn around the neck opening and cuffs.

As for general construction—here is where circular knitting (my fave) comes into play. The dropped-shoulder sweater is the simplest of all garments, consisting of a large tube of knitting that goes from lower edge to shoulder top, and two smaller tubes shaped gently from narrow cuff to wide upper arm for the sleeves. No worry about armhole shaping. No worry about purling back in color pattern. Just lovely knitting—around and around. The armholes are then cut open and the sleeves sewn in.

Norwegian dropped-shoulder sleeves vary from the British Guernsey dropped-shoulder style in that the stitches are not picked up around the armhole and knitted down to the cuff. If you worked the Norwegian sleeves in this manner, the color pattern would give you away. The stitches would be standing on their heads and not match the body pattern (unless, of course, the sweater body has also been knitted from the top down). So you begin at the cuff, and increase regularly: 2 stitches about every 4th or 5th round. When the sleeve is long enough, the top is approximately 50 percent of the body circumference. This generous proportion is in the style of the original garments, but, naturally, may be adjusted according to taste.

So. The body is completed, and all the stitches have been transferred to a piece of wool; the sleeves are finished and match each other. Now, on a large, flat surface, measure the top of the sleeve against the exact side of the body. Darn in a bright scarlet piece of wool to denote the bottom of the armhole. Run a basting "thread" (piece of wool) the length off the armhole, making sure not to veer out of the one vertical stitch you have chosen as the side "seam." With a small stitch and loose tension, machine stitch once (or twice) each side of the basting thread. You now cut down the basting. Gasp! The opening seems larger than the sleeve top! Not to worry—that is the nature of the knitting; once cut, it tends to take a deep breath and expand. Allow approximately one third of the body width for each shoulder and the remaining one third for the neck opening. Sew up the shoulder seams to create an armhole. Pin the sleeve to the body and sew it in from the right side. Because of the relationship of stitches to rows (you are sewing sleeve stitches to body rows) you may either sew a sleeve stitch to a "piece of body"—easing the body to the sleeve when necessary. Or you may choose to (rather laboriously) count the 5 stitches to 7 rows ratio and sew *1:1, 1:2, 1:1, 1:2, 1:1; rep from *.

To the above basic guidelines, there are a myriad of small, satisfying finishing details and techniques you can add. The cut edge of the armhole may bother you. For this problem there are several solutions.

You may gently steam the cut edge towards the sleeve (it wants to fold back on the body, but bend it to your will), and sew it down neatly with herringbone stitch.

If you do not mind a bit of added thickness, you may knit a narrow strip of fabric and appliqué it over the cut edge. Or, when the sleeve has been completed, do not bind off, but continue to knit around (in one color) for a few inches. This will serve as a built-in facing to be sewn down over the cut edge when the time comes. To this last option there are several sub-options: you may want stockinette or reverse stockinette to show on the inside. Also, to obviate the bulk a bit, I like to switch to a lighter-weight wool for the facing.

Traditional Norwegian hand-knit sweater made of natural cream and black wool.

You may weave the shoulders invisibly, but this is generally not recommended for a fairly hefty sweater, as the weight of the sleeves will tend to drag and stretch them. You may like the three-needle bind-off worked from the inside; it looks rather like weaving from a distance, but has a nice firm bound-off edge hidden inside. Or—make no bones about the fact of a seam, and accentuate it by binding off the body stitches and sewing the bound-off seams together. This maneuver may be further accentuated by the addition of a third color. How about finishing the black and cream sleeve and body tops by binding off in bright red and sewing the bound-off seams in red. The use of a third color was (I believe) introduced in lieu of the embroidered felt for decoration.

Your neck treatment choices include: boatneck, hem, turtleneck or a "Norwegian neck," which is simply a flap of garter stitch knitted onto the back edge of the neck opening. After a few inches, bind off and fold the corners of the flap to the front neck edge. Sew them down.

These traditional garments are such a pleasure to knit—and their timeless appearance is so handsome to behold—that I do hope you will consider following in the well-worn needle-path of the scores of enterprising knitters before you. After all, isn't historical continuity one of the most appealing parts of our ancient craft? ⌒

Emma's Bohus Legacy

by Elizabeth Zimmermann

Bohus knitting started in 1939 with hand-knitted socks and mittens, developed into the most beguiling sweaters and caps, and then melted away with the death of Emma Jacobson in 1967. If you have a Bohus sweater or cap on your shelf, preserve it reverently and leave it to a museum in your will.

The province of Bohuslan is in southwest Sweden and has many quarries. In the 1930s, trade was slow and many stonecutters were out of work. Their wives went to Göteborg to ask Emma Jacobson, the governor's wife, for help. It was Emma who thought of combining the knitting skills of the country women with her own gift for color and design. She supplied wool and designs, and the miners' wives knitted socks and mittens. The items were then sold to various dealers, and the profits went to the knitters.

As time passed, this cottage industry grew to include sweaters designed by Emma and a bevy of artists who became attracted to the organization. Among them were Vera

In our century, we've experienced the special birth and demise of a beautiful folk art: Bohus knitting. Pronounced boo-hus, the "u" in "hus" being that extraordinary Swedish "u," not quite the French "u," but near enough. Do you know how to do the French "u"? Say "ee," and leave your tongue where it is as you move your lips into a kiss. You've got it!

Bjurström, Anna-Lisa Mannheimer Lunn, Annika Malmström-Bladini, Kerstin Olson and Karin Ivarsson.

Emma's designs were worked geometrically with two colors of wool, but gradually sweaters were embellished with yokes and decorations of unimaginable beauty in a multiplicity of colors in both knit and purl stitches. In order to do justice to these designs, the very best materials were necessary. Wool was brought from Finland and sent to Italy to be specially spun and sometimes mixed with rabbit hair.

The lovely Bohus garments became world-famous, and tourists (among them me) flocked to the dear little shop on the main street in Göteborg. All I (foolish woman) thought that I could afford was a lovely cap decorated with black, rust, brown, blue, light brown and orange on a natural gray background. It has been worn and worn for thirty years and has, of course, faded. But on the inside, one can still decipher the original colors (I'm liable to wear it either side out).

Sometimes I'm strongly tempted to try and make out the exact mixture of colors and knit, purl and slipped stitches which blend to make the design, but I pull myself up short. Those directions surely exist, somewhere, and one day Bohus designs will resurrect.

For the moment, they've vanished, with their blend of design, texture and color (sometimes a new color will be purled on a stockinette stitch's right side). You must resist the impulse to copy. Emma and her designers must be left to rest in peace with their lovely work.

Those who have inquiring minds and the gift of creation (which we all possess) may like to take advantage of the following notes:

1. Use the very best wool/rabbit hair yarn you can find.

2. Work in the round, using a 24"/60cm needle for sweaters and a 16"/40cm needle for caps.

3. Keep the designs as small and simple as possible.

4. Vary the colors as you will, but *never* work with more than two colors at once.

5. Never carry the wool more than 5 stitches.

6. Occasionally use purled stitches, spaced regularly, when changing to a new color.

7. When you feel it's absolutely necessary to use three colors in one round, don't. The third color may have a round all to itself, the other stitches being slipped (purlwise, of course) between its incidence.

In 1969, Bohus closed its doors. It was impossible to find another Emma who would work for the love of it. The quarries prospered, and therefore, the knitters no longer needed money. And, perhaps the public started to long for large, loose, squarish sweaters. Who can tell? But Bohus knitting still lives in collections, in museums, in special boxes—wrapped in tissue paper, to be worn on ceremonial occasions.

Art Deco labels identify authentic Bohus sweaters, which are treasured by their owners.

Seemingly Seams

Clever ploys for knitters in the round

by Elizabeth Zimmermann

A Phoney Seam may be added as a finishing touch to a seamless garment knitted on circular needles. "Phoney" was one of a generous handful of words I had to learn when immigrating to the United States. After all these years, I just looked it up. It is derived from Irish: a brass ring sold as a gold one! Well!

This brings me to circular knitting, which to my mind is the ideal way to knit a garment—in the mode of the ancient, traditional knitters from all cultures—as it avoids sewing-up, which is very frequently a nuisance, since knitting in pieces demands certain skills with which a knitter is not necessarily endowed, and into which I will not go. We circular knitters have to endure occasional bits of guff from back-and-forth knitters about our lack of seams; they have been heard to remark that our sweaters "don't hang right."

Let us, then, master the simple but beguiling art of adding fold lines (or Phoney Seams) to our knitted circular garments at the underarms of the body and sleeves by

The art of improvising elegant-looking fold lines on circular knits is quite simple and effective. Here is a basic technique plus a couple of variations.

means of the humble crochet hook. (They could be made by slipping the "seam" stitch every second round, but this is not always easy to remember, so let's save the whole technique as an exciting reward to be indulged in when all the knitting is done and naught remains but the finishing.)

Before casting-off, or weaving at the underarms, find the exact center-underarm stitch on body and sleeves. At these points drop this center stitch all the way down to the ribbing or hem. You have achieved a formidable runner, or "ladder." Put a crochet hook through the lowest stitch and hook the first two threads of the ladder through it. Then one thread through the two. Then two through the one. And so on up to the top. You have made a Phoney Seam and—notice how reluctantly the stitch dropped down—you have probably eliminated forever the trauma about dropped stitches.

There are now one-third fewer rows or rounds on this vertical stitch, which makes it hump itself up slightly in a positively magic fashion. It will *stay* humped up, looking as if it were pressed in for the life of the garment, providing easy folding and an elegant appearance.

There are two variations of this technique if you are working in garter stitch. The rate of hooking up will be faster: *two threads through two threads* all the way up. This yields a single, vertical stockinette-stitch seam line, which adds a snappy, tailored look to a garter-stitch garment.

The second variation was discovered at Knitting Camp, and is useful if you seek a *reversible* Phoney Seam on garter-stitch knitting. After the stitch has been dropped (this is for garter stitch *only*), you will find that your "ladder" will easily divide into two sections: a series of *front* and *back* strands. Now, hook up all the front strands on the right side, one at a time (which in reality is every other strand), then hook up all the back strands on the wrong side, one at a time (which is also every other strand). Reversible Phoney Seam! This method will be thicker than the other two, and will *not* cause the fabric to fold.

Phoney Seams needn't only be used for seam lines. I have also used them as practical and decorative vertical lines in the design of a sweater. In one instance, where the spokes of a yoke-decreasing began on my Box-the-Compass design (using that lovely double-decrease of slip two together knitwise, knit one, pass two slip stitches over), I was displeased by the small bump that appeared where the double-decrease suddenly began in the middle of a field of stockinette stitch. The solution was to install Phoney Seams all the way up the body of the sweater (first having let the stitch run down, of course) which melted into the double-decreases, eliminated the bumps and added immeasurably to the styling of the garment.

Phoney Seams are very effective on either stockinette stitch or garter stitch, but they are not applicable for color or texture patterns unless planned for in advance.

So, go for the brass ring! Try Phoney Seams. ⌒

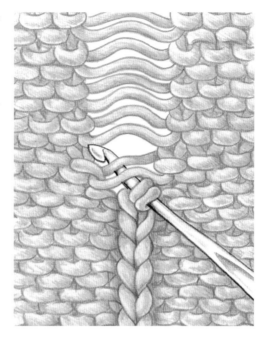

To create a Phoney Seam, drop a stitch and crochet it back up the ladder. On garter stitch, the Phoney Seam is hooked up two threads at once.

Essay: The Moebius Ring

Knitting a twisted circle of intrigue

by Elizabeth Zimmermann

It has been advanced that its principle embodies the Riddle of the Universe.

The collar of this sweater, from the Winter 2001/02 issue, is a Moebius ring.

Some years ago at a knitting workshop in the Twin Cities, a voice piped up asking if I had any opinion on the Moebius Ring. I admitted ignorance, and the questioner proceeded to perform a piece of sheer magic: She showed us a long strip of paper (a yard long by 2 inches wide), gave it half a twist and taped the ends firmly together. Alright, we said, so what? Alright, she said, which is the inside and which the outside of this paper circle? She placed her finger on the "front," and without removing it from that surface, traced the entire circle, inside and out, and lo! The front and back were the same…try it and see. She showed us that the right-hand edge of the piece of paper (or the left-hand one if you prefer) was *the only edge it had*. We were struck practically speechless; this demonstration had all the earmarks of a miracle.

We were told that this ring was the discovery of an 18th-century German mathematician/topologist, August Ferdinand Moebius. The theory has been advanced that its principle embodies the riddle of the universe, and this certainly makes sense to me, ignorant of science as I am. However, I am not ignorant of knitting, and my second thought was—why not knit one?

Since I produce nearly all my knitting on circular needles, I could not resist casting stitches onto a round needle, then "join being careful *to twist*." Alas, that does not work, as it gives the knitting a 360-degree spiral when only a 180-degree turn is required. Try again. With a #10/6mm needle, I cast on some stitches in 2-ply Icelandic wool and knitted straight for about 55"/140cm, gave it half a twist (180 degrees), wove the beginning to the end, and produced—wonders—the Moebius Ring.

To knit your own Moebius Ring you have several texture-stitches to choose from. Be sure you select a reversible one (as both sides of the ring will show at the same time), and consider the ease with which the stitch will weave to itself. We have made them in garter stitch, mistake stitch, lace, seed stitch and ribbing. It is garter stitch I recommend, as it is simple to knit and can be woven perfectly. A beginner can make a strip of garter stitch, twist it, connect the ends, and produce the Riddle of the Universe for a very first project!

The selvage (singular!), when completed, looks a bit lonesome. You may border it with I-cord; either built-in or applied in a contrasting color; I offer directions for both.

This is the warmest imaginable piece of headgear. Put it around your head as a scarf; the twist will lie nice and flat under your coat. Or, allow the twist to twist and pull the resulting loop over your head for a combination scarf/hat.

THE ENDLESS SEAMLESS ONE-SURFACED ONE-EDGED SCARF/HAT

Materials: About 9oz. of thick wool, or 4oz. of thin wool. A largish needle (#8–10/5–6mm); for once gauge

is not critical. Cast on about 8–10" worth of stitches. Use invisible cast on, or be prepared to pick out regular casting on to facilitate weaving when finished. Work back and forth in all knit.

Built-in I-cord border: *K to last 3 sts, wool forward (wyif), slip 3 purlwise, turn. Repeat from *.

At about 50–55", pull out the invisible casting on (or unpick regular casting on) to reveal a row of stitches. Give one end of the piece half a turn and weave.

To heighten the mysterious appearance of the ring, you may want to edge it in a contrasting color with applied I-cord. In that case, omit the purlwise slipped stitches. Slip each first stitch and knit each last stitch. When piece is finished and woven, with a smaller double-pointed needle, pick up one stitch for each ridge (about 12 at a time). At right-hand edge of double-pointed needle, cast on 3 sts. *K2, slip 1, k1 picked-up stitch, psso. Replace the 3 sts onto left-hand needle and repeat from *. This makes a spectacular selvage and you arrive back where you started—yes! Only one edge! Weave the 3 I-cord stitches to each other. That's it. ⌒

Above directions were previously in Elizabeth Zimmermann's *Wool Gathering* and are reprinted by permission of Schoolhouse Press, 6899 Cary Bluff, Pittsville, WI 54466.

The Design Process, Part 1

How sweater patterns begin to take shape

by Margaret Bruzelius

This is the first in a series of four articles on the art of sweater design. The first one explores the "dialogue" between a designer and her yarns.

The first question people ask when they find out that I design sweaters is, "Where do you get your ideas?" Of course nearby sources, such as motifs in a rug, architectural details or designs from old magazines or knitting books can all give rise to new ideas. This process is part of a designer's stock in trade: At least half of the work is simply keeping his or her eyes open for inspiration.

But there is also a more subtle and important design process: understanding the yarn itself. This process is inherently sensuous: It involves squeezing the skein, rolling one strand between your fingers, smelling it, even listening to it when you squeeze it. (Some yarns have a wonderful crunch). Any successful knit design requires that the yarn be suited to the garment, and if you look at it closely, the yarn will tell you how it should best be used. It is the yarn's message to the knitter.

I remember, for example, being given an assignment to sketch and swatch for a novelty summer yarn, a slightly nubby rayon and cotton mix. I struggled and struggled but produced nothing that I thought was particularly good. A few days later, I met another designer wearing a beautiful sweater. "What a great sweater," I said. "What's the yarn?" To my dismay, she named the yarn with which I had struggled for a week—to her, it had spoken loudly and clearly, while I had never gotten the message at all.

Sketches and swatches are often, however, the appropriate beginning for a design. When you have decided on the yarn or yarns, you must experiment with different stitches and needle sizes. If you have thought of some interesting detail, you usually try it out in your swatch, which is where the dialogue between designer and yarn takes place. When you are swatching, you are envisioning how a yarn will work in a particular garment, how it will react to a certain kind of stitch, even how it will wear in the future. It's better to learn on the swatch that the yarn splits than on the garment. You may well want to use it anyway, but you might want to avoid difficult

stitches that will show the splitting or slow you down. When I design, I discard many swatches because they don't look as attractive as I thought they would, but even though I don't use them, the swatches teach me more and more about the yarn.

With your yarn, pattern books and needles of different sizes handy, you can begin to design. Describing the process according to each fiber, I will try to show how I work and what cues I take from each type of yarn.

WOOL

This fiber is the knitter's friend—warm, resilient, ranging from the softest, finest lamb's wool to the thickest, coarsest yarns still stuck with burrs. In fact, wool is so familiar that our dialogues have been reduced to the sort of inchoate "uh-huhs" that punctuate the conversation of old friends; we don't need to say everything out loud. But there is still a process of getting to know the new varieties, and it seems as though there's always one available.

I begin by squeezing and smelling the skein—the scent of wool is so enticing that I always want to knit right away. Then I look at the yarn: Is it tightly spun, with strands that have a very defined line, or loosely spun, with the fibers emerging softly and giving it a blurrier look? Is it fine or heavy? This examination tells me which needle size to use, and gives me an idea of what stitch patterns I could try. A beautifully defined yarn, for example, could be wonderful in plain stockinette stitch, because the strength of its line will give this or any other standard stitch such clarity that it will look bold and exciting. Or, if I want to be fancy—and knit designers always do—I could use a Guernsey pattern or a knit/purl combination, because the pattern will stand out very clearly. A very fine yarn will make me think of lace, because its fineness calls for a delicate stitch and because such a stitch will make the work go faster. A really heavy yarn will make me think of jackets for shepherds in the mountains—something heavy and warm to snuggle into on a cold day in the country.

Whatever the weight, wool's resiliency allows tremendous freedom in design. It will not stretch out like other fibers, which means that I can design something large and heavy without worrying that it will grow as it is worn. Wool's ability to hold its shape is also an important consideration if I am thinking of a pattern that needs to be blocked out—it will remain that way. Wool generally wears well, without pilling excessively or fraying in normal wear. As a result, almost any design is possible. I even like designing with wool for summer—soft and light lamb's wool yarns make terrific light sweaters to fight that air conditioning chill—but I am usually frustrated by the modern knitter's horror of knitting on size 3/3¼mm needles.

Today, technological advances have given wool even greater flexibility. The wonderful new Superwash wools, for instance, make it much more practical than previously for use in children's designs. (I am convinced, with no scientific basis, that more people could wear wool as adults if they got used to it as children.) It seems that there are also more soft wools that can lie against the skin without making it itch. Consider, too, the many exciting combinations of wool and other fibers. My favorite is wool and silk, which has a luster and definition that suffuse everything you make it in. The wonderful wiry heathers have some of that Scottish Highland feel to them—not yarns to be worn close to the skin, but yarns full of character, with a crisp hand that perks up color patterns and makes bold textures stand out. Heavy, almost rope-like wools make me think of short, boxy jackets with deep pockets and high collars. And because wool takes color well, a designer can take advantage of a wide palette.

COTTON

This is probably the second largest category of yarn. Like wool, it's a great year-round fiber, even though you see it mostly in the summer. Cotton, which soaks up color and can have tremendous luster, lends itself to the brilliant sweaters we want to have when the sun is out. But squeezing a skein tells me a few other things as well. First, it is not as resilient as wool, so large sweaters can stretch. I usually solve this problem by throwing them in the washing machine and dryer, something you should attempt only after testing the process on a swatch. Cotton's comparative lack of resiliency can sometimes also lead to sizing problems, as adding width to a sweater will also add weight, making the garment appear droopy instead of full. These problems, however, can usually be solved by substituting a more loosely spun yarn for a denser one.

In general, cottons are divided into three categories: shiny, usually mercerized; unmercerized; and novelties, often mixes of cotton and another fiber (acrylic and rayon are two favorites), which have little nubs or knots or other kinds of decoration on them. The shiny yarns usually say lace to me, and since we associate cotton with summer, lace means cool for hot days. Because I am a designer with a yen for plain yarns, I usually combine these with novelties, perhaps in a striped or yoke effect. I

love cables in cotton, but since cotton gets heavy and will stretch, I plan to block out cotton cables more than wool cables. This gives width without adding weight. There is also a way to do ribs to avoid undue stretching: I usually work a twisted rib, which holds better than the usual stitch. I work fewer stitches in the rib than I might for a wool sweater, and add them back in when I begin the body. And if I'm really desperate, I'll use one of the new elastic yarns and thread it through the back of the finished rib to help pull it in. (Remember to run the washer/dryer test on a swatch with the elastic if you plan this method of care.) But, finally, my attitude toward cotton's stretch is to design around it. I don't try to make ribs pull in a lot because I know they won't stay, and besides, summer sweaters should be loose.

Because cotton has such strength of definition, I also think details: collars, plackets, pockets and little lace trims. And since it's washable, I love to work it in white, which combines with cotton's crispness to create a clean, fresh look—the perfect antidote to summer wilt.

Cotton's easy care and affinity for color also make it the yarn of choice for children's clothing. When sizes are small, weight is usually not a problem, and you may even be glad if the sweater stretches out for a few more months' wear. I have used it successfully for little hats to be worn under hoods for heavier caps—it's soft and gives another layer of warmth, especially important if your infants were born as bald as mine were.

When designing with cotton, remember that successful dialogue means that you listen. If it's saying, "I'm cotton, I stretch," it's a mistake to respond by saying, "But I want you to be wool."

SILK

Lustrous and, well, silky, a skein of silk has a wonderful crunchy feel, a bite beneath its soft exterior. It shares with cotton an almost total lack of resiliency and is also quite expensive, which means that you don't want to design huge items. Although we wear silk year-round, it is warmer than cotton in the summer, and more fragile. So when I design with it, I think short and small, often considering sleeveless looks or styles with three-quarter-length sleeves, which will help prevent frayed cuffs. Short or capped sleeves also help avoid under-the-arm pilling. Because silk has a natural elegance and takes color wonderfully, I try to design sophisticated tops in brilliant shades that will show off the luster. Here again, delicate cables, which I like to mix with pointelles, both show off the yarn and keep the weight of the sweater down. In addition, cables and slip-stitch patterns will help control stretching, as will the kind of two-color pattern that is worked only one color at a time, because the yarn stretched across the back will control the give of the knitted yarn.

Now that a very groomed look is in fashion, I consider silk a natural for little tops to be worn under a jacket. When working with silk, you can never forget the bite that gives it its character, so that even though it clings to the body it always looks stylish.

RAYON

Shinier than cotton and softer than silk, rayon is seen mostly in blends. To me, it has little individuality, but it certainly adds drape and softness when mixed with other yarns, particularly cotton, which can get stiff. In fact, yarn manufacturers often take advantage of the contrast between matte cotton and shiny rayons with cotton/rayon blends, which have a sparkle and three-dimensional appeal that can enhance any simple stitch.

Like cotton and silk, rayon has little or no resiliency. It is frequently seen in ribbon yarn, where it displays its softness and affinity for color to the fullest. And since the new rayons are usually hand-washable, they don't need as much care as their predecessors.

MOHAIR

With its sturdy fuzziness and love of color, mohair can be used for anything. Like wool, it is resilient, so you can be very inventive and not worry about the yarn supporting the stitch. The fuzziness, however, can obscure delicate stitches, so when I squeeze a skein of mohair, I think of bold, graphic patterns created with texture or color. Because of its springy quality, mohair holds shape well, so it is especially good for all sorts of cables. But it works best when used simply—in strong, not overly complicated patterns. One exception to this is the very fine and not very fuzzy mohair that you can sometimes find—this is a true luxury yarn and makes wonderful laces and delicate patterns.

ALPACA

Soft, warm and silky, alpaca is a dream fiber. It doesn't soak up color as others do, but it has a combination of fuzzy softness and luster that I find irresistible. One of my all-time favorite designs was done in a combination of lightweight alpaca and silk in a lace stitch, in which the luxury of the yarn and the delicacy of the stitch complemented each other in a sweater that was both delicate and warm. Alpaca, in fact, is so warm that textured stitches that hold in a great deal of heat will be too much for most people. Because it is usually quite heavy as well, it is better to think of stitches that don't add a lot of bulk. If you knit in alpaca, you can do a very light stitch, a pointelle or lace, and still end up with a warm sweater. Alpaca also wears well, so you don't have to design around wear points.

CASHMERE, CAMEL'S HAIR, ANGORA

These are the ultimate luxury yarns, and a dream to work with. Cashmere and camel hair are also tough fibers and can be used for almost anything. Angora is more delicate, and its puff-ball fluffiness gives it an enticing, otherworldly quality. Because these yarns are so expensive, I don't get to work with them as much as I would like. But since any yarn that costs a lot is worth special effort, a sweater of mine in these fibers would be highly detailed and take a long time to make. Such gorgeous materials demand attention and love. They should be heirlooms.

SYNTHETICS

There are so many types of synthetics that it is impossible to describe their good and bad points generally. The most important point to remember is that the new ones really are a big improvement over the old. Many of the new acrylics, for example, have superior body and elasticity and do not knit up like cardboard. If you are sending a child to college or someplace else where he or she will have to do the laundry, a good-looking, easy-to-care-for acrylic sweater might be a sensible choice; you can save your efforts in wool for when you're sure he or she won't throw them in the washer and dryer.

Of course, synthetics remain the fibers of choice for people with sensitivity to natural ones. And don't turn away from blends, either—some of the new acrylics have been blended with cotton to give them a new softness and lightness that allow a knitter increased flexibility in designing.

Whatever fiber you use, remember that knitting should be a sensuous and enjoyable experience. Let yourself feel the yarn first: Every minute spent getting to know your material enhances not only your design, but your pleasure. ⌒

The Design Process, Part 2

The basics of sketching and scale-drawing

by Mari Lynn Patrick

In the previous article we introduced our series on designing. This process begins with the yarn—the ultimate inspiration for all sweaters.

In this article, we'll discuss more about yarn selection. Then, before you pick up your needles and actually begin to knit, we'll show you how to sketch your sweater design, taking your body measurements and then making a schematic drawing—a scale drawing on graph paper. Of course, this process wouldn't be complete without the essential step of making a gauge swatch.

In some ways, designing hand knits is a simple process: It follows many of the basic rules you work with each time you knit a sweater. Designing, however, requires that you expand on the basics that you may have been taking for granted.

Selecting your yarn helps you to visualize the finished appearance of the sweater you plan to design. Still, you can make a sketch before or after this step. Knit designing is not an exact science. Be flexible and allow your creativity a chance to grow.

You must, however, make an absolutely accurate gauge swatch, experimenting with *all* the stitch or color patterns that you plan to incorporate in your design.

Once you've chosen your yarn, the route is clear. It goes from sketching to stitch-and-row gauge swatching to rendering a schematic on graph paper.

Next, make a mental or written notation of all your pertinent *body measurements* to ensure the best possible fit. And if you plan to make an intricate colorwork or stitch pattern design, you will have to make a chart detailing your stitch or color patterns.

YARN TYPE/WEIGHT

The more you knit with varieties of yarns, the more you realize that different yarn types and yarn weights give a distinctly different look and "hand" when knit. This is why substituting yarns of the same weight may not work when the yarns are of different types. The best way to learn about yarn types and weights is to knit mounds of swatches for your own swatch library. It is helpful to use a good stitch dictionary with a variety of stitch patterns. Tag each swatch with yarn, needle sizes and gauge information. This will be an enormous help when you begin your design selection. Experiment with a yarn knit on various needle sizes until you are satisfied with the results.

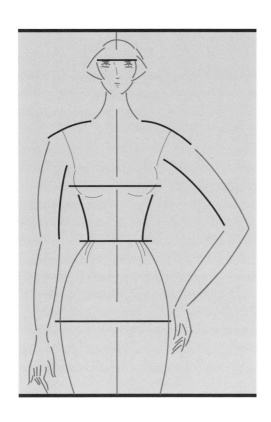

SKETCH

Always remember that a sketch is just a line drawing of how you want your finished sweater to look—it doesn't need to be a sophisticated fashion illustration. The sketch must simply portray the proportions that you want in your finished sweater.

Our model silhouette [left] will help you execute an accurate sketch with the proper proportions. Take tracing paper and place it over the model. Draw the basic outline, then fill in the particulars such as ribbings, sleeve type and neckline. If you are planning to knit complicated patterns at various points, just sketch them in (you'll transfer them to the schematic later with more accurate measurements). This method of sketching may not seem artistic, but the end results will help you determine your design's proper proportions.

GAUGE SWATCH

The gauge swatch is the most crucial part of designing, and it can also be one of the most enjoyable steps in the process. As you experiment with colors, stitches and textures, you can see your ideas take shape. Once you have selected your stitch, you may also want to use your gauge swatch for experimenting with decorative decreases or special edgings.

Make the gauge swatch large enough to see actual finished results. When you work with highly cabled or textured patterns, measurements sometimes change from a small piece of knitting to an actual garment piece such as a back. A 4", 6" or 8" swatch is often needed. Include all of the stitches you plan to use in your swatch, or make several swatches. In designing a cabled sweater, you will need to know both the gauge over the cables and the gauge in reverse or stockinette stitch. You can work in one of two ways: Either take an average gauge over both stitches, or get a separate gauge of each stitch and use these gauges to determine the number of stitches needed for your design. Be careful not to include stitch patterns in your designs that have varying row gauges. Garter stitch, for example, has a different row gauge from stockinette stitch using the same yarn and needle size. If you plan to use these stitches together, it will be necessary to compensate by using short rows. This may be very complicated for a beginning designer.

Fair Isle and colorwork patterns may have stitch and row gauges that differ from stockinette stitch in a solid color. If you plan to incorporate both colorwork and stockinette stitch in a design, you will have to compensate for the difference in gauges. This can be achieved either by changing needle size or the number of stitches used in each pattern band. Generally, the stitch gauge is the most important factor, as it determines your finished sweater width. When working with patterns that are not clearly defined, row gauge is not crucial. However, if your sweater design has a specific repeat or pattern, it is necessary to consider the row gauge when planning the finished total length.

BODY AND FINISHED MEASUREMENTS

A careful calculation of your body measurements is one of the best ways to ensure a custom fit for your design. See sizing chart opposite.

Make a chart of all your body measurements: bust, waist, hips, wrist, upper arm, natural depth of armhole, shoulder width, width of neck at back and sleeve length from wrist to underarm. Take a length measurement from the shoulder at the neck to the waist or desired length. Be sure not to pull the tape measure too tightly when taking these measurements.

Once you have your measurements, you can begin to apply them to your design. In a sweater, the focal point of fit is usually the bust. To get a general idea of fit at the bustline, take a look at the fit chart [opposite page]. Find your bust measurement (shown at the left side of this chart). The measurements at the right of the chart show average measurements for various fits. Subtracting the difference between your bust measurement and the desired fit will give you an amount called *ease*. This term refers to the additional width built into your sweater to allow for comfort. Depending on the amount of ease added, your sweater will be looser or tighter. With a 36" bust, for example, the measurement for a standard-fitting sweater is 38." Thus, to make a standard-fitting sweater, you'll need to add 2" of ease. This is where your creativity as a designer comes in. You can add the 2" of ease throughout the sweater or change the amount of ease at various points—it all depends on the type of style you plan to design. The amount of ease isn't a hard and fast rule.

SCHEMATICS

Once you have completed your sketch, draw a schematic, a more exact rendering, on graph paper [right]. The schematic drawing is necessary to calculate stitches and rows for planning your design. In drawing this diagram, count one square of graph paper as 1" in either direction (width and length). If you were designing a sweater 20" wide with a 3" rib, you would count 20 squares and draw the lower edge line. Mark dots at all the key points (such as neckline curves and cap shaping) that define the shape of the garment. The dots can then be connected as a solid line. Ribbing is usually drawn as it looks, tighter than the actual sweater body. In the above example, you would allow 20 squares for the rib, and draw down 2" (or 2 squares) on either side to account for the depth of the rib. If measuring a fraction, use a fraction of a graph square. Instead of writing out your pattern, you may want to add all the essentials to this graph-paper schematic. This can easily become your working pattern. At this point, work with your stitch and row gauge to plot out the number of ribs or cable repeats needed to fit into the space allowed by the design. It may be necessary to redetermine a cable length or width or rib width to best fit into the look of the sketch. ⁓

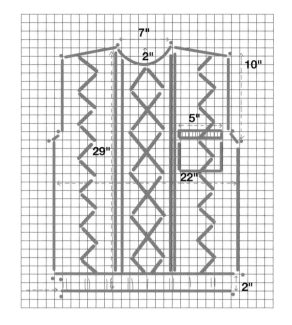

BODY MEASUREMENT	FIT & CORRESPONDING FINISHED BUST MEASUREMENTS				
Bust Sizes	**Very Close-Fitting** A very body-hugging effect	**Close-Fitting** A body-contoured effect	**Standard-Fitting** A body-skimming effect	**Loose-Fitting** A straight-hanging effect	**Oversized** A full, roomy effect
32" (81cm)	**30"** (76cm)	**32–33"** (81–84cm)	**34"** (86cm)	**36"** (91cm)	**37" or more** (94cm or more)
34" (86cm)	**32"** (81cm)	**34–35"** (86–89cm)	**36"** (91cm)	**38"** (96cm)	**39" or more** (99cm or more)
36" (91cm)	**34"** (86cm)	**36–37"** (91–94cm)	**38"** (96cm)	**40"** (101cm)	**41" or more** (104cm or more)
38" (96cm)	**36"** (91cm)	**38–39"** (96–99cm)	**40"** (101cm)	**42"** (106cm)	**43" or more** (109cm or more)
40" (101cm)	**38"** (96cm)	**40–41"** (101–104cm)	**42"** (106cm)	**44"** (112cm)	**45" or more** (114cm or more)

The Design Process, Part 3

Figuring stitch amounts and pattern construction

by Carla S. Patrick

In Part 2 of "The Design Process" [see previous article], you learned how to sketch a sweater, decide on the measurements, plot them on graph paper and make necessary gauge swatches.

Now that the preliminary work is done, you are ready to take the next step—to figure out exactly how to knit the pieces. Continuing to use the design idea sketched in the previous article as an example, we will take you step by step through the calculations.

The first—and absolutely essential—step is to determine your gauge. As shown in the photographs, we have made three different swatches: 1) reverse stockinette stitch (measured on the knit side), 2) the zigzag pattern and 3) the center diamond pattern. Although this may seem tedious and unnecessary, it is crucial to make all three swatches, since gauges may vary over different patterns. You should make the swatch in reverse stockinette stitch first, experimenting with needle sizes until you get the tension

Here are step-by-step instructions on exactly how to work stitch and row gauge into the size and shape requirements of your sweater-in-progress.

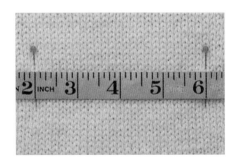

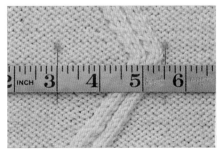

The stockinette stitch gauge, as shown on top, is 6 stitches and 8 rows to 1 inch. The zigzag pattern, below, measured over 16 stitches, equals 2½ inches.

you like. Once you have determined the appropriate needle size, you can then make the other two swatches.

In our example, using a medium-weight wool with a size 6 needle, the gauge over reverse stockinette stitch is 6 stitches and 8 rows to 1". As you can see from the photo, we have measured the entire center cable panel, which is 7" and has 42 stitches. We have done the same with the zigzag pattern over 16 stitches, which equals 2½". The row gauge of these two patterns is identical to the reverse stockinette stitch gauge of 8 rows to 1". This is important to ensure the consistency of the row gauges.

Ordinarily we would begin our calculations with the back of the sweater. But since we want the diamond pattern to end with a full repeat before the front neck shaping, we will start with the front.

Begin by calculating the pattern placement on the front. This will determine the total number of stitches. Use the schematic drawing from your original sketch and place all your patterns and measurements on the drawing, as we have done.

The width of the front piece above the ribbing is 22". Since the diamond panel is going to be in the center of the piece, and we know it measures 7" wide, we can determine the width of the fabric on either side of the diamond panel by subtracting 7" from 22" and dividing by two. Thus 22" minus 7" equals 15", divided by two equals 7½". So there will be 7½" of fabric on each side of the cable.

On each side of the center cable there is a zigzag pattern that is placed in the center of each shoulder. At this point it is necessary to jump ahead to figure out the width of each shoulder after the armhole decreases. The two shoulders plus the neck width add up to the cross back (measurement from shoulder to shoulder), which we know to be 20". The neck width is 7" on the schematic. Therefore, 20" minus 7" equals 13", divided by two equals 6½" for each shoulder.

To center the zigzag pattern on the shoulders, subtract 2½" (the width of the zigzag in the gauge swatch) from 6½". The result is 4", which divided by two equals 2". Work 2" in reverse stockinette stitch on either side of the zigzag above the armholes, and 3" at the side edges below the armholes. As you can see, the width of the sweater is determined by the particular patterns and their gauges.

The row gauge of the patterns is important in determining the length of the sweater. In our example, the row gauge is 8 rows to 1". The desired total length is 30". When you subtract the 2" of ribbing, that leaves 28" for the length of the cable patterns. One full diamond cable repeat is 52 rows. Divide that by 8 (rows per inch), and the result is 6½"—the total height of one diamond pattern.

Let's start with five repeats of the diamond. By multiplying 5 times 6½" we find that our length above the ribbing (not including the neck drop) will be 32½", which according to our schematic is much too long. Four full repeats would give us 26". That leaves exactly 2" to work the neck shaping. However, if it doesn't work out so perfectly, it may be necessary to adjust the finished length of the piece in order to fit in a full repeat, or you can add or subtract ribbing from the lower edge if it's only a matter of an inch or so.

Now you are ready to draw the patterns on the schematic and determine the number of stitches you will need by using the various stitch gauges. As you can see from the schematic, there will be a total of 134 stitches and 22" above the ribbing: 18 stitches (3") in reverse stockinette stitch (rev St st), 16 stitches (2½") in zigzag pattern, 12 stitches (2") in rev St st, 42 stitches (7") in center cable pattern, 12 stitches (2") in

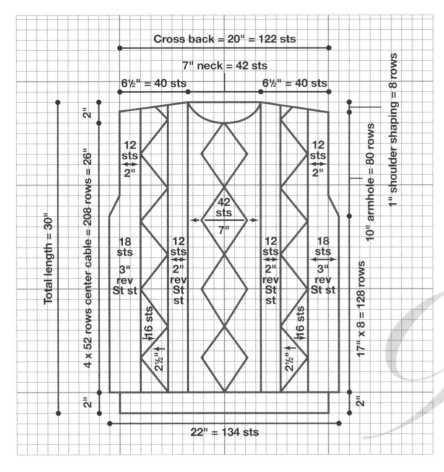

The schematic shows a total of 134 stitches, measuring 22 inches in width, above the ribbing. On either side of a 42-stitch center-cable pattern are 12 stitches in reverse stockinette, then 16 stitches in zigzag, and, at the edges, 18 stitches in reverse stockinette.

rev St st, 16 stitches (2½") in zigzag pattern, 18 stitches (3") in rev St st.

To shape the armholes, decrease 6 stitches (1") on each side for a cross back measurement of 20". For the angled armhole, we decreased 1 stitch each side every other row six times for a total of 122 stitches. Next, figure out the shoulder and neck shaping. For each shoulder you are decreasing 40 stitches (6½"). The shoulder depth is 8 rows (1"). Since you can only bind off from one shoulder on every other row (at the beginning of the row) you need to divide the stitches as evenly as possible over 4 rows. So you bind off 10 stitches from each shoulder edge four times.

The neck shaping is more difficult to calculate. You know that you need to decrease 42 stitches in 16 rows (2") while creating a nice curve. Experiment with graph paper until you find the right curve. To see the actual curve, knitter's graph paper is especially helpful since it corresponds to the actual gauge. For a more general approach, bind off about 3" to 4" worth of stitches at the center, then divide the remaining decreases in half. It is best to bind off 2 to 4 stitches a few times, then 1 stitch until you finish the shaping. For our example, bind off the center 24 stitches (4"), which leaves 9 stitches each side to decrease in 14 rows. After that, bind off from each side 3 stitches once, 2 stitches once, then decrease 1 stitch every other row four times for a total of 42 stitches bound off in 14 rows. Work the 2 remaining rows even. This process takes a little trial and error. When calculating any shaping, be sure always to keep in mind both the stitch and row gauges of each pattern used, and how decreasing in the various patterns will affect the look of the finished piece.

The back piece is worked the same as the front, omitting the neck shaping.

Now that you know the basics of converting inches to stitches, figuring the sleeve is quite simple. Since it is knitted entirely in reverse stockinette stitch, only one gauge is involved.

There are just a few points to remember when working out the sleeve. To get the most accurate sleeve length, take your measurement from the center back neck to the wrist. Subtract half the cross back measurement (10") from this total measurement, add about 1" for ease, and you have your total sleeve length.

As this style has an angled armhole, the width at the top of the sleeve should be twice the armhole depth (10" times 2 equals 20").

You should also shape the top 1" (8 rows) of the sleeve exactly like the armhole shaping—that is, bind off 1 stitch at each end every other row 6 times.

To be sure that your cuff is not too loose or too tight, make a small swatch in ribbing and base the number of stitches on this gauge. ⌒

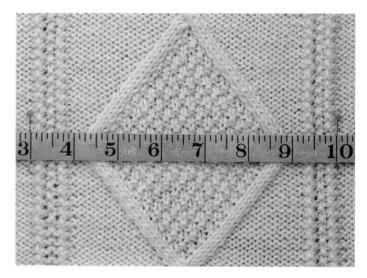

Gauge tends to vary with different patterns, even when yarn and needle size remain the same. So it's essential to measure all patterns in a sweater. Shown here is the entire center cable pattern, which measures 7 inches and has 42 stitches. To get the most accurate reading, do not use the edge of the tape measure, and make sure it is straight.

The Design Process, Part 4

Detailing the finishing phases of sweatermaking

by Nancy J. Thomas

We have been covering the techniques and the sources of inspiration you need to create your own sweater designs. Now, with yarn in hand, you're ready to knit. But before you start knitting, read the following tips, which will make finishing your sweater a breeze.

WHILE KNITTING. When you sew your knit pieces together, they should link together perfectly, and for that reason it is important to measure carefully as you work. If the back is even two or three rows longer than the front, the pieces won't fit together smoothly when you make your seams. Working a selvage stitch at the edges will give you a good base for seaming [see Chapter 4]. Just remember not to include the selvage stitches in your measurements, as these stitches are designed to become part of the seam when your sweater is finished.

The way you bind off at upper edges also helps you to create a smooth seam. A bind-off from the right side of the work makes a neat edge that can be easily sewn. When working shoulder shaping over several rows on the front and back pieces, carefully match your bind-offs for a neater shoulder seam. Working short rows at the shoulder edge rather than binding off stitches makes a smoother seam [see Chapter 7]. When you

Don't drop your guard at the finish line. A great sweater depends on carefully planned edgings, blocking and seaming...the last in a series of articles.

bind off cables, make sure that you do so close to a cable twist, or decrease stitches as you bind off. Otherwise, the seam will spread and your finished measurement will be wider than planned.

GETTING READY TO FINISH. Careful finishing is the most important step in the creation of a professional-looking design. Begin by choosing your sewing yarn. This is usually the yarn from your sweater, but if the sweater yarn is textured, an untwisted roving or a bouclé, it will be necessary to choose some other flat yarn to sew your pieces together. Just remember to pick one of a similar color and with the same fiber content as your original yarn.

Check your pieces for any mistakes or dropped stitches. It is easier to correct errors at this point than after all the seams are sewn. Don't work in your ends yet. If you wait until you have sewn your sweater together, you can work the ends into the seams, rather than weaving the ends into your actual sweater pieces.

BLOCKING. Begin blocking, as we have with our sample sweater, by pinning the pieces to the exact measurements. Don't just guess the measurements. Use your tape measure. Use pins with colored plastic heads, or T-pins that won't get buried in the pieces and become difficult to remove once the knitting is dry. Have enough pins on hand so that you can place them very closely together (about 1"/2.5cm apart). If you don't use enough pins, your seams will scallop and create a wobbly edge for seaming. Don't stretch out the ribbing, unless your design has a straight ribbing rather than one which is pulled in. Pin your pieces on a padded surface. You don't need to have a special blocking board; any flat, thickly padded surface (such as a bed covered with fabric or a towel) will do.

There are several blocking methods, but we find the wet blocking method the best for most sweaters. Always check the yarn ball band before you block. A non-washable yarn should not be wet blocked. Pressing with a dry iron would be a better method. Experiment with a swatch before you work on your actual sweater pieces. You can also use your swatch to test yarn for colorfastness. If the yarn is not colorfast, block with a dry iron. To wet block, begin by spraying each piece with a water sprayer. If necessary, cover the pieces with another cloth to keep your knitting clean as it dries. Allow the pieces to dry thoroughly before removing the pins. You may not be able to block the entire sweater at one time. Take time to block one or two pieces well rather than squeeze the entire sweater onto too small a space.

BEFORE SEAMING. Baste your blocked pieces and try on your garment before the final sewing. This will allow you to see how your finished design will fit. Assuming that you have planned your sweater carefully, major changes should be unnecessary at this point. But sometimes what you have designed on paper may need some minor changes.

You may, for example, need to shorten or lengthen sleeves. This requires various steps, depending on the type of sleeves you make. For instance, if you are making a

capped-sleeve sweater, you will have to rip back to the underarm to add or subtract length. On the other hand, if you are making a dropped-shoulder sweater, you can simply work additional length or rip back to the desired length as long as you don't change the width of the upper arm. For either sleeve, if you have to add substantial length, you may need to refigure your sleeve increases rather than have a long piece worked straight which will create too much extra fabric at the underarm. Remember that you'll need to reblock reworked pieces.

If your sweater body is wider than desired, you can adjust its width by making a slightly wider seam. This isn't a good idea if you want to make a major change, since it will result in a very bulky seam.

GREAT SEAMS. How you sew your sweater together is very important. If sewing has presented problems for you in the past, read "Vogue's Finishing School" [see page 102]. Practice on swatches before you begin to sew your sweater.

THE SEWING ORDER. *Shoulders*: A good place to begin sewing your garment together is at the shoulders. This seam is the foundation of your sweater. A good shoulder seam is important to the look of your garment as well as how it will wear. If you're working with a stretchy yarn, you may wish to reinforce and stabilize this area with seam binding, which can be sewn over the seam. To make a firm shoulder seam, try binding off directly from your knitting needles, by knitting the stitches together [see Chapter 4]. Grafting is another method of joining shoulders. Although there is some debate on this subject, the use of grafting at the shoulder in effect creates "no seam," which is less stable. If you plan to work the neckband with a circular needle, sew both shoulders. Otherwise, sew one shoulder (usually the left one) and leave the other open so that you can work the neckband with straight needles.

Neckband: If you work the neckband after sewing the shoulders but before adding the sleeves, you can avoid having to work with the bulk of the whole garment. Usually neckbands are made with needles the same size as those used for the ribbing of the sweater. If you want to design a special type of neckband, you may want to make a swatch with the needle size you plan to use before you work on your sweater. To pick up evenly around the neck, place pins at even intervals and pick up the same number of stitches between each pinned section. Also use this pinning method to make front bands and neckbands on cardigans. To create a smooth transition when working a neckband in a contrasting color, pick up and knit the first row in the main color, then switch to the contrasting color. Neckbands can be made to the desired height and then bound off, or made double the length and then folded over. The most important part of making a neckband is the bind-off. Choose a flexible bind-off to avoid difficulty in putting the sweater on over your head. You can also make neckbands that are worked separately and then are attached to your sweater. This is slightly more difficult and may require your sewing the band on once or twice to achieve the right fit.

Sleeves: The keys to a neatly sewn sleeve top are careful measuring and pinning or basting the sleeve to your body pieces. If you are adding a dropped-shoulder sleeve, measure down on either side of the shoulder to the correct depth and mark this spot. Place the center of the sleeve top at the shoulder seam and then pin each side to the markers. It is best to work on a flat surface. An angled armhole, such as we have worked in our sample sweater, is done in the same way as the dropped shoulder, with the angle of the sleeve pinned to the underarm angle.

If you are making a sweater with a sleeve cap, once your pieces are complete, pin the sleeve cap to the armhole to check the fit before you begin to block or sew. If the cap doesn't fit smoothly into the armhole, you may need to rip back the sleeve cap

and shorten or lengthen its depth. Don't be discouraged if the fit isn't perfect the first time; it happens to even the most seasoned designers.

BUTTONHOLES AND BANDS. Buttonholes should be just large enough to fit around the button. If you make them wider than the button, they may stretch and constantly unbutton. Of course, you can also reinforce the buttonhole with buttonhole stitches after it has been worked. Buttonholes should be spaced fairly closely, or the band will gap and not lie flat when buttoned. A length of grosgrain ribbon, sewn to the back at the button and the buttonhole bands, will reinforce and stabilize your bands. Buttonholes will have to be cut through the ribbon and then secured with buttonhole stitches.

BUTTONS, BAUBLES AND EMBELLISHMENTS. By adding extras such as buttons, beading or embroidery, you can give a sweater your own creative touch. Unusual buttons and beads are available in wood, horn abalone, porcelain, pewter, cloisonné, shell, leather and so on. For special interest, add buttons in the centers of dot motifs or blocks of color. Use buttons to make fake plackets, cuff treatments or shoulder plackets. Crystal beads or pearls placed at the center of cables or on Aran stitches add a twist to an otherwise traditional-looking sweater. Larger color areas can be knit in as you work, but to create final subtle highlights and shading, work additional embroidery and duplicate stitches with accent colors.

In our "Design Process" series, we've equipped you with lots of new knowledge. You are now ready to journey into a new world of knitting. You may not always be completely satisfied with the results, but each design will teach you something that you didn't know before. You can incorporate these learning experiences into other more successful sweaters, and eventually, working out your own designs will become second nature. ⌒

One-Piece Knitted-on

by Meg Swansen

There are scores of ways to add or incorporate different cardigan edgings into a sweater, and this article will narrowly focus on one of those methods: knitting a one-piece garter-stitch button band onto the cut edge of a circular stocking-stitch sweater. This final addition is fraught with activity and is a rewarding finale to all the hours spent on the garment itself. Also, by knitting the edge directly onto the sweater, you won't have to guess how long to make the strip and can dispense with the sewing.

After the center front steek has been cut, you are ready to knit up all the edge stitches onto one needle: up one side, around the neck and down the other side. Which knit-up method will you use? (By the way, I use the term "knit-up" to describe picking up and knitting as one fluid move: put the needle into a portion of one stitch and hook the working wool back through.)

Isolate a single vertical stitch that runs, uninterrupted, up the front edge to the neck shaping. (I always anticipate this and include a designated knit-up stitch in my original steek allowance, keeping it in the background color throughout.) You may now knit into the L or R half of that vertical stitch, or you may decide to go through both halves of the stitch, or you may dive down through the fabric (either between the two halves of a stitch, or between two stitches) and hook the working wool up from below. The latter is the best way to eliminate distortion of any stitches; it is also ideal if you are working in a contrasting color and want to obviate wrong-side blips.

However, if you want the border to be the same color as the knit-up stitch, begin at the lower left corner and knit up into the left-hand side of the chosen stitch—this not only leaves the right half of the stitch as a pretty little outline detail along the edge but also produces the first garter-stitch ridge that addresses the body most snugly. (If I were to work from the lower *right* corner, there would be a stocking-stitch gap between the body and the border. Yes, I know, picky, picky—but to me, these little details, which most likely will

never be noticed by anyone, are one of the best parts of knitting.)

So you've decided which stitch to knit into, which knit-up method to use and where to begin. Now you will be knitting garter stitch (square) perpendicularly onto stocking stitch (oblong), and you want the border to lie in perfect relationship to the body—neither drooping below the bottom of the sweater nor scrunching up. Elizabeth Zimmermann determined that, when knitting with wool, the perfect ratio in this instance is 2 to 3. So, using a 40"/100cm circular needle, knit into body stitch #1 and #2; skip #3. Knit into #4 and #5; skip #6, and so on. Two stitches for every three rounds.

When you reach the top of the front edge at the neck, you will turn a corner and work in the same direction as the body fabric, so abandon the 2 to 3 ratio and work 1 to 1 across that horizontal plane, then back to 2 to 3 for the side of the neck, 1 to 1 across the back of the neck and mirror image along the other side.

You now have masses of stitches all knitted up onto one needle—both front borders and neck stitches combined—and the sweater front is curled into a circle. Knit back and forth in garter stitch, shaping the neck and adding buttonholes as you go.

MITERED CORNERS: Unless you have made a V-neck, you will want a sharp turn at the top of each front edge. Mark the exact corner stitch (here is where you can flip a coin to choose between the last front edge stitch or the first horizontal neck stitch; match your choice on the other corner) and work an increase on each side of the marked stitch every other row. I put a coilless pin into the corner stitch so I remember to work the increases every time the pin faces me.

If you have shaped a square neck, you may produce a corresponding dart at the inner corners by working a double decrease at that spot every second row (knit to within 1 stitch of the marker, slip 2 tog k'wise, k 1, p2sso).

DETAIL: You may keep the marked corner stitches themselves in stocking stitch by purling them on the inside.

NECK SHAPING: To keep the neck back from flaring,

A garter-stitch border with mitered corners at the neck.

Cardigan Border

Knit-Up Methods

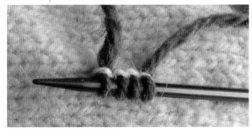

Insert the needle into the **RIGHT SIDE** of each stitch.

Insert the needle into the **LEFT SIDE** of each stitch.

Insert the needle **BETWEEN** each of the stitches.

The result of the pick-up into the **RIGHT SIDE** of each stitch.

The result of the pick-up into the **LEFT SIDE** of each stitch.

Insert the needle **DOWN** through the fabric and hook the wool **UP** from below.

work a subtle decrease after the first or second ridge: K3, K2tog from shoulder to shoulder to eliminate about 1"/2.5cm worth of stitches more or less evenly spaced.

BUTTONHOLES: Most knitters have their favorite buttonhole, and you can find a variety of choices in the various knitting compendiums. If you are still searching for your favorite, experiment with some likely-looking candidates on a swatch and weigh ease of execution against final appearance.

To the common question "How do I figure out how many stitches to put between each buttonhole?" I have an intriguing answer, the brainchild of Mary Rowe (author of the wonderful book *Knitted Tams*), who presented it to us at Knitting Camp in 1984:

$$S = \frac{N - (H \times B) - E}{B - 1}$$

S = the # of stitches between buttonholes

N = the total # of sts on the front edge

H = # of sts used to work each buttonhole

B = total # of buttonholes

E = # of sts at either end

Neat, huh? Thanks, Mary.

BINDING OFF: This is a critical decision, because the final edge must correspond to the vertical tension of the rest of the button band. Sometimes I will bind off in purl, or use a larger-size needle. Or I may use I-cord binding off. In any case, after about 5 or 6 inches (12.5 to 15cm) worth of selvage has been produced, I look at it with a jaundiced eye. Is it pulling up? Is it sagging, or is it just right? Make any necessary adjustments by changing needle size.

I have two favorite methods of binding off. Both give a tidy finish to garter stitch, and both are "unventions" of Elizabeth Zimmermann's.

EZ's **sewn binding off** blends perfectly with garter stitch and is exceedingly elastic even when worked firmly: With a blunt sewing-up needle (not a tapestry needle), go into the first 2 sts on the L needle from R to L and pull the wool through. Now, * go into the first stitch on the L needle from L to R and slip it off. Go into the next 2 sts from R to L and pull the wool through. Repeat from * across all stitches.

EZ's **two- (or three-) stitch I-cord binding off** produces a surprising and beautiful little tube of stocking stitch along the selvage. With working wool, make 2 (or 3) backward loops onto your L needle. *K1 (or 2), k 2 tog tbl (being the last cord stitch and one of the raw sts to be bound off). Replace the 2 (or 3) sts to L needle and repeat from *. You can speed up by not replacing the last stitch; leave it on the R needle and insert the L needle into it and knit. Yes, it will then be twisted, but maintain consistency and you will find that it looks very handsome.

Whichever method of binding off you use, brace yourself for great excitement at the top corners as you watch that rather amorphous lump transform itself into a nice, crisp 90-degree angle.

Done. Neaten the edges, sew on buttons and block. ~

Seven Sleeve Caps

A guide to basic shapes and armholes

by Mari Lynn Patrick

For several years dropped shoulders have dominated the fashion scene. With the return of fit, sleeve caps are once again an essential part of design.

Until recently, the T-square look in sleeve fit and design was the uniform for sweater fashion. As sweaters became more loose-fitting, with dropped shoulders halfway to the elbow, sleeve tops became wider and wider, and shaping almost disappeared. But straight or extended dolman sleeves, always easy to make and wear, are fading in fashion importance. Now that clothes are fitting body contours more closely, we're seeing a return to classic armholes with shaped and full-fashioned sleeve caps.

Here's a guide to all the basic shape categories.

1. STRAIGHT ARMHOLE/SLEEVE. This sleeve top has a straight edge. Sewn along the straight edge of the body pieces, it forms the T-square look. The width of the top of the sleeve is the total depth of the front and back armholes. Since the armhole isn't shaped, the armhole depth should be dropped a minimum of 2½–3"/6.5–7.5cm from the actual body measurement to ensure an easy, non-clinging fit. To place the sleeve accurately, divide the top-of-sleeve measurement by half, and place markers this number of inches down from the shoulders on front and back. Sew the shoulders, then sew the tops of the sleeves to the armholes between the markers.

A straight sleeve is usually knit from the cuff edge to the top edge. This sleeve can also be worked from seam to seam. The advantage of this method is that the stitches run in the same direction as the body when sewn to the sweater and therefore the stitch or color pattern appear as a continuous motif.

To design a sleeve of this type, cast on about 1"/2.5cm worth of stitches. As you work, continue to cast on stitches at the right edge (for left sleeve) and the left edge (for right sleeve) until the desired sleeve length (minus the cuff) is reached. Work until the short edge is the needed width at the wrist. Then bind off the stitches to correspond to those cast on. The long edge must measure the total armhole depth

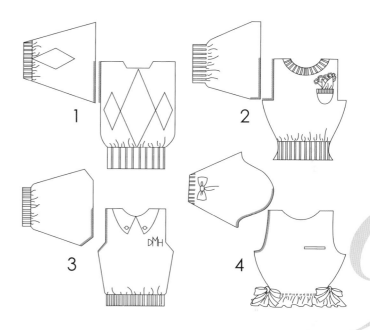

and is sewn to the armhole edges of the front and back. Pick up stitches along the short edge for the cuff ribbing and work the usual way.

2. SQUARE ARMHOLE/STRAIGHT SLEEVE. This sleeve is similar in appearance to the straight style, but with less bulk at the underarm. It is particularly well suited to the addition of shoulder pads. The average width to bind off for the armhole is 2"/5cm. You must work a corresponding 2"/5cm straight at the sleeve top after you complete all sleeve increases. Sew the top (bound-off edge) of the sleeve to the straight edge of the armhole, and then sew the 2"/5cm that was worked straight on the sleeve to the 2"/5cm of the armhole bind-off.

For both styles 1 and 2, you can pick up stitches along the straight edge of the armhole and work the sleeve down to the cuff edge.

3. ANGLED ARMHOLE/SLEEVE. Very common in classic menswear and full-fashioned sweaters, this armhole shaping is often accompanied by a straight front shoulder and a deep, sloped back shoulder. Again, it gives a broader line at the top of

the sleeve without the bulk of a straight sleeve. Since the armhole is angled, it provides more ease of movement. The average decrease for this armhole is also 2"/5cm over a 2"/5cm slope, with corresponding sleeve decreases. The straight portion of the sleeve top must match the straight sections of the front and back armholes.

4. SHAPED ARMHOLE/SET-IN SLEEVE. The set-in sleeve is not only the most classic form of shaping, but offers numerous style possibilities, from a very shallow but broad cap (most frequently used in men's sweaters and easy-fitting women's sweaters) to a very high but narrow cap (used for close-fitting women's sleeves). Set-in sleeves, however, are also the most difficult to plan out. They require careful calculation, graphing, and sometimes even ripping out before you get a perfectly shaped sleeve to fit into the front and back of an armhole. Here are a few tips on shaping the most basic armhole/sleeve cap:

Usually, the front and back armholes are decreases 2–3"/5–7.5cm in from the edge and over a slope of 2"/5cm or more. To get the curve of the armhole, you bind off approximately 1"/2.5cm worth of stitches at once, then decrease the remaining stitches gradually. You begin the sleeve cap by making bind-offs and decreases corresponding to those used on the front and back armholes. After that, the shape of the sleeve cap varies. When you look at the sleeve cut in half lengthwise, the measurement of the depth of the sleeve cap, plus one half the top of the sleeve cap, must add up to the armhole depth of the front or back. The top of the cap can be 2–5"/5–12.5cm in width, which is bound off all at once. Once you determine the width at the top, divide that measurement in half and subtract it from the armhole length of the front or the back. This measurement will be the depth of the sleeve cap.

Puffed sleeves also fall into this category. The armhole shaping is the same as described above. The sleeve cap differs only in that it is deeper and wider at the top, usually by 1–3"/2.5–7.5cm, depending on how puffed you want the sleeve to be. You gather the extra fabric at the top of the sleeve before setting it into the armhole.

5. RAGLAN ARMHOLE/SLEEVE. A raglan armhole is usually seen as a straight angled line going from the underarm to the neck. Sometimes ½"/1.5cm or so is bound off straight at the armhole before beginning the raglan shaping. The sleeve raglan must match the front and back raglan shaping (that is, it must have the same number of rows). The top of the sleeve forms part of the neck [Figure 5A].

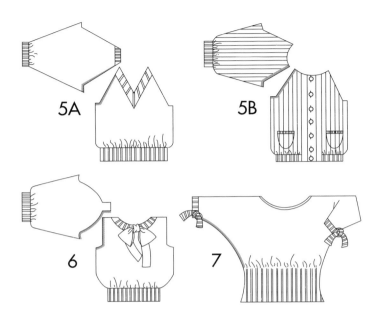

For an easier fit at the front neck, you can make the front neck and armhole shorter than the back neck and armhole by 1"/2.5cm [Figure 5B]. When you do this, you must work the sleeves with a slanted top so that they fit the front and back armholes. In other words, one side of the sleeve raglan is longer (to correspond to the back), and the other side is shorter (to correspond to the front). To shape the top 1–2"/2.5–5cm, you bind off stitches from the front (shorter) edge. The front edge of the left sleeve is at the beginning of the wrong-side rows. Conversely, the front edge of the right sleeve is at the beginning of the right-side rows.

Frequently, raglan decreases are worked 2 to 3 stitches inside each edge for a decorative finish, called full-fashioning.

6. SADDLE YOKE ARMHOLE/SLEEVE. The same shaping principle for the set-in sleeves applies to the armhole and sleeve of the saddle shoulder style. The only difference is that the front and back armholes are shorter by 1–1½"/2.5–4cm to accommodate the saddle shoulder portion of the sleeve. The top of the sleeve, which is worked straight to fit along the top of the shoulder edge, is usually 2–3"/5–7.5cm wide. The top of the saddle shoulder will also form part of the neck.

7. DOLMAN SLEEVE. The dolman sleeve, which was recently fashionable, has always been a classic shaping for evening sweaters and other lightweight dressy sweaters. Actually an extension of the main body pieces, the dolman is worked by increasing stitches, then casting on stitches in larger numbers to obtain the desired curve. It is important to plan the shaping carefully with a graph or paper pattern.

SLEEVE LENGTH: It's often difficult to determine sleeve lengths on any of the styles without shaped sleeve caps. The lengths will vary from style to style depending on the *width* of the body pieces. For the most accurate calculation, measure from your own center-back-neck to wrist (or wherever you want the sleeve to end), and subtract about 2"/5cm or so for stretch. Then divide the width of the back-neck measurement in half and add it to the shoulder measurement. Subtract this number from your center-back to wrist measurement, and you'll know how long to make your sleeve.

SETTING IN SLEEVES: A neatly set-in sleeve is one of the marks of distinction of a knitting perfectionist. In each of the examples outlined here, the setting in of sleeves requires some pre-planning and skill. The sleeve almost always has more fabric to be eased into the armhole; either because of its curves or simply because the stretching of the stitches across is greater than the elasticity of the rows lengthwise.

Sew in sleeves after the shoulder seams have been joined and before the side and sleeve seams are sewn. That way you can lay the pieces out flat and be sure that the sleeve caps are eased evenly into the armhole.

With large T-pins or a contrast strand of yarn, line up the center of the sleeve cap with the shoulder seam and the two sets of armhole bind-offs (or armhole markers). Then baste or pin the remainder of the sleeve cap into the armhole carefully, easing in extra sleeve fabric.

Whether you use the invisible seam, crochet slip stitch method [see "Vogue's Finishing School," p. 102], or your own chosen finishing method, be sure that the seam is worked with small, fairly close stitches for a neat and even seam that will hold up through many years of washing and wearing. ⌒

The Role of Ribbing

by Deborah Newton

Very often forming the foundation and support for a sweater's shape, a fine, firmly ribbed cuff or lower edge helps a favorite sweater last for years. A loose, sloppy ribbing tends to wear out long before the body of an otherwise carefully made garment. The elasticity of the combination of knit and purl stitches (the elements of most ribbing) prevents stretching out of the edges, which tend to get the most wear. Ribbing insures that edges lie flat, hugging the body for good fit. Stitches that have a tendency to curl, such as stockinette, are anchored by ribbing.

The following is conceived to direct both the beginner and experienced knitter in the fine points of ribbing: As a general rule, DON'T SKIMP ON THE RIBBING! Keep in mind that most elastic ribbings are at least 2¼"/6cm deep.

And if you are a beginner or have difficulty distinguishing between a knit stitch and a purl stitch on the ribbed edge, remember the following:

• SOME YARNS WORK BETTER FOR RIBBING THAN OTHERS. It's best to choose a smooth yarn with some of its own elasticity for your early attempts at ribbing—often a fleck of tweed or the curl of a novelty yarn obscures the definition of

The important role that ribbing plays in sweater design, construction and fit should be learned early on by knitters. After all, sweaters have ribbed edges for good reason!

the knit and purl stitches. Plain wool yarns, durable and resilient, usually result in crisp, even ribbing, and you don't need to take special precautions when knitting them. On the other hand, if you are working with a soft, loose cotton yarn or a fancy novelty yarn, you may need to work much tighter and on smaller needles to insure that your ribbing retains as much elasticity as possible.

• WHEN SUBSTITUTING ONE YARN FOR ANOTHER, ALWAYS MAKE A TEST SWATCH OF RIBBING as well as the stitch pattern used for the body of the sweater. It pays to test and compare first!

• EXPERIMENT ON THE SLEEVE. If you find it difficult to begin your ribbing with a large number of stitches, work one sleeve (which has a ribbing with relatively few stitches) before attempting ribbing on the larger front and back pieces.

• AS A BEGINNER, ALWAYS CHOOSE A PATTERN THAT USES A SIMPLE K1, P1 RIB OR A K2, P2 RIB. For k1, p1 ribbing, knit the first stitch and purl the second, and repeat this process across the row. If there is an even number of stitches, you will end the row with a purl stitch; with an odd number of stitches, you will end with a knit stitch.

• BEFORE YOU BEGIN THE NEXT ROW, STOP AND ANALYZE WHAT YOU HAVE DONE. If you purled the last stitch, KNIT the first stitch of your next row. If you knitted the last stitch, PURL the first stitch of your next row. Now, look carefully at your stitches and you may never need worry again about odd-and-even-numbered rows. If the first stitch below the loop on the left-hand needle has the appearance of a smooth V, then knit this stitch. If the first stitch has a bump below the loop on the left-hand needle, purl this stitch.

• PASS THE YARN FROM BACK TO FRONT AFTER A KNIT STITCH, AND FROM FRONT TO BACK AFTER A PURL STITCH. And remember to pass the yarn BETWEEN the needles; don't lay the strand OVER the needle when changing stitches. This is especially important for you beginners to remember. If you are conscious of this, you will never add an extra stitch to your row accidentally.

In the beginning, if you count your stitches at the end of every row, and analyze your work, your ribbing will proceed well and soon you won't even have to think about it.

In addition to these hints, there are several basic rules for both beginners and experienced knitters that apply to the working of most ribbings.

First, almost all ribbed edges should be worked in needles at least two sizes—sometimes three sizes—smaller than the needles required for the main body of the sweater. If the needles you need to obtain the gauge of the main (body) pattern of the sweater are different in size from the ones suggested, be sure to adjust your ribbing needle size accordingly. It is better to use smaller needles if you are unsure, so that the ribbing will cling firmly and hold its shape after repeated wearing and washing.

One of the most important things to remember when knitting a ribbing is to work all stitches with a firm tension. Because the yarn strand changes position between the needles when changing from knit to purl stitches and vice versa, it is essential to pull the yarn firmly between the stitches when the position changes. Otherwise a slackening will occur between the ribs.

Even the most experienced knitters may have difficulty with ribbing at necklines and along front bands of cardigans. Yet if the stitches are picked up correctly along these edges the ribbing can proceed quite easily. Measure your edge and divide this figure (number of inches) into the number of stitches there are to be picked up. This will give you an idea of how many stitches you should pick up each inch (you may mark off the inches with pins if you desire).

When working ribbing around a neckline, be sure that the stitches at each side are symmetrically placed—if you are working a k2, p2 rib and a k2 rib falls at the right shoulder seam, take care when picking up the stitches to count so that a k2 rib falls at the left shoulder. When making a large turtleneck or cowl neck, you can use larger needles for the last half of the collar to give a looser, more draped effect.

When the ribbing is finished, take care to bind off LOOSELY in a pattern. For example, with a k1, p1 rib, you would knit the first knit stitch, purl the next stitch and then pass the knit stitch over the purl stitch. Continue in this manner until all stitches are bound off. Some knitters like to use a much larger needle and bind off firmly. Experiment to see what works best for you.

When working a ribbed band along the fronts of a cardigan, it is important to pick up the correct number of stitches. If you pick up too many, the band will sag; if you don't pick up enough, the band will pull in. If your pattern doesn't give you the number of stitches to pick up along the front bands, in most cases, pick up 2 stitches for every 3 rows. This will result in a neat, even edge. Use your original gauge swatch for experimenting and practicing.

As you get more experienced, you may like to replace the simple k1, p1 ribbing in your sweater instructions with more intricate or decorative ribbing. For instance, a row of small twisted cables separated by one or two purl stitches can be almost as easy as a k2, p2 ribbing—but far more impressive! Remember that all ribbings are NOT interchangeable. If you want a lower edge that is firm and durable, don't choose an open, lacy rib—save it for that dressier top to make a prettier neckline edging.

If you do decide to substitute a ribbing, be sure to make a swatch of BOTH the pattern's ribbing, and the one you select. Do at least a 4"/10cm swatch over the same number of stitches to compare the two. If your new ribbing seems looser than the original, you might want to cast on fewer stitches than were originally suggested, or try smaller needles. And, conversely, if your ribbing seems too tight, then cast on more stitches or try larger needles.

by Meg Swansen

As you are knitting a jacket, how do you find the exact location for the pocket? How far should it be from the lower edge? From the front border? How wide across the top? Here is Elizabeth Zimmermann's practical answer: Knit the entire jacket and put it on. Now put your hands in the imaginary pockets. Stop. Aha—there! That's where I want to put my hand. Mark the center of that spot and insert an Afterthought Pocket.

What about socks? Do you know precisely where the heel will fall, knitted either from the top or from the toe? Knit the sock perfectly straight and try it on. Mark the center of where your heel bulges out and knit an Afterthought Heel.

And mittens. Just where will the base of the thumb be in relation to the rest of the hand? Try on the finished, thumbless mitten and feel around for the "crotch" between your thumb and forefinger. Mark it and knit an Afterthought Thumb [see page 166].

I learned all of the above from Elizabeth, who gave the technique its very appropriate name. We'll deal first with the Snip Method in plain stockinette stitch.

After you have marked the place for the pocket (or heel or thumb), decide how many stitches wide it will be and snip half a stitch in the middle of the predetermined width. I learned both of those lessons the hard way by snipping through more than one strand (ouch!)—and snipping at the far edge of the would-be opening, which left no proper length of wool to be darned in. Now you can pull out the snipped row—half a stitch at a time—in either direction until total wanted width is reached, which provides a long tail for neatening up each corner when you are done. You will have an upper and lower row of raw stitches, and it is a simple matter of picking them up and completing the item as follows:

POCKET Pick up the lower stitches and finish them off with a rolled edge of stockinette stitch, a noncurling edge of garter stitch, seed stitch or ribbing, or an I-Cord border. Then put the upper raw stitches on a needle and knit the flat pocket back and forth. As pockets are used, they tend to become a bit droopy, so it is a good idea to

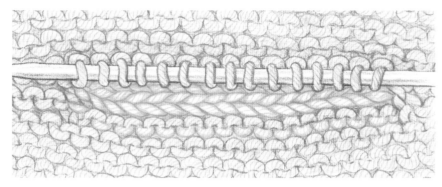

After snipping and unraveling, the upper raw stitches are placed on a needle. The lower raw stitches have been picked up and cast off in I-cord.

make a very narrow opening—just wide enough to slip your hand through—and widen the pocket as you go as follows: After about 1"/2.5cm, begin to increase at each edge, every other row, until the pocket is good and roomy. Now work straight to wanted depth and either half-weave the raw stitch to the inside of the fabric and tack down the edges or cast off (loosely) and sew down all three edges. Another trick: Keep 4 to 6 stitches of the pocket edge in garter stitch to prevent it from curling. Make the inside of the pocket smooth stockinette stitch for your hand and the back will be reverse-stockinette stitch to match the rest of the garment. Darn in all ends. I much prefer this single-layer pocket to the one that is worked as a tube, which creates a triple thickness and can be rather bulgy. (Algie met a bear, the bear was bulgy, the bulge was Algie.)

HEEL If you have knit the sock from the top and shaped a "regular" tapered toe (decreases on either side and woven across to the end), you may now—with double-pointed needles or two circulars—pick up all the raw heel stitches you can find, plus an extra stitch at each "corner" (pick up a loose strand and twist it as you put it onto the needle) and knit another toe. Great fun. As to how many stitches to unpick: Very generally speaking, a heel opening uses half the circumference of the sock.

THUMB As above, with double-pointed needles (or two circulars), pick up all stitches in sight, plus 2 "corner" loosenesses, and knit thumb to desired length, decreasing slightly during the last few rounds. If you are not following a specific pattern that tells you how many thumb stitches you need, you can estimate that the number to ravel may be about 20 percent of the whole: A 56-stitch mitten might have an 11-stitch thumb base times 2, plus 2 corner stitches: 24 stitches altogether.

If you work an Afterthought anything into a color or texture pattern, try to arrange the Afterthought part to occur during a plain row/round. If you must plow right through the middle of a color pattern (by snipping a half-stitch of each color involved in that row/round), you will be confronted with an interesting and rather mysterious sight: the lower stitches will be fully recognizable, but the upper stitches will have only an occasional familiar stitch, connected by looping strands of both colors. I usually grab the lower stitches first, then pick up a like number of upper "stitches," turning the loops into stitches by twisting them. If you are raveling through traveling stitches or other complex textures, it might be a good idea to test it on a swatch first so you can be properly braced.

An alternate method is often called The Thumb Trick. The disadvantage is that you must decide the exact location and width as you knit the garment. Once that is established, knit the future opening stitches in a contrasting color. Replace the stitches to the left needle and reknit them with the working wool. When you are ready to deal with it, remove the contrasting color thread and, faced with all the live stitches, proceed as above.

This technique makes it easy to replace a worn-out heel, toe or thumb by simply ripping out the tired section and reknitting.

P.S.: If you discover you have miscalculated the location after you have finished a Snip Method Afterthought something, weave the raw stitches back together again and snip anew. Magic. ⌒

Afterthought Thumbs

Mittens with or without thumbs

by Elizabeth Zimmermann

For the last ten years or so, a common sight has been that of teen-to-middle-aged citizens clad in jogging shoes, jogging suits and jogging gloves trotting along the edges of our roads (when no sidewalks are available) with determined but happy faces. In cooler to icy conditions, delete "happy"; their hands are cold and their thumbs *freeze*, they say. You say, slip your thumb out of its mitten thumb and warm it up with your fingers. They say no; they don't want to.

Well, my friend Becky was moaning to her brother Mark on this subject, and he came up with the idea of a *thumbless* mitten, which he propounded to me. Dandy, I said, immediately realizing (as a knitting designer) how this would simplify mitten knitting for willing but beginning knitters. So I made a pair, and Becky was delighted. I added the *curled tip*, the organic characteristics of which had been on my mind for some years. As soon as I completed the prototype and slipped it on, the fingers approved.

And of course, if and when *thumblessness* ceases to charm, the adding of an *afterthought thumb* is just the matter of the snip of a single stitch at the thumb knuckle, the unraveling of this thread in both directions for 6 or 7 stitches, the placing of the

Thumbless mittens with curved tips are ideal for keeping joggers' hands warm. Add thumb and they return to their traditional function.

resulting 13 or 15 stitches on three needles, and the knitting around on them for an inch or so. (By the same token, if the mitten wearer becomes a jogger, the thumb can be ripped out and the stitches woven to make a *jogger mitten*.)

Make the mitten cuffs wide so that they will envelope the jacket cuff. I long ago came to the conclusion that the wind likes to blow past the mitten cuff and *up* the sleeve, and that confronted with a coat-cuff-enveloping gauntlet, it reckons that that's too much trouble and will go and find some other arm to make uncomfortable.

You have your choice of thumb treatment: When you have worked as far at the thumb joint (around 3"/8cm from the wrist or thereabout), take a length of contrasting color wool and with it knit 5 to 6 stitches. Replace them on the left-hand needle, leaving the ends hanging down on the outside; reknit them in the mitten color and continue around the hand. When the mitten is finished, remove the contrasting color, and about 11 or 13 stitches will be revealed. Pick them up on three double-pointed needles and knit the thumb as described in the directions. Even when you have twisted the corner stitches on the thumb, there is occasionally still a looseness; tighten one side with the wool hanging there, and the other side with another piece of wool. Some knitters find that shaping out for the thumb by gradually increasing below (a thumb gusset) gives a better fit, but I rarely bother with this, since knitting is so flexible and elastic that it shapes itself.

Don't worry if the mitten is too big; if it's made in wool the first few snowballs will cause it to shape itself to the individual hand. In fact, those who knit for some saltwater fisherman often deliberately make the mitten enormous, drop it into boiling saltwater and boil it down to size. (This is with *wool*, of course; I don't know what boiling does to synthetics.)

Instructions for mittens: *Size*: Adult. *Gauge*: 20 sts to 4"/10cm in St st. *Materials*: 3oz/90g main color (MC), small amount of contrasting color (CC). 1 circular needle 11½"/29cm long. 1 set of 4 double-pointed needles (dpn). All needles in size to obtain given gauge.

Start with rolled border: With circular needle and MC, cast on 47 sts. Join and k 6 rnds (wrong side of work). Turn and k 2 rnds in CC. Beg pat as foll: *K3, MC, k1, CC; rep from * around until 3"/8cm has been worked in pat. (The pattern will spiral.) K 2 more rnds in CC, then change to MC and p 6 rnds. *K2, k2tog; rep from *, end k3 on next rnd—36 sts. Work even for 5½"/14cm (or desired length to tip of little finger). *Mark* 1 st at center back. K to within 1 st of it and work a double decrease as foll: Sl 2 tog knitwise, k1, pass 2 sl sts over k st. Rep this *every* rnd until 18 sts remain. Fold them tog, side to side, and join them by *weaving* (or *Kitchener stitch*)— curled tip complete. (Kids are delighted if you sew on two of those "eyes" from the notion counter.)

Optional thumb: Try on mitten: *Snip* 1 st (thumb-knuckle). Unravel in both directions for a total of 7 sts (which will reveal 15 sts). Pick up the 15 released sts (twisting the loose corner sts) on 3 dpn, starting at the palm end, and leaving a 4–5"/10–13cm end to strengthen this sensitive spot. K for about 15–20 tiny rnds. Break wool, thread through all 15 sts and fasten securely (maybe skimming the wool down to the left-hand side of the thumb to strengthen this corner). ⌐

The Angle on Shaping

How to figure out increases and decreases

by Mari Lynn Patrick

Have you ever wanted to lengthen or shorten a sleeve, or change a round neck into a V-neck, but found yourself intimidated by the prospect of recalculating the increases or decreases?

This article will give you a mathematical formula for figuring increases and decreases. Then, it will explain how the placement of these can alter the angle of the piece.

Before beginning you only need to know two things: the gauge, and the width and length you want the finished piece to be. With these you can determine the number of stitches you will have before and after shaping, and the number of rows within which the shaping will take place.

To determine the number of stitches, simply multiply the width measurement by the stitch gauge. To determine the number of rows, multiply the depth measurement by the row gauge.

While the following examples describe decreases, the formula also applies to increases. In both examples the gauge is 6 stitches and 8 rows to 1". Note that all measurements are in inches only.

When and how frequently you increase and decrease determines the slant of your knitting. Here's an easy-to-follow formula.

DECREASING AT EVEN INTERVALS

Let's start with the simplest case. In this example, suppose you want the width measurement before shaping to be 15", and the width measurement after shaping to be 1¾", with a total length of 10".

Now translate these measurements to stitches and rows. Thus 15" x 6 (stitch gauge) = 90 stitches before the shaping. Then 1¾" x 6 = 10.5, which round to 10 stitches after the shaping. And 10" x 8 (row gauge) = 80 rows in which to work the shaping—in this case, decreasing.

It follows that 90 – 10 = 80 stitches to be decreased (or 40 on each side) in 80 rows. Now divide the total number of rows by the number of times you need to decrease on one side. Thus 80 divided by 40 = 2, which means you work the decrease each side every other row 40 times [Figure A].

DECREASING AT UNEVEN INTERVALS

In the second example, suppose you want the width measurement before shaping to be 17", and the width measurement after shaping to be 3", with total length of 8".

Now translate these measurements to stitches and rows. Thus 17" x 6 (stitch gauge) = 102 stitches before the shaping. Then 3" x 6 = 18 stitches after the shaping. And 8" x 8" (row gauge) = 64 rows in which to work the shaping—in this case, decreasing.

It follows that 102 – 18 = 84 stitches to be decreased (or 42 each side) in 64 rows. Now divide the total number of rows by the number of times you need to decrease one side. Thus 64 divided by 42 = 1.523.

Since that is not an even number, you have to vary the number of rows between decreases. Decreasing 1 stitch on each side every other row 42 times will result in 84 stitches decreased, but over 84 rows—20 rows *more* than the 64 that are necessary. Therefore, on 20 of the rows worked, you should decrease 1 stitch on each side *every* row (for a total of 40 stitches). On the remaining 44 rows, the decreases are worked *every other* row 22 times (for a total of 44 stitches). Now to double check the math:

40 sts dec'd in 20 rows

<u>44 sts dec'd in 44 rows</u>

84 sts dec'd in 64 rows

PLACEMENT OF UNEVEN DECREASES

You can place the decreases in a number of ways. When combining fast-slanting (more frequent) decreases with slower-slanting (less frequent) ones, the fast-slanting decreases may come first [Figure B]. Using our second sample, work the 20 decreases *every* row first, then the remaining 22 decreases *every other* row.

If, on the other hand, the slower-slanting come first [Figure C], work the 22 decreases every other row, then the remaining 20 decreases every row.

As a third option, you can alternate the faster- with the slower-slanting decreases for an even slant. In this case, work 1 decrease every row once, then 1 decrease every other row once, and continue to alternate every row and every other row, working the last 2 every other row. ⌒

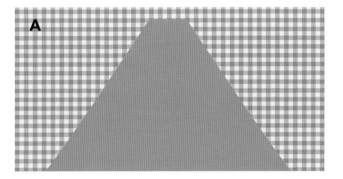

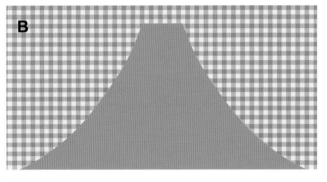

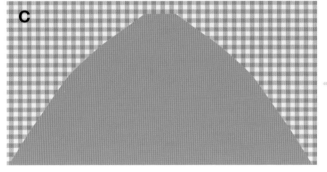

These three angles differ only in the placement of the decreases: at even intervals (A); fast-slanting first, then slower (B); slower followed by faster slanting (C).

Knitted Bust Darts

How to achieve a more stylish, comfortable fit

by Cindy Polfer

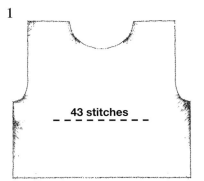

1

43 stitches

Measure the distance between your bust points and draw onto your schematic, adding 1½" to the line between the points.

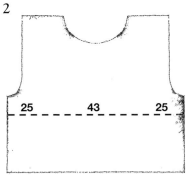

2

25   43   25

The distance on either side of the total bust point line to the side edges is the width of your bust darts.

Use this technique to shape the fabric of your sweater, for smoother lines, a fitted look—and no more gaping at the armholes.

Darts can be an effective way to achieve fullness in specific areas of a garment.

Actually, knitted darts aren't really darts at all. Unlike sewn darts, which require the removal of fabric, knitted darts are shaped fabric formed by short rows. The best fabrics in which to make short rows are stockinette, garter or reverse stockinette stitch because short rows interrupt the pattern.

Bust darts help eliminate gaping at the armhole. And by allowing more fullness at the bust while keeping the side seam measurement constant, they prevent the garment from hiking up in front.

Here are instructions for placing and knitting bust darts. (Our example, using arbitrary figures, illustrates the step-by-step process.) Before beginning to knit, you will need to determine your stitch and row gauge as well as certain measurements. To make this process easier, use an existing schematic, or draw one.

Example: Bust darts will be placed into a garment with 93 stitches across the front and with a stitch gauge of 16 stitches and 21 rows to 4", or 4 stitches and 5.25 rows to 1". (These calculations are given in inches only.)

1. Measure the distance between your bust points, and draw these points on your schematic [Figure 1], adding 1½" to the line between them, so that the tip of the dart doesn't fall directly on the bust point. The darts should fall in line with the bust points.

Example: The measurement between bust points is 9", and we add 1½". The result: 9" + 1½" = 10½".

2. Multiply the result from step 1 by the stitch gauge to get the number of stitches to be placed between the darts. If the total number of stitches across the front is odd, make the number of stitches between the darts odd as well. If it is even, make the number of stitches between the darts even. Add or subtract 1 stitch if necessary.

Example: Our stitch gauge is 4 stitches = 1". It follows that 10½" x 4 stitches = 42 stitches. Since our front has 93 stitches—an odd number—we need to add 1 to the 42 stitches. The result: 42 + 1 = 43 stitches in the center front between the darts.

3. Decide how deep you want the dart. (An average depth would be 1" to 1½".) A good way to do this is to measure the amount that your sweater usually hikes up in front. Then multiply this measurement by the row gauge to determine the number of rows needed for the depth of the dart. This must be an even number. If it isn't, round it to the nearest even number.

Example: We will put in a dart 1" deep. It follows that 1" x 5.25 rows per inch = 5.25 rows (rounded to 6 rows). Six extra short rows will be worked into the front across the bustline to complete our darts.

4. Since short rows are worked in a series of "steps" that are equal on each side, divide in half the number of extra short rows needed for the dart.

Example: 6 ÷ 2 = 3. Our darts will be 6 rows with 3 "steps" on each side.

5. Now calculate the number of stitches in each of the 3 "steps." First, subtract the number of stitches between the darts from the total number of stitches across the front.

Example: 93 – 43 = 50 stitches.

6. Divide in half the result from step 5.

Example: 50 ÷ 2 = 25 stitches. There will be 25 stitches on each side for the darts [Figure 2].

Double check: 25 stitches (left dart) + 43 stitches (center) + 25 stitches (right dart) = 93 stitches.

7. Divide the number of stitches in each dart by the number of "steps" calculated in step 4. Many times this number will not divide evenly. Round off the result into increments of whole stitches as evenly as possible.

Example: Divide 25 by 3 "steps." The result: 9 + 8 + 8 = 25 stitches.

Now that the front is divided into a series of "steps," you are ready to knit the darts. To shape the short rows, knit only part of a row, turn the work, and then work back in the opposite direction. We give instructions on the following page for working short rows by hand and machine.

HAND-KNITTING THE DARTS

Complete your garment to the point where you wish to begin the darts. Referring to Figure 3, work the following short rows. (The numbers in parentheses are taken from our example.)

Short row 1: Work the row until you have the number of stitches in the first step remaining unworked (9). Wrap the next stitch (see instructions below for wrapping both knit and purl stitches). After turning your work, work the next partial row in the opposite direction. (Remember to turn the work each time you wrap a stitch.)

Short row 2: Repeat short row 1.

3

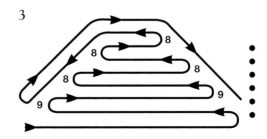

Short row 3: Work the row until you have the number of stitches in the first step plus the second step unworked (9 + 8 = 17 stitches). Wrap the next stitch.

Short row 4: Repeat short row 3.

Short row 5: Work the row until you have the number of stitches in the first, second and third steps unworked (9 + 8 + 8 = 25 stitches). Wrap the next stitch.

Short row 6: Repeat short row 5.

You have now completed the bust dart. Knit to the very edge of the garment on the next 2 rows, hiding the wraps as you come to them. Follow the instructions below for hiding the wrap (knit or purl side, depending on whether you are knitting or purling).

At the underarm, measure the length along the side seam of the garment. The 6 extra rows knitted into the center do not count in the total rows to the underarm. ⁓

SHORT-ROW WRAPPING

To prevent holes when making short rows, wrap a knit or a purl stitch before turning the work. After completing all the short rows, you must hide the wraps.

TO WRAP A KNIT STITCH

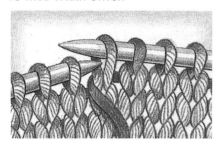

1. With the yarn in the back, slip the next stitch purlwise. Move the yarn between the needles to the front of the work.

2. Slip the same stitch back to the left needle. Now 1 stitch is wrapped. Turn the work, bringing the yarn to the purl side between the needles.

3. To hide the wrap, work to the wrapped stitch. Insert the right needle under the wrap and knitwise into the wrapped stitch. Knit them together.

TO WRAP A PURL STITCH

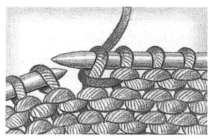

1. With the yarn at the front, slip the next stitch purlwise. Move the yarn between the needles to the back of the work.

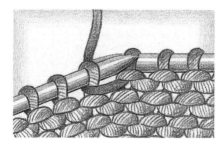

2. Slip the same stitch back to the left needle. Now 1 stitch is wrapped. Turn the work, bringing the yarn back to the purl side between the needles.

3. To hide the wrap, insert the right needle from behind into the back loop of the wrap, and place it on the left needle, as shown. Purl it together with the stitch on the left needle.

Sizing Up Sweaters

by Carla S. Patrick

The silhouettes that best suit the full-figured woman should be somewhat loose—just skimming the bust and hips, and never binding at the armholes or too tight in the sleeves. Dolman sleeves, or straight, dropped shoulder sleeves are a safe bet because they allow for extra room around the bust and upper arm. Do not choose a body-hugging style with small, set-in sleeves, or puff sleeves, which can accentuate broad shoulders. But do consider that a broadened shoulder line will balance and offset a wide hip line. Classic, semifitted styles are suitable as long as they provide at least 3–4"/7.5–10cm of ease to *your* body measurements.

If you have large hips, tunic-length sweaters, usually covering the hips, are the best choices. Short, boxy sweaters that hit just below the waist will only make your hips look boxy, too.

You love sweaters, but you are not a "model" size? Don't despair, and don't deny yourself the style and comfort of today's great sweaters. Figure flattery and good fit can be yours if you follow our easy tips for style and yarn selection and instruction adjustments, to fit *your* size and fashion appetite.

Look for V-necks, soft, drapey cowls or wide, scooped necklines to show off those collarbones. Any kind of interesting collar detail, such as an asymmetrical closure, gentle ruffles or pretty lace collars will frame your throat and draw the eye upward to your face.

Once you've decided on the silhouette, consider the stitch and pattern details. Vertical or diagonal stripes or pattern stitches are good choices for a slimming, elongating effect. We all know that obvious horizontal stripes and patterns accentuate width. Stay away from stitches that tend to pull in and cling to the body, such as ribbings or lots of cables. Smooth or lightly textured stitches are best, such as stockinette stitch, seed stitch, basketweave, small, spaced cables, etc. Avoid very bulky stitches or excessive details like chunky cables, lots of ruffles, etc. These only add bulk and extra width to the sweater—and to your silhouette! And keep in mind that on your first attempt to alter a pattern, you will have more success if you start with a simple style with no complicated shaping and simple stitch patterns (such as stockinette stitch). Practice on these kinds of styles before attempting to change a more complicated pattern like one with a great deal of colorwork or intricate patterns.

Carefully consider your choice of yarn for making a larger size sweater. A larger garment means MORE knitted fabric. Therefore, the fabric should be as lightweight as possible. This is best achieved with lighter-weight yarns, such as sport and worsted weights. Also, yarns with a pliant, soft hand, such as silk or rayon blends, Shetland or lamb's wool, give the fabric a more supple, drapey effect. Bulky or highly textured yarns will add excess volume, making for a heavy, thick sweater that will probably be less than flattering. An important note to remember: be sure to buy more yarn than is required for the largest size in the instructions.

Color is also an important consideration. Black is always slimming. And autumn's rich, classic darks like navy, charcoal gray, chocolate brown, hunter green and deep burgundy also lend themselves to figure flattery. Go ahead and indulge in pretty, muted pastels like crystal aqua, powder pinks and peaches, and a whole range of soft gray to beige neutrals. Matching the sweater color to your favorite skirt or pants gives a head-to-toe lean, tonal look. With all the exciting yarns available today, finding colors to match other garments in your wardrobe should be a snap!

Once you have chosen your sweater style and yarn, you'll need to decide on the finished measurements of your sweater. The easiest and most accurate way to determine the finished size is to find a sweater in your closet that you know fits well and looks good on you. Lay this garment flat on a firm surface, and, using a tape measure, note the following measurements: Bust from side seam to side seam, plus cross back after armhole shaping; hips or lower edge of sweater; length from shoulder to lower edge; armhole depth; width at upper arm of sleeve; length of sleeve; cuff width; shoulder width or width from armhole seam to seam; and back neck width. These measurements should reflect your ideal FINISHED MEASUREMENTS. Compare them to your BODY measurements at the same points, and the difference should reflect the amount of ease you want in the sweater. Keep both sets of measurements as a guide when adjusting your instructions and for making future sweaters. Now you're ready to begin altering the instructions to your measurements and desired size. Although the instructions are not given in your size, with patience and a few simple rules, you can size up to make the sweater of your dreams. As an example, let's use a pattern that goes up to a 38" bust. The largest size given in the instructions is for a size 38"/96cm bust, with a finished measurement of 40"/101cm. Obviously, this allows for 2"/5cm of ease. Let's say you have a 44"/112cm bust, so proportionately you would want to add 3"/7.5cm of ease for a finished bust measurement of 47"/119cm. Following are the steps necessary to alter this pattern to your desired size:

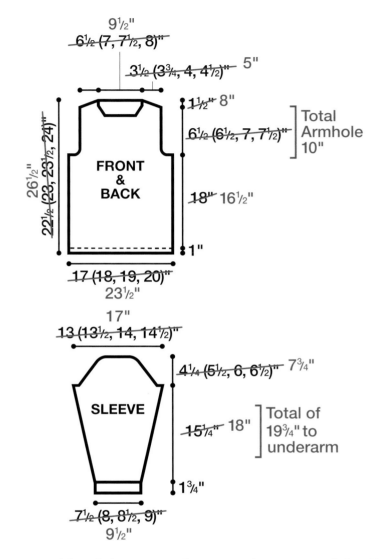

1. Read through the entire set of instructions first to get a good idea of how all the pieces are made.

2. GET THE GAUGE! You must knit a test swatch of at least 4"/10cm square, changing needle size if necessary to obtain both the stitch and row gauges given in the pattern. In this particular pattern the gauge is 16 stitches and 20 rows to 4"/10cm (or 4 stitches and 5 rows to 1"/2.5cm) over stockinette stitch using size 9/5.5mm needles.

3. Write in the finished measurements you want on the measurement diagram (schematic) provided at the end of the instructions.

4. Calculate, if necessary, the number of stitches you will need according to the gauge. It is best to jot down all calculations before beginning to knit. Note: the calculations in this section are figured according to INCHES only.

BACK: Since the new finished bust measurement is 47", the back should measure half this number, which is 23½", multiplied by 4 (because gauge is 4 stitches to 1") = 94 stitches (sts). Therefore, you must cast on 94 sts for your back piece. Work in the pattern following instructions until desired length to underarm: Here work until back measures 16½" from turning ridge. Before figuring the armhole shaping, see what your cross back measurement is after the armhole. In this case it is 19½" (see diagram) x 4 = 78 sts should be left. Therefore, 94 – 78 = 16 sts must be decreased at armhole. The first bind-off sts usually are the same as in the instructions. However, if you need to decrease many more sts than called for in the original instruction, you can bind off an extra 2 or 3 sts at the beginning of the armhole. For our example we will use the same bind-off as in the pattern, which states: "Bind off 4 sts at beg of next 2 rows." Now you have 8 more sts to decrease (4 sts each side). The instructions say to "dec 1 st each side every other row 3 times." This only decreases 6 sts (3 each side), therefore you must work decreases every other row one more time for a total of 8 sts decreased. Now continue on 78 sts for desired armhole depth 10". Now calculate your back of neck: 9½" x 4 = 38 sts which must be left at center back after shoulder shaping. Therefore, 78 – 38 = 40 sts (20 sts each side) to be decreased for shoulder. The shoulder shaping in the instructions is done in 6 rows, therefore bind off 6 sts at beginning of next 2 rows (12 sts) and 7 sts at beginning of next 4 rows (28 sts): (12) + (28) = 40 sts decreased in 6 rows. You may have to do some trial-and-error math to work out your own personal neck and shoulder shaping.

FRONT: Work the front same as back until desired length to beginning of neck (the schematic shows your neck to be dropped 2" from the first shoulder bind-off, therefore 10" – 2" = 8". Work until armhole measures 8". To figure your front neck shaping, you must be sure to end up with the same number of sts for the shoulder after the neck decreases as on the back (in this case, there are 20 sts for each shoulder). Keep the decreases at the side of the neck the same as the instructions. (In this instruction it is "dec 1 st at each neck edge every other row 3 times.") You have

78 sts after the armhole minus 40 sts for shoulders minus 6 sts decreased at neck edges equal 32 sts to be bound-off at center neck.

SLEEVES: Your desired wrist measurement is 9½" x 4 = 38 sts to cast on. Your width at upper arm is 17" x 4 = 68 sts. There are no increases in the cuff, which is approximately 1¾" in the cording pattern. Your length to the underarm is 19¾" – 1¾" = 18" x 5 = 90 rows. Therefore 68 – 38 = 30 sts to be increased in 90 rows, so increase 1 st each end every 6th row 15 times (6 x 15 = 90 rows).

CAP SHAPING: Always bind off the same number of sts as on the first 2 rows of the armhole shaping for back and front; in this case, bind off 4 sts at the beginning of next 2 rows and there are 60 sts left. The last bind-off at the top of the cap should measure approximately the same as the original pattern: we will use 18 sts which equal 4½". You now must decide the depth of your sleeve cap based on the measurement for either the front or back armhole: Your armhole measures 10", the top of your cap is 4½" which you must divide by 2 equaling 2¼", therefore 10" – 2¼" = 7¾". Usually in the last ½" to 1" of the cap you bind off ½" to 1" each side. Let's bind off 1" or 4 sts each side (8 sts bound off in all) at beginning of next 4 rows (which is approximately 1" long). Now subtract this 1" depth from the remaining sleeve cap which is 7¾" to get 6¾" or 33¾" rows rounded to 34 rows as the depth of your cap before your last bind-offs. Now subtract the sts at the top of the cap (18) plus the bound-off sts before the cap (8) from the sts remaining after the first armhole bind-off: 60 – 18 – 8= 34 sts to be decreased in 34 rows, so "dec 1 st each end every other row 17 times."

COLLAR: Since this particular collar is made separately from the top down, you may want to figure the collar after you have finished making the rest of the sweater. In this case, measure around the entire neck edge of your finished sweater (adding an extra inch since the bound-off edge tends to pull in), and multiply this measurement by 4 to get the number of stitches you need at the end of the collar. To figure the number of stitches you'll need to cast on, read the pattern backwards, making the increases to correspond to the decreases, until you end up with your final increase (which will become your first decrease as you make the collar).

Once you've discovered how simple it is to select and alter patterns, a whole new world of knitting will be opened to you! ⌐

Designing for

by Margery Winter

It probably won't surprise you to learn that 52 percent of American women are 5'4" or shorter, and that 49 percent wear size 14 or larger. Yet fashion designers seem oblivious to these statistics. Season after season, they design ready-to-wear expressly for the "perfect" size 10.

A few years ago, this wasn't such a problem. Seventh Avenue, reflecting a strong Japanese influence, was producing one-size-fits-all garments. Most women found an oversized, dropped-shoulder sweater to be a flattering style. Taking the cue from Norma Kamali, they added football-player shoulder pads, making the bust, waist and hips look smaller. Completing the look with a pair of high heels, they created an illusion of long and lean.

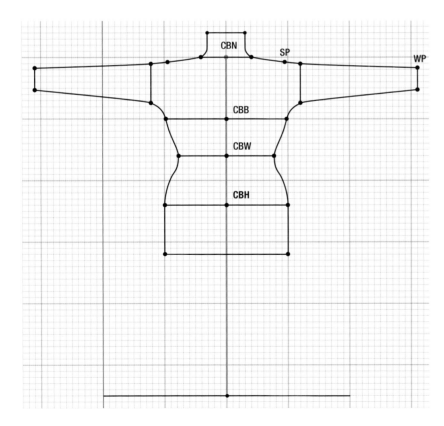

So it is understandable that women are reluctant to give up their shoulder pads. But inevitable changes have taken place in fashion. Today the fit is truer. The bodice is shaped, and the sleeve cap has returned. The waist is emphasized, shoulders are smaller and sloped, the hemline went way up and is once again falling.

If you can buy clothes off the rack—that is, if your size is from 6 to 12, with no need for alterations—then you can knit from existing sweater patterns without adjusting the fit.

If you do have fit problems, however, the following method of drafting a basic sloper (a flat pattern representing your exact fit) will open up a whole world of wardrobe possibilities. It will enable you to design and execute sweaters that fit perfectly and look great.

TO PLOT YOUR BASIC SLOPER

Materials:

- Graph paper–10 squares per inch
- Eraser
- Pencil
- Fiberglass tape measure
- See-through plastic ruler
- Red pencil

Special Sizes

Begin by having someone take your measurements—measuring honestly and accurately without tugging on the tape measure—and then plot them on graph paper. Let one square equal one inch. The information that follows is given in inch measurements only. (Unless otherwise specified, mark all dots on the graph paper with a regular sharp pencil.) With tape measure and graph paper handy, plot your basic sloper as follows:

1. The starting point is the center back neck (CBN) which is the most prominent bone at the base of the neck. Mark it toward the top center of the graph in red pencil. Now locate your center back neck and, with tape measure, measure the distance from there to the floor. Mark the floor point on the graph paper, and draw a vertical red line from the CBN to the floor point. Then draw a horizontal line to indicate the floor.

2. Locate your center back waist (CBW). Measure the distance from your CBN to your CBW, and mark the CBW on the graph paper. Draw a horizontal line, half your waist measurement in length, at the CBW, centering it over the vertical red line.

3. Locate your center back at hips (CBH). Measure the distance from your CBN to your CBH, and mark the CBH on the graph paper. Draw a horizontal line, half your hip measurement in length, at the CBH, centering it over the vertical red line. (Note: If the measurement at your thighs is wider than your hips, use the thigh measurement.)

4. Locate your center back at bust (CBB). Measure the distance from your CBN to your CBB, and mark the CBB on the graph paper. Draw a horizontal line, half your bust measurement in length, at the CBB, centering it over the vertical red line.

5. Measure your neck. On the graph paper, draw a horizontal line half that measurement in length, centering it over the CBN.

6. Locate your shoulder point (SP), at the shoulder joint. Measure the distance from that point to the CBN. Then on graph paper, count down one square to account for shoulder slope, and mark the SP. Draw a line from the SP to the point at the outer edge of the neck.

7. Extend your arm straight out to the side, perpendicular to your body. Placing the tape measure along your arm, measure the distance from your CBN to your wrist. Mark the wrist point (WP) on the graph paper, counting down two squares from CBN. Then draw a line connecting that point to the SP.

8. Locate the fullest part of your upper arm. Measure the distance from that part to the SP. On the graph paper, mark the point where your upper arm is the fullest on the line between the SP and the wrist. (It should be at least 3 inches from the SP.) Now draw a vertical line, half of the measurement of the fullest part of your upper arm in length, extending down from the point just marked.

9. Measure your wrist. Draw a line, half of that measurement in length, extending down from WP on the graph paper. Mark the corresponding points for the opposite arm.

10. Finally, draw your body shape on the graph paper by connecting the points at either end of the hipline, the waistline, the bustline and so on. Extend the line 8" down from the hip points and draw a horizontal line connecting these lines. You have completed your own basic sloper according to your specific measurements. You are ready to design a sweater that will fit and flatter you.

ALL ABOUT EASE

Ease is the amount of extra fabric added to a sweater beyond your basic body measurements to allow for comfort and freedom of movement. You can get away with slightly less ease in knits than in woven fabrics, because knits have built-in stretch. Still, when knitting garments in larger sizes, it is always better to err on the side of too much rather than too little.

As a rule of thumb, you should add 3½" to the total bust measurement, 1" to the total waist measurement and 2¾" to the total hip measurement in order to achieve the average amount of ease. (Note: The total measurement is twice the measurement of one piece of your garment.)

By adding to or subtracting from average, however, you can use ease to create style and silhouette. This, in fact, is one of the most creative parts of drafting a schematic.

TO DESIGN YOUR SWEATER

Take a piece of tracing paper and lay it over your sloper. Fasten it at the corners with masking tape. To decide on the amount of ease you want for your sweater, sketch the sweater on the tracing paper over the sloper. In this way, you can clearly see how its proportions will relate to the proportions of your body. You can place motifs, colorwork, stripes or Aran stitch panels by drawing them on the tracing paper. You can also determine button size and placement, as well as the shaping of the necklines, collars, armholes and sleeves.

Now you can begin a swatch to select the right knitted fabric for your sweater— or, if you prefer, you can swatch before you sketch. The order of the creative process is up to you. You may start with a wonderful button, which may suggest a cardigan, which then suggests a fabric, and so on.

When you make a swatch, keep in mind that the weight of the garment is usually supported at the neck and shoulders, and it drapes from there. Too much knitted fabric in a heavy yarn may be too much for the neck and shoulders to support. You should use yarn that is light enough and has a firm enough tensile strength to support the garment.

Referring to our series on designing [see pages 144 to 155], you can write instructions from your schematic and gauge swatch and you're ready to go. ⌣

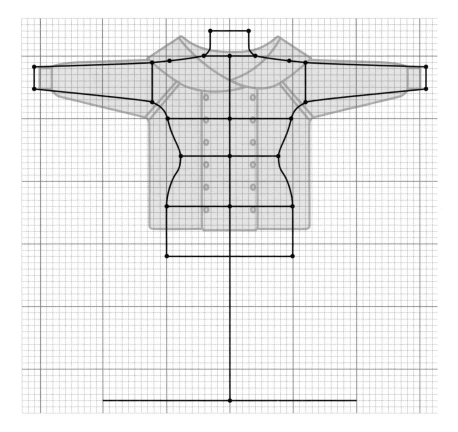

Pattern Alterations

Easy-to-follow guidelines for getting a better fit

by Mari Lynn Patrick

There are many "fit" reasons for altering existing patterns—perhaps updating a fashion silhouette, or rearranging a detail such as a cuff or neckline. Some alterations are necessary when your body type doesn't fit that of the sweater pattern. But probably the best reason is to customize a design to your own taste. All it requires is some knowledge and experience.

When we speak of altering a pattern, we mean minor changes, which should not be confused with the complexity of garment redesigning. Most alterations are simple and can even be done by beginners.

When making alterations, first take your measurements, then compare them to the schematic drawing. Do you need to shorten your sleeves? Is the sweater too long or short? Based on your measurements and the schematic drawing from the pattern, you can probably make these adjustments easily. But do you need to change the bust or hip width? Before attempting these changes, read our information on ease. (Note: All measurements in this article are given in inches only. For metric conversions, divide the number of inches by .394.)

Want to shorten a sweater? Increase its hip size or sleeves before you knit it? Here's a handy how-to guide even beginners can follow.

MEASURING UP

For the truly customized garment, you need to work with specific body measurements. Don't automatically make the size you usually wear, since sizes vary greatly with the garment style.

1) **Bust measurement**: Measure your bust around the fullest part, making sure the tape is not drawn too tightly.

2) **Waist measurement**: Measure your natural waistline, where your skirt or belt encircles you. Although this measurement is not frequently needed for hand-knitting, it is helpful as a reference point.

3) **Hip measurement**: Again, measure around the fullest point, which is usually 7–9" below the waist.

4) **Armhole depth**: With your arm extended, measure from the armpit to the center of your shoulder.

5) **Cuff width**: This is the circumference of your wrist.

6) **Upper arm**: This is another circumference, measured at the widest point.

7) **Sleeve length to underarm**: Take this measurement from your wrist along the inside of your arm to the center of your armpit.

8) **Cross back**: Take this measurement across the top of your back from the inside shoulder edge to shoulder edge.

9) **Sweater length**: To determine the desired length, measure down from the highest point of your shoulder.

MEASUREMENT COMPARISON AND EASE

Now compare each of your measurements to each of the corresponding numbers on the schematic pattern pieces. Remember that back or front pieces represent half of your body's circumference at those points. the extra inches included in the schematic drawing's measurements are called "ease." If, for example, the finished bust size is 42" on a pattern to fit a 34" bust, that means that there are 8" of ease added to the bust, giving a loose and easy fit. If you wish to keep this fit, but your bust measures 38", you will want to add the same 8" of ease. Your finished measurement will thus be 46".

To further understand the definition of ease, take a look at the fit chart [page 149].

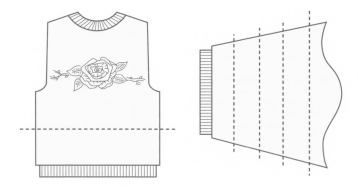

In a piece of knitting with straight sides—as in the front panel above—you can lengthen or shorten anywhere after the ribbing and below the armholes. For side-shaped garments—a sleeve here—the adjustments must be evenly spaced along the piece.

When you determine the ease added or subtracted, you may decide to make a size different from the one you normally wear.

GAUGE

Gauge is the formula for all of your calculations and must be taken and followed carefully before knitting. Since it is easier to work with 1" increments, if you have a gauge given over 4", break it down to 1". A gauge of 20 stitches and 28 rows = 4", for instance, would become 5 stitches and 7 rows = 1". When making any adjustments, you would need to add or subtract 5 stitches (for changes in width) or 7 rows (for changes in length) for each 1". Of course, many gauges break down into fractional numbers per inch—22 stitches = 4" would be 5½ stitches = 1". It is easy enough to use a calculator and round off numbers, but tabulate all calculations carefully to avoid confusion. Also, be sure to keep pattern repeats or stitch multiples in mind along with your gauge calculation.

PATTERN STITCHES

Before attempting these alterations, consider the feasibility of adjusting a stitch or colorwork pattern. When adjusting a colorwork pattern, you need to know if a specific color repeat must begin and end at a determined point. With stitch patterns, note whether there is a large stitch multiple—in excess, for example, of 6 or 8 stitches. This is important information, since a complete multiple must be added or subtracted if you are planning to resize. Also, must the pattern end on a certain row at the underarm, either for the purpose of matching the sleeve or for correct continuance of the pattern after the armhole shaping? Or are there wide panels of vertical cables with all the stitch alteration taking place on the outside edges? If the style is highly designed, intricately shaped or has a large motif, it might better be left unaltered.

ALTERING THE PIECES

1) **Bust alteration**: Length and bust measurement are critical to the fit of every garment. These measurements are always stated in the preface to each *Vogue Knitting* instruction to aid you in choosing the right size. (The size that the model is wearing is also given in the caption to show you the way the style "hangs.")

2) **Waist alteration**: Unless the sweater is tightly shaped, a waist measurement rarely calls for adjustment. If you do need to alter this measurement, check the ease used in the existing pattern and apply it to your own measurement. Be aware that altering waist shaping is complex.

3) **Hip alteration**: Many sweater styles run in a straight line from bust to hip. If you are making a long sweater that falls at or below your hips, compare the finished bust measurement to your own hip measurement. It is best to keep these measurements roughly the same on your garment. If your hips are much wider than your bust—say, 38" and 34", respectively—you should make the bust measurement larger (to fit a 36" or even 38" size) to correspond to the width of your hips. This will maintain the silhouette of your sweater.

4) **Armhole alteration**: When changing the depth of an armhole, also consider the shape of the sleeve top, since the sleeve shaping corresponds directly to the armhole shaping and depth.

4a) **Sleeve alterations**: The areas that can be adjusted on a sleeve comprise the overall length and the width at the cuff and the upper arm. Keep in mind that these adjustments are easiest for simple patterns and that it is best to avoid drastic changes to the shaped sleeve caps.

5) **Width at the lower edge**: Since the cuff width has very small variation from size to size, keep any changes close to the existing numbers.

6) **Width at the upper arm**: This measurement will correspond to the top-of-the-sleeve measurement after all the increases are completed.

6a) **Cap-sleeve style**: To figure the sleeve width at the upper arm, use your body measurement and add approximately the same ease as for the bust. This will differ from style to style, but this ease formula will give you an approximate number to work with.

6b) **Straight-sleeve style**: Since this measurement reflects the top-of-the-sleeve measurement, it is best calculated as twice the armhole depth. First decide what you wish the armhole depth to be, and then multiply by two to get the top-of-the-sleeve measurement. For a 10" armhole, for example, the top of a straight sleeve would measure 20".

7) **Length to underarm**: Your own measurement to the underarm will correspond exactly to that of sleeves with shaped caps. Always remember that when making any

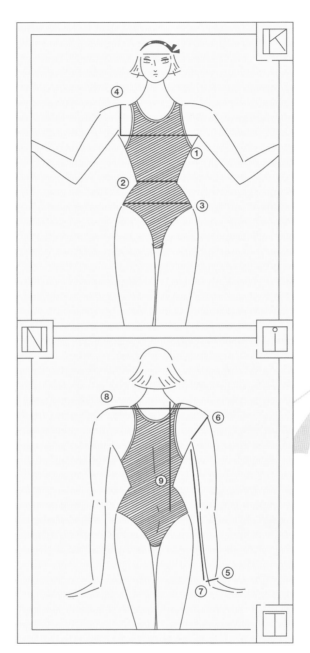

Use a good dressmaker's tape measure to take measurements and ask a friend for help: It's difficult to measure yourself accurately.

length alterations, you must take into account the number of rows necessary to work the increases. Calculate this number carefully with your row gauge to determine the increase frequency, and be sure to get a smooth slant up to the underarm. If you have to increase 40 stitches to the underarm (20 increase rows) and the increases are made every 6th row or in 120 rows by shortening your sleeve, you will have fewer than 120 rows in which to make your increases. If you decrease your sweater to 90 rows in depth, then it is best to work your increases every 4th row or a total of 80 rows. If necessary, you can also work out a combination of every 4th and 6th row.

7a) **Length of a straight sleeve**: The width of the sweater will determine the length of a straight sleeve. Generally, the wider the body of the sweater, the shorter the sleeve, since more of the body falls off the shoulder.

8) **Cross-back alteration**: This measurement is a combination of that of both shoulders and the neck. On your sweater, it will correlate to the measurement across the sweater *after* shaping the armhole. When making adjustments to this measurement, you must change the number of stitches for the shoulder and neck.

8a & b) **Neck and shoulder alteration**: Take a look at the schematic pattern pieces for any of the styles in this issue, and you will see fractional differences among sizes—if any—in the neck shaping. The largest difference between one side and another is usually worked into the shoulder area; keep this in mind when resizing a sweater at this point of fit. Although a variety of neck styles is available for hand-knit garments with varying neck widths, you should stay fairly close to the given numbers if you want to get the same look as the photo of your chosen style.

9) **Total length alteration**: The total length of a garment—the measurement taken from the inside neck edge (top-of-the-shoulder slope) to the lower edge—is one of the easiest measurements to adjust. It is accomplished readily because most patterns are worked vertically by inches and only occasionally by rows (as in the case of horizontal bands or stripes). You should lengthen or shorten the garment before the underarm. Avoid any alteration in the armhole area, which will require more complicated work in the sleeve-cap shaping. ⌒

TIPS

- You may want to use graph paper to redraw your schematic pieces and make notes on the planned changes.
- If alterations to your sweater involve edges, as in a cardigan, you will have to recalculate the number of stitches to be picked up.
- When changing the length of a cardigan, you may have to respace your buttonholes and, in some cases, add or subtract buttons. Remember that too few buttons will cause your band to gap.
- When making neckline alterations, you must also refigure the number of stitches to be picked up for a neckband or collar.
- If you are making changes to the main gauge of the body of your sweater, make a swatch of your ribbing to make sure that it will correspond to your new gauge.

Sizing Up the Situation

Knitting for kids' sizes 4–14

by Mari Lynn Patrick

The first step to getting the right fit is to learn how to properly measure your child and understand how to relate his or her measurements to those in the pattern. You'll need five key dimensions: chest, waist, hip, upper arm and back waist length. These and a few other measurements are described in detail below. To take them you'll need a cloth tape measure and a pad and pencil to record the measurements. You'll get the best results if you measure the child in his or her undergarments or over light, close-fitting clothing. Keep the tape snug, but not tight.

Once you've taken the necessary measurements, compare your child's measurements to those on the chart on page 185. Base your size choice on the child's chest measurement; you can make adjustments to the other areas as needed. For example, if your 6-year-old has a 30"/76cm chest (standard for a size 12), but a back waist length of 10½"/26.5cm (standard for a size 6), choose a size 12. Since most kids' styles do not have waist shaping, you'll simply need to knit fewer rows to achieve the correct length. The difference in sleeve length between the two sizes is 3½"/9cm, but the difference in armhole depth also needs to be addressed. Increasing the frequency of sleeve shaping

Tall and slim, short and chubby, lean and leggy—kids come in all shapes and sizes, and those shapes and sizes are ever changing. Choosing the right size for a child who's growing faster than you can click your needles can be a challenge, but with a little planning and a sense of how children's knits are sized, you're guaranteed a garment that fits right and looks great.

from every 6th row to every 4th row, for example, will shorten the number of rows needed to complete the sleeve while keeping the armhole depth in proportion. For styles with dropped shoulder sleeves, the center back neck to wrist is the critical measurement. In this case, the sleeve length may need some alteration. For changes in the upper arm measurement, follow either the upper arm and armhole measurements for size 6 or size 8. Measuring your child—and even clothes that fit well—are your best parameters.

Keep in mind that your child's body measurements may differ from the finished garment measurements given in the knitting pattern. That's because finished garments measurements allow for ease—the amount of wearing room built into the design to achieve a certain fit. Check the description of the garment given in the instructions; most will include one of the following terms: **Close-fitting** styles hug the body snugly and usually reflect an addition of no more than 2"/5cm to the standard body measurements. **Standard-fitting** styles have a classic, roomier fit——2–4"/5–10cm more than the standard body measurements. **Loose-fitting** garments lean toward the oversized with 5–7"/12.5–18cm or more of ease added to the body. **Oversized** garments allow for more than 8"/20.5cm of ease. If these descriptions are not given in the instructions, a quick comparison of the finished garment measurements to those on the standard sizing chart will give you an idea of how much extra room is or isn't included in the style and how the garment will fit your child.

The next factor to consider is the time it will take you to make the garment. The child who was a chubby size 4 when you started knitting may go through a growth spurt that brings him up to a long and lean size 6. When in doubt, go for the next size up. You'll also want to factor the season into the sizing. That Aran sweater you started in December won't be much good if it's finished in May…unless, of course, you've sized it to fit the child for the following winter!

Last but not least, consider the child's own style. Most kids like their clothes roomy, but a style-conscious teen may prefer a body-hugging fit. Get to know what the child likes; with so many fabulous knits to choose from, you're sure to find one that is suitable.

MEASURE UP

When designing a garment, the pivotal point is the chest measurement; this number will determine several other measurements. For example, in a sweater with straight armholes, the shoulders will vary in width to accommodate extra ease in the chest, while the neck measurements will remain fairly close-fitting. Determine the sleeve length by subtracting half of the cross-back measurement from the total length to the wrist. In a style with cut-in armholes and a classic fit at the shoulders, the cross-back measurement is important and should be adhered to as carefully as possible for a close body fit, with extra ease for an off-the-shoulder fit.

CIRCUMFERENCE MEASUREMENTS

A. Use this measurement as your guide for selecting garment size, as it is much easier to alter the length of a garment than the width. Slide the tape measure up under the underarms and measure around the chest.

B. This measurement is necessary for skirts, pants and structured garments that dip in at the waist. Measure around the natural waistline.

C. This measurement is necessary to ensure that the sweater does not hug the hips

too tightly. It usually differs little from the chest measurement. Measure around the hips at the widest part.

D. The upper arm measurement will have a fair amount of ease added to it for the most comfortable fit. This is especially true for a dropped-shoulder-style sleeve. Measure around the upper arm at the widest part.

E. The wrist shows a very small difference between the various sizes, and ease will often be added for a comfortable fit. Measure around the wrist bone.

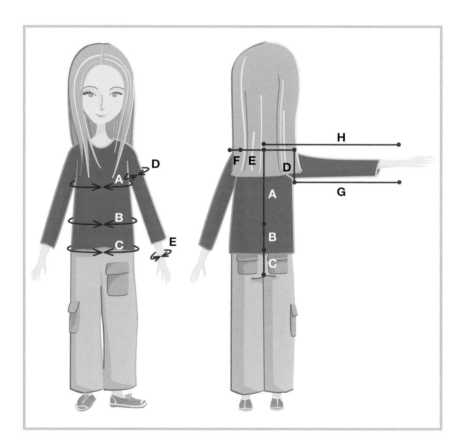

CIRCUMFERENCE MEASUREMENTS
A Chest
B Waist
C Hip
D Upper Arm
E Wrist

LENGTH & WIDTH MEASUREMENTS
A Back Waist Length
B Waist to High Hip
C High Hip to Lower Hip
D Armhole Depth
E Back Neck Width
F Shoulder Width
G Sleeve Length at Underarm
H Center Back Neck to Wrist

LENGTH AND WIDTH MEASUREMENTS

A. BACK WAIST LENGTH

Shoulder slope (usually ½"–1"/1–2.5cm), which may or may not be worked into children's styles, is included in the measurement. Measure from the prominent bone at the base of the neck to the natural waistline.

B. AND C. WAIST TO HIP

Measure from the waistline to the high point of the hipbone. Add this measurement to the back waist length to determine the standard sweater length for your child. For a tunic-length garment, measure to the lower point of the hipbone (C) and add to the back waist length (A).

D. ARMHOLE DEPTH

You'll need to add a bit of ease here for a comfortable fit. The only time you would want to match the actual body measurement is when knitting a tank top. In that style, the skinny straps will stretch with the weight of the garment, and you will need to keep depth to a minimum. Measure from the top outside edge of the shoulder to the base of the underarm.

E. BACK NECK WIDTH

To determine the neck width, measure across the back of the neck. For a close-fitting neckline, adhere closely to this measurement; for a looser fit, or to allow for the addition of a collar, add more ease to the measurement.

F. SHOULDER WIDTH

Measure across the shoulders to the beginning of the arm socket. Add the two shoulders to the neck to determine the actual cross-back measurement.

G. SLEEVE LENGTH AT UNDERARM

This measurement is necessary for sleeves with shaped sleeve caps or raglans, but it can be skipped for sleeves that are set in straight across the armhole edge. Measure from the beginning of the underarm along the inside of the arm to the point at which you wish the sleeve to hit the wrist.

H. CENTER BACK NECK TO WRIST

To take this measurement, have the child hold his or her arm out straight to the side and measure along the outside of the arm, from the center of the back neck out to the wrist. Once you have this measurement, calculate the precise sleeve length for a dropped-shoulder garment by dividing the cross-back measurement in half, then subtracting that figure from the full center back neck to wrist measurement.

BODY MEASUREMENTS						
Children's sizes	4	6	8	10	12	14
Approximate height Metric equivalent (cm)	3'4" 102	3'10" 116	4'3" 129	4'5" 134	4'9" 145	5' 152
Approximate weight	40lbs	50lbs	60lbs	65lbs	85lbs	95lbs
Chest	23" 58	24" 61	26" 66	28" 71	30" 76	32" 81
Cross back	9¾" 25	10¼" 26	10¾" 27	11¼" 28.5	12" 30.5	12¼" 31
Armhole depth	4¾" 12	5" 12.5	5½" 14	6" 15	6½" 16.5	7" 18
Neck	3½" 9	3½" 9	3¾" 9.5	4" 10	4" 10	4" 10
Back-waist length	9½" 24	10½" 26.5	12½" 32	14" 35.5	15" 38	15½" 39.5
Center-back neck to wrist	18½" 47	20" 51	21½" 54.5	23½" 59.5	25½" 65	27" 68.5
Waist	21" 53	22" 56	23" 58.5	24" 61	25½" 65	26½" 67
Hip	24" 61	26" 66	28" 71	30" 76	32" 81	34" 86
Upper arm	7½" 19	8" 20.5	8½" 21.5	9" 23	9½" 24	10" 25.5
Wrist	5½" 14	5½" 14	5¾" 14.5	6" 15	6" 15	6" 15
Sleeve length	10½" 26.5	11½" 29	12½" 31.5	13½" 34	15" 38	16" 40.5

Size Matters

Style, fit and finishing: the essential elements for a made-to-measure man's sweater

By Mari Lynn Patrick

Sweaters have been a men's-wear fashion favorite since the 1920s, when the Prince of Wales was spotted wearing a stylish Fair Isle at the St. Andrews Golf Club. Before long, Arans and Guernseys, once the wardrobe staple of sailors and fishermen, were making their way to Main Street. In the '50s, tailored cardigans, snug-fitting vests and classic V-neck pullovers were all the rage. By the '90s, "casual Fridays" and a general loosening up of the dress code paved the way for a more relaxed approach to sweater styling; shapes became more boxy; and a push for natural fibers brought about demand for cozy wools and comfortable cottons. Today, as the fashion world seeks to please an ever-more-sophisticated consumer, the concurrent crazes for retro styling, comfort and high-performance fibers mean that the sweater choices for men are bigger and better than ever.

THE ELEMENTS OF STYLE

Men's wear has come a long way from staid knit designs in somber tones of olive, brown and gray. As elsewhere in the fashion world, color is making a big splash, and while the majority of men are not ready to embrace the hot pinks, oranges and other neon brights that have been making their way down the fashion runways, they are finding room in their closets for more intense colorations and fabulously textured patterns.

When it comes to color, almost anything goes. A growing concern for the environment has resulted in the ever-increasing popularity of green—everything from subtle moss shades to brilliant flashes of lime. Neon brights borrowed from performance gear are showing up as accents in stripes and on collars, cuffs and plackets. No longer content to be fashion's wallflowers, browns, denim blues, indigo and other rich, earthbound colors are also making their presence known in deeper, more saturated shades. Color, too, is crossing the gender line, as traditionally feminine shades of pink, and especially lavender and purple, make their way onto the men's-wear scene.

Texture is the touchstone of the season for women and for men. Deep ribbing, chunky cables and sculptural patternwork in cushy cottons, tweedy wools and other bulky, fleecy yarns are big news. Though confined for the moment to the truly fashion-forward few, fringed and furry yarns and other novelties are also making headway in the men's department. Indulgence is another buzzword for the 21st century, so don't be surprised to find classic crew necks and cardigans worked in luxury fibers such as cashmere, alpaca and ultrafine Merino. Silhouettes are all over the map, from formfitting pullovers in boldly patterned designs to slouchy deconstructed styles accented with slits and slashes. When it comes to the details, fine ribbing, drawstrings, zipper closures and thin stripes, both vertical and horizontal, move front and center. Of course, old favorites still endure—there's always room for a traditional Aran (though this season's version will be worked up in a superchunky yarn or bold color), fabulous Fair Isle or classic cardigan.

SIZE IT RIGHT

Once sweater style is determined, it's time to pay attention to achieving a perfect fit. Men's sweaters aren't just oversized versions of their female counterparts. As is the case with women's styles, the chest measurement is the pivotal sweater fitting point for men. While men's styles can run the gamut from formfitting to oversized, the most flattering (and comfortable) silhouette is a relaxed design with about 4"–6"/10–15cm of ease added to the chest measurement. To determine chest size, place a tape measure around the widest part of the chest and record the measurement.

When it comes to a comfortable fit, length is as important as width. After all, a sweater that's too short or too long is just as likely to remain buried in the depths of the closet as one that's too tight. Keep length in proportion to the person who will be wearing the sweater. Short and small-framed men look best when the length from the highest point of the shoulder to the lower edge is about 25"/64cm. For tall and large-framed men, 29.5"/75cm is best. Those of more average build fall somewhere in between. For the best fit, make length adjustments below the underarm.

You'll also want to pay close attention to the fit of the sleeve. Deep, easy-fit armholes and wide upper-arm measurements best accommodate a man's broad shoulders and physique. To determine the length of straight sleeves, subtract the center back neck to cuff measurement (the actual body measurement—see chart opposite) from half the cross back measurement.

Adequate neck drop and width are crucial for comfort and a professional-looking finish. Classic crew necks are the most popular style, but don't overlook fashionable alternatives such as turtlenecks, polo collars and split-neck designs. Firm ribbed neckbands, either deep or shallow, are great basics, but neat rolled edges also provide a simple finish. For a round neck, keep the neck drop to 2–2.5"/5–6.5cm; for a V neck, 4–5"/10–12.5cm is best. For the back neck, a width of 6–8"/15–19cm is the most flattering. For turtlenecks, keep the depth at 6.5"/16.5cm or less—this will eliminate excess fabric.

A FINE FINISH

Neat and even finishing is the hallmark of all well-made hand knits. Since details are kept to a minimum in most men's sweaters, a professional finish is even more important—after all, there's nothing to distract from a poorly stitched seam or sloppy cuffs and hems. The finishing techniques to use depend on the style of both the garment and the person who will be wearing it. Today's trend is toward simple self-finishing and a looser fit, but traditionalists will prefer tailored finishes, snug cuff and close-fitting ribbing. ⌒

SIZING CHART: MEN'S SWEATERS

SIZE	SMALL 34	36	MEDIUM 38	40	LARGE 42	44	X-LARGE 46	48	XX-LARGE 50	52
CHEST (in)	34	36	38	42	42	44	46	48	50	52
(cm)	86	91.5	96.5	101.5	106.5	111.5	116.5	122	127	132
WAIST	28	30	32	34	36	39	42	44	46	48
	71	76	81	86	91.5	99	106.5	111.5	116.5	122
HIP	35	37	39	41	43	45	47	49	51	53
	89	94	99	104	109	114	119	124.5	129.5	134.5
CROSS BACK	15.5	16	16.5	17	17.5	18	18.5	19	19.5	20
	39.5	40.5	42	43	44.5	45.5	47	48	49.5	50.5
SHOULDER	5	5.25	5.5	5.5	5.5	6	6	6	6.25	6.25
	12.5	13.5	14	14	14	15	15	15	16	16
NECK: SHIRT SIZE	14	14.5	15	15.5	16	16.5	17	17.5	18	18.5
	35.5	36.5	38	39.5	40.5	42	43	44.5	45.5	47
ARMHOLE DEPTH	8	8.5	9	9.5	10	10.5	11	11.5	11.5	12
	20.5	21.5	23	24	25.4	26.5	28	29	29	30.5
SLEEVE TO UNDERARM	17.5	18	18.5	19	19.5	20	20	20.5	20.5	20.5
	44.5	45.5	47	48	49.5	50.5	50.5	52	52	52
BACK LENGTH	26	26.25	26.5	26.75	27	27.25	27.5	28	29	29.5
	66	66.5	67.5	68	68.5	69	69.5	71	73.5	75
CENTER BACK NECK TO CUFF	32	32.5	33	33.5	34	34.5	35	35.5	36	36.5
	81	82.5	83.5	85	86	87.5	89	90	91.5	92.5

The table of body measurements for men reflects the standard sizing that is used for men's garments. These are actual body measurements, not knitted measurements, and are taken on the body with a tape measure. The amount of ease (inches/cm added to the body measurement for wearable ease) in men's styling is often from 4–6"/10–15cm in the circumference measurements.

By Anne Marie Soto

A FIGURE ANALYSIS

The crucial difference between Petite and Misses' sizes is the length of the garment. In ready-to-wear, that difference may vary slightly from manufacturer to manufacturer. In patterns for home-sewing, however, both Miss and Miss Petite sizes have been standardized. Thus the measurements in home-sewing patterns can serve as useful guidelines for altering Misses' knitting instructions to suit your smaller frame.

Here are some of the ways in which Petite sizes differ from their corresponding Misses' sizes:

• For Petites, the back waist length (from the neck base to the waist in back) is 1"/2.5cm shorter.

• The hipline (at the fullest part of the hip) is 2"/5cm higher—it's 7"/18cm below the waist for Petites, compared to 9"/23cm below the waist for Misses. As a result, the length of a finished Petite sweater (measured from the waistline to the hemline at the center back) is 2"/5cm shorter.

• The sleeve length for Petites is 1¼"/3cm shorter.

• The Petite shoulder (from the back of the neck to the joint where the shoulder and upper arm meet) is ⅛"/3mm narrower.

In trying to translate standard knitting instructions for your size, you may be tempted simply to knit everything shorter, but this seldom solves the problem. The reason is that length adjustments must be made in proportion to the total garment. The diagrams that accompany this article will show you how to make length adjustments. Remember to make them on both the back and front pieces of the garment.

The extent of the adjustments will depend on the design of the garment. If the garment has no armhole shaping (as in dropped shoulders or angled armholes, for example), you can limit the adjustments to two zones: across the upper chest and near the lower edge. But a shaped garment that is hip length or longer will need to be shortened in all three zones: across the upper chest, in the midriff area, and at the hipline or along the lower edge of the garment.

The colors are gorgeous, the gauge is perfect and the technical execution is flawless. Yet the final result is a sweater that overwhelms your figure. If you're under 5'4", this scenario may sound all too familiar. That's because your petite proportions don't match the 5'4" to 5'6" figure that is the standard for most sweaters, including those in *Vogue Knitting*. This doesn't mean, however, that you are sentenced to a lifetime of ill-fitting garments. Good fit can be yours if you start with figure-friendly styles, then learn how to fine-tune them.

If there are buttonholes, recalculate their position, taking the length adjustments into account. You may also want to reduce the number of buttons.

Sleeves, too, require length adjustments. The fitted sleeve has three adjustment zones: the sleeve cap depth; the upper arm (an inch or two (2.5 to 5cm) above the elbow); and the midpoint of the lower arm.

An adjustment to the sleeve cap depth is essential. If you adjust the front and back armhole depth but overlook the sleeve cap, the finished sleeve cap will be too large for the armhole. For more on sleeve cap shaping, see page 159.

SELECT A SUITABLE STYLE

Some styles are inherently unflattering to a diminutive figure. Avoid roomy dolman sleeves, extended shoulders, wide lapels, deliberately oversized fashions, proportions that cut the body in half horizontally, giant patch pockets, exaggerated fullness and excessive details. Beware, too, of the "cutesy" details—such as tiny lace-stitch collars, rows of ruffles and bunches of applied bows—that are too frequently considered the province of Petites. There's nothing appealing about an adult in clothing suited to a little girl!

Instead, choose slim silhouettes that skim the figure. A clean, uncluttered, sophisticated look is best. Look for long, vertical lines that carry the eye upward. Center front bands are universally becoming. A double-breasted style can flatter a slim petite figure, but be careful; it can also make you look shorter and wider.

Although monochromatic color schemes tend to elongate the figure, they don't offer the creative opportunities that most knitters crave. Consider replacing the contrasting colors with contrasting textures. The interplay of same-color yarns with different textural surfaces adds interest to a design without visually breaking the garment lines the way contrasting colors might.

DIMINISH THE DETAILS

Regardless of the style of the sweater, all of its details should be in proportion to your figure. Consider reducing the width of the collar, narrowing the plackets, switching to smaller buttons, and/or scaling down any patch pockets. Even as small a change as ¼"/6mm can make a big difference.

And don't forget the ribbing. If it is too deep, it can make the sweater look off-balance—even if the overall length is exactly right. When shortening the sleeves or the body, consider making part of that adjustment in the ribbed area. As a rule of thumb, subtract ¼" to ⅜"/6mm to 2cm from the depth of the ribbing.

SIMPLIFY THE PATTERN

For petite figures, simpler is generally better. Because the body "canvas" is smaller, a sweater can have the same impact with fewer design features. A profusion of patterns—too many cables, too many color changes, too many different motifs—creates a confusing effect.

A complex color pattern may be more compatible to the petite figure if you eliminate a few of the shades. As an alternative, consider isolating several elements from an appealing pattern, then working them into a solid ground. For example,

choose one eye-catching stripe from an allover Fair Isle design, or cut down on the number of cable variations in an Aran pattern. Avoid large intarsia motifs unless they can be downsized—without losing the basic qualities of the design—by omitting the central stitches.

ARTFUL SUBSTITUTIONS

Although you may love the way that tall, leggy model looks all cuddled up in her bulky sweater, stop and think about how all that yarn will look on your small frame. Overwhelming, right? Still, the basic design may be exactly what you're looking for. If so, consider changing the size of the yarn and needles.

Of course, it's not enough simply to change the yarn. To ensure that the finished garment fits, you must also revise the knitting instructions. Since this requires a fair amount of arithmetic, try it first with a relatively simple design.

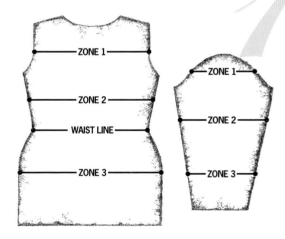

ADJUSTING PATTERN LENGTHS

• When adjusting a fitted body, you will need to adjust all three zones. For an unshaped garment, adjust zones 1 and 3 only.

• The amount you need to shorten will depend on your overall length. For example, you can shorten 1 or 2"/2.5 or 5cm at the hip area, 1"/2.5cm above the waist and ½ to 1"/2 to 2.5cm in the armhole area.

• When adjusting the sleeve length, it may be necessary to recalculate the increasing sequence.

• For set-in sleeves, it is essential to adjust the armhole and sleeve cap.

For example, a bulky yarn on size 11/8mm needles may be too much, but the same pattern executed in a worsted yarn on size 8/5mm needles may be just right.

In general, if the pattern calls for bulky yarn, substitute worsted yarn. If it calls for worsted, substitute sport yarn. And if it calls for sport yarn, substitute fingering yarn.

Here are a few more tips:

- Never, ever make a substitution without first making a gauge swatch to determine both stitch gauge and the row gauge for the new yarn.

- If the knitting instructions provide both measurements, subtract the body measurements from those of the finished sweater. This will tell you how much design ease the garment includes. Design ease is an important factor in maintaining the look of the sweater.

- Next, take your personal body measurements, add the design ease and compare the totals to those in the original instructions.

- Use all this information to revise the knitting instructions, recalculating the cast-on stitches, the increases and decreases, the number of rows and so on.

By downsizing your sweaters, you'll be able to upgrade your wardrobe with knitted garments that are comfortable to wear and truly flattering to your petite figure. ⌒

DOWNSIZING YOUR SWEATER

The Aran pullover shown here, first featured in the Winter 1992/93 issue, need not overwhelm your smaller figure. A few changes in the pattern stitch can downsize the overall look. We've taken 1 stitch from each of the cable ropes for the center cable and 2 stitches from the side cables. As with any adjustment, it is important to check your gauge and calculate the overall width.

Wear and Care

How do the experts care for their fine knitted items? We spoke with representatives of several yarn companies, who were happy to share tricks of the trade.

by Janine Hornicek

The industry insiders interviewed for this article have one thing in common: All emphasize the importance of knitting a gauge swatch, then blocking it in the same way as the final garment. Says Barry Klein of Trendsetter Yarns: "Always knit a swatch and keep it; don't rip it out. Use it not only to determine the gauge but also to test how you'll block and clean your garment."

A blocked, or dressed, swatch will give you the true stitch and row gauge for your knitted fabric (certain stitches, such as lace and cables, change dramatically after blocking); as well, it provides valuable information about the drape of the yarn, and lets you know how the yarn will react to moisture. Cashmere, for instance, softens after washing, and its stitches "bloom" (that is, fill in). Other fibers too change their character or gauge. Notes Margery Winter, creative director of Berroco, Inc.: "After blocking, [some] linen yarns undergo a big change—the length and width of the blocked swatch differ substantially from the measurements on the needle. The only way to determine the gauge is from the blocked swatch."

HANDLE WITH CARE

Yarn manufacturers urge knitters to follow their recommendations for cleaning and blocking. If other methods are being considered—ones that involve steam, heat or any other action that's inconsistent with the yarn's care label, for instance—it's doubly important to do a test. For example, knitters must use caution with synthetics (some may melt), natural fibers such as silk, and fibers that can scorch, like cotton and rayon.

Many fibers—protein, plant and manufactured—can be hand-washed safely. In fact, animal fibers generally benefit from hand-washing, which removes dirt and oils trapped during the manufacturing process. It's the type of dyes used and how those dyes interact with the fibers that determine whether a particular yarn should be washed. (Dyes can often be "set" by adding a tablespoon of white vinegar to water.) Again, test first on a swatch. When working with yarns that are blends of multiple types of fibers, follow the instructions on the ball band.

KINDS OF BLOCKING

Barry Klein considers blocking an essential part of the knitting process. To begin, he wet-blocks a square by spraying the fabric with water, shapes it, pins it and lets it air-dry. To protect the garment, he places the fabric right-side down. Interestingly, a number of yarns—Trendsetter's polyester eyelash for one—should not be blocked at all; instead, he says, just shake them to fluff.

Margery Winter concurs: "I never block [Berroco's] faux-fur 'Zap.' It's sufficient to tease it with a knitting needle and shake it to fluff the fabric." She also skips blocking when the stitch quality of the finished piece is consistent, edges don't curl and the measurements are exact. She adds that some yarns, such as "Plush," don't need blocking because they are completely square and finished right off the needles.

However, Winter hard-blocks garments made from wool, or those with a high percentage of wool or other animal fibers, after assembling them, because hard-blocking evens out and aligns stitches. She hard-blocks linen by dampening it, then steam-ironing it through a pressing cloth. She also hard-blocks cotton and silk blends but cautions knitters to use extra care when blocking silk.

Chuck Desmond, manager of the Jagger Spun Division at Jagger Brothers, Inc., blocks garments right-side up and always wet-blocks items knitted from animal fibers. She recommends briefly soaking garments in water, spinning them without agitation to remove excess moisture, then blocking. Like many of those we spoke with, she suggests placing delicate items such as lace shawls in lingerie bags before spinning so they don't catch on washing machine parts.

Nancy Thomas, editorial director of Lion Brand Yarn, has a different philosophy when it comes to blocking. "Years ago there was a move to more careful blocking: pinning to exact specifications and hard finishing. But with the proliferation of more yarn blends, heavy blocking is no longer as necessary." She doesn't steam garments made from blends of manufactured and animal fibers, and yarns such as Lion Brand's "Glitterspun" don't need blocking at all. Usually, she just sews garments together, though she may lightly spray them with water. Thomas steam-blocks seams from the inside of the garment and does other blocking from the outside.

CLEANING KNITTED GARMENTS

The following instructions apply to all of the fibers for which hand-washing is recommended. (Remember: Protein fibers and silk are most vulnerable when wet.) Fill a clean basin with cool to tepid water and a gentle cleanser made specifically for washing wool and other fine fibers, or a gentle pH-neutral, dye-free detergent. Gently squish the water through the garment—never twist or wring—and let it soak. Let the water out of the basin and, supporting the fabric with your hands, gently press it against the sides and bottom of the bowl to remove excess water. If the detergent needs to be rinsed out, refill the basin and repeat the process. Place the garment in a washing machine (use a lingerie bag if necessary) and briefly spin without agitation to remove much of the excess water. Support the garment when you remove it, shape, and lay flat to dry.

HOW THE EXPERTS DO IT

Chuck Desmond uses Eucalan, a pH-neutral, biodegradable cleansing agent that doesn't need rinsing, for items made from animal fibers. Because protein fibers should not be wet for long periods of time, she briefly spins them in a washer. For tough stains that are embedded in the fibers, such as oil and grease, she recommends dry cleaning.

Some yarns can be trickier to clean. For example, Desmond notes that Jagger Spun's lace-weight wool/silk "Zephyr" should be dry-cleaned, because wool and silk fibers handle dye differently. (Dyes tend to sit on top of silk fibers and may be less resistant to fading in light and water than pure wool.)

For hand-washing garments, Barry Klein recommends using a mild dye-free detergent such as Dreft or Ivory Snow (some harsh detergents, including Woolite,

contain acid). He adds: "Put a little Vidal Sassoon finishing rinse in the final rinse water when washing mohair to soften it up. But always test this on your swatch first." He notes that garments made from multiple fibers can be safely "air fluffed" in a dryer without heat; in some cases, low heat may be used.

Like Chuck Desmond, Nancy Thomas prefers a no-rinse wool wash. She fills her washing machine with water, adding wool wash as it fills, and lets her garments soak for half an hour. She then spins most of the water out, not allowing the machine to agitate. Occasionally she'll place knitted items such as afghans in the dryer for a few minutes, at a low temperature, to help eliminate some of the moisture. Thomas also recommends placing items that can be damaged by the spinning motion of a washing machine in a pillowcase or lingerie bag for protection.

STORAGE

All of the yarn company representatives stress the importance of making sure garments are absolutely clean before they are stored, because moths, carpet beetles and other fiber-eating pests are attracted to stained fibers. Make sure too that they are perfectly dry: damp fibers will mildew and rot. Margery Winter stores knitted items in ventilated plastic hampers in her closet, with tissue paper between the layers. Chuck Desmond folds garments flat and places them between acid-free tissue paper (available from dry cleaners) in a cedar chest or in plastic sweater boxes with a cedar block or chips near them (a cotton ball soaked in natural lavender oil also works). "Clothes should not be kept in plastic bags, but plastic sweater boxes will allow some air circulation," she notes. Always store clothes made from natural fibers away from light.

Barry Klein recommends storing knitted garments on a shelf in a dark corner of a closet. He says that zippered bags should never be used, nor should any garment be placed inside sealed plastic, because animals fibers (wool and the like) need to breathe or their characteristics will change. If there is a concern about moths or other fiber-eating pests, a piece of cedar may be hung in the closet.

When in doubt, consult with your dry cleaner for ideas about the long-term storage of special garments. ⌐

BLOCKING AND CLEANING RECOMMENDATIONS

These recommendations are based on information from a variety of sources, including *Principles of Knitting*, by June Hemmons Hiatt; *Vogue Knitting: The Ultimate Knitting Book*, from the editors of *Vogue Knitting*; and other highly respected sources, including trade association Web sites. Note: The recommendations apply to yarns that contain only one fiber, or fibers with compatible care methods. If the ball band specifies a cleaning or blocking method that differs from the one recommended below, follow the care instructions on the band. Where hand-washing is recommended, refer to the instructions herein.

PROTEIN FIBERS

Alpaca Hand-wash. Blocking: Steam-block or damp (wet) block

Angora Hand-wash. Blocking: Wet-block by spraying

Cashmere Hand-wash (this fiber is more susceptible to alkalis than is wool; use extra care when washing). Blocking: Wet-block, or dry-block with steam (test temperature on swatch)

Mohair Hand-wash. Can be briefly air fluffed in a dryer without heat. Blocking: Wet-block by spraying

Wool Hand-wash; can be machine-washed and dried if labeled "Superwash." Blocking: Wet-block, or dry-block with warm steam

PLANT FIBERS

Cotton Machine-washable using soap or detergent; can be machine-dried, which will help restore its original shape. Dry completely before storing. Blocking: Wet-block, or block with steam. Use caution—scorching will occur if steam is too hot

Linen Can be washed with non-alkali soap or dry-cleaned; can also be dried in a hot dryer, then ironed. Dry completely before storing. Blocking: Wet-block, or dry-block with warm or hot steam

Silk Hand-wash using a pH-neutral detergent, or dry-clean. If appropriate, use steam and a moderate iron temperature. Note: Moisture weakens silk fiber. Blocking: Steam-block at a moderate temperature setting; be sure to test on your swatch

SYNTHETICS PRODUCED FROM WOOD PULP

Rayon Wash with a mild pH-neutral detergent; alkalis and dry heat can cause damage; will scorch if the heat used to press it is too high. Rayon weakens when wet and must be dried completely before storing. Blocking: Wet-block by spraying, unless contraindicated by ball-band instructions

Lycocell Lycocell—trade name Tencel—is a manufactured fiber made from cellulose (wood pulp) using a process different from that used for rayon. Found in many yarns, Lycocell can be hand- or machine-washed and dry-cleaned; the fibers with which it is combined determine the cleaning and blocking methods. For more information about this fiber, visit www.tencel.com. Blocking: Use the method specified for the types of fibers with which it is blended

SYNTHETICS

Most synthetic fibers, including nylon, acrylic and polyester, as well as metallic yarns, are produced in various ways; recommendations for cleaning and blocking vary. Follow the instructions provided on the ball bands.

Tender Loving Care

by Marge Raphaelson

GENERAL CARE TIPS

• Save a few yards of yarn from your project, wind into a "butterfly" and attach securely to an inside seam. It will "age" with the sweater and insure a color match if you ever need to mend.

• In a pinch, you can also use your gauge swatch for mending, but we recommend saving it so you can test blocking, spot cleaning and washing/drying methods on it.

• Try not to wear the same garment two days in a row. Time between wearing allows the fibers to return to their original position, drop wrinkles and be refreshed by moisture in the air.

• Your handmades should never be hung on a hanger (or hook or back of chair) even briefly. This will pull the garment out of shape.

• Garments worn next to the skin will need more frequent attention than crews or cardigans worn over a blouse. Remember to check them (especially neckline and cuffs) after each wearing for makeup or other soil.

• Most hand-knit garments will benefit from a good brushing with a soft clothes

A handmade knitted or crocheted garment is truly a labor of love. With every single stitch formed by hand, and all the hours spent…don't mistreat your finished garments! Natural fiber and blended yarns such as wools and wool blends, angoras and mohairs, are inherently resilient, and all your winter hand knits will benefit from proper between-wear and between-season care.

brush. To avoid snagging loopy knits or garments made with bouclé yarns, a good shaking out will suffice.

• Flat knits or fuzzy yarns sometimes "pill," especially where surfaces rub together—at the underside of a sleeve, for example. Most times, a thorough, gentle brushing or a going-over with sticky tape will do the trick. In extreme cases, you might try the following: Lay the garment flat and pull the knit slightly taut, then lightly run a safety razor just above the surface, "shaving" off the pills. DON'T try this if you're rushing on your way to work, or with anything other that flat knits.

• It's a good idea to trace a garment outline on heavy paper, or write down detailed measurements before you clean it for the first time. This will aid in blocking or pressing to the original shape.

• Always spot clean a garment between wearings so stains won't set. You can use dry cleaning solvent or a little soap and water—test for results on your gauge swatch.

• Mending should always be done before cleaning, but try to do it as soon as you notice a flaw. Pulls can be fixed by easing the thread into the surrounding stitches with a crochet hook. Fix snags by pulling through to the wrong side with a crochet hook or pin. If thread is broken, knot on wrong side (not too tightly!). For bigger mending jobs, use your "butterfly" or gauge swatch yarn.

CLEANING

The most important information is found on the skein band. Save it, or write the information down somewhere. If more than one type of yarn was used in the garment, use the gentlest method recommended. Whether a garment is machine-washable, hand-washable or dry-cleanable, you should be able to keep major cleanings down to a few times a year with good between-wear care.

• When hand-washing, turn garment inside out (button to help keep shape), fill basin with lukewarm water and mild soap (not detergent). Unless the sweater is unusually dirty, use only a little soap—water is the important cleanser. Let sweater soak for a few minutes, then gently swish it around in the suds. Don't pull or twist the sweater—the less it's handled, the better. Rinse in lukewarm water three or four times until water is clear and there are no traces of soap. Press out excess water from the sweater using the side of the basin. Roll sweater in a thick towel to absorb excess water, supporting it with your hands to avoid stretching.

• Some new wool yarns and blends can be machine-washed. Use lukewarm water and mild soap.

• If your sweater is dry-cleanable only, advise your cleaner of the fiber content. A skein band may also identify one of several solvents recommended for cleaning.

DRYING AND BLOCKING/IRONING

Once your garment is clean, proper drying and care will guarantee a good-as-new garment. Avoid too-fast or too-slow drying; both can damage fibers.

• Always dry sweaters flat on a towel or rack away from heat or sun, which can shrink fibers, make them brittle or discolor them.

• If blocking, pull gently to shape using your paper pattern or written

measurements. As the sweater dries, periodically coax it into shape. In rare cases, you may need to pin to shape. If so, be sure to use rustproof pins.

• To help reshape a highly styled sweater, put crushed, acid-free tissue paper where shaping is needed—turtleneck, puffed shoulder, peplum.

• For heavy garments like outerwear, slip an extra towel in between sweater front and back to speed drying.

• Never iron sweaters made from 100% acrylic yarns; they can stretch permanently out of shape. These are the true wash-and-wear fibers and never even need blocking.

• If you must press out wrinkles, keep it light! Use a damp cloth between the iron and the wrong side of the garment, being careful not to touch the surface of the garment with the iron. Ribbings or raised patterns should never be pressed.

STORAGE

Proper between-season storage is extremely important. One moth can do a lot of damage, and giving your garments a good "summer vacation" can add years to their useful life.

• Don't put sweaters away dirty; this attracts moths. Spot clean, brush and air. You shouldn't need moth crystals or balls, but if you do, use them sparingly and don't sprinkle them directly onto the sweaters.

• Empty pockets, button buttons, shape collars and ruffles. The more time you take now with your sweaters, the less fussing you'll have to do when you want to wear them again.

• Always store handmades folded on a shelf, in a drawer or in a cedar chest (be sure to allow them plenty of room to "breathe"). Acid-free tissue paper between the folds will help prevent wrinkles.

• If you store sweaters in plastic bags, punch a few holes in the bags so air can circulate. Better yet, buy the stackable, ventilated clear plastic boxes you can find in the closet shop of your department store.

If you're ever tempted to toss a sweater over the bedpost or ignore a stain until a more convenient time, just think of the hours it would take to replace it, or even to restore it to its original condition. The best care will prolong the life of your precious handmade for many years! ~

Holey Wars

Attacking the archenemy of woolen sweaters

by Elizabeth Zimmermann

Yes, I insist on knitting only with pure *Wool*. In the face of wool's countless benefits, the single drawback is a small price to pay. What is that one disadvantage? M--hs. After all these years, I still cannot bring myself to tap out that word, a word that conjures aversion and terror—but also a certain amount of smugness. Is it tempting Providence to make that statement? Me, who has been m--hless in this old schoolhouse for the past twenty years? And it bursting with scores of sweaters, let alone the stacks of wool, fleece and winter garments indispensable to our climate? Well, the truth is that I've not always lived in this state of bliss.

About fifty years ago, we actually *imported* a British member of the above-mentioned tribe in my husband's best suit, and were stricken with guilt and apprehension. *It* was well-stricken, too, with a flyswat, and apparently before it produced any descendants, since we never played host to any more of the species.

I immediately laid in a large stock of m--hballs and scattered them around liberally, and also habituated myself to storing winter stuff in plastic bags, just then coming into style, with the unbelievable result that, to date, we have remained uninvaded.

All very well, you say, but suppose someone came to call, and flung down her old fur coat, and its inhabitants snuck out and crept into my wool room, let alone my sweater shelves? Well, I should look pretty silly after the above boasting, but I guess I'd lay in another 50lb bag of m--hballs and hope for the best. Better still, there's the cedar-chest. No m--h would even spend the weekend there, or in the cedar closet. Either of them is available if you're fortunate enough to have a family member handy with a hammer and nails. Be sure to use Eastern Red Cedar (as opposed to Western Cedar), as it is the most aromatic and effective.

A surefire killer of m--hs in all their stages is to put the suspect garment (or skeins or fleece) into the freezer for four to five days, a treatment that no form of *This* insect can survive. Also, when washing your woolen garment (always wash before storing, since body oils and dirt attract the dreaded m--h) add a drop of cedar oil, available in most health-food stores, to the final rinse water. This is not a lethal treatment, but will make m--hs think twice about setting up housekeeping. Unbleached, undyed wools do contain oil (lanolin) that is gourmet food for m--hs. Take extra precautions with this wool—it's worth it.

Now, let's explore Nature's side of this whole squalid business: It's not the *müth* (as Peter Seller's Clouseau pronounced it) that does the damage, but the dainty little baby caterpillars that come from the m--h that comes from the fur coat. *Go After Those Müth*, as they flit around looking for a home. They are very erratic flyers, not easy to stalk and smack at, although a flyswat is useful if you have one handy. Once hatched, all the caterpillars care about is munching around in your beloved woolens in order eventually to spin a cocoon from which will emerge another m--h that will flap around, mate and lay more eggs, which will hatch into caterpillars that will gnaw on your best woolens. Ad Infinitum. And the result is—*Müth-Holes*.

Dealing with müth-holes is frustrating in the extreme, since they usually involve two or three, or even more, threads of your knitted garment. Weaving in a repair job (which would be duck soup if the creature had seen fit to gnaw through just *one* thread) can be tantamount to booking a room in the Bin. Again, I must stress prevention, but when all else fails, consult the classic *Mary Thomas's Knitting Book* for marvelously clear drawings on repairing large holes.

Speaking of mending: In spite of the skill you use for the job, and the fact that you still have some of the same wool in which you knitted the garment, it is sometimes unsuccessful because the "new" bit of wool used for the repair is noticeably different in color and perhaps texture. This is because the sweater has been worn and washed for years, while the repair thread is still pristine. Aha! Here is an invaluable trick I learned from Barbara Abbey: Upon completion of the garment, take about two yards of the wool and skim it from lower edge to armhole (and back again) at the inside of the sweater. This two-yard length will then go through the same wash and wear as the garment, and will match perfectly should a patch ever become necessary. On the other hand, if the m--h has had the thoughtfulness to gnaw where a pocket would come in handy…need I finish this sentence?

I will go the extra mile to knit with incomparable Wool, but keep in mind that this natural fiber does have a natural enemy. ⌒

Essay: Of Knits and Men

by Donna Bulseco

Knitting has come a long way, baby: Just ask any man who has taken up a pair of size 8 needles and a skein of wool to create a sweater, a scarf or a wool cap with his own bare hands. And there are a surprising number of them you could ask, from the boy next door and the fireman down the block to the vascular surgeon who keeps his fingers nimble perfecting his cables.

Isaac Mizrahi devoted a segment to knitting on his Oxygen Media television show; it's a hobby he's enjoyed since childhood. Designers Marc Jacobs and Todd Oldham use their hands-on knitting experience to create the gorgeous hand knits in their collections. The Web site knitting.about.com has a "Men Who Knit" link, complete with photos of handsome dudes who knit one, purl one, making sweaters for themselves and their wives, onesies for their new babies or afghans for their pals. The buzz has even extended to celebrities: You know that knitting has really arrived on the red carpet when rumors circulate that such stars as Robert De Niro and Russell Crowe knit. (Okay, it's just a rumor. But hey, guys—it's never too late to start!)

Ask any man who knits why he does it, and you'll hear many of the same reasons women give for engaging in the craft: it's a stress reliever, a way to pass the time and a source of creative expression. Though there's little stigma attached to men who enjoy the craft, many acknowledge that they've encountered at times a certain amount of curiosity and social stereotyping. They've raised eyebrows; some have endured teasing from friends and family and even been called sissies. Many of them knit only in private, or were so secretive they didn't tell anyone about their hobby until they had something to show for their efforts. Still, their interest never waned, because they loved knitting. And from the look of many of their finished projects, adversity has certainly begotten originality and devotion to the craft.

Canadian actor Kirk Dunn learned to knit to impress a girlfriend some fourteen years ago. "I always thought knitting was cool," says Dunn. "Because it involves mathematics, spatial relations and counting as well as color, texture and aesthetics, it seemed like the perfect marriage between the sciences and fine art." At first, he kept his knitting a secret, gleaning the basics from an old Patons *How to Knit* book. He was adept enough to create an Icelandic Lopi sweater in "nice thick wool" while practicing lines for a children's play about, appropriately enough, gender stereotyping entitled *Girls Can! Boys Can!*

Today, Dunn practices what he preached so many years ago in that play—he clocks in knitting time at home in Toronto while taking care of his two young children. Last year, he knit a pair of green-and-blue variegated socks for his wife; a cardigan with blue diamonds and roses for his young daughter; and a huge 5-foot scarf using leftover yarn in hundreds of colors. "Knitting is a labor of love," says the actor, who rarely knits anything for himself. "I conceive a project for a person, choosing yarn and developing a pattern, and then I make it. It takes time and energy." One project he remembers fondly is a sweater he knit for his father, a minister, that featured two-toned, geometric orange and blue crosses. It was so vibrant, it caught the attention of renowned knitwear designer Kaffe Fassett, and Dunn was offered the chance to apprentice at Fassett's studio in London, a lifelong dream.

A shared characteristic of male knitters is that many learn by the book, then ignore the instructions, preferring instead to wing it by making up patterns, stitches and a gauge of their own. David Powers is a prime example of someone who moved quickly beyond the *America's Knitting Book* he learned by, and today he's creative and technically savvy enough to write his own how-to manual. "I don't follow what everyone else does," says Powers, who has lived in New York City for more than twenty years. "Everything I've knit has been from my own patterns. I never overdesign. Most people combine six or seven knitting ideas into a project, but when you do that, you end up with a beast."

Douglas Weiss, director of design research for Limited Design Services, picked up a book to learn "how to get the yarn on and how to get it off," then raced ahead to make a bright red, gray and chartreuse scarf inspired by a gorgeous one by Dries van Noten he'd seen at Barneys New York. Now, he's confident enough to strike out on his own, designing a scarf that picks up a beautiful palette found in *The Designer's Guide to Color*, which he uses in his job.

For most men who do it, knitting fuels creativity, but they also like the way it calms them down. When Peter Alvarez opened his own hair salon near Colorful Stitches, a yarn shop in Lenox, Massachusetts, he never guessed that he would find respite from the frenetic pace of his business right next door. "Knitting is very peaceful—it's a way to pass the time," says Alvarez, whose first project was a gray cashmere hat done on circular needles. His daughter Priscilla likes to brag about his accomplishments, showing a photo of her handsome dad in an impressive navy mohair cowl neck that took him six months to finish.

In the "Men Who Knit" forum on knitting.about.com, John Sutton, who took up knitting while serving on a U.S. Navy ship, reveals how he loves "watching this thing of my own making grow slowly—sometimes too slowly— in my hands. I love finding a color combination that works. And I love the results, the satisfaction of being able to say, 'I made it myself,' which is even more special because so few people expect to hear it from a man."

Amir Toos, senior vice president of production for the design house Badgley Mischka, thinks of knitting as "a form of meditation." The father of three, he just finished a onesie in silk-and-wool tweed yarn for his infant daughter, trimming it at the waist with eyelet threaded with red leather cord.

Even though knitting is primarily a solitary activity, most men enjoy its social benefits. For almost two years, David Powers, who lives in New York's trendy TriBeCa neighborhood, spent part of his day knitting at the World Financial Center in lower Manhattan, now closed as a result of the events of September 11. "Tourists would sneak photos of me, workers would stop to gauge my progress, and passersby would strike up conversations," says Powers.

Another New York City knitter, Andrew Flynn, joined a knitting group to hone his skills. "I'm a little too self-conscious to knit in public," he says, but the group, which meets once a month, helps build his confidence when he hits a snag or drops a stitch. He finished an aqua wool scarf for his niece and is on to a putty-colored "very Calvin Klein" sweater for himself, a fitting creation for the head art director at *Women's Wear Daily*.

Composer Richard Rodney Bennett, who created the music for the movie *Four Weddings and a Funeral* and is currently writing a saxophone quartet, was a member of the Big Apple Knitting Guild in New York for almost ten years. He attended lectures by knitting professionals given at the Guild and enjoyed the lively meetings. "When Kaffe [Fassett]'s first book came out, it was a passport into the world of knitting. I loved the technical side of it—cabling, manipulating colors—but was never really that tied to the idea of making sweaters," says Bennett. His knitting was an exploration of color and texture, much like the paintings he does nowadays. And although he's given away most of his yarn and needles to pursue art, he remains friends with those he met during his knitting odyssey.

"Boy Genius" is the way knitwear designer Nancy Winarick describes her pal Isaac Mizrahi, with whom she worked for many years developing hand-knit sweaters for his fashion collections. Their friendship led to a knitting collaboration on his TV show. "We knit matching monogrammed twinsets for Isaac and his dog Harry. Isaac knit his own in camel's hair on size 5/3.75mm needles, and I did Harry's," she says. Mizrahi, who was taught by his mother, is a very good knitter, but he relies on Nancy—his "knit doctor"—whenever he goes on a knitting binge.

Vive la différence! And may many more boy geniuses catch the knitting bug. ⁓

A Look-in on

Awards and accolades are nothing new to Perry Ellis. His innate design sense has kept him ahead of the fashion forefront for the five short years he has headed his own companies and for the ten preceding years that he was design director for John Meyer of Norwich, sportswear designer for the Vera Companies and designer of his own line for Portfolio.

Perry has won three Coty Awards (the Academy Awards of fashion), two for women's sportswear and one for his men's-wear collection. He was voted into the Coty Hall of Fame in 1981, one of the highest honors in the fashion industry. That same year, he was selected as one of the three designers to receive the Council of Fashion Designers' premier American Sportswear Award.

He received the Neiman Marcus Award for Distinguished Service in the Field of Fashion in 1979 and became the subject of worldwide acclaim in 1980 when he was chosen to represent the United States at the "Best 5, '81" international fashion presentation in Tokyo. And in 1982 he received both the CFDA Award for men's wear and the EARNIE award for children's wear. That's quite a collection of honors to

Perry Ellis, more than any other American designer, has been responsible for the resurgence in popularity of hand knits that we have seen in the last few years. His use of cables in simple shapes with tweeded yarns became a kind of trademark for him. And now you can make these true signature pieces from his rave-winning collection, to add a dash of Perry Ellis fashion originality to *your* wardrobe.

receive over a four-year period, but it's not surprising, for Perry has an adventurous and witty approach to design that blends the classic with the innovative—a combination that's bound to be noticed.

Perry also is known for his personal honesty and natural ease…elements that are an integral part of his designs. He is opposed to fashion mandates and is a firm believer that clothes are completely an individual matter. He strives to offer fashion options and to pique our *own* sense of fashion innovation, to make us think about ways of putting things together that we hadn't thought about before.

Perry's ability to mix the functional with the fanciful is part of what brought him such instant recognition, along with his courage to be different. Perry Ellis has added a lot of spirit to American fashion, not just with his marvelous sweaters, but with all his other endeavors, too.

Perry Ellis

Perry's path to fame has been as creative as are his designs. His B.A., from the College of William and Mary, is in business, and his M.A., from New York University, is in retailing. When he finished his education, he became a buyer for Miller and Rhoads, a department store in Richmond, Virginia. It was not long before his own flair for design emerged, however, and he began making specific fashion suggestions to manufacturers on how to improve their lines. His contributions helped create best-sellers and soon he and the manufacturers realized that in addition to excellent business and merchandising skills, he possessed a very special design talent.

It is that talent that we are pleased to bring you in this fashion year of the sweater, and we know you'll have as much fun knitting your own Perry Ellis originals as you will have wearing them.

Perry Ellis died in 1986. His design sensibility continues to influence the fashion world through Perry Ellis International, which designs, licenses and markets both women's and men's fashions.

This Perry Ellis design appeared in the Winter 1990/91 issue.

Pierrot: Knitting Wizard

by Donna Gould

While this mercurial designer is a bit mysterious about the details of his past (he's worked as a model, actor, musician and nanny), Pierrot sums up his history in one sentence: "Everything I've learned has led me to where I am now." He grew up in Lyon, France, in a house without indoor plumbing. But his mother made sure her children were well educated and taught him to knit when he was 9. "I suffered a soccer injury and was bedridden for a month," he says. "I was driving my mother crazy, and she thought knitting would calm me down."

On his own at a young age, he traveled continuously and spent a good deal of time in Paris, where he was exposed to the punk movement and club scene. He designed clothes under the "Pierrot" label and sold them to boutiques in New York, where he eventually moved at the invitation of a friend. Immersed in the downtown art and design community, he worked several jobs while trying to establish his design business.

"I didn't have the space to do sewing and sample making, so to make ends meet I started knitting sweaters and built up a private clientele," he says. Word spread, and by 1999 he was designing knits for rising star Miguel Adrover, whom he befriended while

Pierre Carrilero—known to the design world as Pierrot—never went to design school and often claims to know nothing about fashion. But his sharp wit and intricately crafted knits have made him a legend in knitting circles—and won raves from trendsetting stores and style icons like Sarah Jessica Parker (who donned his clothes in *Sex and the City*) and Kim Basinger (who sported his pink cardigan in the film *The Door in the Floor*).

working at Horn, Adrover's now defunct East Village boutique.

But the boyishly exuberant Pierrot had his own vision, and before long he was presenting his unique designs, the first time as part of a group show during New York's Spring 2000 Fashion Week. His first solo collection debuted in the fall of 2001, a highly anticipated show that was creative, quirky—and a raving success. "Next thing I knew, I had a financial backer, a PR company and my own studio," he says.

Inspired by American culture and the unique beauty of the female form, Pierrot has made it his goal to offer wearable clothes that still have a creative edge. Last year he parted ways with his backers and is currently producing collections on his own. "I have always designed and knitted my own samples, and this fall I branched out into wovens," he says. "I am proud to say I did the entire collection myself—the patterns, samples, everything—in yarns from Zegna Baruffa." The press proclaimed it his strongest effort yet, and stores like Barneys New York immediately placed orders.

Pierrot says this collection was inspired by "a very strict but sexy style" that was popular in the late 1950s. "It's an inspiration that is very dear to me because my mother used to dress like this—in pencil skirts and slim pants and chic sweaters." He reproduced the full look, complete with hand-knit intarsia ski sweaters and ladylike pointelles like the pretty pink cape featured here.

Despite his success, Pierrot confesses that he still has a lot to learn about his craft. "I'm not very technical or innovative. I just use a lot of imagination," says the designer, who learns from other knitters as well as from his own mistakes. "At this point in my career, I really want to experiment with knitting and see what else it can do," he adds. "But I'm humble enough to know that I will never know everything."

Today this self-described city boy commutes to Manhattan from his country house near Kingston, New York, where he likes to relax and entertain. "I still love shopping in the city," he says, "but here I am far removed from being a designer. And I love that, too." ⌐

Following a successful runway show during New York's Fall 2005 Fashion Week, Pierrot launched a line of women's clothing for the QVC Network called "Voila by Pierrot." He continues to create exclusive knits for stores in Paris and his hometown of Lyon, France, and is currently at work on his next collection.

Pierrot credits the fabulously feminine styles his mother once wore as inspiration for the strict-but-sexy shapes he sent down the fall catwalk—including the lacy pink cape shown here, first featured in the Fall 2004 issue.

Martin Storey and

by Donna Gould

Inventive. Romantic. Fanciful. And just a little offbeat. Two of the hottest designers around talk about their love affair with knitting—and the style they call their own.

MARTIN STOREY

Martin Storey believes in luck. In fact, he attributes every stage of his successful career to it. "It was only through chance that I discovered I could actually study fashion at university," says the designer, who is quickly redefining the image of Jaeger Handknits.

Raised on a farm in Yorkshire, England, Storey learned to knit in grade school. He was expected to assume responsibility for running the farm, but his keen interest in knitting prevailed. His father encouraged him to follow his dream—Storey's first stroke of luck.

He studied fashion design at Middlesex University in the early 1980s, a heady time on the London fashion scene. A decision to include a few hand knits in his final student collection rekindled his interest in the craft. But Storey claims it was once again "pure chance" that led him to his first job, at a design studio called Artworks, where his inventive creations were a big hit. He worked with owners Jane and Patrick Gottelier for fifteen years, doing everything from making patterns to inventing new stitches—a challenge he enjoys to this day.

Storey considers designing for Jaeger Handknits a fantastic opportunity. "Jaeger is part of Rowan Yarns, and for the first time in my life I enjoy the luxury of having yarns made to my specifications," says the designer, who has the enviable task of creating pieces that showcase the

Martin Storey's I-cord fringed pullover appeared in the Winter 2002 issue.

yarns introduced each season. In addition to adding a bit of panache to Jaeger's traditional English look, he is infusing the classics with color and wit—his trademark "English eccentricity"—to appeal to the younger customer. "Right now, hand knitting is riding the crest of a wave, and we need to tempt customers with new ideas."

His design for VK [below] is a case in point. "I'm always trying to find new ways to introduce texture into knitting, whether it's with stitches or embellishments like sequins, beading, even coins," Storey says. "This season I'm using luxurious yarns as trims on simple garments." His cowl-neck pullover, knit in Rowan's lustrous "Mohair Art," is trimmed with fanciful I-cord fringe. "The I-cord method creates a thick three-dimensional fringe that goes off in all directions when it's knit into the cuffs and hem. It's quirky and fun to wear."

He travels often for work, but these days Storey is content to stick close to his London home, enjoying life's simple pleasures—gardening, swimming, visiting museums and galleries. He has no desire to return to the family farm, confessing, "I'd rather go to the seaside and enjoy the peace and tranquillity. With a little luck, maybe it will happen."

JAMES COVIELLO

Though James Coviello's name is probably familiar to you, you could know it from any number of places. Since he began designing in 1987, he has created hats bearing his own label as well as those of designers ranging from Geoffrey Beene to Todd Oldham. He has designed knit dresses under the name Coviello & Erickson. And today he creates knitwear collections for Anna Sui and produces his own apparel collection—complete with hats.

His love affair with knitting began soon after he graduated from the Parsons School of Design in New York and launched his hat collection. "I wanted to make some

James Coviello: Men at Work

This James Coviello design was featured in the Winter 2002 issue.

his collections with a group of South American hand knitters whom he describes as some of the best in the world. "I'm a designer, but because I know how to knit and sew I understand the technical aspects of how things are made. I think that puts me way ahead of the game."

Known for his sophisticated color combinations and intricate stitches, the designer says that the quality and attention to detail found in vintage clothing inspire his romantic, slightly quirky styles. He also has a library stocked with a vast number of reference books, and his design featured here [left] began with an idea he first saw in a book on counterpanes. "I liked the idea of mixing classic cable stitches in a basic body, and also making it feminine," says Coviello. "The book featured a sampler with a beautiful ruffle that was knit in the opposite direction." Developing the swatch was difficult and required the help of his Peruvian samplemakers and a talented knitter friend. "The finished sweater, knit in a thick yarn on large needles, is a bit of a challenge. But the result is classic, unusual—and well worth the effort!"

Coviello divides his time between Manhattan and a historic house in upstate New York that he is slowly restoring. He loves to travel, and when he's away on business, he often schedules side trips to such places as Beijing, Buenos Aires, Bangkok and the famous ruins of Machu Picchu in Peru. "Relaxing on a beach is not for me," says the designer, who confesses that his creativity needs constant stimulation. "I'm always incredibly busy—and I wouldn't have it any other way."

knit hats and had never done any knitting or crocheting," says Coviello. "I met an expert knitter who taught me the basics but also encouraged me to do my own sweater collection. She became my mentor and introduced me to the beauty of the craft."

He loves the fact that knitting allows him to create a garment and its fabric simultaneously. "Given all of the yarns and stitches that exist, the ideas are limitless if you're a good knitter." Too busy these days to knit samples himself, Coviello develops

Martin Storey left his role as head designer for Jaeger Handknits to lead the design of Rowan's RYC Classic Collection of hand knits, launched in February 2005. He currently produces four pattern brochures a season for the line. Today James Coviello sells to more than forty specialty boutiques and department stores throughout the world. In 2003, he began designing a collection of affordable hand knits and home furnishings for the Spiegel Catalog, which is sold exclusively through Spiegel's Big Book.

Design Principals: Kaffe Fassett, Brandon Mably

by Donna Gould
A PAINTER'S PALETTE

Kaffe Fassett is known for his signature knitwear designs: intricate intarsias and elaborate patterns rendered in layers of glorious color. But *VK* readers may not know that Kaffe's unique sense of color and design has inspired legions of devoted fans—and brought him recognition worldwide as an expert on color and craft. "I'm a painter, knitter, quilter, needle artist and designer," he says, "but my approach to every discipline is the same—manipulating pattern and seeing how color comes alive in different forms."

Until age 28, Kaffe devoted his life to painting. Born in San Francisco, he won a scholarship to the School of the Museum of Fine Arts in Boston at age 19—but left after three months to paint in London, where he took up residence in 1964.

He had no experience with needlework but was often drawn to the richly patterned textiles he saw in museums and flea markets. "As a painter, I often tried to render them," he says, "but I had an urge to move from the canvas to something someone could wear." During a visit to a Scottish woolen mill, Kaffe succumbed to the

Knitters around the world covet their evocative and inventive designs. But while Kaffe Fassett, Brandon Mably and Vladimir Teriokhin share a passion for knitting, they have traveled vastly different roads to success. A peek into their intriguing pasts reveals their surprising artistic roots.

"exquisitely subtle colors" of the yarns, bought twenty shades and some knitting needles, and was taught to knit by a fellow passenger on the train ride home. "I got the gist of it, and from there I taught myself."

His first design appeared in *VK*, in 1986, and he went on to produce commercial collections for designers Bill Gibb and Missoni. Celebrities such as Barbra Streisand, Shirley MacLaine and Lauren Bacall have collected his one-of-a-kind knits, and in 1988 he became the first living textile artist to have a one-man show at London's Victoria and Albert Museum.

Kaffe has traveled extensively and communicated his design philosophy through numerous workshops, television and radio lectures, books and videos. He has been interviewed countless times on the subjects of color and design and has inspired thousands of crafters to incorporate vibrant colors into their projects. "Color is my inspiration," Kaffe says. "When it comes to knitting, it's about using big, strong geometrics and as rich and complex a color palette as possible."

KAFFE ON COLOR:

• Don't be afraid of color—why limit yourself to just one shade of red when you can use seventeen? Layering colors will give your work resonance, so strive for a rich texture, even if it's worked in fifty shades of gray.

• Let your yarns inspire you. Make collections of yarn and display them in a basket where you can see them. I often open a drawer of yarn to organize it, and next thing I know I'm sitting down to knit.

and *Vladimir Teriokhin*

He often designs "right in the middle," beginning with one idea but letting the piece develop as he's working. "When I knit, I work as a painter," he explains. "In my workshops, I tell people to pretend they're painters and to just let the dreamy part of themselves take over." He believes that knitting is not cerebral—it is intuitive. "Don't do it with your brain; just let your hands take over."

To make it simpler to layer in countless shades of color, Kaffe developed a technique for knitting-in the ends of yarn as he goes along. "This saves knitters hours of laborious darning in when they're done knitting," he says. "When introducing a new color, leave ends of about 3 inches [8cm] on the old and new yarns. Work the next two stitches with the new yarn, holding both ends in your left hand; lay them over the working yarn; and work the next stitch. Now insert the right-hand needle into the next stitch as usual, then bring the ends up over the point of the right-hand needle and work this stitch past the ends."

Calling himself "an old hippie," Kaffe says he prefers clothes that are romantic and intriguing. For this issue, Kaffe shied away from doing a classic crew- or V-neck sweater. Instead, he created a lush jacket with a generous shape, inspired by one that was given to him by his sister Holly, whom Kaffe describes as "a sensational knitter who bakes wonderful pies and runs our family business."

Describing the design for the jacket as a combination of abstract shapes and colors, Kaffe began by choosing hues that struck his fancy. "I pulled to-

gether a mix of juicy watermelon pinks, rich browns, swimming-pool blues and lapis lazuli," he says, and then sat down and started knitting. "I just designed it as I knit. One of the things I love most about knitting is that you never know how something is going to turn out. It could be a disaster, but you'll always come away from each project having learned something new."

He encourages knitters to take advantage of all the wonderful yarns available today. He has a preference for the sophisticated palette of Rowan yarns, saying, "They know what I'm all about. They have gorgeous shades, and their natural-fiber yarns are wonderful." For years Kaffe's designs have appeared on the pages of the company's pattern books, which revolutionized the industry by introducing imaginative designs to knitters of all ages.

Kaffe's limitless drive to create has led him to branch out into other mediums, including tapestry, fabric weaving, quilting and mosaics, and he has published a highly popular series of how-to books on each. Over the years, he has never stopped painting, and says that his style has evolved as a result of his work in other media: "There's a glow and intensity to my work that I've learned from textiles." But he says that knitting offers him the greatest creative freedom. "When I sit down to paint, I have something in front of me to get me going. It's more limiting," he explains. "But when I'm knitting, I feel fearless and free. Knitting is living row by row."

Kaffe Fassett in a colorblock jacket he designed, featured in the Special 2002 issue.

Brandon Mably models a turtleneck sweater he designed for the Special 2002 issue.

A CHEF'S PASSION

Brandon Mably is crazy about color and design. He remembers being mesmerized by the yarns displayed in—of all places—the local candy shop while growing up in a small seaside town in south Wales. "Next to the glass jars filled with candies were shelves and cabinets bulging with vivid knitting yarns, all arranged by color," Brandon recalls. "That's what always caught my attention."

While pursuing a career in the food industry in London in the early 1980s, Brandon had a chance meeting with Kaffe Fassett and made a radical shift, turning in his pots and pans for knitting needles. "I walked into Kaffe's studio—which was overflowing with baskets of yarn, Turkish carpets, Chinese ceramics and needlework cushions—and knew in an instant that I wanted to be part of that world."

Brandon became Kaffe's studio manager and Kaffe became Brandon's mentor, encouraging him to create his own designs. Eventually, Brandon started teaching the Kaffe Fassett knitting workshops, which led to the discovery that he enjoyed helping people connect with their innate sense of color and design.

Ironically, Brandon says that he doesn't consider himself a teacher. "My job is to encourage knitters to let go of their fears. I want them to learn to play, to be children again, to make mistakes." One of the first things he urges knitters to do is to experiment with combinations of dark and light hues and observe what they can do to one another. "Light shades can just kiss dark ones, and that's often what gives a garment dimension."

Anyone who attends a Kaffe Fassett workshop must know how to knit, since Brandon rarely focuses on technique. "Sooner or later, beginning knitters will get tired of making a mess and will learn to clean up their technique. I want to focus on helping knitters open up the gates, not bog them down with worry."

Conducting the workshops requires constant travel, and Brandon says it is a continuous source of his inspiration. "I'm exposed to new and exciting happenings all the time, and I soak it up like a sponge." He thrives on visual stimulation and asks his students to look at the patterns in things around them for inspiration: "A border on a carpet or a design on a porcelain vase can trigger an idea." The sport of rugby inspired his design for this issue. "I knit it in a lightweight yarn, and instead of using black or gray—those safe colors men usually go for—I gave it lots of color."

Admitting that his approach to technique is "quite basic," Brandon describes his style as simple, strong and clean. "I have a very practical mind, and I try to strip out complexity so that things are not too fussy. It's a look that's pure and contemporary but also nostalgic." As an example, he cites a sweater he designed for the Winter 2000/01 issue of VK. "I called it 'Nantucket,' my inspiration. I started with color— seaside colors, weathered cottages, white laundry hanging on a line." He distilled the images into an abstract design featuring a series of vertical lines and chevron shapes that represent seagulls. "It was like a domino effect, with one thing leading to another. Any devoted knitter can do it, just by letting his imagination run wild."

In the process of learning to knit, Brandon found that cables, fancy stitches and intricate shapes distracted from the impact he wanted to make. "I don't really know how to knit cables," he confesses. "I prefer to stick to a simple stocking stitch and basic shapes that can be sized easily, and that's what we do in the workshops."

When knitting designs that use many colors, he offers knitters the following tip for speed—and for preserving their sanity: "The different-colored yarns invariably get tangled at the back of the work, so I rarely have balls or bobbins attached," he says. "Instead, I break off short lengths of 2 to 3 feet [60 to 100cm], depending on the area to be covered. As they get tangled, it's easy just to pull through the color you want." When more color is needed, "You simply tie on another length, knitting-in the ends as you work," he adds.

Brandon is fascinated by the varied backgrounds of the people who attend the workshops. "Last fall, Kaffe and I did a book tour and I taught workshops in twenty-one cities around the world. It was challenging to work with people from so many different places and cultures. One thing I've discovered is that people don't knit out of necessity but rather as a form of meditation. Professional people knit to give time back to themselves."

While he enjoys knitting gifts for others, his busy schedule prevents him from knitting for himself. "My work is my life, and I love it," he adds. "Since September 11, I've been thinking a lot about how fragile life is. And if you have a God-given talent, you shouldn't waste it. You should express it."

BRANDON ON DESIGN:

• When working with color, it's important to focus on what you're doing. Watch what happens as you knit and connect with what you are creating. Let the colors take control and enjoy the idea that the finished product can end up looking very different from what it was in the beginning.

• Pin up your knitting, step back and look at it as you're going along—just like a painter does. You'll be amazed at how putting your work in a different perspective can affect what you see and influence your choices.

A DANCER'S DISCIPLINE

Vladimir Teriokhin confesses that his greatest design challenge is staying focused. "I want to design a lot of things at once, and it often gets me into trouble," he laughs. "In ballet, you learn to stay away from a certain spot on the stage because it's slippery—and I need to remember that!"

Vladimir frequently mentions dance and design in the same sentence, and it is no coincidence. In 1969, he was among 20,000 9-year-olds who auditioned

for the prestigious Bolshoi Ballet Academy School in Moscow—and one of only twenty selected. He spent the next ten years studying and performing with the Bolshoi, during which time he met and married the world-renowned ballerina Elena Stepaneko. The couple had successful dance careers in the former Soviet Union, but decided to travel to New York City in 1989 and start a new life.

Vladimir continued his ballet career, dancing with the Los Angeles Classical Ballet Company, but after twenty years he felt it was time to do something else. "In Russia, I spent years studying art history and design, and had experience designing ballet costumes," he explains. Gradually, he launched a second career as a designer—with a focus on knitwear. "I have always found knitwear to be the most interesting aspect of fashion. I learned to knit from my grandma and have been doing it my whole life."

He began working freelance and created commercial collections for a succession of top designers, including Donna Karan, OSCAR by Oscar de la Renta, Isaac Mizrahi and Ralph Lauren. "I did my first job for Ralph Lauren in 1998," he says. "They needed several sweaters for a fashion show and asked me if I could produce them in a week!" He met the deadline—and one design made the cover of *Women's Wear Daily*. Vladimir's ability to perform under pressure—and deliver an impeccable product—cemented a relationship with Lauren that continues today.

He opened his own company, Vlad Knitwear, in the mid '90s and discovered the joy and freedom of designing for himself. His signature hand knits are a reflection of his dancer's aesthetic: elegant, fluid and often sensual in shape or texture. Ancient symbols and icons—from South American prints to Japanese characters to Egyptian hieroglyphs—serve as his inspiration, but his interpretations are uniquely modern. "Knitwear has a long tradition, and I like the challenge of trying to create something totally new," he says.

When creating a new piece, he always knits swatches first and then draws the instructions on graph paper before knitting a complete garment. To learn new techniques, Vladimir often copies motifs that other designers have created—and he advises knitters to do the same. "As I try to figure out how something was created, I learn something new. It's like in painting or fashion design, where students learn by copying from the masters over and over."

Vladimir strives for the highest standards of quality in every piece he designs and believes that knitters would benefit from giving themselves the same challenge. "All it takes to produce something beautiful is desire and experience," he says, adding that practice really does make the difference. "When you are knitting and you reach a section you think is difficult, knit a few practice swatches first, then incorporate it into the design."

In addition to creating exotic patterns and textures, Vladimir is always looking for unique yarns with which to create them. "I love Japanese paper," he says, "and I decided that I wanted to re-create it in yarn." He searched for months and finally found an Italian paper yarn. "I used a crochet hook to stitch it, keeping it very loose and open, and then pressed it flat. It was perfect!" he says with childlike glee. He has worked with everything from satin tape to a yarn so hairy it looked like fur when knit into a coat, and he encourages knitters to take chances and experiment.

Vladimir compares the creative process to a flower slowly opening. "When I get an assignment from *VK*, I usually put it away for a few days and let ideas come to me," he says. He then researches his ideas, often by visiting museums or consulting his "library"—a collection of books, magazines, fabric and color swatches that he uses for inspiration. In creating designs for this issue, he looked for traditional patterns with an antique feel. "Men's wear is always pretty conservative," he explains. "I wanted to do something classic but give it a modern edge."

The former ballet star says that his work keeps him so busy he doesn't miss dancing. "Ballet gave me the discipline and training to be a designer," he says, and he's so devoted to his craft that he spent last New Year's Eve knitting a few last-minute samples—while on vacation in the Bahamas. "Designing a collection is just like performing," he concludes. "When the tickets are sold and the audience is in their seats, you can't say you're too tired or need a vacation. Somehow you find the energy and emotion to do your best." ~

This Vladimir Teriokhin design appeared in the Special 2002 issue.

VLADIMIR ON KNITTING:

• Quality is essential. No matter what you are making, use the best materials possible—yarns that look and feel wonderful—and knit it to the best of your ability.

• If you're ready to start, just do it. Knitting is like starting a new relationship—be honest and open and move ahead fearlessly. Then trust your instincts, and your guardian angels, to guide you.

In addition to giving workshops on knitting and colorwork throughout the world, Kaffe Fassett and Brandon Mably contribute regularly to numerous publications and knitwear collections. Fassett has authored several new books, most recently *Kaffe Fassett's Museum Quilts* (2005) and *Kaffe Fassett's Pattern Library* (2003); Mably's *Knitting Color* (Sixth&Spring Books), a collection of travel essays and original designs inspired by his travels, was published in October 2006. Vladimir Teriokhin continues to be the mastermind behind the knitwear collections of fashion luminaries such as Vera Wang and Oscar de la Renta. His designs appear frequently in *Vogue Knitting*.

Zimmermann's Own: Meg Swansen

by John Birmingham

It's hard to imagine anyone who would seem to fit the phrase "born knitter" better than Meg Swansen. As daughter of the legendary Elizabeth Zimmermann, Meg learned to knit at the age of 6, literally on her mother's knee. By 7, she was beginning to master short rows. Throughout childhood, she was surrounded by wool and all the accoutrements of the craft.

Yet Meg did surprisingly little knitting while she was growing up. "I was amply supplied with sweaters," she explains. "My mother kept churning them out, so I had no incentive to knit."

Before settling on knitting as a way of life, Meg traveled extensively. And that, too, seems part of her heritage. Her Bavarian father, Arnold Zimmermann, and her British mother emigrated from England to New York, where Meg was born. From there, the family moved to New Hope, Pennsylvania, and then to Milwaukee. After finishing high school, Meg ski-bummed for two years in Maine and California before attending art school in Munich, West Germany.

In 1964, back in New York, she married composer Chris Swansen, and soon her first

"I keep hearing about a return to traditional knitting. Of course, I've never really left it."

This Meg Swansen design first appeared in the Special 2002 issue.

knitting commissions came from celebrated jazz musicians like Gary Burton and Stan Getz. Later Meg ran a yarn shop in New Hope. Then, after moving again to upstate New York, she went into business with her mother, selling wool and knitting supplies by mail order.

Today Meg and Chris live in the rural setting of Pittsville, Wisconsin. They have a son and a daughter in college: Cully, a physics major, and Liesl, who studies languages (appropriately enough, since she was responsible for the family's rather cryptic nicknames, such as "Swand" for Meg). Over the years, the Swansens have expanded their home, a one-room frame schoolhouse, to include a "wool room" as well as high-tech video and audio studios. But in other ways, their life remains enviably simple. Meg grinds her own wheat to bake bread. In the winter, she often goes cross-country skiing—right out the back door and onto the bluff.

Now that Elizabeth has retired, Meg has taken over the helm of their mail-order business, the Knitting Camp summer workshop, and Schoolhouse Press, which publishes her mother's books. Last summer she worked with Elizabeth on *Knitting Around*, both the book and video series. Recently she has also begun collaborating with Elizabeth on her column for *VK*.

Of course, Meg Swansen has long played a prominent role in the knitting world. Through magazines and workshops, she has earned a reputation as a resourceful designer and an expert on technique. Not to mention one of the fastest knitters around.

JB: Do you remember your first knitting project?

MS: My first actual project—aside from practice squares and things—was a scarf for Auntie Pete, who was my mother's father's sister. I was 6 or 7. I remember doing the scarf in garter stitch, but it wasn't just a straight garter-stitch strip. Instead, Elizabeth had me round it in the back so that it was shaped like a horseshoe. And I remember doing short rows—isn't that peculiar—for my very first project. Of course, we didn't know about wrapping in those days; we did it according to Mary Thomas, just slipping the first stitch on the way back. But I was *very* pleased with myself...you know, making this U-shaped thing that would fit *organically* around the neck of my aunt, whom I'd never met.

Were you always passionate about knitting?

No. As a matter of fact, I got exceedingly bored with it after that scarf. I don't remember knitting anything all through the rest of grade school. Then, in high school, I reached the stage where girls knitted sweaters for their boyfriends, and that rekindled my interest. After that, the word got out. Hand-knit sweaters were fairly popular, and I started doing swaps. Through my art teacher, I knew some painters in Milwaukee who were quite good. But I couldn't afford to buy their paintings, so we worked out barters.

What about after high school?

Around 1961, I went to an art school in Germany to study drawing. Of course, the real reason for going to Germany was to meet my relatives, whom I'd never set eyes on before. I stayed with my father's sister, who lived outside Munich, and I commuted into the city to go to school.

At one point during that period, we had a holiday, and one of the other students invited me to her home in Reykjavik. So we took a freighter from Hamburg to Iceland, where we spent about six weeks. And that's where I stumbled upon this incredible Icelandic wool. It was unknown in America at the time and only sparsely known in Europe. I knitted a couple of sweaters while I was there, and sent wheels of wool back to my mother in Wisconsin. And she started importing it. I really got excited about the Icelandic wool. It was a fiber I'd never come across before, and the possibilities seemed endless.

Why did the Icelandic wool appeal to you so much?

The sheep of Iceland are unlike any other in the world. The staple of their wool is extraordinarily long, which means the wool doesn't need to be spun. So you get wheels—they call them "wheels" or "plates" or "cheeses"—of wool that is just drawn out into a roving. And you can knit directly from the wheel, which enables you to knit in a single strand or two, three or more strands together.

You're a strict devotee of the circular needle?

Yes. That's partly brainwashing from my mother; it's been ingrained in me from the word go. Of course, it's also logical and makes sense. It's just the most pleasant way for me to knit.

What's your position on symbolcraft?

I love it. In fact, when I'm working a lace pattern from a book in which the instructions are written out, the first thing I do is chart it for myself. It's so much easier for me in the long run. When it's written out in lines and lines of text, you can't see where you are. Whereas, if it's charted on a graph, you can *see* the pattern. You can see where the traveling stitches are, and where the yarn overs are. You can see where you're headed and where you've been. So, to me, it's become almost mandatory to take the time to chart it out.

Do you take a systematic approach to design?

Not at all. I'm simply in awe of people like Deborah Newton—as far as I can tell, from the things she has written about designing, she has the entire garment mapped out before she casts on. My approach isn't like that at all. When I cast on, I have a rudimentary idea of where I'm heading, and then all kinds of things occur to me along the way. Of course, not all of those ideas work out; I do a lot of ripping. But I get my best ideas while the work is in progress.

Can you think of a technique that really came to you as a revelation?

Knitting back backwards [see page 121]. This is a very useful technique for things like popcorns on an Aran, or the entrelac stitch, or putting in short rows across the back of the neck. When you're making a popcorn on an Aran, for instance, you have to knit five, turn, purl five, turn, knit five...and it's bothersome to keep turning around. So I purl back from the right side.

I discovered the technique as I was purling back, by peering over the top of the needles to see what happens on the right side when you purl back. How is the needle going into the stitch? Which way is the wool wrapping around the needle? Once you have that figured out, duplicate those moves on the right side, and you're knitting back backwards.

Now I do it at every opportunity. And since my discovery, Lizbeth Upitis, the author of that marvelous book *Latvian Mittens*, has carried it even further. She made a Fair Isle, knitting the body in the round. And when she got to the armholes, she decided to forget about steeks and cutting and all that stuff. She did the front and back separately, but still never purled back in color pattern. She has completed a Fair Isle by knitting forward and backward from the armholes up.

What trends do you see in knitting?

I keep hearing about a return to traditional knitting. Of course, I've never really left it, so that's naturally what leaps to my eye whenever I look at books or magazines. On the other hand, the British designers are still going strong, with intarsia, flowers and that sort of thing. So it seems that the two trends are running simultaneously—which is a boon for knitters. After all, the greatest thing is to have options, to have it all at your feet so you can pick and choose whatever appeals to you.

Obviously Elizabeth has been a great inspiration to you. What other knitters have influenced you?

I have a number of knitting heroines. Gladys Thompson is one. And Mary Thomas. And Barbara Walker. I also admire Alice Starmore. And I love Kaffe—first of all, because he's a wonderful person, and then for his inspired use of color. His attitude toward technique is a lot more casual than mine; he doesn't care, for instance, if a knot pops through on the right side of his knitting. In order to knit a Kaffe Fassett sweater, you have to do a mental hiccup and adjust your whole attitude toward knitting. And I think that's wonderful; he's breathed new life into the craft for so many people.

Tell us more about Gladys Thompson.

She's the author of *Patterns for Guernseys, Jerseys and Arans*, which is the classic book of its kind. There are now five or six books about Arans and Guernseys, but Gladys Thompson's was the first. She was the one who followed guys around the docks along the British coast and scribbled patterns off the backs of the sweaters they were

wearing. She really made an effort to get these historic garments down on paper.

She and Elizabeth corresponded before Gladys died. Through that, we found out that the Aran part of the book—for which it was first famous—was actually stuck on as an afterthought. The publisher wanted more, so she added an Aran chapter…. Oh, and the patterns had all been written to be knitted in the round, which was the traditional mode for making Guernseys and Jerseys. Then the British publisher made her rewrite the entire book with directions for flat pieces to be sewn up, because "that's the way the British knit nowadays." Let's hear it for history, huh? But this was so typical—to alter history according to the current fashion.

What's your favorite aspect of knitting camp?

The flow of ideas. We draw knitters from every corner of the United States, and without exception, each one is considered insane by her family and friends. Ostensibly they come to touch the hem of Elizabeth's garment; she has become a legend in her own time, and they just want to be proximal to her. But while they do learn a lot from us, I think they learn equally—if not more—from each other.

How does your philosophy differ from Elizabeth's?

I think they're pretty much the same. I share her belief in knitting for enjoyment above all else…and trying to keep it easy. Because I do think that knitting is mainly a pleasure, and the fact that it turns out to be useful is just a wonderful bonus.

Meg's beloved partner, Chris, died in 1995, and Elizabeth followed in 1999. To deal with her grief, Meg submerged herself in work. Since this profile was published, she has authored a book with Interweave Press, *Handknitting with Meg Swansen*, and produced twenty-two books through Schoolhouse Press, including reprints of all seven of Barbara G. Walker's indispensible books, which had languished out of print for years.

Meg has also expanded to four weeks per year of Knitting Camps, built an extensive new Web site, started offering a free electronic newsletter, converted her and Elizabeth's videos to DVD, and built a large new warehouse/office building just down the hill from the original Schoolhouse.

Karen Allen Knits

by Alice Rose Hurley

Karen Allen likes doing things in living color—and her way. She played feisty Marion Ravenwood opposite Harrison Ford's Indiana Jones in the blockbuster adventure film *Raiders of the Lost Ark* and costarred in *Starman*, a sci-fi love story. She grows an eclectic mix of peonies, lilies, grasses and ferns near the converted Massachusetts barn she calls home, far from the frantic pace of city life. And she knits in living color, too, thinking outside the skein with unconventional palettes and patterns.

The sweater Allen is shown wearing below was machine-knit, inspired by a pattern she liked from British designers Jamie and Jesse Seaton, who are favorites of hers, along with Kaffe Fassett and Annabel Fox. "I used [the Seatons'] graph and changed the colors extremely," says Allen. "I love the look of antique rugs, whose colors slightly change because the dyes were inconsistent. Those rugmakers changed colors by necessity, but I do it by choice." She reversed the original pattern, which featured pastel designs on a dark field, by choosing off-white and beige colors as the background for dramatic

Actress Karen Allen followed her love of knitting from childhood to Hollywood—and now has her own dream-come-true knitwear design studio in the tranquil Berkshire Mountains.

Karen Allen modeling a sweater and scarf she designed.

geometric flowers. The striped cuffs are another addition. "I often do borders on cuffs," she says. "As they say, God is in the details." She ticks off the colors in the scarf she is also wearing like a proud winemaker listing her winning vintages: "burgundy, a really brilliant red, tawny brown-gold and merlot," along with turquoises, olives and celery green. The repeating pattern reminds her of the melodies of the classic Hindu ragas she was listening to at the time it was knit.

Even Allen's scarf lengths and styles are surprising and unconventional. "I tend to knit one of two lengths: either a 6-footer you can wrap around yourself and make a major part of your wardrobe, or a 4½-foot shorty [like the one shown at left] to wear over a sweater." One of her favorite ways to wear the shorty is to hold it closed with a 4-inch hair pick instead of wrapping it. "A pick slides through beautifully and doesn't damage the yarn," she says.

Her bold, vivid knitwear designs, which tread where few have before, sport colorful names like Cat's Eye, Zanzibar, Flying Cloud and San Blas (named for the islands where Kuna Indian women appliqué fabrics). "Ideas tumble out one after the other," says Allen. "I design the pattern and the name follows."

Sometimes, she would lug two big suitcases filled with yarn to movie sets and knit for fellow cast or crew members, especially those expecting babies. "I constantly knit on the set," says Allen. "I have an unbelievable amount of yarn in my possession that I've collected from all over the world." She was often reluctant to put down her needles when called before the camera. "Sometimes they would knock on the door and I'd think, Maybe I'm enjoying this more than I am being an actor."

Now she's pursuing her dream to do something she has loved with a passion since she picked up her first knitting needles at age 5, following in the footsteps of her grandmother Florence. Allen and her family spent summers at the family farm in the tiny town of Jerseyville, Illinois, where Florence would sit and knit happily. "My grandmother was a knitter extraordinaire, and I was very close to her," says Allen. "She constantly knit afghans, sweaters, slippers and scarves, and then sent them off to people."

As a little girl, Allen found fabric stores as appealing as most kids find candy stores. "I was always very, very interested in anything that had to with textiles and design. In a fabric store, it felt as though someone had dropped me off at Disneyland." Her family moved about every year (her Dad was an FBI agent), hopscotching around the country, from Illinois to Tennessee, New Jersey, Pennsylvania—one reason, perhaps, why the comfort and continuity of knitting have always been so important to her.

"Some people like to say knitting is boring, but it's such a calming, centering thing to do," says Allen, who also founded a yoga school. "And it's very portable, which is great because we're all on the move so much. It also creates a sense of generosity when you make things for other people. A baby sweater gets passed down and becomes an heirloom."

Speaking of baby sweaters, it's no surprise that Allen doesn't knit hers (including the ones she once made for her own son, now a teenager) in traditional baby blues and pastel pinks. She won't give up her visionary sense of color, even when making garments for tykes. "I'm not a pastel kind of girl—those colors just don't interest me," says Allen. "But I like heathery versions of pastels. I don't like pink, but I like rose. I don't like baby green, but I love olives and deep chartreuse. I don't like baby blue at all, but I love a heathery turquoise."

Allen started Monterey Fiber Arts, a textile and knitwear design studio, in January 2004 after studying machine knitting at the Fashion Institute of Technology in New York City. Her teacher and mentor there, Marian Grealish-Forino, has come to the rescue several times since. "Marian has trekked to Massachusetts to help me when the machines are acting quirky; things go wrong mechanically or with the computer. But once you get the hang of it, it's pretty spectacular what you can do with them."

At her studio, Allen has five knitting machines (one of them named Flo) and is assisted by two women. "I work with 200 needles, the largest bed you can have on a Brother 910 home knitting machine," she says. Most of her pieces combine machine knitting with hand-finishing techniques. Her yarns of choice: Jagger-Spun and Igea merino wool, Loro Piana Italian cashmere, and Todd & Duncan's Scottish cashmere. "I like to knit with fine wools, not heavy, chunky ones," says Allen. Wherever she travels, she grabs a copy of the Yellow Pages first thing and looks under "Yarn." In New York City, she loves to shop at The Yarn Co., praising its selection, classes and sense of community. At home in Lenox, she visits Colorful Stitches for its vast array of high-quality fibers.

"When you knit by hand, your only limitations are your imagination and your palette. The machines have mechanical limitations, but I'm finding ways to turn those into strengths. I do not want to give up on color. I love it too much," says Allen. "The difference between hand and machine is that it's very, very difficult to make a living knitting only by hand. The sweater I'm wearing now would probably cost $1,000 even if I paid myself 10 cents an hour."

What's next? More roles—and more work she loves. "I will always, for the rest of my life, think of myself as an actor. But knitting was honestly my first love. How wonderful that I actually get to do something that makes me so happy." ⌐

In May 2005, Allen opened a store in Great Barrington, Massachusetts, called Karen Allen – Fiber Arts, also the name of her cashmere knitwear company. Her line of cashmere sweaters, scarves, hats and gloves is sold in stores across the country. See more of her work at karenallen-fiberarts.com.

Knitting Is Total Bliss:

Two needles and a ball of yarn are pure heaven for Britain's favorite children's knitwear designer.

by Gail Goldie

Like the designer herself, Debbie Bliss's knits combine a great sense of humor with a discerning eye for detail. Her charming children's sweaters and knitted toys have earned her the devotion of knitting fans on both sides of the Atlantic—all of whom were delighted when she extended her talents to include adult styles.

FLOWER POWER

Debbie began her love affair with yarn and needles while completing a Fashion and Textile fine art course at the N.E. London Polytechnical College in 1971. There, under the influence of her tutor, she concentrated on machine knitting for two years. Inspired by artist Claes Oldenburg's soft sculptures, she began using wire, plaster of Paris and yarn dyed to mimic gradations on a cane to create whimsical knitted plants and trees. The designs were sold at Christopher Strangeways in World's End—the hub of Chelsea's arts and crafts movement—where pop star Elton John bought one of her "cheese plants." The innovative "One Off" department at Liberty, London's famous Regent Street store, also began selling her knitted daffodils, arum lilies, irises and wonderful cascading Lurex

This Debbie Bliss design first appeared in the Winter 2004 issue.

fuchsias. Debbie jokes that her labor-intensive work at the time was basically "nonprofit"—there were no grants available in those days to help aspiring artists and entrepreneurs.

Luckily, magazine editorials showcasing her designs soon brought wider recognition. In the mid-'70s, publisher Mitchell Beazley appointed Debbie contributing editor on a book project called *Wild Knitting*. Debbie designed the book jacket cover and contributed several of her whimsical designs, including cocktail hats, ties styled like sardine tins, a knitted garden and, perhaps the most innovative, a child's raincoat made from a bin liner and embellished with knit-in beads.

FASHION FORWARD

Debbie's move from sculpture to hand-knitted garments began with magazine commissions for unstructured sweaters. Strongly influenced by artist Sonia Delauney,

her first was a stunning knit for *Woman* magazine worked in Sirdar yarn with blocks of color on the sleeves. Supported by her mother's encouragement (and numerous cups of coffee) she mastered the intricacies of garment patternmaking. In 1978 she became press officer for Hayfield Yarns—a position she held for fifteen years. Working with other designers, she interpreted current fashion into editorial knits. The job involved close contact with fashion editors, which led to several book commissions.

TURNING POINT

Debbie met her filmmaker husband, Barry, when she was 17. Friends for many years, they finally married in 1982. Three years later, the birth of son Billy had a defining effect on Debbie's career. Inspired by the joys (and challenges) of motherhood, she decided to turn her attention to kids' knits. The birth of daughter Eleanor five years later further bolstered her interest.

Initially, Ebury, Debbie's publisher, did not share her enthusiasm for kid's knits, believing people "weren't interested in knitting for children." Fortunately, an editor's faith in Debbie convinced Ebury otherwise, and her first book, *Baby Knits*, hit the bookshelves in 1988. It was a rousing success and was soon picked up for distribution in the U.S. Debbie began work on a string of bestselling titles, releasing two books a year.

The late 1990s saw the U.K. launch of *How to Knit*. Following the ethos "If I can do it, anyone can," Debbie demystifies knitting in a series of workshops, taking the complete beginner through the early stages and building confidence in more experienced knitters worried about color and texture. Other subjects include lace, entrelac, how to design a basic sweater and decorative details.

MOVING AHEAD

Like many women, Debbie juggles family and home with a busy workload. Since 1993 she has been the commissioning editor for knitting designs at *Woman's Weekly*, and

Autumn '99 will see the launch of her ready-to-wear collection of newborn knits for Baby Gap. As if all this weren't enough, she found time to open her own shop, in London.

Debbie holds knitting and design classes at the shop, around the U.K. and abroad. Her aim is to rekindle enthusiasm in young knitters. In no way dogmatic, she happily admits there may be more than one way to achieve a technique, but passes on her advice and expertise as to the method she has found the best. She believes it is both exciting and important to experiment rather than just stick to conventional patterns. While currently inspired by American folk art and patchwork, Debbie also loves the U.K.'s traditional Aran and fisherman patterns, finding more fulfillment in the development of Aran stitches than colorwork. When we met she had just returned from book signing and lecturing at the Creative Sewing & Needlecraft Festival in Toronto and had been asked to return by the Royal Ontario Museum. With all that's, going on in her busy life, she managed to squeeze in time to design two adorable kids' knits exclusively for *VK*. ⌣

Since this profile was first published, Bliss has closed her London store and successfully launched her own brand of classic hand-knitting yarns. She continues to design prolifically, contributing to various magazines and pattern booklets and authoring numerous books, most recently *Simply Baby* (2006); her next book, *Special Family Knits*, is scheduled to hit stores in Spring 2007.

Lily Chin, the Knitting

by John Birmingham

"I was always an angry, rebellious youth, and that affects my philosophy of design, which is to reinvent things...."

"I can't stand that granny image of knitting," says Lily Chin, a confirmed New Yorker in her late twenties who has been designing for more than a decade. "And I'm doing my best to change it. That's why I like to dress outrageously and to take my knitting with me."

A self-appointed agent provocateur of the knitting world, Chin clearly strives to shock. But she also aims to educate. She conducts workshops around the country, writes a regular column on design techniques for *Knitter's* magazine, and favors a controlled, analytical approach to knitting. Even her designs are didactic in that they prod knitters to rethink their craft. Take, for example, her innovative draped designs. As Chin points out, they show how a knitted fabric can be made to drape gracefully, "at a diagonal instead of on the vertical."

At the same time, her draped sweaters—inspired by a look she first noticed in the collections of Romeo Gigli—reveal Chin's attitude toward fashion. "I'm very fashion-oriented," she says. "Some people discount it, because the trends change so quickly. But fashion is a cultural indicator. It says something about us, and that's why it keeps changing."

Chin's fashion bent dates back to childhood. "I grew up in the New York *schmatta* business," she explains. Her mother, a Chinese immigrant, worked as a sample maker on Seventh Avenue, and from the age of 13, Lily spent summers as an "assistant bookkeeper and general gofer" at her mother's firm, where she learned how garments were pieced together. She later attended the prestigious Bronx High School of Science. Along the way, she crocheted much of her own wardrobe.

"I loved looking at clothes in magazines, but couldn't afford the prices," she says. "So to me, handcrafts were an economic necessity. Plus, they gave me a chance to make micro-miniskirts, and my mom couldn't complain, because I'd say, 'But mom, I made it myself!'"

Today Chin designs knitwear for magazines at her Greenwich Village apartment, which she shares with her fiancé Clifford Pearson, an editor and architecture critic. The apartment reflects diverse interests—a Picasso print hangs next to the B-movie poster; in various corners are three knitting machines; names on the bookshelves range from Margaret Atwood to Marguerite Duras. It's late afternoon as this interview begins. Chin, chicly subdued in black tights and tunic, is just starting her day.

JB: How does living in New York affect your designs?
LC: It keeps me in touch with fashion—not the fashion industry, but what people are wearing on the street. I like to get a feeling for the zeitgeist around me. In fact, most of my fashion ideas come from being out there and seeing what people are up to. And so many trends begin on the streets of New York. Right now, for instance, the '60s look is big among fashion designers. Well, I was wearing white go-go boots and miniskirts back in 1984.

Which other ideas came up from the streets?
When I was a dancer, we would go out wearing our tights from class, along with an oversized sweater. That was as early as '82. Eventually designers picked up on it, and now that silhouette—a big sweater with little, spindly legs—is part of the mainstream lexicon. As a matter of fact, I designed some knitted leggings in the early '80s, but they were never published. They may have been too outré for the time.

What's you most unusual source of inspiration?
Architecture. Do you know the Bayard Building on Bleecker Street? It's the only Louis Sullivan building in New York. I took one look at it and said, Woah! Sullivan is the father of modernism, really. Rather than adding ornaments to hide things, he brought the structure out into the open, enabling you to see the beams that hold up the building. And I've done the same thing with some of my designs. [Chin points to her version of an Aran fisherman's sweater.] Here, for instance, I use color to bring out the structure, so you can see exactly what's happening.

Is there a usual starting point for your designs?

What I call "creative problem solving." That's when you want to do something, but you have a certain set of givens to overcome. If I were using a thin yarn and wanted to make a jacket, I might use cable stitches, which condense the fabric and thicken it. Or if I were using cable stitches and wanted to make a standard-fitting sweater with drape, I might loosen up the gauge by using larger needles. It's a matter of looking for ways to compensate for those givens. One thing leads logically to another.

When have you used "creative problem solving"?

One time I wanted to make a scarf in cables. Usually the back of a cable is the "wrong" side, and it looks like a mangled mess. But I wanted that side to be presentable, because both would be exposed. So I found a way to compensate. I probably wasn't the first to come up with this concept, but I think I was the first to analyze it and get it published. The idea is, if you rib everything, the back is the same as the front. So if you cable rib stitches—knit, purl; knit, purl—both sides will look alike. It's a very simple concept. Even beginners can use it.

What else does your design process entail?

My work follows a series of developmental stages. I usually experiment by making swatches; that can save as much as a week of work. I'll do several variations on a theme, trying different stitches, perhaps knitting something in a thick yarn and then again in a thinner yarn. I spend almost as much time planning a design as I do knitting it up.

This Lily Chin design first appeared in the Fall 2001 issue.

Is there a preconception about knitting that you'd like to see abolished?

The idea that sweaters all have to be constructed one way— in pieces, from the bottom up. There are advantages to that method. But if you don't think of each project as a jigsaw puzzle, things can really take off in different directions.

Do you see any limits to what can be done with knitting?

Obviously there are certain things you can't do. Even with a fine-gauge machine, you can't achieve the crispness of a starched white blouse. But I do think that knitting is extremely versatile. As a matter of fact, I'm thinking of knitting a man's suit. I plan to do it on the machine, using a weaving thread to keep the fabric from stretching. Sure, knitting has its limitations. But not too many.

Since this article was published, Lily has created runway samples for designers such as Isaac Mizrahi, Vera Wang, Diane von Furstenburg and Ralph Lauren. Her handiwork has graced celebrities and supermodels from Raquel Welch to Cindy Crawford.

She has written four books on knitting and crochet and has won two international contests (2002 and 2004). Dubbed the world's fastest crocheter, she has made numerous TV appearances and is a regular on the DIY Network's *Knitty Gritty*. Most recently, Lily has started her own line of yarn and patterns, the Lily Chin Signature Collection.

A Pattern for Success:

by Polly Roberts

Mari Lynn's ability to produce original samples, as well as precise written instructions, keeps her in great demand.

She sees knitting not just as a way to make a sweater, but as an opportunity to create the fabric, style and fit of a garment all at once. In fact, the prospect of complete creative control led Mari Lynn Patrick to choose knitting as a career—when she was only 12. Now in her mid-thirties, Mari Lynn already boasts 17 years of experience as a prolific designer, technical writer and frequent contributor to yarn companies and knitting magazines.

Adept at both knitting and crochet, she admits knitting is her first love. She first learned to knit and crochet at the age of 7 from her Prussian grandmother. "People from her background did a lot of 'white work' or crochet, cutwork, embroidery and lace," Mari Lynn explains. "She would visit us in the summers and be doing a crocheted lace edge on a handkerchief or making a bedspread, and I'd ask her to show me how. I was thoroughly interested."

Stacks of *Vogue Knitting* magazines at a friend's house provided another early influence. "I thought, gee, I'd like to design clothing. But I wasn't even thinking of sweaters—I wanted to approximate what you could buy in ready-to-wear, like a dress or a coat or an ensemble. This was in the '60s, so the shapes were simpler, but they were all lined and had zippers and darts."

Soon the budding designer immersed herself in sketching and designing. Her first couture customers were her sister's Barbie dolls. From the outset, Mari Lynn had a keen interest in head-to-

This Mari Lynn Patrick design first appeared in the Holiday 2006 issue.

toe design. "I also designed shoes, but didn't feel any control over that because I didn't know how to make them. But since I could knit, I thought I could be a knitting designer. I loved making something from scratch that I could control. To create the fabric as well as the design and shape and size—that was very exciting to me."

Finding higher education in knitting proved difficult. Not content to study the craft as a mere adjunct to a fashion design curriculum, Mari Lynn finally turned up a few schools in Great Britain that offered programs devoted entirely to knitting.

In the meantime, she attended the University of Massachusetts, studying art, literature and languages. "But I couldn't imagine doing anything in those areas," she says. "So when I was a sophomore, I applied to Leicester Polytechnic in the midlands of England. It was nine-to-five knitting—not hand-knitting, but machine-knitting and textile technology. I learned about textile and fiber testing for knitting, making knitted fabrics, cutting and sewing knitted fabrics, dyeing knitting yarns, mathematical and scientific tests on knitting yarns…it was total immersion."

A year later, she came home to finish college. The University of Massachusetts gave her credit for the year abroad, with an independent degree in textiles. So in her senior year she returned to studying languages, which led to the sideline as pattern translator.

"Translating has been very helpful to me, because there's a bigger variety of stitches, techniques and finishes in France and Italy," says Mari Lynn. "I've gotten a fuller understanding of different approaches.

Mari Lynn Patrick

Her career started with jobs at American Thread and, later, Columbia Minerva. There she learned the value of measuring, charting, testing, proofreading, checking and checking again. "It was a good way to learn to write instructions. I don't think the yarn companies today are doing that kind of intensive in-house training, and young people just aren't learning pattern writing."

Mari Lynn's ability to produce original designs and beautiful samples, as well as precise written instructions, keeps her in great demand. Over the years she has worked for almost every major yarn company and craft magazine, including designing and writing articles for *Vogue Knitting* beginning with the 1982 Fall/Winter issue. Now, because her pattern-writing skills are becoming so rare, she finds herself writing more than knitting.

"I like to write probably as much as I like to knit, and the more challenging, the better," she says. "It's very important to me that a design be makable and that someone else can understand and digest it. And for my own satisfaction, it's fun to find the answers—it's like working out a puzzle—and then write it in a clear and concise way."

As Mari Lynn sees it, knitting is alive and well, with lots of young talent coming along. "It may not attract a huge following, but the people who are involved are totally involved and think about knitting day and night." Still, she worries that the scarcity of good technical writers will lead to patterns that are confusing and frustrating—possibly discouraging new converts. "There are very few people who can really do it well. You have to orchestrate a lot of elements at once while concentrating on individual things; and it requires concise writing skills, as well as a certain mathematical ability."

She favors a classic approach to design, shying away from exaggerations of style and fit. "I avoid highly slanted or curved fit. I don't feel it's appropriate to knitting. The knit stitch has a life, stretch and contour all its own. So the shaping I do is a bit more graceful; it lets the knitting itself take over.

"But I probably do more shaping than anyone else, and there are ways to shape and improve fit: interior curved bust shaping, back darts, front darts…. Then there are extended sloped front shoulders that fit onto a shallow back shoulder. That makes the shoulder portion of a jacket fit better and keeps the neck in place, too. It's the same way ready-to-wear is cut…and the armhole is cut deeper in front than in back; that way the sleeves are shaped differently."

Because fit and shape can't really be evaluated until a garment is finished, Mari Lynn is highly disciplined about charting her designs. "I work from a schematic diagram—I adjust all the lines on graph paper until I feel it's exactly what I've sketched. Then I just count the squares, follow the curves, and measure and plot the increases and decreases, It's a precise, simplistic approach, and everyone can do it."

To save time, Mari Lynn plots and writes out the pattern before starting to knit. "It's very useful—because then as you're going along, if you make changes or there's a better way, you can note it on the spot. And when it's finished, you have a thorough pattern guide and there's no confusion."

Mari Lynn pays special attention to finishing. "You're spending so much time to make something, I feel finishing is very important. I join from the right side, matching stitch to stitch, and tend to use a selvage stitch that will disappear to the inside. I often weight or thickly finish edges with interior hand-knit facings so that the edges fit and lie flat. And I always innovate edges and try something I haven't done before."

Since she enjoys using a wide variety of techniques, Mari Lynn encourages fellow knitters to explore new ones as well. "I would like to see people get into more sophisticated patterns and approaches to knitting clothing," she says.

And what is there left for such a dedicated knitting pro to explore? "Someday I want to make filet crochet curtains and beautiful bedspreads," says Mari Lynn, "like my grandmother did." ⌒

Mari Lynn continues to design prolifically, and her designs and patterns appear regularly in all major hand-knitting publications.

Nicky Knits: Nicky Epstein

by Daryl Brower

Daryl Brower: You turn out an amazing amount of work. What fuels your creativity?

Nicky Epstein: I have this physical need to have yarn and needles in my hands. If I don't knit, it hurts.

So how did it all begin?

My grandmother taught me to cast on, but I actually learned to knit from a Spanish woman in my neighborhood. I taught her English and she taught me how to do stripes, colorwork and motif knitting.

Have you always wanted to be a designer?

Actually, no. I wanted to be a commercial or fine artist. I became a designer because I wanted to win a set of knitting needles.

You wanted what?

Needles. I'm very serious about them—I have hundreds of pairs lying around my apartment. Back in 1981, McCall's *Needlecraft* magazine ran a sweater contest, and one of the prizes was a set of needles. The deadline was looming, but I was on my way to the

With scores of sweater and afghan designs in print and seven books under her belt, Nicky Epstein is one of the most prolific knitters working today. She uses yarn and needles in endlessly innovative ways to sculpt flowers, ruffles, corded closures and other embellishments, turning simple sweaters, hats and afghans into three-dimensional works of art. *Vogue Knitting* got her to set down her needles just long enough to talk about knitting, designing and her book *Knitting On the Edge* (Sixth&Spring Books), which hit bookshelves in the spring of 2004.

This Nicky Epstein design first appeared in the Fall 2004 issue.

California desert to work on a television commercial. I pulled over at a yarn shop, grabbed the first skeins I found and worked on the sweater for the entire journey. I finished it, tossed it in the mail and promptly forgot about it. Several months later the publisher called to tell me that I'd won first prize—$500—and asked me to design more sweaters for the magazine.

You must have been thrilled.

What I really wanted to know was whether I could still have the needles. It was the first thing I asked. The editors teased me about it for years.

So did you get them?

Yes—and I still have them. I also got my first lesson in meeting a deadline: I was asked to submit designs for two more sweaters in a week.

And you managed to do it?

I'm fast. I use long aluminum needles, anchoring one under my armpit and keeping the stitches close to the tips. I think wooden ones are beautiful, but they are too slow for me.

Sounds like you work well under pressure.

KNIT TIPS FROM NICKY

- Bobbles and popcorn stitches can be added after the piece is finished. Knit the bobble, then pull the cast-on and bind-off tails to the wrong side of the work and tie them on. Draw the loose ends back through the bobble and cut them off.
- I-cord can be quickly constructed with circular needles. Simply slide the stitches from tip to tip as you would with double points.
- A sure way to keep track of stitches that look similar on both sides is to remember which side of the needle the cast-on tail is on. If you're using the knitting-on method, for example, the tail will be on the left side of the needle when the right side of the work is facing you.
- Save wear and tear on favorite paperback knitting books or patterns by laminating the covers. You can also have the book spiral-bound so that the pages lie flat.
- For intarsia motifs with multiple colors, use long strands or butterfly ties in lieu of bobbins. If they tangle, you can simply pull the yarn through to separate the strands.

I do. In fact, that's how I came up with the idea for knitted frogs. I was frantic to finish a piece that was due the next day, and the editors wanted frog closures. I didn't have the time to shop for them, so I stitched up some I-cord and just started coiling and playing with it until I got something I liked.

So necessity truly is the mother of invention.

Right. And figuring out a new way to do something is a kind of artistic expression. It upsets me when people say that everything has been done before. This would be a very boring world if that were true. Creativity is simply a matter of viewing something familiar from a new angle.

Is that how the embellishments and edgings that define your design style come about?

I've always been fascinated by edgings—they're like frames around a painting. And I enjoy the challenge of figuring out how to create them. I lay a piece of edging down on the floor, twist it a certain way, and suddenly it's a flower. I don't like to give up on an idea. If I don't like the way it's going, I don't ditch the project and start over. Instead, I see if I can turn it into something else. Some of my best hats started as

sweaters. The average head measures 20 inches, and so does the average sweater back. Knit it up about 7 inches, seam it together and you've got a hat.

Now I know what do with all those half-finished sweaters I have lying around. You're obviously not the kind of designer who's afraid to share techniques and ideas.

I don't see the point in trade secrets. I get a big kick out of seeing my designs, or elements of them, on the street, and I love sharing what I know. I teach a class on attaching bobbles, and it's like magic when everyone gets it.

Your books fill a similar need.

Well, if I'm going to write a book, I want it to be one that I would use myself—something that I can reach for time and again for inspiration as well as technical instruction.

Knitting On the Edge includes how many different trims?

Three hundred fifty—all the ruffles, laces, fringes and picots I've used over the years and then some. There's nothing like it out there. Some of the designs are my own; others are classics I've updated and given a new twist. I wanted to give knitters a one-stop-shopping resource for fabulous finishes.

Anything else in the works?

I'm finishing up a book called *Barbie & Me*, which includes doll-, child- and adult-size patterns. After that, I'll be pulling together *Knitting Over the Edge*, which will cover all the fabulous things I couldn't fit in *Knitting On the Edge*.

Any parting advice for budding designers?

Always go for the extra touch that makes your project a showstopper. Most of all, believe in your work and enjoy it!

Of course, I can't let you go without asking the question that every interview has to include.

What inspires me? Chocolate. And knitting in the nude. ⌒

Nicky has followed up on the phenomenal success of *Knitting On the Edge* with two bestselling sequels, *Knitting Over the Edge* (2005) and *Knitting Beyond the Edge* (2006), and with *Nicky Epstein's Knitted Flowers* (2006). Her *Knitting Never Felt Better: The Definitive Guide to Fabulous Felting*, will appear in June 2007 (all published by Sixth&Spring Books). Nicky continues to teach and give workshops across the U.S. and around the world.

Inside Design: Norah Gaughan

by Daryl Brower

You won't find too many knitting books with a foreword written by a physicist, but then again, there aren't too many knitting designers like Norah Gaughan. With an art-filled childhood (both of her parents were illustrators) and a lifelong love of math and science (she earned a biology degree from Brown) behind her, Gaughan puts hard science on equal footing with creative expression in her first book, *Knitting Nature*.

Daryl Brower: You are so well known and so well received in the knitting industry that it's hard to believe *Knitting Nature* is your first book. Did you find the experience of designing for yourself different from that of designing for someone else?

Norah Gaughan: I've had designs featured in different knitting books, but this is the first book that's all mine. Doing it was a liberating experience. Most of my career has been spent working for yarn companies or for magazines, and while there's certainly some artistic freedom in that, you are designing within a set of specifications: Use this yarn, appeal to this customer, interpret this theme. With this book I could focus on what I wanted to do.

And what was that?

Experiment. The publishers really gave me free rein to come up with an idea for the book, which was exciting. I was browsing in a store and came across a copy of *The Self-Made Tapestry*, a book about pattern formations in nature written by the physicist Philip Ball. It demonstrates how patterns like spirals appear again and again in seemingly unrelated situations—hurricanes and sunflowers, for

instance. That got me thinking about how these forms could be knitted.

In the introduction to *Knitting Nature* you talk jokingly about leading a double life, one divided between equal interests in art and science. Can you explain that a little more?

Art was the big focus in my family. My parents were both artists [her mother, Phoebe, is well known in art and needlework circles], and there was always paint and paper and fabric around the house. We were all encouraged to use it any way we liked.

Sounds fun.

It was. I loved making things. But I was also very interested in math and science. I liked studying these subjects, and they came easily to me. I loved art too, but I thought it was hard. I had to work at it.

Your mother does a lot of illustrations for needlework books and magazines. Was knitting something you grew up with?

Needlework, yes; knitting, no. My mom and grandmother taught me to crochet when I was very young, and I loved to embroider and sew, but I didn't learn to knit until I was 14. I spent a summer with a friend in Princeton and she introduced me to it.

Were you instantly hooked?

Yes, but I was also incredibly frustrated. I was, and still am, a perfectionist, so I cried whenever I couldn't understand a pattern. And since no one in my house knew how to knit, I really didn't have anyone to help me.

You've obviously managed to work past that. How?

My mother bought me a copy of *Knitting Without Tears*.

And?

And I stopped crying. Elizabeth Zimmermann made it all make sense to me, and I found that I enjoyed knitting very

This Norah Gaughan design first appeared in the Spring/Summer 2005 issue.

much. So I started working out my own designs. When I was in high school my mother helped me get one of those designs published in a needlework magazine she worked for.

Did you decide then that you wanted to be a designer?

No, not really. I'd always been interested in math and science, so I decided to study biology at Brown, not because I planned on doing anything with it, but because I liked to study and the topic interested me.

So you became a bio major for fun?

I suppose so. You know, I grew up in a household where working freelance was the norm. Neither of my parents ever had a "regular" job, but they always had plenty of work and they liked what they were doing. So I never had this feeling that you were supposed to worry about what you were going to do with whatever degree you earned. You were supposed to study because it interested you and you were furthering your knowledge of something you enjoyed.

The world might be a happier place if more people thought like that. What about the art, though? Did you miss that?

I did, so I started taking art classes too. And I ended up with an undergraduate degree in biology with a concentration in studio art. I was still knitting, so after I graduated I answered an ad for a sample knitter and began working with Margery Winter and Deborah Newton. Deborah started recommending me to editors for design assignments, and Margery taught me much more about designing. And the work just snowballed from there. I swatched ready-to-wear for a few companies, designed for Adrienne Vittadini and eventually became the design director at JCA. Now I'm the design director at Berroco and am working with Margery again.

Do you have any regrets about not pursuing a career in science?

In the beginning I was very conflicted about it. I went to college at a time when the whole idea that women could and should be pursuing fields that were male-dominated was being pushed hard, and underlying that was the sense that nothing that might be construed as woman's work had value. So when I found myself knitting for a living, I sometimes had to fight this inner voice that said, "You should be doing something more serious."

But you ignored that voice.

I absolutely loved knitting, and my parents encouraged my creativity and were very supportive. They never gave me the sense that I'd wasted their money by going to Brown "only" to end up designing sweaters. Their feeling was that I'd accomplish something with what I'd learned, whether I used it directly or not. And with my book, I feel like I've really brought my math and science side and my artistic side together.

Is science where you find your design inspiration?

In a sense. What I like is a challenge. I started by making up new twisted stitches and cables—I like the logic of them. Then I went on to experiment with construction, trying to find different ways to piece a sweater together. And to these I added everyday observation. The spirals in the book, for instance, came from a river that I pass on my way to work every morning. I'd see these swirls of foam and the vortices they made, and I began to think about how those swirl patterns repeat and grow and how they could be re-created in yarn.

You like the complexity?

My designs look complex, but they're actually not. The underlying structure is basically one motif that repeats over and over. I like to keep things logical so you can remember where you are and what you're doing as you go along.

So anyone can knit these designs?

It may take some technical expertise to master one of these motifs, but once you have it down, you can just go with it. It's one idea that gets repeated and expanded upon until it becomes something else entirely. And that's an exciting thing to experiment with. You never know where it will take you.

NORAH'S FAVORITE...

YARN: My interest is primarily in textures you can create with different stitches, not in the yarn itself. So I tend to prefer the more classic styles of yarn. I also like the springiness that natural fibers such as wool provide. I think using a fiber like this does make a difference in the stitch quality you get.

PLACE TO KNIT: In the winter I knit in my sunroom—in front of the TV. In summer it's in the Adirondack chair in my backyard, listening to podcasts on my iPod.

by Gail Goldie

Born in Cambridgeshire, England, in 1945, Sasha Kagan is the proud daughter of a talented English seamstress and a Russian engineering translator. A childhood spent knitting and sewing at her mother's side instilled a passion for pattern and an inherent understanding of the textiles that would inspire her for years to come.

Sasha's parents encouraged her to put her artistic skills to work on a professional path. In 1965, Sasha entered the Exeter College of Art to train as a painter, emerging three years later with a diploma in art and design. Her paintings of this period are an early indication of the passion for the pattern repeats and layering of colors that would later emerge in her knitwear designs. Continuing her academic career, Sasha moved on to the Royal College of Art in London, where she studied printmaking. Courses in etching, lithography and silkscreening further fueled what she terms an "obsession" with repeats. "They're therapeutic and calming," Sasha explains. "Finding the repeat in a pattern and recreating it over and over is very soothing." Sasha found herself discovering beauty in the simplest of objects and began using them in her work. One amazing silkscreen print from this period features and enlarged stockinette-stitch

Sasha Kagan:

With a knack for color artistry, an acute sense of the world around her and a keen business acumen, British designer Sasha Kagan has turned her creative desires into a smashing success.

pattern worked in varying colors; another, a 25"/63cm-square lithograph, is a fantastic study of blades of grass. Fascinated by flowers, leaves, repeating organic forms and layering of images, Sasha began combining colors and shapes and playing with textures—an exploration that continues in her current knitwear design.

CHANGING CLIMATES

Sasha earned her master's degree from the Royal College of Art in 1971 and embarked on a short teaching stint. By that time married with one child, she soon realized that quality of life was more important to her than financial security. Deciding that she'd had enough of the "teeming metroland" that was London, she moved her young family to a remote area of Wales. Soon discovering that "one cannot live on fresh air alone," Sasha began to earn money knitting sweaters for family and friends. These early clients encouraged her work, and in 1974 she packed a suitcase with samples and headed back to London, cold-calling on shops to assess the commercial viability of her knit designs.

The timing couldn't have been better. Fashion's love affair with hand knits was growing, and Carnaby Street (situated in the heart of London's West End) was

This Sasha Kagan design first appeared in the Fall 2006 issue.

A Country Classic

becoming a Mecca for trendsetting fashion aficionados. Sasha showed her designs to a friend who had made a successful career of making and selling Liberty-print shirts. He immediately recognized their potential and encouraged her to show her work to Browns, an influential fashion shop on South Moulton Street well known for its support of young, cutting-edge designers. The Browns staff fell in love with her designs (the sweaters, inspired by '40s Fair Isles and worked in zigzag and optical blocks, sported cutaway armholes and twisted ribs on the welts, arm- and neck-bands) and commissioned six pullovers. The first few designs were a hit. As customers eagerly snapped them off the shelves, Sasha had to hire knitters to keep up with the demand. Back in Wales, she set up a design studio adjacent to her whitewashed timber-framed house, and a thriving cottage industry was born.

Sasha was also indulging her talent as a freelance costume designer by dressing the cast of the famed Black Box Theatre Company for productions at the Round House in London and Sussex University—a sideline which soon led to commissions from other theater groups. All the while, her knitwear business was steadily growing. By this time, Sasha and her band of tireless knitters were not only supplying finished sweaters to shops, they were selling them direct at exhibitions and shows. Sasha was now producing two seasonal collections a year and retailers in the U.S. were clamoring for her designs. Before long, her knits were sashaying down the runways during New York's Fashion Week and filling the racks at top-name shops such as Sportsworks, Top Drawer and Billy Martin in New York; Madrigal and Three Bags Full in California; Bramhall & Dunn and Erica Wilson on Nantucket Island; and Gildas in Massachusetts.

Intent on providing home knitters with access to designer style, Sasha began providing mail-order kits that contained everything needed to create a Sasha Kagan original: top-quality yarn, buttons and the Sasha Kagan label. Knitters couldn't get enough—and still can't. In the U.K. her kits are eagerly sought after at exhibitions such as the Chelsea Craft Fair and the Knitting & Stitching Shows, while fans on both sides of the Atlantic eagerly watch their mailboxes for Sasha's latest mail-order brochure.

Breathing vitality into her classic designs with her signature twisted ribs, Sasha became a master at blending contemporary style with enduring appeal. Her "Hawthorne Jacket" and a ruched '40s sweater design are immortalized in the permanent exhibition at London's Victoria and Albert Museum, the bastion of costumes and textiles. Her enthusiasm for knits and knitting is infectious—making her in constant demand for lectures. Knitters are constantly asking for more, and Sasha obliges, publishing patterns in books and magazines (she's created at least 13 exquisite designs for *VK*).

HOME GROWN

Where does the inspiration for these enduring classics come from? The Welsh countryside, for one. Sasha's studio, set on a thickly wooded hillside and surrounded by thirteen acres of breathtaking scenery, provides an endless source of ideas. Using her innate sense of rhythm and lyricism—along with her proficiency as a colorist—Sasha translates the growth cycle of plants, flowers and the ever-changing seasons into her signature knitwear designs. "I aspire to make my designs both a delight to knit and a delight to wear," she explains. She takes what she terms a "holistic approach" to design, regarding buttons and trims as an integral part of the whole sweater, rather than mere finishing touches. Extending this philosophy, she has turned her business into a way of life. By keeping home, studio and office all in one location, Sasha has worked out a wonderful balance between creative fulfillment, family and career. She truly loves what she does and it shows through in the finished product. "Knitwear is something to be made with love and care and worn with pride," she points out. "A sweater is more than a fashion statement, it's a friend in one's wardrobe." ⌒

Recently Sasha had a one-woman show at the Victoria and Albert Museum titled "Country." She has done coast-to-coast workshop tours of the United States and teaches frequently in Great Britain. Seeing the need for a how-to book for the next generation, she wrote *Ready, Set, Knit*. Her latest book, *Crochet Inspiration (*Sixth&Spring Books), will be published in the spring of 2007. In 2007 she will also give "Crazy Crochet" workshops and tour the USA, sharing her spin on crochet.

Kristin Nicholas: Master

by Lisa Morse

William Morris, the great 19th-century textile designer, once said, "Have nothing…that you do not know to be useful, or believe to be beautiful." It is a simple, direct sentiment, one that master knitter Kristin Nicholas tries to live by. As an expert craftswoman, Nicholas is primarily interested in combining the useful with the beautiful—the practical with the fanciful.

Nicholas was destined to knit. She comes from a long line of craftswomen. Her great-grandmother, Anna Klara Roessler, was prolific tatter, crocheter and needleworker. Her grandmother, Frieda Roessler Nicholas, an expert needleworker and baker, worked at a hosiery mill before raising a family.

Her mother, Nancy Nicholas, is probably the most important influence in her daughter's creative life. Nancy taught Kristin to sew when she was 8. Under her mother's tutelage, the child developed her talent for fine sewing techniques and details. In her senior year of high school, Nicholas won New Jersey's highest 4-H sewing award before she began her undergraduate work at the University of Delaware, where she majored in textile and clothing design.

"I will not tire of the first loves of my life…textiles, sewing and knitting."

Continuing her education at Oregon State University in 1979, Nicholas entered an exchange program. "I had just finished a hand-spinning class and had a lot of yarn. I always wanted my projects to be useful, so I asked my fiber arts professor, Pat Sparks, about knitting. She suggested that I buy a copy of *Knitting Without Tears* by Elizabeth Zimmermann and a *Mon Tricot* stitch glossary. I traveled back to the East Coast by train, and at the end of my journey had perfected the techniques."

Nicholas received a master's degree in textiles and clothing at Colorado State University and then moved to New York to pursue a career in textile manufacturing. While in Oregon, Nicholas had met Mark Duprey. Their relationship continued when both moved back to the East Coast. But there was a long distance between them—Nicholas lived in New Jersey and worked in New York, and Mark lived in northern Massachusetts on his family's dairy farm while working as a veterinary pharmaceutical salesman. While commuting on weekends to be together, they decided to embark on a joint project to raise Romney sheep. Mark cared for the sheep and Kristen used their wool to design simple sweaters. From there, Nicholas developed a mail-order catalog business, Eden Trail, through which she sold her yarn and patterns.

Knitter of the '90s

This Kristin Nicholas design first appeared in the Fall 2006 issue.

In the spring of 1984, Nicholas, weary of commuting and wanting to spend more time with Mark, took a job at a small mill in Lowell, Massachusetts, that had a fledgling hand-knitting yarn division. Before too long, that tiny division grew into Classic Elite Yarns. Nicholas now had an important position at a young company and was able to settle down with Mark.

At Classic Elite Yarns, Nicholas started out designing classic patterns: traditional sweaters with simple cables and detailing. She made her mark through her use of colors. Her sophisticated color sense challenged the experienced knitter's palette while simultaneously attracting the beginner knitter.

Practical values have influenced Nicholas's designs throughout her career. Her sweaters have an easy-to-wear unisex styling that gives them a wonderfully timeless quality. The semi-rural lifestyle she shares with Mark in northern Massachusetts has also helped to give her work its unique flavor. "I grew up with gardens," says Nicholas. "I always wanted to live on a farm. While I tend my gardens of perennials, herbs and vegetables, my mind always goes back to color and form—the color of the fruits, the texture and grace of the vines—it never fails to stimulate my creativity."

A profound love of nature has always been present in her life as well as in her work. Indeed, the two worlds overlap. On the weekends, she and Mark tend to their still-growing flock of sheep. During the lambing season, they bottle-feed baby lambs in their kitchen. They also shear their wool once a year and take it to market. Nicholas still has some spun for herself, to make, as she puts it, "those rugged sweaters that will last a lifetime."

For her third pattern collection, in 1987, Nicholas began using color to celebrate ethnic patterning in her sweaters. By 1991, she had developed the first of the World Knits Collection—small, portable projects promoting colorwork and ethnic motifs.

She even used traditional ethnic knitting techniques for these kits. "I developed these ethnic patterns so that the average knitter can take a pattern and develop their own color palette, choose their own motifs and make the project a personal reflection of their own tastes. I find designing these kits very satisfying because I have had so many people come up to me and say 'I never thought I could do it, but I did.' These small projects breed self-confidence."

Nicholas is constantly encouraging knitters to design on their own. She feels that most knitters simply lack the confidence and that the key to overcoming this is swatching. She personally knits all of her own swatches with the yarn she has chosen for the project. "This way, I know the parameters of the stitch, if it is fun to do. If a stitch is difficult or not a joy to knit or if the gauge is too dense, I'll work on it until it's right. I won't put it into one of my designs just because I like it. I have to feel that the knitter will enjoy doing it too."

Nicholas recognizes her need to keep growing as an artist. She doesn't know what creative project will interest her next, although it is likely to involve the folk and decorative arts. She feels confident that her artistic growth will continue to carry over into her hand-knitting designs. Above all, she hopes to encourage knitters to better their own skills and to teach friends and children what they have learned. As Nicholas says, "every knitter, crocheter and needleworker is a textile designer in their own right, and they too should explore all the avenues open to them. Otherwise, these great crafts may be lost to future generations." ⌐

After the birth of daughter Julia in 1998, Kristin's family moved to western Massachusetts to pursue their dream of living in the country. They found an old farmhouse built in 1751 in the middle of an abandoned apple orchard. They now have 160 sheep, two pigs, forty chickens, nine cats and two very enthusiastic Border collies. In 2004 their home was profiled in *Country Home* magazine.

Kristin left Classic Elite in 2000 and started writing books. She co-authored *Knitting for Baby* with Melanie Falick, wrote *Kids' Embroidery* and *Colorful Stitchery*, and is working on a new knitting book to be published in the summer of 2007.

She continues to design for magazines, including *Vogue Knitting*. Nashua Handknits distributes her designer line of yarn, named Julia (after her daughter), throughout the USA, and JVA distributes her crewel stitchery designs.

Newton's Law: Deborah Newton

by Nancy Brumback

The first rule of designing, says this virtuoso of the craft, is to trust your own instincts.

If the knitter's challenge is to visualize a finished garment while tending to tiny details, Deborah Newton is unquestionably a master. Few knitwear designers bring together all the elements—pattern, texture, shaping—in such technically accomplished sweaters. Yet Newton's role model isn't a knitter. She is Barbara Matheson, a theater costume designer.

After graduation from Rhode Island College as an English major, Newton took a job as a costume design assistant in her alma mater's theater department. Matheson, the department's costume designer, "has a strong sense of design process, of taking a garment from the original inspiration to the sketch, then from the fabric to construction," says Newton. "She is adept in every one of these areas. I have great respect for her ability to do all those things, and that influenced me a great deal. I wanted to be able to understand every aspect of the process."

That commitment to "process"—to "working through an idea and following it step by step"—has given Newton the confidence to tackle and master knitting, designing and sketching. "The process itself becomes your teacher," she explains.

Today Newton designs sweaters for many yarn companies and magazines, and she does find inspiration for her knitwear patterns in theater costumes. But a career in costume design never appealed to her. "I prefer a slower, more confined art form," she says. "Costume design was too broad for me."

She took up knitting in 1980, in part because knitted garments were fashionable at the time. Almost immediately, she designed a sweater on her own, teaching herself from books. Since she liked the design, a turtleneck variation on an Irish knit in wine-colored wool, she sent it to a crafts magazine, which used the sweater in a fashion feature. That initial success inspired her to come up with other designs, and at the age of 28, just two years after she started knitting, Deborah Newton decided to become a freelance knitwear designer.

Both she and Paul Di Filippo, the science fiction writer with whom she has lived

This Deborah Newton design first appeared in the Fall 2005 issue.

for fifteen years, are now freelance workers, and their Providence, Rhode Island, home overflows with the paraphernalia of their careers. "Our best work is done when both of us are in the house," she notes. Although Di Filippo doesn't knit—"he tried once but gained stitches"—Newton considers him a major contributor to her work. From the outset, she says, he has "allowed me the freedom" and provided the support to develop her design career.

Newton's work habits have changed since the beginning. "When I first became a freelance designer, I knitted up all the garments to send to editors and yarn companies. It would take me three weeks to do one," she says. She now works with four or five women who make the garments to her instructions. "The best part of my job has been working with other knitters who are excited about what they do."

To work effectively with those knitters, she developed "a sketch and swatching technique to convey the design idea. I didn't know how to sketch, so I had to learn. I developed a sort of cartoony style, and the swatch reinforced the idea."

More recently, Newton has applied that determination and learning process to writing. Her first book, *Designing Knitwear*, is set to be published early in 1992. With this volume, she hopes to encourage even beginning knitters to experiment, to break away from patterns and create their own garments.

"Because I began knowing nothing, I realized designing was something anyone could do," she says. "That's the whole focus of my book—what is designing, how to recognize an idea…. I went through the same process with the book as with designing. It's like learning anything. You just go slowly from one step to the next."

Newton hopes *Designing Knitwear* will help knitters trust their own instincts. "I would rather see someone wearing one of my sweaters that they had changed a little than one knit exactly to the pattern. It's a matter of taking what interests you and doing something with it, of taking that first step. Designing is a matter of learning to see, of opening up to what is around you. Inspiration is a deliberate, slow noticing of things."

The inspiration for her early designs came from pattern dictionaries, especially those compiled by Barbara Walker. "Her books were a tremendous influence," says Newton. "If they hadn't been available to me, I would probably have taken a different design path, perhaps with more emphasis on colorwork."

In developing a design from pattern books, she adds, "you start to play with the traditional patterns. What happens if I increase the number of stitches in each repeat, or elongate the pattern? Or you can mix several patterns with the same theme together in one garment."

Still, she emphasizes, inspiration can come from anywhere. "People think creative people invent things. That's not true. They just draw from the net of visual stimuli around them." With pictures of non-knitted garments and other objects that have attracted her attention, Newton's book illustrates "how to take inspiration from the world around you and use it in knitting."

But while the inspiration and idea are important, the swatch remains the most critical part of Newton's work. "You can have an idea, but you can't be too firmly attached to it," she says. "When you get the yarn in your hands and start working with it, you have to be open enough to see what's happening. Your mind has to let go of preconceived notions you might have had before you began. When you focus on the stitch in the swatch, that's when things start to happen. It's very exciting, especially when you let go and just enjoy what interests you."

For this reason, Newton typically devotes two or three hours a day to swatching. "An idea doesn't happen if it doesn't work in the swatch," she explains. "You have to be able to knit it, or that idea isn't real."

She advises knitters to make "as strong and finished" a swatch as possible, and to do everything to the swatch that will be done to the finished garment. "The swatch is your safety net. It teaches you everything you need to know about that garment. If the swatch works, the garment will work."

Newton is known for her intricate patterns and careful garment construction. The designer acknowledges her interest in detail, but adds she is moving away from the intricate patterns which marked her previous work. "People will be surprised I designed several of the garments in the book," she says, citing a colorwork coat and sweater with bold graphics and larger areas of color blocks.

Such designs reflect her growing interest in the colors and shapes of traditional ethnic garments from Africa, South America, Japan and China, as well as the designs of the '20s and '30s. But while she is drawn to bright colors, especially oranges and golds, she refuses to be limited. "All colors interest me. I work in many palettes."

Newton notes that the simpler designs she is producing now may also be more in keeping with the time demands on knitters. "It's tough for people to find time to knit now. I feel I have a commitment to my readership to acknowledge their reality."

Finishing is the part of knitting Newton likes best. "I never let anyone else do it—putting the pieces together, weaving in the ends. To me, that's the end of the process, and I want to be there. When a garment is all done, when it's perfect, it will never look that good again."

Beyond knitting, her interests include her garden, her family (who live nearby), her neighborhood, and any travel she and Di Filippo can fit in. She devours magazines, especially European fashion magazines.

Newton starts each day at 6 A.M. with an hour-long walk. And, even though her office is at home, she has imposed on herself the discipline of a nine-to-five schedule. "I no longer work at night," she notes.

Now that her book is finished—that particular process took three years—Newton hopes to design and sell one-of-a-kind garments while continuing to develop knitwear patterns for yarn companies and magazines. Although known for her expertise at construction, she is increasingly interested in colorwork, as well as in developing patterns based on woven ethnic fabrics. "I'd like to do some fulled pieces featuring colorwork," she adds.

As Newton sees it, this evolution is only natural to her growth as a knitwear designer. "I realize people become attached to a style and want a designer to *be* that style. But what I am doing at the moment is what I am. My likes and interests have expanded over the years. For a designer, such change is inevitable." ⌒

Newton has been living in Providence, Rhode Island, with writer Paul Di Filippo for almost thirty years. She is still designing knitwear of all sorts, and she and her brother also make maps for their family business, Maps for the Classroom. Her 1992 book *Designing Knitwear* is still in print, with over 30,000 copies sold. Newton has been a serious yoga student for a long time, and that daily yoga practice now shapes her schedule more than anything else. Yarn and knitting still continue to fascinate her.

Jane Slicer-Smith:

by Deborah Soden

This Jane Slicer-Smith design first appeared in the Winter 2005/06 issue.

Don't tell international knitwear designer Jane Slicer-Smith she can't do something—such negativity would never occur to her. After all, this is a woman who knit a three-quarter-length Aran coat—without a pattern or instructions—the very first time she picked up a pair of knitting needles; a woman who chose to backpack through hottest Africa for sixteen weeks on a traveling scholarship from the British Wool Council when most recipients were opting for Paris or New York. And this is the woman who moved from Britain—the heart of the wool industry—to Australia to start a hand-knitwear business even though her university lecturers told her she would never make a living in such a niche market.

More than two decades after ignoring that advice, Slicer-Smith and her business, Signatur Handknits, are more popular than ever. And now, hand-knitting aficionados in North America are enjoying what legions of loyal fans in Sydney and nearby cities have been privy to since Slicer-Smith first burst on the scene: her designs and custom yarns are now available as finished garments (found at exclusive boutiques in New York, San Francisco and Los Angeles) and as kits in yarn shops across America and online via her Web site, www.sigknit.com.

Born in Bradford, England, Slicer-Smith parlayed her passion for color and texture into a degree (with honors) in knitwear design. She started designing professionally in 1980 while still at Trent University in Nottingham, and won the traveling scholarship the same year. She chose Africa as her destination for the chance to absorb firsthand the colors and culture of the land that inspired the designs for which she won her school's Award of Color.

"Seeing fashion in the raw was a fantastic experience," Slicer-Smith says. "We were in the middle of nowhere, at times not even knowing if we were headed toward Kenya or Uganda. And in Egypt, at the Cairo Museum, I was able to see one of the world's

A Colorful Life

oldest examples of hand knitting in chain mail. I found inspiration at every turn."

In 1982, following her African adventure, Slicer-Smith headed to Australia, intending to visit friends she'd met on her trip. The holiday turned into a career. She started her own label, selling finished garments at Sydney's funky Paddington Bazaar markets, through a chain of tourist shops and at private shows that continue today as a valuable source of customer feedback.

From her Australian base, she also spent three years working with a Japanese spinner, designing for books, promotional fashion shows and magazines. "Japan was a fantastic experience, but I yearned for fewer design limitations and more color, which is as important to me as the design itself. Establishing my own label and designing with only the best yarns in colors of my choice are what designing is all about," she says.

Her color obsession began at a young age. While she didn't tackle that Aran coat until she was 17, she got an early education in color and fashion from her seamstress grandmother and commercial artist/fashion illustrator mother. "My grandmother taught me how to cut patterns. My Barbie doll wore ballroom dresses I designed. Both my parents worked, so to entertain me, my grandmother would get out the easel and oils and we'd paint. And when I was 10, my mother gave me free rein to decorate my room with orange, purple and lime green paint. I guess that's why I like yarns that aren't fancy—they allow me to put my own color combinations together."

Those early influences still shine through. "Color is what makes Signatur different. I'm a little precious about my designs and color combinations. To pick five colorways, I probably knit twelve. There are three to nine colorways in each design, from single-color designs to my 'Living Reef' pattern, which includes more than twenty colors.

"By creating my own yarns and kits, I have control over color and design," she continues. "After twenty years of doing it myself, I didn't want to give up that independence. The kits also help ensure that the correct yarn is used. My signature swing coat drapes the way it's supposed to because I've chosen the correct yarn. Kits also let me include detailed instructions, allowing the knitter to make size variations to achieve the correct fit."

Slicer-Smith is more than a fashion designer; she is an artist, and knitting gives her the chance to create works of art. "I chose to study knitwear design because it is so much more than just fashion. It allows you to create your fabric as well as establish your own style. It's about creating your own pattern instead of the yarn doing it for you."

Slicer-Smith's can-do attitude has led her down a new path. In 2000, she fulfilled a dream of launching her own line of merino wool yarn, which carries the Woolmark quality stamp.

"Australian merino pure new wool is the best in the world, and instantly changes a knitter's perception of wool," she says. "Like most Australian fine wool, it's spun with an extra twist to protect the fine, soft fibers. This twisting also enhances the natural luster of the yarn, but what really sets it apart is the drape it achieves in my swing-coat designs."

The timelessness of her designs and the high quality of her yarn have led to some interesting "complaints" from her customers. "Some are wearing sweaters that are twenty years old—they never wear out! People in London, Paris and New York have all told me that strangers stop them on the streets to ask them about their sweaters. One woman was stopped so many times on a sightseeing trip that her husband made her take hers off!" ⌐

Jane introduced Signatur Knitting Kits and Finished Garments to the USA in 2000. In addition she has helped launch the Signatur Collection for Trendsetter Yarns. The goal of the Signatur patterns and yarns is to appeal to new knitters. "The range began with some very simple designs, taking two scarves into a capelet, using simple stitch patterns and a decrease, teaching knitters to count stitches and rows and work a decrease." Jane's passion for color led her to introduce mitered squares ranging from simple to sophisticated.

Life is constantly busy for Jane; one bonus of living in Sydney and selling in both hemispheres is that there are two winters each year. "I am really fortunate. I have a passion for my work and I travel and meet people who share my passions.... Ideas are no problem; I just need a few more days in the week! In fact it's now 7:15 P.M. and time to cook dinner, after which out comes the knitting, of course."

The Fine Art of Knitting:

by Katherine Rich

Knitting has been a part of Margaret Stove's life for as long as she can remember. "My grandmother taught me to knit when I was a girl and it has been my life ever since," she recalls. "I learned the European style of quick knitting, which has been very useful with my more detailed and labor-intensive designs." On Victory Day in 1945, 5-year-old Margaret passed her grandmother's "test of efficiency" in knit stitches and was allowed to "graduate" to purling. "I can still vividly recall [Grandmother] telling me to knit the 'V's for Victory and to purl the crosses—the latter being formed by the loop of the purled stitches," she reminisces in *Creating Original Hand-knitting Lace*. That moment instilled in her a lifelong fascination with stitch, design and shape.

Like many New Zealand women of her generation, Margaret knitted for economic and climatic reasons. Winter can be cold in New Zealand, and with a husband and four children all needing warm clothes, hand-spinning and hand-knitting were a sensible way to keep the family warm. But for Margaret, knitting went beyond the practical. Her grandmother's fireside stories of the traditional shawls from the Shetland Isles, so fine in

"There is nothing that makes its way more directly to the soul than beauty," said 18th-century English writer Joseph Addison. Looking at the delicately detailed designs of Margaret Stove, one has to agree. This accomplished knitter, spinner and designer has changed the way the world looks at lace knitting.

This Margaret Stove design first appeared in the Holiday 2003 issue.

construction that they could be pulled through a wedding ring, kindled a fascination with fine lace knitting.

Her love of the craft drew her to search for new and interesting lace designs. As she dug through pattern books, she found that not only had designs progressed little since the 1940s, but also that understanding of the craft was very limited. "I realized that I was working established designs without really understanding them," she explains. "But once you deconstruct the patterns and understand the lace, the world is your oyster in terms of new designs." She embarked on a path of investigation and development, and is now credited with establishing the recorded history of lace knitting and considerably advancing its design. She has authored an impressive lineup of craft books and papers, including *Creating Original Hand-knitted Lace* and *Merino: Hand-spinning, Dyeing and Working with Merino and Superfine Wools*.

While the roots of her lace knitting are firmly grounded in the Northern hemisphere, Margaret has built on the tradition and given it a distinctly Pacific feel. New Zealand, with its scenic landscapes and waterways—especially the dramatic

Margaret Stove

seascapes of the port town of Lyttelton where she lives—provides much of the stimulus. Native plants, such as the rata and fern, as well as fish and birds have been incorporated into a number of trademark nature-oriented designs. The centuries-old carvings and weavings of the Maori, the native people of New Zealand, are also a constant source of inspiration. Many of her designs, such as "Kaimoana," which means "food from the sea," bear Maori names.

Margaret's profile within the knitting industry has grown steadily over her impressive career, but her "big break" came in 1982 when Princess Diana was pregnant with her first child. A group of New Zealand fine-wool sheep breeders provided Margaret with New Zealand merino and asked her to design and knit a christening shawl fit for a king. Young Prince William was photographed swaddled in the shawl on many occasions. This simple gift from New Zealand increased the profile of Margaret Stove and lace knitting dramatically, a trend that has continued to build over the last 18 years.

Like many craftswomen, Margaret discovered a way to combine business with pleasure. She now runs a successful business marketing charts, hand-knitted lace kits, and a range of lace-weight merino yarns. Her Artisan brand yarns are the result of her search for a wool fine enough to use in her intricate designs. "I had been spinning yarns using coarse crossbred sheep fleece and was unhappy with the result," she explains. "Quite by accident, a friend gave me a merino fleece to try and I've used mostly superfine merino yarns since." Working with this fleece, Margaret developed a new spinning technique (which she now teaches in her workshops) that produces a light, airy yarn. Today, the business looks set to become a family affair. Margaret spends a good three months out of the year traveling overseas for workshops and lectures, so her daughter, Christine Sullivan, has taken over in her absence.

Christine's involvement has allowed Margaret more time for her true passion—teaching. In her classes, she manages to impart not just the technical aspects of lace knitting but a true love and understanding of it as an art form. Margaret's teaching philosophy is very personal. She prefers that her students discover what they want to do with the craft rather than become "clones" of herself. One of her courses, "Understanding the Mysteries of Knitting Lace from Charts," has been very popular with a diverse group of craftspeople. As she notes, "Once people unlock some of these secrets, they can be applied to a variety of end products: bobbin lace, crochet and knitting."

Readers who sometimes struggle with their knitting can take heart in Margaret's conviction that anyone, regardless of skill level, has the potential to be creative. "Artistic expression is unique," she stresses. "It is up to a good teacher to unlock that potential." It's a philosophy she's put into action in her recent teaching tour of the United Kingdom, Europe and the United States. The tour has been a whirlwind of activity. At press time, the highlight was her visit to Orenburg, Russia—famed for the intricate mohair shawls that have been produced there since the time of Catherine the Great. Here she was an official guest of the Museum of Arts and Culture. The tour ends in Kent, Washington, but Margaret has no plans to set aside her needles. "Sometimes with my teaching and business I don't have time for my own work," she explains. "I look forward to taking some time out for thinking and designing. It will be a treat to focus on my own projects."

For Margaret Stove, working with yarn is more than a craft, it's a way of life. As the Maori would say, "Arohanui" to you, Margaret—much love and best wishes.

For the last three years, Margaret has been studying full-time for a bachelor of fine arts degree in printmaking at the Ilam School of Fine Arts at the University of Canterbury in New Zealand. She is also completing her third book, which will focus on shawls. In addition to featuring original shawl patterns, it will include the story of a 150-year-old Shetland shawl that suffered moth damage, and the process she followed to repair it and to work out the pattern. Margaret also teaches and lectures worldwide.

In Loving Memory:

On November 30, 1999, the knitting world lost a friend, mentor and visionary when Elizabeth Zimmermann, who revolutionized the art of knitting, died at a hospital in Marshfield, Wisconsin.

Born Elizabeth Lloyd-Jones near London, England, in 1910, Elizabeth spent her childhood in the English countryside surrounded by women who knit. "One of my earliest memories has always been of a day when I pestered my mother to teach me how to knit," she recalls in her book *Knitting Around* (published by Schoolhouse Press). "'Well,' said my mother, 'If you're good all day today, I'll teach you to knit tomorrow.'" She also recalls her "Auntie Pete" showing her how to knit a sock: "Off I went, on to the cliffs, to knit, and had the time of my life.

"Later that day, Auntie Pete demanded her knitting back, so as to be able to get on with it herself, and gently commented on its looseness where one needle had joined another. I was cut to the quick, but said nothing, possibly having instinctively realized My Life Was Starting. When she ripped out my few rows, my little heart almost broke. But I'd learned HOW TO KNIT, and have never stopped since."

At age 17, she went to art school in Lausanne, Switzerland, and was then accepted into a pre-Akadamie Art School in Munich, Germany. Her knitting accompanied her. "I soon evolved this idea of knitting away on sweaters and jerseys which I then exchanged at the wool shop for more wool and a little change to knit models which I could exchange at the wool shops for more wool. Ad infinitum. It was very rewarding to see my knitted pieces exhibited in the shop-window at pleasing prices."

She met her husband, Arnold, in Germany in 1930. She had had a skiing accident and was sent flowers by a male friend. Arnold, a coworker of the friend, caught sight of the thank-you card she had sent and was intrigued by "the funny Limey handwriting (in bright green ink, no less)." They went to visit a recuperating Elizabeth and it was love at first sight.

They married in England in 1937 and immigrated to New York, moving several times before settling in Wisconsin. In 1955, Elizabeth began submitting knitting designs to *Woman's Day*. Annoyed with editors who translated her kindly writing style into standard Symbolcraft instruction, she started her own hand-knitting newsletter and established Schoolhouse Press, a successful mail-order business that sells knitting supplies, books and videos. In 1957, she introduced the U.S. to its first commercially published Aran sweater pattern via the *Vogue Pattern Book*, the sister publication of *Vogue Knitting* magazine. By 1964 she was hosting *The Busy Knitter*, a half-hour knitting program on Milwaukee Public Television that proved so successful that its follow-up, *The Busy Knitter II*, enjoyed nationwide syndication.

Elizabeth shared her skills and enthusiasm with others in workshops and classes, and in 1974 she established "Knitting Camp" in Shell Lake, Wisconsin. Her books *Knitting Without Tears*, *Knitting Around*, *Knitters' Almanac* and *Knitting Workshop* are treasured by knitters around the world and are still available through Schoolhouse Press. She inspired us with her beautiful and timeless Norwegian Pullovers, Shetland Yoke Sweaters, Aran Jackets, and Moccasin Socks and changed the way we thought about knitting with innovations such as an entirely seamless sweater knit in the round, Moebius Ring Scarves [see page 142], incredible reversible sweaters that fold into a wearable shape, and her mathematical system for determining sweater proportions [see page 126].

Elizabeth taught us to trust our instincts, revel in our creativity, and above all, find joy in the simple act of knitting. She will be greatly missed.

Elizabeth Zimmermann

1910–1999

FROM MEG SWANSEN

Dear Knitters,

Since my mother's death a few weeks ago, I have received a staggering amount of mail and gifts from all over the world. I could fill these pages with heartfelt and articulate quotes in an attempt to convey the enormous impact Elizabeth Zimmermann had on the knitting world over the past four decades, but it seems more fitting to quote EZ herself.

Here, from the final pages of her second book, *Knitters' Almanac*, are words that seem applicable now—at the end of her life, the end of the year and the end of the millennium….

—Meg Swansen

"Envoi. You and I have strung one another, and our knitting, around and through the seasons. Now Christmas Eve, Christmas Day, even Boxing Day are behind us. The year is running down.

These few days between Christmas and the New Year are for holding the breath, for sitting still and observing, for summoning energies against the future. There is a hush, unbroken even by the click of knitting-needles, although perhaps by turning of the pages of the beautiful new Christmas books. The house still shines from its pre-holiday scrubbing, meals are simple and we are snowed in.

Soon the tree will come down and the ornaments will be put away for another year. To me this is one of the most touching of the annual rites; much more so than that of putting up the tree when all is festivity and excitement. Where shall we all be when these boxes are opened again? What is about to befall? What joys are in store? We are thankful for the past year and hold a good thought over the next.

The small battered tree-baubles—mementos of how many years, remaining members of how many sets—may now spend fifty weeks under the garage rafters, at the mercy of wax-melting heat and enterprising mice, until their High Season returns.

The manger, with its precious German waxen Holy Family, shepherd, donkey and horn-less cow; its eight Holy Three Kings, picked up at Woolworth's over the years because they were irresistible; its two china snow-babies who sledded and rolled down the icing of my childhood's Christmas cakes, and the rest of its heterogeneous inhabitants, is dismantled. It was made of scrap lumber and an orange crate for our first American Christmas, thirty-six years ago. The roof lifts off, the sides pull out and it folds flat—this in preparation for the many moves we knew we would be making.

I reconnoitered in my wool-room yesterday; it is full of possibilities for the New Year. Another Aran perhaps, to start off with? Should it blow tradition and be hooded? Six pairs of socks for the Old Man? Cushion covers? A shawl with a ten-inch lace border and perhaps design the border myself? A huge afghan to keep one's knees warm whiles being knitted?...

By this time next year some of these will have been achieved, and some scorned and abandoned. Some as yet undreamed-of whims will have taken shape. I'm ready for them; my mind is open, my wool-room full of wool, my needles poised, my brain spinning like a Catherine-wheel. There are plenty of pencils—I think—and where did I see that old block of squared paper?

My word, such good fortune. I can only hope the same for you." ᔓ

Index

A

Acrylic, 30, 31
Afterthought additions, 164–165
Afterthought thumbs, 166–167
Allen, Karen, 214–215
Allover traveling cable, 84
Alpaca
  blocking and cleaning, 193
  designing a sweater, 146
Alteration of pattern, 179–180
American knitting, 13
American method, 56
Angora
  blocking and cleaning, 193
  designing a sweater, 146
Animal fiber, 191–192
Aran
  history of, 12–13
  for men's sweaters, 186
  for petite sizes, 189, 190
Armhole
  binding off, 85
  kids' sizes, 185
  knit from to create sleeve, 91–92
  measurement of depth, 180
  men's sizes, 187
  pattern alteration and, 181
  shaped pick-ups, 92
  straight pick-ups, 92
Aunt Jean's invisible jog. See Invisible jog
Austrian cast-on variation, 79

B

Backstitch seam, 103
Backward loop cast-on method, 76–77
Backwards, knitting, 19, 20, 121–122
Basting, 102
Bavarian twisted stitch, 79, 94
Binding off
  basic method, 83
  crocheted method, 84
  decrease method, 84
  I-cord method, 158
  picot edge method, 85
  seam method, 85
  sewn, 158
  sloped method, 100
  suspended method, 84
  three-needle, 108
  three-needle method, 85
  tips for, 85
  when working in ribbing, 163
  See also Casting off
Bliss, Debbie, 216–217
Blocking
  following recommendations for, 191
  knitted garments, 195
  linen, 191
  process of, 116–117
  shoulder seams, 92
  sweater, 102
  sweatermaking, 153–154
  types of, 191–192
  wool, 34, 51
Blunt-wool needle, 104
Boatneck hem, 111
Bohus knitting, 138–139
Box-the-compass design, 141
Bust/chest
  kids' sizes, 185
  measurement of, 179
  men's sizes, 187
  pattern alteration and, 180–181
Bust dart
  hand knitting, 171–172
  placement of, 171
  purpose of, 170
  short-row wrapping, 172
Buttonhole
  backward loop cast-on method, 76
  one-row, 20
  stitches between, 157
  sweatermaking, 155
  tips for improving, 114–115
  types of, 115

C

Cable
  allover traveling, 84
  correcting reversed, 90
  creating without cable needle, 94–95
  decoding, 59
  vertical, 85
  wayward, 96–97
Cable cast-on method, 73
Cable twist, 85
Camel's hair, 146
Cardigan
  centering a color pattern, 124
  edging, 156
Carrilero, Pierre, 202–203
Cashmere, 31
  best use for, 36–37
  blocking and cleaning, 193
  caring for, 37, 191
  designing a sweater, 146
  as look of luxury, 35
  quality of, 36, 37
Casting off

Latvian method, 81
tubular method, 20
  See also Binding off
Casting on
  Austrian variation, 79
  backward loop method, 76
  cable method, 73
  elastic long-tail method, 82
  German twisted method, 82
  invisible, 20
  knitted-on method, 78
  Latvian method, 80
  long-tail method, 76–77, 78
  open method, 74
  provisional, 20
  purl variation, 79
  regular old method, 76
  simple method, 72
  single needle, 76
  thumb method, 72
  tubular method, 20, 74
  Turkish method, 74
  two-needle method, 73
  two strand method, 76
Center-back-neck-to-cuff measurement, 93
Chart
  fit captions and finished bust measurements, 149
  mosaic pattern, 66–67
  reading colorwork, 64
  understanding, 62–63
  veering off, 96
  working pattern, 64–65
Chenille, 30
Chin, Lily, 218–219
Circular knit, 51
Circular knitting
  avoiding seams, 140–141
  creating sleeve, 92

  easing the tension, 133
  invisible jog, 134–135
Circular needle, 131
Cleaning knitted garments, 192, 195
Close-fitting style, 183
Color
  for full-figured woman, 174
  Kaffe Fassett on, 206
  for men's sweaters, 186
  motif for Fair Isle, 128
  for petite sizes, 189
Color-knitting technique, 132–133
Color pattern
  centering, 123–125
  sweatermaking for full-figured woman, 174
  See also Fair Isle
Continental method, 56
Copyright
  expiration of, 68–69
  fair use, 68
  garments of copyrighted pattern, 69–70
  photocopying of material, 70
  posting pattern on blog, 71
  protection of material, 69
Cord
  free standing I-cord, 98
  I-cord, 19, 20, 58, 109, 143, 158
Cotton yarn, 30, 31
  blocking and cleaning, 193
  caring for, 191
  designing a sweater, 145
  hard-blocking, 191
  organic, 42
Coviello, James, 204–205
Crocheted bind-off, 84

Credits and Permissions

p. 8: Photographs by (from left, top row to bottom): Rudy Molacek, Torkil Gudnason, Alan Cresto, Arthur Elgort, Patrick Demarchelier, Andrea Blanch, Jeff Lipsky, Jim Jordan, Paul Amato.

p. 10: Photographs by: 1. Francesco Scavallo. 2. Michael O'Brien. 3. Hiromasa. 4. Patrick Demarchelier. 5–8. Paul Amato.

p. 11: Bildarchiv Preussischer Kulturbesitz/Art Resource, NY.

p. 14–15: Photographs by Matt Valentine.

p. 19, 99, 109, 141, 165: Illustrations by Phoebe Gaughan.

p. 19–20, 57, 72–74, 83–85, 86–89, 101, 103, 105, 172: Illustrations by Kate Simunek, Chapman Bounford and Associates (UK), originally published in *Vogue Knitting: The Ultimate Knitting Book*, © 2002 SOHO Publishing Co., and *Vogue Knitting Quick Reference*, © 2002 Sixth&Spring Books.

p. 22: Image by (c) Corbis.

p. 24–25: V&A Images/Victoria and Albert Museum.

p. 27: From the collection "Verses from 1929 On," by Ogden Nash, from the book *Many Long Years Ago*, published by Little, Brown. Copyright © 1936 by Ogden Nash, renewed. Reprinted by permission of Curtis Brown, Ltd.

p. 28: Bridgeman Art Library/Leeds City Museums and Galleries.

p. 30: Photograph by Brian Kraus.

p. 34: Original illustrations by Michelle Laporte; redrawn by Phoebe Gaughan.

p. 35: Photograph courtesy of Stefano Moscardi, Natural Fantasy. Originally published in *Luxury Knitting*, © 2005 Sixth&Spring Books.

p. 39–40, 97, 150, 152, 222: Photographs by Jack Deutsch.

p. 49, 101, 107, 115: Photographs by Jack Deutsch, originally published in *Vogue Knitting Quick Reference*.

p. 59–60, 63, 65, 67, 93, 113, 116, 135, 151, 169, 174, 176, 178, 189: Illustrations by Jane Fay.

p. 75: Photograph by Marcus Tullis.

p. 77–79, 82: Illustrations by Martin Laksman.

p. 81: Photographs courtesy of Meg Swansen.

p. 91, 142, 203–205, 211, 214, 216, 219–220: Photographs by Paul Amato.

p. 95: Photograph by Bobb Connors.

p. 111, 121: Original illustrations by Joni Coniglio; redrawn by Phoebe Gaughan.

p. 124, 125: Illustrations by Meg Swansen.

p. 126: Illustration by Elizabeth Zimmermann, from *Knitting Workshop*.

p. 129, 226, 229, 234: Photographs by Rose Callahan.

p. 137: Photograph courtesy of norwegianwool.com.

p. 139: Sweaters from the collections of Angela Rotondi and Virginia Stotz.

p. 148–149, 159–160, 180–181: Original illustrations by Diana Huff; redrawn by Jane Fay.

p. 156–158: Photographs by Meg Swansen.

p. 170–171: Original illustrations by Joni Coniglio; redrawn by Jane Fay.

p. 184: Illustrations by Carol Ruzicka.

p. 190: Photograph by Patrick Demarchelier.

p. 201: Photograph by Eric Boman.

p. 207–208, 210: Photographs by Tom Wool.

p. 224: Photograph by Marco Zambelli.

p. 231, 236: Photographs by Jim Jordan (JimJordanPhotography.com).

p. 239: Photo by Walter Sheffer, courtesy of Meg Swansen.